School Finance in Transition

List of Contributors

Stephen M. Barro
Charles S. Benson
Joel S. Berke
R. Stephen Browning
Alan K. Campbell
David K. Cohen
Dennis A. Gilbert
Robert J. Goettel
Robert W. Hartman
Henry M. Levin
David C. Long
Arnold J. Meltsner
Robert T. Nakamura
John Pincus
Robert D. Reischauer

A Rand Educational Policy Study

School Finance in Transition

The Courts and Educational Reform

Edited by **John Pincus**

Ballinger Publishing Company • **Cambridge, Mass.**
A Subsidiary of J.B. Lippincott Company

International Standard Book Number: 0-88410-156-8

Library of Congress Catalog Card Number: 74-7299

Printed in the United States of America.

Library of Congress Cataloging in Publication Data

Pincus, John A.
  School finance in transition.

  1. Education—United States—Finance. 2. Educational equalization—
United States. I. Title.
LB2825.P49   379'.13'0973   74-7299
ISBN 0-88410-156-8

Contents

Preface

In August 1971, the California Supreme Court ruled in the case of *Serrano vs. Priest* that the existing system of school finance in California was in violation of both federal and state constitutions, holding that school funding could not depend upon the property wealth of individual school districts, but only on the wealth of the state as a whole. This decision implied a major change in American school finance, which almost universally allows each district to determine, partly on the basis of local property wealth, the level of financial support for local schools.

Serrano was rapidly followed by a number of other cases in state and federal courts throughout the country. In the spring of 1973, the U.S. Supreme Court ruled in one of these cases, *Rodriguez vs. San Antonio Independent School District*, that the existing system of school finance was not in violation of the Fourteenth Amendment of the federal Constitution. However, this decision did not foreclose the possibility of a major restructuring of American school finance. Most state constitutions contain language that might be consistent with the lower court decisions in *Serrano* and *Rodriguez*. In 1973, for example, the New Jersey Supreme Court ruled that the existing system of school finance violated the state's constitution, and the U.S. Supreme Court refused to review that ruling. A California court held in 1974 that, on the facts, the state's school finance system violates the California constitution.

In view of the substantial nature of the reforms that would be in order should the *Serrano* principle be upheld widely, The Ford Foundation, during 1971 and 1972, commissioned a number of studies of the impact of school finance reform, including this volume. The Rand Corporation was asked to call upon a number of specialists in education and public finance to write a connected series of essays discussing the legal, financial, educational, and social implications of the recent school finance cases.

I wish to thank all of my collaborators for their patience in the inevitable revising of chapters brought about by various policy changes that took place while the book was being written—notably the U.S. Supreme Court decision in the *Rodriguez* case, which was announced just before the original completion of the manuscript in the spring of 1973. Although we could have gone ahead and published the volume at that time, we felt that it would be more useful for students of the subject and policymakers in state legislatures and executive branches if the book reflected the effects of the *Rodriguez* case on public policy.

The list of people who merit acknowledgments for helping us to produce this book is too long to include here, but, in addition to the coauthors of the book, I must mention James Kelly of The Ford Foundation, who believed that a volume like this might play a useful part as a background for public policy.

School Finance in Transition

Chapter One

School Finance in Transition: The Background

John Pincus
The Rand Corporation

School administrators, state legislators and their staffs, and academic specialists in school finance have for decades discussed the inequities produced by the link between property taxes and school finance. The issue is important because schooling is by far the largest item in state and local public finance (about $60 billion annually), and the local property tax is the chief source of public school funds in the United States.[1] Existing inequities stem from the great variation among school districts in value of taxable property per student, their so-called per capita tax base. There are also variations in other relevant aspects of school finance—costs of doing business, scale of operations, degree of competition for property tax base by city and county government, and customary standards of educational expenditure.

One result of these variations has been a tremendous diversity of school spending among states (from $500 per pupil in Alabama to $1300 per pupil in New York) and within states (in California, one district spends $577 per pupil while another spends $1232; in Texas the range is from $264 to $5334). There is also a wide interstate and intrastate disparity in tax burdens for education. State and local revenues for education range from 4 percent of personal income in Alabama and Rhode Island, to more than 6 percent in Vermont and Utah. The diversity principally reflects interstate and intrastate differences in local property wealth per student and the relative importance that districts and states attach to education finance. Despite the persistence of these disparities, and the evident inequity, as of 1971, most states had undertaken no serious effort to equalize per capita school spending among districts, and the federal government has not yet tried to equalize spending among states.[2]

To move toward more equal spending per district, state governments would have to redistribute funds from rich districts to poor ones. But this effort would raise serious political opposition from representatives of wealthy districts. State legislatures have therefore avoided direct confrontation on this issue, and characteristically settled for a modest step toward equalization in the form of foundation plans, which tend to help the poorest school districts without helping average districts or seriously penalizing wealthy ones (see Chapter 2). There was simply no political support for more thoroughgoing measures of equalization at the state government level.

During the 1960s forces were under way tending to affect the political balance. President Johnson's Great Society programs of 1964-65 were based largely on the theme of equal opportunity as a device for overcoming poverty. Education and training were perceived as the principal equalizing forces for society. Yet it was evident that property-rich school districts maintained an enormous advantage in available resources.

Once equality of educational opportunity became a topic of general public interest, government-financed studies began raising questions about both the effectiveness of compensatory education and the fairness of distribution of federal compensatory education funds. The Coleman Report[3] showed wide differences in per capita spending on education, but it also cast doubt on whether these differences in spending were associated with differences in student achievement. This finding was largely ignored by policymakers until the end of the 1960s. Meanwhile, federal task forces studying the administration of compensatory education, under Title 1 of the Elementary and Secondary Education Act of 1965, found that in many cases federal funds were not flowing to the intended recipients—disadvantaged students—but throughout the recipient school districts through substitution of funds.

By the end of the 1960s, advocates of school finance reform sensed that the surge of interest in equal educational opportunity might provide a more receptive atmosphere for reform legislation. From 1969 on, legislation was introduced in a number of states (notably California, Michigan, and New York) that would have instituted statewide property tax systems, aimed toward equalization of per capita spending throughout the state. Most such legislation would have allowed local districts to supplement the basic state distribution through additional local property taxation, but state aid would have represented a much higher floor to district spending than under present foundation programs, thereby reducing interdistrict inequalities.

But none of this legislation was ratified, thanks to the combined opposition of wealthy districts, which did not want to transfer funds to poorer districts, and of agricultural interests, whose property is often under-assessed now and might not presently fall under a statewide tax system. Despite these setbacks, it was clear that state legislators were more receptive in the 1970s to the idea of school finance reform than in the past. In 1972 in California, for example, the legislature authorized a substantial increase in the statewide foundation program, financed largely by sales tax increases.

Several writers (notably Arthur Wise, Harold Horowitz, and J.E. Coons and associates) meanwhile suggested that the present system of school finance was unconstitutional and therefore subject to challenge in the courts.[4] Several cases were brought to trial at the end of the decade (see Chapter 3). In August 1971 the California Supreme Court held, in the case of *Serrano v. Priest*, that the California system of school finance violated both the California and the U.S. Constitutions in that it "Invidiously discriminates against the poor because it makes the quality of a child's education a function of the wealth of his parents and neighbors,"[5] and remanded the case to a lower court. Subsequent cases in Minnesota, Texas, and New Jersey affirmed the same constitutional principle, including a state constitutional provision in the New Jersey case. The Texas case, *Rodriguez v. San Antonio Independent School District*, was heard on appeal by the U.S. Supreme Court in 1972.

The Court's decision, announced in March 1973, reversed the lower court's decision in *Rodriguez* by a 5-4 vote, with Justice Powell delivering the decision.[6] His main points were:

1. This is not a proper case in which to examine a State's laws under standards of strict judicial scrutiny, since that test is reserved for cases involving laws that operate to the disadvantage of suspect classes or interfere with the exercise of fundamental rights and liberties explicitly or implicitly protected by the Constitution.

(a) The Texas system does not disadvantage any suspect class. It has not been shown to discriminate against any definable class of "poor" people or to occasion discriminations depending on the relative wealth of the families in any district. And, insofar as the financing system disadvantages those who, disregarding their individual income characteristics, reside in comparatively poor school districts, the resulting class cannot be said to be suspect.

(b) Nor does the Texas school-financing system impermissibly interfere with the exercise of a "fundamental" right or liberty. Though education is one of the most important services performed by the State, it is not within the limited category of rights recognized by this Court as guaranteed by the Constitution. Even if some identifiable quantum of education is arguably entitled to constitutional protection to make meaningful the exercise of other constitutional rights, here there is no showing that the Texas system fails to provide the basic minimal skills necessary for that purpose.

(c) Moreover, this is an inappropriate case in which to invoke strict scrutiny since it involves the most delicate and difficult questions of local taxation, fiscal planning, educational policy, and federalism, considerations counseling a more restrained form of review.

2. The Texas system does not violate the Equal Protection Clause of the Fourteenth Amendment. Though concededly imperfect, the system bears a rational relationship to a legitimate state purpose.

> While assuring basic education for every child in the State, it permits
> and encourages participation in and significant control of each
> district's schools at the local level.

Justice Powell concluded the decision by stating:

> We hardly need add that this Court's action today is not to be
> viewed as placing its judicial imprimatur on the status quo. The need
> is apparent for reform in tax systems which may have relied too long
> and too heavily on the local property tax. And certainly innovative
> new thinking as to public education, its methods and its funding is
> necessary to assure both a higher level of quality and greater
> uniformity of opportunity. These matters merit the continued
> attention of the scholars who already have contributed much by
> their challenges. But the ultimate solutions must come from the
> lawmakers and from the democratic pressures of those who elect
> them.

In one of the dissenting opinions, Justice Marshall said:

> The majority's decision represents an abrupt departure from the
> mainstream of recent state and Federal court decisions concerning
> the unconstitutionality of state educational financing schemes
> dependent on local wealth. More unfortunately, though, the majori-
> ty's holding can only be seen as a retreat from our historic
> commitment to equality of educational opportunity and as unsup-
> portable acquiescence in a system which deprives children in their
> earliest years of the chance to reach their full potential as citizens.

The effect of the Supreme Court decision in *Rodriguez* was to rule
out the Fourteenth Amendment as a legal basis for school finance reform. The
decision did not, however, rule out comparable provisions in state constitutions
as a basis for decision.

In the same week as the *Rodriguez* decision, the New Jersey
Supreme Court upheld a lower court's decision in *Robinson v. Cahill*, affirming
that the present system of school finance conflicts with the New Jersey
constitution, which requires that "the legislation shall provide for the maintenance and support of a thorough and efficient system of support for free public
schools." In other words, as the law now stands, decisions about the legality of
the present school finance system are to be decided state by state. If enough states
follow the *Robinson v. Cahill* and *Serrano v. Priest* precedents, then even those
states where no constitutional basis for school finance reform is found may well,
through legislative action, seek to reform their own systems. However, it is still
too early to predict how many states will follow the *Robinson v. Cahill*
precedent.

If "fiscal neutrality" (the approach recommended by Coons et al., and apparently affirmed in *Serrano v. Priest*, in a Michigan case [*Miliken v. Green*] , and other cases) eventually prevails in a number of states, then different school districts will no longer receive varying per capita revenues for any given tax rate. Apparently the only acceptable method for one school district to spend more than another, whatever the difference in per capita tax base, would be by imposing a higher tax rate. This implies that the only acceptable response to *Serrano* is either equal spending per student throughout the state, or equal spending per student throughout the state for any given local tax rate, irrespective of tax base—the so-called power-equalizing approach. A California Superior Court decision of April 1974, upholding *Serrano* on the facts, maintains the strictness of this approach, and even goes beyond it by calling for virtual equalization of spending per student throughout the state. The decision suggests that the state government should use its revenues to equalize differences in property tax yields as between districts that are rich and poor in property wealth.

The changes that would be required under a strict interpretation of *Serrano* and similar cases are probably greater than the political system can quickly tolerate (see Chapter 9), so some modification is likely that allows limited variation or a high foundation level of support. Otherwise, widespread evasion of the intent of *Serrano* and similar cases should be expected on the part of rich districts (see Chapter 6).

A number of writers have pointed out that the recent court cases do not necessarily provide for equal educational opportunity among social or economic classes, but only for greater equality in spending among school districts (see Chapters 9 and 10). In many states, districts with high per capita tax bases have many poor families, while those with low per capita tax bases may have many middle-class families. Therefore, equalization of school district spending may not lead to any substantial increase in the relative share of school resources going to disadvantaged students (see Chapters 6, 9 and 10). In other words, disadvantaged students in urban areas are, on the average, probably located in cities of average per capita property wealth. This is most likely because cities with large concentrations of poor people—white, black, or brown—may have a substantial commercial or industrial tax base that compensates for the lower per capita value of residential property (e.g., Oakland, Washington, D.C.).

What, then, are the implications of the court cases for equal educational opportunity? In the states concerned, they will clearly promote the flow of resources to poor districts, those in rural areas, working-class suburbs, or many small towns. They will probably result in a larger resource flow to the schools, because any leveling process that takes place among school districts will have to increase the total of state and local funds flowing to the schools. The school finance legislation passed in 1972 by the California legislature (see Chapter 9), and that proposed by the Fleischmann Commission (see Chapter 5), appointed to draw up new school finance legislation for New York state, both point in that direction.[7] To the extent that such an increase means greater equality of educational opportunity, *Serrano* will bring in its wake benefits for disadvantaged students.

But the extent of the benefit remains in doubt. The Coleman Report and succeeding studies[8] have indicated that per capita school spending and related measures, such as class size, bear very little relation to academic achievement as measured by standardized test scores (see Chapter 10). Yet few parents would willingly accept a sharp reduction in school spending on the basis of these data. Standardized tests measure only a small proportion of the aims of schooling, and that imperfectly. Even if it could be shown that differences in per capita spending did not substantially affect school testing results, parents and students would probably prefer the higher level of amenities made possible by larger school budgets—for example, smaller classes, better physical plant, more special services, such as counseling or health care.

But more money for schools means more taxes and a change in the incidence of taxes. How should or can more spending be financed? There are a number of possibilities, all of them including a relative increase in statewide funding, whether through property, sales, or income taxes (see Chapter 4). Each alternative implies a different level and incidence of taxation from those now prevailing. The greater the changes in level and incidence, the less feasible they are politically (see Chapter 9). There will therefore be pressure, if *Serrano* is upheld, on both the courts and the federal government, to reduce the political costs of the fiscal neutrality doctrine. The pressure on the courts will be to allow limited variation or a high foundation program as substitutes for strict fiscal neutrality. The pressure on the federal government will take the form of asking for more "no strings" federal aid to school districts to help pay for the costs of leveling up. The Nixon administration's proposed special educational revenue-sharing fund might offer a convenient focus for such efforts.

The fiscal neutrality cases are all based on a state government's treatment of its citizens. These cases therefore make no provision for remedying *interstate* differences in school spending per student, which vary by a range of nearly four to one among the states that spend most and least for schooling. Whether the fiscal neutrality cases are upheld in enough states or not, there is sure to be pressure on Congress to apply the fiscal neutrality principle, loosely defined, to interstate inequalities in school spending.

Let us assume that, through a protracted process of adjudication and political negotiation, interdistrict and interstate differences in school spending are substantially reduced over the next decade through a leveling up process. Who will benefit and who will pay?

The most evident beneficiaries are: (1) school teachers and administrators in the less wealthy districts, whose salaries will presumably rise and whose numbers will increase with the availablity of more funds; (2) taxpayers in less wealthy districts, who will benefit through some combination of lower taxes and greater school revenues per local tax dollar. The obvious losers for converse reasons are teachers, school administrators, and taxpayers in wealthy school districts. Also, to the extent we believe that educational outcomes, however defined, improve with an increase in resources, benefits will flow to the students in districts that level up. Two chapters in this volume contest this conclusion. Chapter 6 argues that educational progress requires greater community control, which will not be forthcoming. Chapter 10 argues that there is no evidence that more money improves school outcomes, and also that under the fiscal neutrality cases, it will be property-poor *districts*, not poor students, that will benefit most, so that even if money could be shown to have favorable effects, the neediest students would benefit insufficiently from fiscal neutrality.

On the tax incidence side, the effects of these cases, and of any interstate equalization that may occur, is unclear. Intrastate equalization will presumably be financed by property and sales taxes, which are probably somewhat regressive in effect (although as Chapter 4 points out, there may be some progressivity over a range of property tax levels), or by state income tax, which is either neutral or progressive. Any federal aid forthcoming is presumably largely financed by progressive income taxation, although the exact degree of progressivity remains in question.

Whatever the distribution of financial and educational costs and benefits, it seems unlikely, on the basis of current research results, that the fiscal neutrality cases will have an important effect on children's cognitive skills.[9] There seems to be rather strong evidence that heredity and the nonschool environment are the principal determinants of academic achievement for the great majority of children. To the extent that school factors do play a part, the Coleman Report indicates that the socioeconomic status of one's classmates is the most important single factor. This is not to say that schools as now organized are providing optimal educational benefits. It may be that schools could do much more than they presently do to help children achieve, particularly those in academic difficulty. However, the effects to date of concerted efforts to improve educational outcomes, such as compensatory education under Title 1 of the Elementary and Secondary Education Act of 1965, have been unimpressive. A number of writers have claimed that this record does not reflect children's capacity to learn, but rather the inability of educational bureaucracies to tailor their approach to the needs of specific clienteles (see Chapters 6 and 7). They have proposed that what the schools need is not so much more money, but a more adaptable bureaucracy.[10]

Some change in bureaucratic behavior may follow under fiscal neutrality by shifting the locus of responsibility for school finance from the local district to the state (see Chapter 7). However, there is no assurance that this change will result in more innovative and effective approaches to education, whether of rich or poor children. There is no substantial evidence to support the contention that state departments of education or local school boards, free from their current concern with school finance, will be more able to develop a responsive educational bureaucracy than they are now. Nor is there much evidence that new educational approaches have much effect on cognitive outcomes, as measured by standardized tests. It is not known how much these results reflect inadequacies in measurement rather than defects of new educational methods. Nor, for that matter, do we know why innovations apparently succeed at one time and place and fail at others.

For all of these reasons, the educational effects of fiscal neutrality are unpredictable. The argument in favor of fiscal neutrality rests largely on equity grounds, albeit on a peculiar form—equity among school districts within a state, rather than equity among individuals or preferred treatment for those in greatest educational need. It is a matter of debate whether a transfer of funds from rich to poor school districts will result in greater funding for disadvantaged students. It seems likely that fiscal neutrality, if adopted, will be the last major reform to take place in American public schools for some time. In the past two decades, the public schools have been successively hit by rapid growth; compulsory school integration; federal assumption of significant responsibility for educational finance; the systematic development of compensatory education programs; and large-scale experiments, such as Head Start, Follow Through, performance contracting, educational vouchers, bilingual education, Sesame Street, and the Electric Company.

The federal government, the sponsor of most of these initiatives, has found large-scale efforts at planned change in the public schools, largely disappointing in results. Therefore, in 1972-73, two federal policy initiatives signaled a change in direction. First, because educational research to date was considered a poor guide to policy, a new large-scale policy research effort was launched under the aegis of a new HEW agency, the National Institute of Education (NIE). Second, pending more promising research and development results from NIE, the federal government decided to abolish a number of categorical aid programs and instead introduced legislation that would pass an equivalent sum on to school districts in the form of revenue sharing, a method that offers no stimulus to innovation in the schools. Presumably, as NIE and other research provide promising educational innovations, federal support for planned change in the schools will increase. But this will not happen soon, considering how primitive our knowledge is and how long it takes to test out innovations in the educational marketplace, where results may often be measured in decades.

The fiscal neutrality cases, and any subsequent attempts to extend the principle to interstate equalization, mark a sort of milestone. If improvement in the quality of schooling does not follow from these cases, then it is arguably unlikely to follow from any other major change during the current decade, simply because no likely engine of change is emerging to supplant the courts and the federal government as catalysts, however imperfect the final outcome of their efforts may appear.

THE ROLE OF THIS STUDY

The fiscal neutrality cases imply at least potentially major changes in local and state fiscal roles, in governance of the schools, in equality of educational opportunity (as measured by dollar inputs), and, possibly, in the eventual federal role in school finance. As noted above, these changes may turn out to be less sweeping than the court decisions, at first perusal, imply. Nonetheless, they represent the potentially most important national policy change in public education since the school desegregation cases of the 1950s and the passage of the Elementary and Secondary Education Act of 1965. This book attempts to give a perspective on the financial and educational implications of the recent court cases.

What Are the Real Alternatives?

In Chapter 2, Stephen M. Barro sets out the range of alternative approaches to school finance that would be compatible with the fiscal neutrality cases. Barro points out that it is not yet clear either *what* is to be equalized per pupil: expenditures, school resources, or educational outcomes; or what *degree* of equalization is required: uniform provision of funds, fiscal neutrality, limited variation, or a guaranteed minimum provision. He discusses the implications of each approach as policy options.

Barro describes the existing state-local school finance system, including the elements that lead to inequities in taxing and spending. Several strategies could be adopted to reduce these inequalities, ranging from full state funding to state aid that would vary inversely in proportion to localities' ability to raise funds. The principal post-*Serrano* alternatives that have been discussed are full state funding and district power-equalizing, which would allow each district to choose its preferred tax rate and receive school funds according to a schedule linking tax rates to entitlements of dollars received per pupil. (Transfers between the state and districts would make up the difference between tax proceeds and dollar entitlements, assuring equal receipts for equal tax effort among districts.) These two extreme alternatives can be combined in various forms, providing for a state-funded base program, plus local supplementation under state-mandated procedures. Under such alternatives, state policy would be used to make several choices, including the level of the base program, the level of statewide taxation imposed, and the nature of the supplementation schedule that relates local tax effort to provision of supplementary school funds.

Much of the discussion of equitable school taxation revolves around appropriate property tax levels. Barro points out that it might be more appropriate to make equity judgments on the basis of definitions of local effort based on income rather than on property wealth, on the grounds that retired homeowners, for example, are overtaxed because they are wealth-rich and income-poor. Either property taxes or income taxes could be used to raise funds under an income-based definition of effort. He points out that it would be possible to work to greater equalization through another device—reduction of tax base disparities. This could be accomplished by:

1. Removing commercial and industrial property from the local tax base, thereby removing an important source of interdistrict tax-base disparities as a source of inequality;
2. Switching to a local income tax base; or
3. Reorganizing districts into units that would be more equal in property tax base.

Finally, Barro discusses the ways in which local districts are likely to respond to the incentives provided by a new school finance system. He demonstrates that under each of the major reform alternatives, some districts would lose financially, and some gain, in different ways, depending on the alternatives adopted. He concludes that the fiscal neutrality cases will, in any event, lead to increases in school spending statewide because of the political need to level up.

THE LEGAL SITUATION

Serrano vs. Priest and *Rodriguez vs. San Antonio Independent School District* are two of a group of nearly fifty cases that have been brought to trial, alleging violations of the Fourteenth Amendment and similar provisions of state constitutions that require a state to extend equal protection of the laws to its citizens. R. Stephen Browning and David C. Long, in Chapter 3, trace the development of current legal doctrine and examine its legal implications and its implications for educational policy and for legislation.

The U.S. Supreme Court decision in *Rodriguez* states that existing inequities in school finance do not violate the United States Constitution. What will the effect of this decision be on the role and the activity of courts and legislatures in school finance reform? Browning and Long point out that *Rodriguez* has clearly shifted the focus of school finance reform from the federal courts to state courts and state legislatures.

Browning and Long begin by reviewing the history of court action in respect to equal educational opportunity. In a landmark case, *McInnis v. Ogilvie*, a federal court held that the courts could not direct state school finance systems to allocate funds on the basis of "educational needs" because these were undefinable. The failure of reform in *McInnis* led to the development of the fiscal neutrality doctrine. The first case decided under the fiscal neutrality doctrine was *Serrano v. Priest* in which the California Supreme Court held that "[the California] funding scheme invidiously discriminates against the poor because it makes the quality of a child's education a function of the wealth of their parents and neighbors." The State Supreme Court returned the case to the Superior Court for trial on the facts and in April 1974, the Superior Court affirmed that the California system of school finance was unconstitutional. This decision implies that not only the California school finance systems but that of many states whose constitutions contain equal protection clauses are probably invalid.

The court held that defendants' arguments that plaintiffs' education was adequate were irrelevant, and stated that the level of resource inputs was the appropriate standard of comparison, rather than such outcome measures as academic achievement. The decision reaffirmed the 1971 *Serrano* finding that education is a fundamental interest under the state consitution, meriting the strict scrutiny standard established for equal protection cases.

A New Jersey case was decided by the State Supreme Court on somewhat different grounds: namely, that the statewide system of funding schools resulted in children in some districts receiving an education that was less than "thorough and efficient" as required by the state constitution.

Browning and Long review the U.S. Supreme Court's argument in *Rodriguez* stressing Justice Powell's argument that the Texas school system did not operate to the particular disadvantage of the poor since the taxing and spending system was based on districts not people. Although the court refused to view the facts in the case as demonstrating that wealthy children benefit systematically and poor children are deprived systematically by the operation of the school finance system, the court left open the question about whether relative wealth might provide a proper base for claiming violations of the Fourteenth Amendment. Another point that Browning and Long emphasize is the Supreme Court's refusal to find that education is a "fundamental interest" under the federal constitution. It is not clear however from the Court decision in *Rodriguez* whether the Court would ban *any* inequities that may result from state or local property tax systems.

In light of *Rodriguez*, however, the authors contend that the state courts and state legislatures will be the principal forums for school finance reform efforts. The three key cases in the state courts (*Serrano v. Priest, Millikan v. Green,* and *Robinson v. Cahill*) each imply somewhat different approaches to reforms, and future cases may support or reject plaintiffs on relatively new terrain.

In closing Browning and Long contend that both state courts and state legislatures are likely to maintain a pace of activity that will promote school finance reform. However, they argue litigation is likely to slow down in order to allow state legislatures time to act in the absence of court pressures.

TAX POLICIES

In Chapter 4, Robert W. Hartman and Robert D. Reischauer discuss the implications of the fiscal neutrality cases for tax policy. After describing the present school finance system, which derives, nationally (with wide variation among states), 7 percent of its funding from the federal government, 41 percent from state government, and 52 percent from local revenues, the authors attempt to judge the tax incidence of existing school revenues. Generally speaking, the federal share is financed by progressive taxation, the state share is raised by taxes that may on the average be roughly proportional to taxpayer income, and the local share, financed largely by property taxes, may be regressive, proportional or progressive, depending on such factors as the extent to which the incidence of the property tax actually falls on owners and renters, or on the nature of local tax assessment practices, or on the extent to which localities use taxes on sales or income to supplement the property tax.

The authors predict that states will require all districts to establish minimum per student spending levels higher than those now mandated by states, providing for add-ons through some form of district power equalizing. Raising the state minimum to the level now enjoyed by each state's 70th percentile student (starting with students who are in districts with the lowest funding levels in the state and going up to the students who are in districts with the highest funding levels), would impose additional costs to the states of about $3 billion ($60 per student) averaged nationwide. This burden, although large in total, is, the authors state, "well within the bounds of what states can afford when a high-effort state constitutes the standard of comparison or when new sources of revenue such as general revenue sharing are taken into account."

If we accept the proposition that fiscally neutral systems will consist of a higher state-mandated minimum spending level plus an add-on based on district power equalizing through a common tax base, or similar approaches, what will the effects on the tax burden be? If the add-on portion starts out as self-financing, any subsequent increases in the common tax base will increase state costs, normally at the expense of high-spending districts. It is not possible to predict exactly how school district spending and taxes will change in each district if the state combines raising the common tax base with reducing statewide minimum support. The authors classify probable responsiveness according to the initial position of the district and to the degree to which its spending responds to changes in income (changes in the state-financed minimum) and in the price of education (changes in the add-on rates of the school finance system).

Under this type of system, a local district's tax and expenditure levels will increase or decrease according to the district's relative preference for education and its perception of whether "outsiders" really bear the property tax burden. Given the present amount of available knowledge about educational preferences and the incidence of property taxes, we cannot now predict in advance what any particular school district will do as far as local effort is concerned.

How would state financing of the prospective increases in state school spending affect taxpayers? On the basis of New York State data, Hartman and Reischauer estimate: (1) a state property tax would fall most heavily on New York City; (2) a state income tax would fall most heavily on wealthy suburban counties and least heavily on rural areas; (3) a state sales tax would fall most heavily on rural areas. It is harder to estimate how alternative tax sources would affect individuals living in these districts, except for such obvious factors as the greater burden of state income taxes on rich people, and the greater burden of state sales taxes on the less wealthy. But the net incidence is hard to estimate if we also try to include the effects of corresponding reductions in property taxes, whose incidence is unclear. If commercial and industrial property were taxed statewide and only residential property were subject to local taxation, then the existing range of variation in the property tax base would be substantially reduced. If localities substituted income or sales taxes for property taxes, then current rankings would change and some "rich" districts would become "poor" and vice versa.

There could be some important secondary effects resulting from changes in taxation. Decreases in property taxation would raise all real estate values. A statewide property tax would tend to lower property values in rich districts and raise them in poor ones. Statewide property taxation would also result over time in elimination of industrial enclaves and other property tax havens.

THE TRANSITION TO FISCAL NEUTRALITY

In Chapter 5 Charles Benson discusses how the requirements of the fiscal neutrality cases can be brought into being considering the present fiscal and political constraints. His analysis of the transition process is based on recent proposals that have been advanced for full state funding in New York (in the Fleischman Commission report of 1972) and district power equalizing in California (in the Senate Select Committee report of 1972).

In the New York proposal, all low-spending districts would be brought up to the 65th percentile of operating expenditures per student per year. Districts above the 65th percentile could continue to maintain their present outlays per student, but they could not increase spending until the basic statewide level rose to the high-spending district's own level, which would then move ahead in step with other districts (in response to progressive state-mandated increases in the basic funding level). Certain categories of expenditures (transportation, school lunches, debt service) would be fully funded by the state in all districts. Under the New York version of full state funding, equal sums would be made available for each student unless there were educational reasons for variations in spending (cost differences, special needs of students, and so on). The New York proposals would have been funded by a statewide property tax, with a so-called circuit-breaker provision that would set a ceiling on the tax to be paid by low-income families.

The California proposals would be based on district power equalizing (DPE), with full state funding provided only for categorical aid along the lines suggested in the New York report. But in the California proposal, fiscal neutrality is achieved by allowing a district to choose any tax rate it wants, subject to specified floor and ceiling rates. The district would receive a specified per student revenue independent of the local tax base. The actual schedule chosen was designed to provide for decreasing revenue growth per unit tax increase beyond a specified "normal expenditure point ($700 per student)" to prevent too great an increase in state costs.

Benson cites four major problems of transition under both the New York and California proposals.

The danger that wealthy families may desert the public schools. Under present arrangements, wealthy people form their own school districts (Beverly Hills, Pound Ridge), which are private to the extent that property values are too high for poor people to enter. Under the Fleischmann report version of full state funding, rich districts cannot reduce their public school spending rates by sending their children to private schools instead, but they will pay lower property tax rates than before. Under district power equalizing, the greater the average value of property, the greater the temptation to set a low tax rate (which would still transfer some funds to poor school districts) and send children to private schools. In general, the larger the state share, the more likely rich families are to remain in the public school system; and the larger the federal and state income tax credit allowed for private school tuition, the more likely rich families are to leave the public school system.

Definition of public education expenditures. Under district power equalizing, rich districts have an incentive to shift educational expenditures from the school budget (where they have to transfer tax receipts to poor districts) to the city budget (where they do not have to make such transfers), whereas poor districts would have the opposite incentive. Thus Beverly Hills would have an incentive to shift school library expenses from school to city budget, while a "poor" district would have an incentive to shift the city library to the school budget, and would also have an incentive to spend money on education rather than other city expenditures, because the relative price of schooling is reduced. This could work, as Benson explains, to the disadvantage of poor children.

Poor households in property-rich districts. Under district power equalizing, rich districts will have to raise their property taxes, thereby imposing heavy financial burdens on poor families in those districts. Some circuit-breaker approach of the type recommended in the Fleischmann report seems necessary to prevent such inequities.

Financial requirements of large cities. Large cities generally have high per-student tax bases. Therefore, under schemes compatible with fiscal neutrality, large cities would have to raise their tax rates. But it is argued that large cities place more demands on local taxpayers for noneducational expenditures than other municipalities. On the other hand, large cities would tend to benefit under the New York and California proposals for full state financing of categorical aid (including compensatory education) and under the circuit-breaker provisions.

EFFECTS ON RESOURCE USE AND EDUCATIONAL OUTCOME

Chapters 2-5 raise and attempt to respond to questions about the effects of the fiscal neutrality cases on financing and the law; in Chapter 6 Henry M. Levin addresses the question of what the cases will do for schools and students. Levin, like most other observers, assumes that the cases, if upheld, will lead to more spending on education and certainly to more in poor districts. He contends, however, that neither the increase in spending nor the concomitant equalization is likely to produce the improvements in educational quality for poor children that the courts have sought. In this respect he agrees with David Cohen, who in Chapter 10 discusses the relation between school finance and social policy.

For Levin, the difficulty lies in the ways schools are administered and in the institutional interests that are served by the existing administrative structure. How the money is actually used and what outcomes it produces will be affected most strongly by the decisionmaking structure of the educational system.

In theory, additional funding should affect schooling outcomes by providing more and different resources that will be used to improve the outcomes of schooling. But, Levin points out, a number of factors conspire to prevent this outcome. First there is disagreement over the aims of schooling. Second, even if there were agreement about aims, in general we do not know how more and different resources can be used to improve outcomes. Third, the incentives that teachers and administrators face are not associated with student performance.

How, then, will additional funds for the benefit of poor students actually be spent? Levin argues that school district response is affected by six constituencies: (1) local taxpayers; (2) parents of disadvantaged students; (3) disadvantaged students; (4) the school board; (5) teachers; (6) school administrators. The power of the second and third groups is quite low because they are poorly organized and usually do not have enough electoral, economic, or social influences to affect the behavior of the other groups. The first group, taxpayers, seeking on the whole to keep their taxes down, have only a moderate amount of power, because they do not directly intervene in school policy and taxes are typically only one of several issues influencing their votes in school board elections. School boards, the fourth group, do have substantial power, but their principal goal is to minimize conflict, to avoid disruptive clashes in the conduct of the schools. Teachers, the fifth group, are a powerful organized force, seeking smaller class sizes, higher wages, and fringe benefits. In their organized capacity, therefore, teachers translate funds for disadvantaged students into increased employment benefits for themselves. School administrators, also a powerful group, tend to use additional funds for expanding district staff in ways designed to minimize conflict.

Various coalitions may develop among these six groups, notably between taxpayers and the school board, and between teachers and administrators. The results are likely to include heavy pressure to attract a maximum of federal and state funds, and to devote any increases in funds to job benefits for educators. Disadvantaged parents and students are unlikely to be able to form advantageous coalitions and are therefore likely to benefit least from increased resources. The evidence from the published evaluations of the federally financed compensatory education programs (Title I) supports the conclusions of this model of school district behavior. Very few of the benefits of Title I programs went to disadvantaged children; much of the money was used to aid taxpayers and school district employees.

Given the present distribution of power, Levin concludes that increases in school funds generated by the fiscal neutrality cases will, in like manner, be used to provide benefits for educators rather than poor students. In that sense, he says, compensatory education has not failed; it has never been tried. Nonetheless, the fiscal neutrality cases should be upheld because they at least offer the potential for more equal education, if child-centered educational policies should eventually be adopted at the school district level.

THE POLITICS OF FISCAL NEUTRALITY

In Chapter 7, Alan K. Campbell and Dennis A. Gilbert generally agree with Levin that decisionmaking power will continue to rest in the hands of professional educators and middle-class taxpayers. Will there, however, be an increase in state control as a consequence of increased state funding? Present studies indicate that the relation between the state share of finance and control of local educational policy is slight. The "no politics" tradition of American education has tended to give much of the political power in education to educational professionals. Because there is no sustained organized opposition to public education, the professionals have had substantial freedom of action, both at the school-district level and the state level. At the state level, surveys indicate that the state education agencies are relatively independent from the governor and the legislature. However, they are traditionally weak in administration, which has been justified by the ideology of "local control" in public education.

At the state level, the state agencies' constituencies are organizations of school board members, and of administrators and teachers, as well as public interest groups such as parent-teacher associations. These groups have traditionally worked closely together at the state level to promote benefits including increased funding for education. This consensus is now breaking up, with considerable fragmentation of interest groups. The result is to increase state legislators' freedom of action to work in favor of their own constituencies.

The federal government has entered the public education field somewhat reluctantly, because of congressional concerns for the political pressures that would be produced by general aid to education. They have preferred to provide categorical aid, distributed through state education agencies, which has tended to strengthen the state agencies' hand in public education policy.

How will fiscal neutrality affect the governance of the schools in such domains as finance, personnel and curriculum? In finance, rich districts are likely to use their influence at the state level to oppose full state funding in favor of permissive variations at the local district level. The politically powerful middle- and upper-class suburban districts are likely to be strong advocates of perpetuating quality differentials. These pressures may be strong enough to push the courts toward allowing discretionary variation in full state funding schemes, despite the evident conflict with equal protection doctrines. The same suburban districts are likely to oppose district power equalizing, because it will lead to higher tax rates for rich districts.

In the short run, implementing *Serrano* and other decisions will mean more money for education because equality of treatment will have to be produced by a leveling up process. In the long run, however, state control of school finance may mean slower increases in spending because teacher organizations will not be able to play one district off against another as they now do. Of course, if teacher and administrator organizations are able to develop strong statewide political power, legislatures may be forced to provide substantial increases, but given the increasing fragmentation of educational interest groups, this is an unlikely outcome in most states.

In respect to curriculum, the changes are likely to be less sweeping. School boards will have to devote less of their time to finances, but it is not clear that they will devote more time to curriculum. As in the past, professional educators will tend to dominate curriculum policy. However, there is likely to be a relative increase in the influence of education professionals at the state level, with a consequent increase in emphasis on statewide curriculum evaluation and development. Such a tendency will be strongly resisted by local professionals, but not with complete success. In respect to personnel practices, the states already have substantial authority over teacher certification. The most marked changes in personnel policy are likely to be in pay scales. The additional funds produced by leveling up under the equal protection cases will go to higher pay for teachers and administrators as well as for larger staffs. On the other hand, as noted above, in the long run teacher organizations are likely to have less influence over state legislatures than over local school boards.

If the rich districts are able to exert enough influence, the state role in education will not substantially change existing decisionmaking authority and processes. In these circumstances, there will be very little change in the operation of the system. If full state funding is adopted, the result may be a new, state-operated, decentralized state educational structure, perhaps with regional agencies operating as intermediaries between school districts and the state education agencies. In either event, a substantial share of the decision-making power will remain with the educational professionals, as in the past.

CATEGORICAL AID AND FISCAL NEUTRALITY

In Chapter 8, Joel S. Berke and Robert J. Goettel point out that the courts have avoided discussion of categorical aid. This aid consists of earmarked revenue sources, usually provided by state or federal agencies, that are addressed to specific purposes, such as transportation, programs for disadvantaged, handicapped or gifted students, school lunch programs, and so on. The authors point out that some categorical programs may violate fiscal neutrality, for example by requiring matching funds from local districts without reference to differences in district wealth. Categorical programs potentially provide the allowance for differences in educational need that was rejected by the court in *McInnis v. Ogilvie.*

Categorical aid is designed as a method for higher jurisdictions to respond to needs that are not randomly or equally distributed at the local level, such as for transportation or compensatory education. It also is a way for state and federal governments to encourage practices in local districts that represent the interests of these broader jurisdictions. Funding for innovative practices or compensatory education are cases in point. Finally—in theory at least—they allow higher jurisdictions to evaluate the performance of local districts in conducting programs that are considered to be of special importance.

As now offered, categorical aids are sometimes positively correlated with district wealth (for example, fast-growing wealthy schools may get a disproportionate share of construction aid), but they do offer the school system an opportunity to meet the educational needs criteria that *Serrano* and *Rodriguez* presumably permit but fail to provide for directly.

The sources of differential need include differences in population density, in population age distribution and in percentage of school-age children attending public schools, in percentages of handicapped and disadvantaged students, and in school construction needs. Equalizing formulas can in effect be a source of categorical aid by offering extra amounts of state aid per pupil for students with specified characteristics.

Berke and Goettel review the national pattern of state categorical aid. More than one-sixth of all state aid to local districts is categorical, mostly in the form of flat grants for school construction, special education, transportation, vocational education, and compensatory education, in that order. The authors describe current initiatives in categorical aid being proposed in California, Florida, Michigan, Minnesota, and New York.

Federal categorical aid has been provided in a variety of forms since 1917, when aid to vocational education was initiated. Thereafter, successively introduced were free lunch programs, aid to areas with large numbers of federal employees, post-Sputnik aid to improve the quality of America's technical skills, and aid for the poor and for educational innovation under the Elementary and Secondary Education Act of 1965. These programs have a variety of goals: (1) helping districts cope with effects of situations that are national in scope (for example, aid to children of migrant workers); (2) national goals not perceived by local districts (for example, school lunches); (3) situations where there are important externalities or economies of scale (for example, research and development or aid to teacher training institutions); (4) interstate equalization.

Federal aid, consisting of nearly 100 separate programs, ranges from 2.5 percent (Iowa) to 26 percent (Mississippi) of total state education spending. The aid is generally focused most heavily on central cities and rural areas, minorities, the poor, and low achievers. In total, the federal government provides about 7 percent of all public school expenditures. The actual ways that funds are used reflect preferences of state and local administrators, because the public education system is too decentralized to allow effective federal control of local policy.

Current proposals for revising federal aid include untied federal block grants, special education revenue-sharing (essentially the creation of several broad categorical grant areas by drastic reduction of the present number of categories), and general aid contingent on adoption of equalizing policies by the states. Each presents its own strengths and weaknesses.

So far, local school administrators have been able to use categorical aid to suit their own purposes. Although this often frustrates federal and state purposes, it is not evident that federal and state agencies can allocate funds more effectively than district administrators.

These political questions are reinforced by legal questions about categorical aid. Does categorical aid have to be fiscally neutral? Berke and Goettel conclude that it does, thereby disallowing unequalized matching programs.

Recent court cases carry the implication that special categories of students may require special treatment. Thereby categorical aid may eventually provide an educational-needs rationale to complement the fiscal neutrality principle proposed in *Serrano* and *Rodriguez*.

POLITICAL IMPLICATIONS: A CASE STUDY

Despite the evident inequity of most state school-finance systems, change has been slow to come. The inequalities produced by current foundation programs create a group of districts with vested interests, and the fragmentation of educational interest groups and the geographical decentralization of school districts create a variety of interest groups that find it difficult to invite alternatives. These conditions are remarkably similar from state to state.

In Chapter 9, Arnold J. Meltsner and Robert T. Nakamura examine the politics of state financial reform using California as an example. The forces at work will be similar in most states—a fight by beneficiaries of the present system to defend the status quo, an effort by various specific interest groups to obtain adjustments on their behalf, and a continuing debate about appropriate school tax policies. The outcomes will vary by state, as specific political factors interact with the general political features of school finance. The authors predict that, in most states, the result will be relatively minor changes in school finance policy rather than the large-scale reforms anticipated by those who have observed the fiscal neutrality decisions.

Positive results of *Serrano* and other cases will be to direct legislative attention to school finance and to expand the base of political support for reform. However, there is no evidence that the court decisions have provided enough political strength to sweep away the existing legislative paralysis. Nor can the courts by themselves efficiently legislate and administer the reforms they mandate. Since the fiscal neutrality cases leave the legislatures a wide range of options, the legislative solution is likely to turn more on estimates of political feasibility than on conformity to the courts' intent. Therefore, we can expect some lessening of the financial pressure on poor districts, without abandonment of certain privileges for rich ones. Full state funding is politically impossible, as is any large-scale shift in tax policy.

To understand why large changes are unlikely, Meltsner and Nakamura contend, it is necessary to perceive the leading features that characterize state school finance policy. First, rich districts are more likely to succeed in preserving the status quo, which favors their interests, than poor districts are in persuading the state to tax others for their benefit. Second, at the ideological level, many legislators believe that school districts are not accountable, efficient, or responsive to the communities. Therefore, the problem of the schools is perceived as not susceptible to solution by more funds, which the education lobby persistently demands. Third, the concept of equalization raises certain questions of value. Many legislators are uneasy about a concept of fiscal neutrality that appears to place restrictions on the right of well-to-do parents to offer their children as high a quality of public education as the local community wishes to pay for. Given this conflict of values, the "solution" is often inaction. Fourth, school finance reform is a low priority item for most political participants—governors, legislators, teacher organizations, and so on. Only some school finance experts and a few legislators give high priority to reform. When changes are made, they are likely to take the form of marginal changes in the complex structure of categorical aid or foundation plans. The more complex the superstructure of state finance arrangements, the more reluctant legislators will be to undertake sweeping change with unpredictable consequences. Sweeping change is further inhibited because its supporters are disunited as lobbyists, and parents are largely voiceless in their stand on such a complex subject as financial reform. Opponents of change—rich school districts, farmers, and certain business interests—are well organized to defend the interests that are threatened by reform. Partisan politics may also act as an impediment to change—in California, for example, Republican legislators and the governor are less likely than Democrats to support increased state funding for education.

Given these conditions, the authors say that policy must be used to create a coalition of supporters through appropriate appeals to the fragmented interests in the political arena.

> Once a proposal which accommodates a core of supporters is formulated, policy entrepreneurs engage in an exercise of salesmanship and side-payments to gain additional support. The strategy of building coalitions through formulating attractive proposals comes from being aware of the enduring features—paralysis, the second priority, complexity, weak support and strong opposition, and partisanship.

Meltsner and Nakamura discuss California legislative maneuvering during 1971-72, in the wake of *Serrano*. As it turned out, the legislation that was finally approved late in 1972 closely followed the pattern predictable from the enduring features affecting school finance policy. Full state funding was soon ruled out in favor of a modest increase in the existing state share. A modest degree of equalization was provided through raising the state support floor. Property-tax relief was provided for homeowners, in particular for high-tax, low-wealth districts; limitations were also placed on local districts' ability to increase property taxes. The existing tax structure was left undisturbed, as was the existing structure of local control over school districts. No move was made to redistribute the tax base of wealthy districts, and the politically attractive balloon of property-tax relief was tied to the weight of increased state funding.

Were these reforms consistent with *Serrano*? On the face of it, clearly not. No effort was made to make school spending independent of the wealth of neighboring families.

On the other hand, the California type of reform may ultimately be accepted by the courts, abiding with the legislatures' judgment that such reforms represent the maximum feasible change. The authors state their fear that acceptance of such a minimum program by the courts will damage long-run reform prospects that will *automatically* allow for continued improvement without renewed paroxysmal tinkering with the foundation plan. In some respects, the authors' suggestions are consistent with the Fleischmann Report proposals for New York, which provide for automatic upgrading of district spending to the point where statewide uniformity, with categorical exceptions, is achieved. However, Meltsner and Nakamura believe that in California, as in other states, a number of conditions not now in effect would have to be met before such a structural change could be achieved.

SCHOOL FINANCE AND SOCIAL POLICY

In Chapter 10, David K. Cohen considers the fiscal neutrality decisions in the perspective of broader social issues, stemming from the judicial finding that education is a fundamental interest, deserving of special consideration under the Fourteenth Amendment.

Cohen begins by pointing out that in *Serrano*, as in other fiscal neutrality cases, the court argued that reducing the influence of local wealth to serve the interests of property-poor districts would also serve the interests of poor children, and by improving the quality of their education provide them with more equal opportunities for economic and social success. But poor people, Cohen points out, are as likely to live in rich districts as in poor ones, and no one know whether there is any relation between school spending and educational outcomes, for reasons discussed by Levin in Chapter 6.

The central issue that the courts attacked in practice, then, is unfairness in taxation as it affects a district's freedom to choose its preferred level of taxing and spending. The index of ability to pay used by the courts is the property-tax base. But, as has often been pointed out, the incomes of the district's taxpayers and the locality's level of noneducation spending, although overlooked in the fiscal neutrality cases, are also important determinants of a district's capacity to pay for schools. Precisely because income is left out of the fiscal neutrality calculus, the doctrine cannot eliminate the influence of wealth on local school revenues, Cohen argues. Even if income cannot be included in the calculus, because of the many political issues it would raise, some improvement would be achieved by excluding industrial and commercial property from the local tax base.

Cohen attributes the courts' stance to an essentially political calculation—that some equalizing of tax burdens was possible if the issue were presented as one of equity in the distribution of schooling. But, as he points out, satisfying the fourteenth amendment with respect to the distribution of school aid does not necessarily imply fairness in the production of revenue. This leaves a considerable degree of vagueness about exactly what the mandate of these cases is, and reinforces state legislatures' tendencies not to stray from the status quo.

What then is the social significance of the fiscal neutrality cases? The courts have held that equality in the provision of schooling is more important than equality in providing other social services, because education is, in the words of the New Jersey court, "a fundamental interest."

Cohen argues that although there is a connection between years of schooling and economic and social success, it accounts for only a modest part of those outcomes. The evidence leaves some uncertainty about whether education is a fundamental social interest. Even if it is so accepted, there is overwhelming evidence that school expenditures per student exercise little if any independent effect on school outcomes, and still less on chances for social and economic achievement.

It has also been argued that providing a fairer distribution of educational resources will provide a fairer distribution of political influence. As Cohen points out, the evidence indicates that people with more education participate more in politics, but the amount of money spent per student does not have any significant effect on how long people go to school. Furthermore, there is no evidence that high-spending schools develop more politically sophisticated people than low-spending ones. The effect of schooling on children's political learning is quite uniform.

In general, Cohen states, the effects of schooling may be very important, but they are not differential, because the educational system is quite uniform in its basic characteristics. It is the presence or absence of schooling that is important to society rather than its differential qualities.

In light of these considerations, who is likely to benefit from the fiscal neutrality decisions? Educational professionals are likely to gain, as are taxpayers in poor school districts. In a broader perspective, it can be argued that since children in poor districts will receive more resources, benefits will accrue to society as a whole because fiscal neutrality provides citizens with more equal access to public resources. This is a very different argument from those based on the productivity of increased school spending, and is, in a sense, in conflict with that argument.

In conclusion, Cohen points out that there is little support for the contention that the fundamental interest requires fiscal neutrality. Even defining a necessary minimum standard may prove to be difficult in a society where most people already receive at least twelve years of schooling. The political argument for equality tends in the direction of uniform provision rather than minimum provision, but to accept this argument for education without also accepting it for a wide variety of public goods creates substantial difficulties. For example, the notion of power equalizing, discussed in Chapter 2, has the virtue of separating individual wealth from levels of public expenditure, but it raises unavoidable questions about the entire structure of public revenues and spending. These dilemmas are inherent in the fiscal neutrality cases, and are likely to be resolved only by gradual changes in the ways that we think about equality, schooling, and society.

REFERENCES

1. For the United States as a whole in 1972, 52 percent of school funds came from local sources through property tax; 41 percent came from state

government support; and 7 percent from federal support. Almost all the local funds are raised by property taxes.

2. In California, Beverly Hills' per capita tax base is nearly 14 times that of Baldwin Hills; Baldwin Hills has to impose a $5.48 property tax rate to raise $577 per student, but Beverly Hills can raise $1232 per student with a tax rate of only $2.38.

3. J.S. Coleman. et al., *Equality of Educational Opportunity*, U.S. Office of Education, Washington, 1966.

4. Harold Horowitz, "Unseparate But Unequal—The Emerging Fourteenth Amendment Issue in Public School Education," *UCLA Law Review* 13 (1966):1147; Arthur E. Wise, *Rich Schools, Poor Schools: The Promise of Equal Educational Opportunity* (Chicago: University of Chicago Press, 1968); John E. Coons, William H. Clune III, and Stephen Sugarman, *Private Wealth and Public Education* (Cambridge, Mass.: Belknap Press, 1970).

5. 96 Cal. Reporter at 604, 487, p., 2nd at 1244.

6. Supreme Court of The United States, No. 71-1332, San Antonio Independent School District et al., Appellants v. Dimetrio P. Rodriguez et al., March 25, 1973.

7. *Report of the New York State Commission on the Quality, Cost, and Financing of Elementary and Secondary Education*, Albany, 1972.

8. Christopher Jencks et al., *Inequality* (New York: Basic Books, 1972).

9. Harvey A. Averch et al., *How Effective Is Schooling?* (Santa Monica: The Rand Corporation, 1972).

10. John Pincus, *Incentives for Innovation in the Public Schools* (Santa Monica: The Rand Corporation, 1973); R.D. Carlson et al., *Change Processes in the Public Schools* (Eugene: University of Oregon, 1965).

Chapter Two

Alternative Post-Serrano Systems and Their Expenditure Implications

Stephen M. Barro
The Rand Corporation

Although the Supreme Court, in *Rodriguez*, declined to make school finance reform a constitutional imperative, this by no means implies that states will be freed of pressure to modify their systems in directions sought by the *Serrano* and *Rodriguez* plaintiffs. The main practical consequence of the decision is that this pressure is not likely to be applied by or through the federal courts. But there are at least three other ways in which leverage can be exerted to bring about thoroughgoing reform on a state-by-state basis. One important possibility is legal action based on state constitutions, which are explicit about public responsibilities in education while the federal constitution is not. The court rulings obtained by reform forces in New Jersey provide a convincing demonstration of the opportunities that lie along that route.[1] A second possibility is that federal legislation will eventually compel or induce changes of the kind implied by *Serrano* and *Rodriguez*. This could happen if requirements or strong incentives for distributional reform were attached to a program of federal financial aid, as has been suggested in a number of Nixon administration and congressional proposals during 1972 and 1973.[2] The third possibility is that political efforts at the state level will lead to action by state legislatures to develop more equitable financing systems. A number of states have recently taken action to reshape their systems substantially.[3] The fact that these efforts continue now that the threat of federal court action has been removed is cause for optimism about the capacity of states to reform themselves without congressional, judicial, or other external intervention.

If anything, the absence of a national mandate for a particular kind of school finance reform makes it more important to identify and analyze reform alternatives. Had the *Serrano-Rodriguez* guidelines been upheld in detail, states might have had relatively little leeway in designing new systems. As it is, reform mandates by state courts are likely to take varied forms, depending on the wording and interpretation of individual state constitutions and on the present financial pattern in each state. Even greater diversity can be expected where reform takes place as a result of political efforts in state legislatures, rather than in response to court orders. Thus, the present situation is highly fluid. Many reform options need to be considered that would have been excluded or made irrelevant by affirmative Supreme Court action; fewer constraints can be taken as given. There seems to be a real need by policymakers at the state level, and perhaps at the federal level as well, for definition and analysis of the alternatives that have now opened up and for elucidation of their consequences. This chapter and those that follow are intended to provide major pieces of the needed information.

The present chapter is concerned, specifically, with alternative post-*Serrano* school finance systems and their prospective effects on the level and distribution of public school expenditures. Certain aspects of the discussion are oriented toward the situation in California, where the executive, legislative, and judicial arms of state government have been grappling with the issue since the initial *Serrano* decision in August 1971. However, the California emphasis is reflected primarily in the numerical examples and illustrations. Nothing in the discussion of alternatives limits the applicability of the analysis to other states.

The scope of this chapter is limited in two significant respects. First, nothing is said about proposals that depart from the general model of publicly funded, publicly operated elementary and secondary schools. Thus, educational voucher plans are not examined even though advocates view them as potential replacements for existing school finance systems. Nor is any attempt made to analyze plans that would do away with local educational jurisdictions (school districts) as the basic units of financial and administrative organization. Brief reference is made, however, to possible financial implications of school district reorganization. Second, this chapter does not deal with the full range of implications of the alternatives discussed, but leaves many important issues to be explored in later chapters. In particular, a comprehensive treatment of the tax or revenue side of school finance reform will be found in Chapter 4. Analyses of changes in school governance and in education itself that are likely to follow from school finance reform will be found elsewhere in this volume.

The organization of this chapter is as follows: First, alternative interpretations of the "mandate for equalization" are discussed, as laid down or likely to be laid down by the courts, or as it may be defined through the political process. Then, with alternative equalization standards established, existing types of school finance systems are examined to determine why and to what extent they violate those norms. This is followed by a detailed exposition of post-*Serrano* alternatives, which builds on the previous norm-setting and diagnostic exercises. The final section examines likely local responses to different types of alternative systems, and describes, at a general level, the new patterns of expenditure distribution that are likely to emerge.

INTERPRETATION OF THE MANDATE FOR EQUALIZATION

The principal goal of current school finance reform efforts is *equalization*— reduction of existing inequities in access to educational programs and in the tax burdens that must be shouldered to obtain a given level of school support. Long after the first state equal protection ruling (*Serrano*), there remains considerable disagreement about the degree of equalization that such decisions require, or the kind of inequality they permit. This is paralleled by intense controversy among school finance and educational experts, political and educational leaders, and other concerned parties about what forms of equalization—setting aside the legalities—are good public policy. To some extent, these differences revolve around fairly narrow, even technical issues, such as the "correct" way of defining "fiscal ability," "tax effort," and "educational need." At least in equal part, however, they involve basic questions about education—the effectiveness of schooling and its effects on individuals' lives and prospects—and equally basic issues of political philosophy—centralized versus decentralized decisionmaking and the balance between equality and individual or local choice. Conflicting opinions on these issues give rise to a range of interpretations of decisions of the *Serrano* type and, more fundamentally, to diverse formulations of the proper role of the state in equalizing educational opportunity for its citizens.

Looking at the expenditure side of school finance only (neglecting the question of how school tax burdens should be distributed), several points of view emerge on *what* should be equalized and on the *degree* of equalization that an acceptable system should produce. Each set of positions on these two questions constitutes a different interpretation of the equalization mandate.

What Is to be Equalized?

This question has two aspects. First, there is the problem of selecting a target variable for equalization policy. Three possibilities are (1) expenditures per pupil; (2) school resources per pupil; and (3) educational outputs. Next, a decision must be made on how thoroughgoing an equalization policy to pursue: Is the goal to reduce inequality in all categories of per pupil spending, resources, or outcomes, or does it apply only to support for certain functions—such as instruction—or to certain outputs—such as performance in basic skills? To take extreme examples, one could establish as ambitious a goal as minimizing variations in a broad range of educational performance categories, or as narrow a goal as reducing disparities in the amount spent per pupil for teachers. The financial implications are obviously vastly different. Considerations that bear on this choice include, on one hand, the educational and philosophical implications of each possible equalization goal and, on the other, such practical matters as the measurability of the relevant variables and the feasibility of translating each goal into a plan for allocating dollars.

Expenditures per pupil. A policy of equalizing expenditures per pupil raises the fewest practical problems, but it is the least satisfactory on educational and philosophical -grounds. The practical advantages are that (1) measurement problems would be minimal even if a very inclusive definition of per pupil spending were chosen;[4] (2) it would be easy for interested parties—including the courts—to verify the degree of equalization that had been achieved; and (3) translation of the equalization goal into a financial formula would be straightforward since there would be no need to determine dollar implications of redistributing some nonmonetary resource or result. The main shortcomings of such a policy are that by considering only dollars, one would be neglecting both variations in the educational purchasing power of the dollar across jurisdictions and variations in the effects of a "dollar's worth" of education on different types of children. Therefore, despite the advantages of simplicity, expenditure per pupil would be the right target variable only if the goal were to equalize access to tax dollars without regard to either the educational effects or the educational resources those dollars could obtain.

School resources per pupil. From an educational point of view it is clearly more meaningful to give students access to equal amounts of real resources—teachers, materials, facilities, and so on—than to equal numbers of dollars. But to do the former it would be necessary to determine differences in costs of resources from one jurisdiction to another and to make appropriate adjustments in distributing funds. This raises the following practical problems: (1) It is extremely difficult to compare resource costs across districts when there are variations both in prices paid for resources and in resource quality. The difficulty is especially great when it comes to comparing costs of teachers, the most important resource in education. (2) When there are many different types of resources to consider, as would certainly be the case if an inclusive definition of educational resources were adopted, the necessary calculations become complicated and cumbersome.

These difficulties are not likely to be overcome quickly. In particular, the teacher quality problem is likely to remain intractable for some time, since neither an adequate conceptual base (for example, a definition of teacher quality) nor relevant data are now available. This means that interdistrict cost indexes with satisfactory properties can not now be constructed.

Yet there is a strong case for taking cost differentials into account, especially with respect to urban districts where wages and prices are clearly higher, and with respect to certain classes of districts—both urban and rural—where substantial premiums may have to be paid to attract quality staff. To neglect the problem on grounds that quantification is difficult would perpetuate one of the major inequities of existing systems. A feasible interim solution may be to develop rough cost factors for a few broad categories of districts—for example, urban, rural, suburban—and to use those, where appropriate, to modify dollar allocations. It should be possible to assemble enough evidence to define reasonable ranges for these factors, following which the final determinations would depend on educational and political judgment. The results, admittedly, would bear only a general resemblance to true resource equalization. Nevertheless, compared with the alternative of "dollars only," even a crude adjustment process could be expected to produce a substantially closer approximation to equal treatment of pupils.

Educational outcomes. The real philosophical gap appears between those who focus on equalization of school inputs, whether dollars or resources, and those who maintain that the purpose of reform should be to reduce disparities in the results or end products of education. The rationale for the latter view is that schooling is only a means to an end and that, therefore, equalization of resources or programs per se is not of fundamental interest; the proper target of equalization policy is the benefits that are supposed to flow from schooling. This may mean either long-term benefits, such as job opportunities or social status, or immediate results such as the ability to read. In either case, the contention is that dollars or resources should be allocated to produce a "good" distribution of benefits, taking account of the differential effects that given allotments of resources are likely to have when applied to different kinds of children. The last clause is the key: operationally, the goal of equalizing outcomes means an effort to allow for differential educational needs of children when allocating funds. Assuming that this goal is desirable, the practical issue becomes the degree to which such needs can be measured and translated into financial differentials.

A policy of outcome equalization would logically seem to require quantitative knowledge of relationships between resources and outcomes for different types of pupils. With such knowledge, one could say, for example, that poor urban pupils "need" 50 percent greater resource allotments than suburban pupils to reach the same levels of performance. But existing knowledge of input-output relationships is so fragmentary that such statements are out of the question. In fact, a realistic characterization of the current situation would be that (1) we have not defined many relevant dimensions of performance, much less devised ways to measure them; (2) we know very little about quantitative relationships between resources and outcomes; and (3) the best available evidence suggests that even massive redistributions of resources to low-performing children would be unlikely to have large effects on distributions of proximate or long-term results.[5] The last point, in particular, suggests that schemes for eliminating educational inequality through financial reform should be viewed with the utmost skepticism.

On the other hand, there is some basis for believing that there are categories of "disadvantaged" children whose performance would improve if sufficient additional resources were made available. This belief provides the rationale for federal and state compensatory education programs. To the extent that it is well-founded, allocation of additional funds to districts with disadvantaged populations could have the effect of bringing up the lower end of the outcome distribution. The mechanisms for this type of compensatory equalization is simple: all that is necessary is to give greater weight to disadvantaged than to regular pupils in computing each district's fund allocation. Several recent finance reform proposals have included provisions for this type of weighting according to educational need.[6]

At least for the time being, the general proposition that funds should be allocated according to educational needs boils down to the less ambitious proposal that additional funds should be given to districts with educationally disadvantaged pupils. Ideally, we would look to educational research or documented experience for guidance on whom to include in the disadvantaged category and on the size of the need adjustment. Realistically, it will be necessary to rely for some time to come on a combination of educators' and politicians' judgment.

The Unresolved Issue. The various court decisions did not clarify the issue of whether the correct target variable is dollars, dollars adjusted for cost, or dollars adjusted for both cost and educational need. What they seemed to say is that "at least" dollar equalization is required, while allowances for cost and need differentials are not required but are allowed. But this has raised a troubling issue. Studies conducted after *Serrano* have shown that if the real goal is to equalize either resources or resources in relation to needs, equalization of per pupil spending may be a step in the wrong direction. The reason is that many central cities, which have high needs because of their concentrations of poor and minority pupils, already spend more than the average for their respective states. This means that if state authorities pursued simplistic policies of dollar leveling, many high-need districts could be made worse off than before.[7] This is true, ironically, even though many of the equal protection lawsuits were brought in order to aid those very districts.

It remains possible that some state courts will rule that interdistrict variations in costs must be taken into account in new financing systems. But given the negative Supreme Court decisions in pre-*Serrano* cases that cited "needs," it is not likely that there will be a judicial mandate for compensatory equalization.[8] The question, "What is to be equalized?" will have to be fought out politically in the various state legislatures. The answer may determine whether the fundamental goals of school finance reform will be achieved.

What Degree of Equalization is Required?
There has been more concrete discussion of the degree of equalization to be produced than about the specific quantity to be equalized.

Nevertheless, there is considerable room for speculation about the forms that legal or policy criteria may ultimately take in the several states. Four distinct "equalization doctrines" can be identified: (1) uniform provision throughout a state; (2) fiscal neutrality; (3) limited variation in support; and (4) minimum provision. The meaning of these labels can best be conveyed by identifying the kinds of inequality that would and would not be allowed under each one.

Uniform provision. According to this interpretation or policy position, the only type of variation in educational spending per pupil that will (or should) ultimately be permitted among local jurisdictions is variation according to educationally relevant factors. Factors that would legitimately be associated with spending variations might include differences in costs of school resources among localities, differences in costs of educating different types of children, differences in the out-of-school environment that bear on children's educational performance, differences in needs for special services, and differences in availability of specific types of personnel and other resources. Variables that would *not* be permitted to affect spending are local wealth or tax base and local preferences regarding schooling. To have uniform provision, therefore, it would be necessary to establish a centralized system of finance. No one maintains that uniform provision was required or implied by *Serrano*-type rulings, but some contend that the decision of the New Jersey court points strongly toward full statewide equality.[9]

Fiscal neutrality. Fiscal neutrality is the equalization doctrine most closely associated with the equal protection cases. It is expressed by the proposition, "the quality of public education may not be a function of wealth, other than the wealth of the state as a whole."[10] This has been taken to mean that one local jurisdiction may support its schools more generously than another by exerting greater fiscal effort for public schooling, but that each district's ability to support schools must be independent of its own wealth or tax base. Under fiscal neutrality, therefore, expenditures may vary according to differences in local willingness to pay for public schooling, as well as according to the kinds of educationally relevant factors mentioned above.

This immediately raises the questions of how "ability" or "wealth" and "willingness" or "effort" are to be measured. It becomes clear as one searches for answers that there are several versions of fiscal neutrality. The narrowest definition, one that corresponds most closely to the precise language of *Serrano*, is that if the property tax is the source of local funds, then per pupil support may vary with the local school property-tax *rate* (effort), but not with the property tax *base* (wealth).[11] A natural extension is to define both wealth and effort more comprehensively, for example, by using community income as the measure or by taking account of multiple dimensions of wealth. The distinction between income and property value is an important one, because the two are not necessarily closely correlated. Different sets of districts would be losers and gainers, depending on which was chosen.

A troublesome issue concerning fiscal neutrality is that of the separability of effort and wealth. High-tax-base or high-income communities may prove more willing than others to tax themselves for schools even when they are not permitted to take direct advantage of their greater ability to pay. Then, with school spending correlated with wealth, would the fiscal neutrality principle be satisfied? To answer, one must choose between ex post and ex ante concepts of fiscal neutrality. The ex post interpretation is that the actual level of educational support must not correlate with wealth. On that basis, a system that resulted in both higher spending and higher tax effort in wealthy districts would not be acceptable. The ex ante formulation is that the *ability* of a district to support schools should not depend on wealth. This means only that a unit of effort must produce the same support everywhere. In that case a correlation between expenditure and wealth might be acceptable. As a practical matter, systems based on the ex ante notion are much simpler and more likely to be adopted.

Limited variation. In contrast to those who hold to one of the above-mentioned strict equalization principles, there are others who suggest that the *magnitude* of disparities in spending and tax rates permitted under a new system is the key determinant of its legal and/or political acceptability.[12] According to this theory, there would never have been judicial intervention in the school finance field if it were not for the gross inequalities among districts permitted by state laws. If those disparities are sharply reduced, the argument goes, it will no longer be important to show that the new system conforms to some abstract equalization standard or that all vestiges of correlation between wealth and expenditure and wealth and tax rate have been eliminated. Thus, systems that permit wealthy districts to enjoy somewhat higher levels of support and/or somewhat lower tax rates than other districts may be acceptable, provided that those advantages are not "excessive."

It is difficult to be more precise about the degree of variation that would be permissible under this doctrine, except that it would presumably have to be no more than a small fraction of the average level of per pupil support. Quantitative limits could be stated either in terms of the degree of variation (e.g., a maximum coefficient of variation of per pupil spending of no more than 10 percent) or as an interpercentile range (e.g., no more than 15 percent variation in per pupil support between the 10th and 90th percentile districts). Presumably, state courts would have to specify these limits in much the same manner as the Supreme Court was eventually forced to specify numerical limits on inequality in order to implement its equal apportionment rulings.[13]

Minimum provision. The final and most unrestrictive interpretation of the equalization mandate is that every local jurisdiction in a state must simply be guaranteed access on equal terms to an "adequate" level of support for its educational program. This might mean that a state would have to provide sufficient state revenues to each district to finance the "adequate" program, or that it would have to assure each district's ability to finance such a program at a given level of local tax effort. If individual districts chose to spend more per pupil out of locally raised funds than was needed for the "adequate" program, that would be deemed irrelevant to the question of equalization.

So permissive an interpretation cannot be extracted from the wording of the *Serrano*-type rulings. Nevertheless, one can conceive of the "fundamental interest" argument being used, ultimately, to support such a position. It could be claimed that all the vital functions attributed to education by plaintiffs in equal protection cases are valid, but that they are fully accomplished when an "adequate" program is provided. Any additional school support could then be viewed as a consumption good, or luxury, for the pupils concerned, not covered by the fundamental interest umbrella.

The success of this line of argument may depend on whether any substance can be given to the concept of an "adequate" public school program. A state could certainly contend that a guarantee of what was until recently the *average* statewide level of per pupil support to every jurisdiction would constitute adequate provision relative to the wealth of the state as a whole. A wealthy state might even attempt to justify its system by pointing out that all its districts are well supported by *national standards*. Thus, the minimum provision doctrine could be construed very permissably to legitimize systems very similar to those now in use, subject only to a showing by the state that the minimum level of support provided to each district is, in fact, "adequate."

Specific financing formulas that correspond to each of the four equalization doctrines or combinations thereof will be described later in this chapter. But to prepare the groundwork for that discussion, I turn first to an analysis of inequalities and departures from these equalization standards under existing school finance systems.

SOURCES OF INEQUALITY UNDER EXISTING SYSTEMS

Existing school finance systems in most states fail to meet even the least restrictive of the four equalization standards: access to a "minimum adequate" educational program at a uniform price. They fall far short of satisfying more demanding standards such as statewide uniformity of support or fiscal neutrality. In nearly every case, the design of the system makes the financial opportunities available to a school district a function of local taxable wealth. That is, a district with a high tax base is more able than a "poor" district in the same state to enjoy a higher level of per pupil spending, a lower school tax rate, or both.

Intrastate disparities in expenditures and tax rates have been documented in two recent national studies, in numerous official and unofficial reports from individual states, and, of course, in a stream of plaintiffs' briefs in equal protection lawsuits.[14] The California data shown in Table 2-1 illustrate a typical pattern. The data for the first group of districts show that communities with progressively higher tax bases need to pay progressively lower tax rates to support roughly similar levels of spending. The second set of comparisons shows that available support at a given tax rate bears a strong positive relationship to wealth. The third set shows that wealthy districts are simultaneously able to offer more generously financed programs and lower tax rates than districts with less taxable property per pupil. Although California, like many other states, distributes state aid funds in an inverse relationship to wealth in order to compensate for tax base disparities, the data on state aid and local tax revenues in Table 2-1 show that aid does not increase nearly rapidly enough to offset the proportional relationship between local wealth and revenue-raising ability. This is brought out most dramatically by comparing the figures for Compton, a poor black suburb of Los Angeles, and Santa Monica, a predominantly white suburb with a very large tax base. Although Compton gets 2.5 times as much state aid, Santa Monica, which exerts only half the tax effort, is able to spend 20 percent more per pupil.

The most important point, however, is not the magnitude of the spending and tax rate disparities, but that disparities are designed into existing state systems. That is, specific features of the formulas for distributing state aid

Table 2-1.   Expenditures, State Aid, Tax Rates, and Property Values in Selected California School Districts, 1970-71

District	Property Value per Pupil	State Aid per Pupil	Current Expense per Pupil	Tax Rate for Current Purposes
Compton	$ 4790	$ 455	$ 852	6.10%
Alameda	9836	325	848	5.05
Monrovia	12373	316	863	4.74
Long Beach	16142	237	862	3.71
Garden Grove	5813	424	678	4.29
San Diego	10267	327	817	4.22
Downey	13268	301	833	4.25
Newport-Mesa	17876	192	888	4.31
Mt. Diablo	7834	397	844	5.93
San Jose	12360	310	893	4.84
Burbank	24136	216	946	3.43
Santa Monica	29810	183	1025	2.85

Source: *California Public Schools, Selected Statistics*, 1970-71 (Sacramento: California State Department of Education, 1972).

and provisions of the law governing local taxation assure that wealthy districts will have superior financial opportunities. In analyzing the main types of existing systems, our primary purpose is to pinpoint the characteristics that lead to wealth-related advantages. With that information in hand it becomes easier to see how systems must be changed to bring them into compliance with more or less stringent equalization standards.

Types of Systems

In every state but Hawaii, where there is a single statewide educational system, the nonfederal portion of a school district's funds is obtained from a mix of local tax revenues and grants-in-aid from the state government.[15] The local portion consists predominantly of receipts from taxes on real and personal property located within a district's boundaries. Some states allow local use of nonproperty taxes for support of schools, but generally they are of minor importance.[16] The main differences among existing state systems, therefore, have to do with the proportions in which property taxes and state aid funds are relied on to support schools, the forms in which state aid is provided, and the degree of variation in taxable property per pupil among districts. These characteristics are all determined by the state statutes that define school district boundaries, authorize districts to levy taxes, and specify the rules for apportioning state school funds.

In most states, the bulk of the state contribution is distributed in the form of general-purpose grants to school districts, funds that can be used for any category of operating expenses. Usually there are also special-purpose, or categorical, grants for specific educational functions, such as pupil transportation, or for particular categories of pupils, such as handicapped, retarded, or disadvantaged. In this discussion we restrict our attention to general-purpose grants, which are the main focus of current reform efforts.

It is useful at the outset to divide state aid formulas into two broad categories. The first includes all formulas that distribute aid as *lump-sum grants*, without regard to local decisions about school tax rates or overall levels of per pupil spending.[17] There are two important subcategories: the foundation program formula, which distributes state funds in inverse relationship to the local property tax base, and the flat grant formula, which, as its name suggests, allocates essentially the same amount of money per pupil to each district. According to the National Educational Finance Project (NEFP), during school year 1968-69 thirty-four states used the former and seven states used the latter;[18] however, several states operated systems that combined elements of foundation and flat-grant mechanisms, which makes that count only approximate. In any case, the two kinds of lump-sum formulas were used by the great majority of the fifty states.

The second category consists of state systems that incorporate the principle of variable matching, in which the state matches local revenues or shares in total spending at a rate that varies inversely with local wealth. These systems, more commonly described as percentage equalization or guaranteed valuation formulas, were found in eight states in 1968-69, according to the NEFP.[19] The reason for distinguishing them from the lump-sum grant formulas is not that their allocative effects are so different (in fact, side conditions and constraints often restrict the matching effect so severely that they are indistinguishable from lump-sum formulas) but that the variable matching principle itself is a key ingredient of some of the most important post-*Serrano* alternatives.

Foundation Program and Flat-Grant Systems

Texts on school finance generally differentiate between foundation program and flat grant formulas on the basis that the former tend to equalize expenditures among districts and the latter do not. In fact, the basic sources of wealth-related inequality in financial opportunities are the same under both systems. Mathematically, the flat grant formula is merely an extreme case of the more general foundation program formula.

The basic concept underlying the foundation program formula is that any school district, however meager its tax base, should be guaranteed a certain minimum level of revenue per pupil (the "foundation program") provided only that the district exerts a minimum level of effort on its own behalf by imposing at least a stipulated minimum property tax rate. A district's aid entitlement is the difference (if greater than zero) between the foundation level of spending per pupil and the amount per pupil that the district raises locally at the specified minimum rate. Algebraically,

$$S = F - r_0 V,$$

where

S = the amount of state aid per pupil,
F = the foundation amount per pupil established by the state,[20]
r_0 = the minimum tax rate specified by the state, and
V = taxable property per pupil, the local tax base.

The total revenue per pupil, E, obtained by a district under this system is, by definition, the sum of state aid, S, and local property tax revenue, rV, where r is the tax rate (at least equal to r_0) selected by local authorities. Therefore,

$$E = S + rV = F - r_0 V + rV = F + (r - r_0) V.$$

That is, total revenue per pupil equals the foundation amount plus the revenue brought in by imposition of a local tax rate in excess of the minimum required rate, r_0.

The foundation formula has an equalizing effect in that it establishes a negative relationship between the amount of state aid and district wealth. To illustrate, consider a relatively wealthy district with $20,000 assessed value per pupil (AV) and a poor district with only $5000 per pupil.[21] Suppose that the foundation amount is set at $500 per pupil and the minimum tax rate at 2 percent. The wealthy district would be entitled to $500 − (0.02 x $20,000), or $100 per pupil in state aid. The poor district would receive a grant of $500 − (0.02 x $5000), or $400 per pupil. The two districts, although greatly different in wealth, would each be able to provide a $500 educational program at the identical tax rate of 2 percent.

But the equalizing effect of the formula is limited in two respects: First, the formula does nothing to compensate for differences in local ability to augment the foundation program. Thus, if the same two districts each taxed themselves at 4 percent, the district with $20,000 AV would be able to spend $900, while the district with $5000 AV would be able to spend only $600. Second, most states that use the foundation formula have established an aid "floor"—a minimum per-pupil grant to which any district, no matter how wealthy, is entitled. If the floor were set at $200, for example, the district with $20,000 AV, although entitled to only $100 per pupil according to the basic formula, would receive the $200 minimum grant instead. It would then be able to spend $100 more than the poorer district even at the 2 percent minimum tax rate. This significantly reduces the equalizing effect.

Under the flat grant formula there is no minimum tax rate that the district must impose as its contribution to the foundation formula. The state simply distributes a fixed number of dollars, G, for each pupil, and the district is on its own to augment that sum by collecting local taxes. That is, the total revenue available to the district is

$$E = G + rV,$$

where G is the amount of the flat grant per pupil and the other variables are as defined above.[22] Comparing this with the equation for per-pupil spending under the foundation formula, it can be seen that the two have the same form except for the minimum required tax rate, r_0. Putting it differently, the flat grant formula is equivalent to a foundation formula with the minimum required tax rate set at zero.

Taking the same hypothetical districts as in the previous example, and assuming a flat grant of $400, the total revenue obtained at a 2 percent tax rate by districts with $5000 and $20,000 AV is $500 and $800, respectively. In this comparison, therefore, the flat grant program produces greater inequality in financial opportunities than the foundation program formula. On the other hand, it is not correct to conclude that states with flat grant systems always distribute funds less equally than states with foundation systems. Had the amount of the flat grant been higher, say $600 per pupil, then opportunities would be more nearly equal for the two districts, at least over a considerable range of tax rates, than in the foundation formula example. It is correct to state, although we do not prove it, that for a given total amount of state aid, the foundation formula produces smaller expenditures and tax rate disparities than a system of flat grants.

The equalizing effects of alternative systems can be compared by means of a graphic analysis of the financial opportunities that each system makes available to districts with different tax bases. Later we will use that method to examine the properties of proposed post-*Serrano* alternatives. Here, to support the analysis of existing systems and to demonstrate the method itself, we apply it to the foundation program and flat grant formulas.

Figure 2-1 illustrates the properties of the "pure" foundation formula, Figure 2-2 the foundation formula modified by an aid floor, and Figure 2-3 the flat grant formula. Each shows the total revenue per pupil (state aid plus local property-tax revenue) that would be obtained at various tax rates by districts with low (L), average (A), high (H), and, in some cases, very high (VH) tax bases. For the two foundation systems it is assumed that state aid in excess of the aid floor is conditional on district compliance with the minimum-tax-rate requirement. Consequently, opportunity schedules are shown as solid lines only

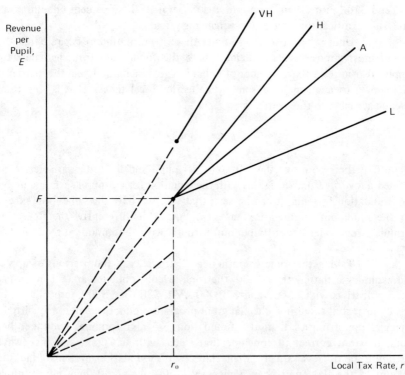

Figure 2-1. Foundation Formula, No Aid Floor.

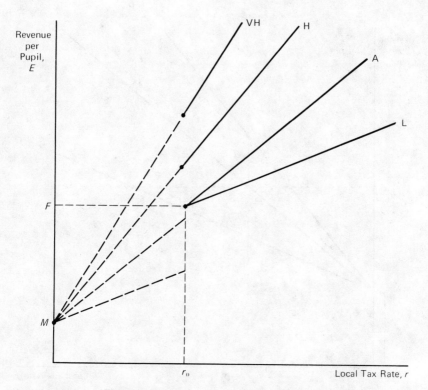

Figure 2-2. Foundation Formula with Aid Floor.

for tax rates equal to or greater than the minimum. Dashed lines indicate the revenues that would be available to districts levying less than the required minimum rates.

Figure 2-1 shows that under a pure foundation formula all districts except the one with the very high (VH) tax base obtain access to the foundation level, F, of spending at the minimum tax rate, r_0. The very wealthy district is able to raise more than F dollars at that tax rate and is permitted under existing state laws to retain the excess. Therefore, even at the minimum expenditure level, access to support is not quite equal: Very wealthy districts enjoy more favorable opportunities than the others. At all tax rates greater than r_0 the opportunities of districts of varying wealth diverge rapidly and the scope for expenditure and tax rate disparities becomes progressively greater.

Figure 2-2 shows that the effect of an aid floor (M) is to give the high-tax-base district (H) more aid than it would have received under the basic formula, thereby permitting it, too, to raise more than F dollars per pupil at the rate r_0. The district with very high wealth also receives a bonus. Thus, introduction of the floor increases financial disparities. The degree of inequality under the foundation program is positively related to (1) the difference between the foundation amount and the actual (average) level of per-pupil spending in

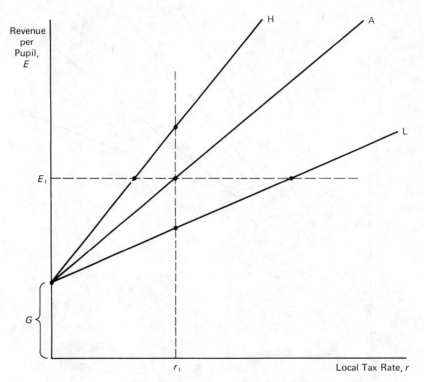

Figure 2-3. Flat Grant Formula.

the state; and (2) the level of the aid floor as a fraction of the foundation amount.

Figure 2-3 illustrates that when districts receive only flat grant aid (G) their financial opportunities are unequal at all positive tax rates. The diagram shows the progressively higher rates needed to obtain a given level of revenue, E_1, as tax base decreases and the progressively higher levels of revenue obtained at a given tax rate, r_1, as tax base increases. The relative amounts raised by richer and poorer districts at a given tax rate depend on the size of the flat grant, G. The higher the grant, the smaller the percentage differences.

Given the above analysis and examples, we can summarize the properties of existing lump-sum systems as follows: first, each formula establishes a certain base level of support that the state undertakes to make available to all districts on equal terms. In the case of the foundation program the base is the stipulated foundation amount, and the "price" of access is the required minimum tax. In the case of the flat grant formula the base is the amount of the flat grant itself, and the "price" is zero. If a district chooses to supplement the base level of support, it must rely entirely on local taxes to do so. (In most states supplementation is not truly optional since the level of the base program is only a fraction of what is needed to provide a "minimum adequate" education according to prevailing standards.) A district's ability to supplement is strictly proportional to local taxable wealth. Therefore, to the extent that districts do supplement, the system guarantees that there will be either a positive correlation between spending and wealth, a negative correlation between tax rate and wealth, or both. In addition, the foundation program as actually applied in the states has less than its theoretical equalizing effect. The combination of an aid floor and a provision that allows wealthy districts to retain excess proceeds from the minimum tax will result in unequal access to even the base level of support.

This formulation points directly to five kinds of changes that would be helpful in reducing or eliminating inequality in existing lump-sum systems.

Make the "price" of the base program the same to all districts. This means either paying for the base program entirely out of state funds, as in the flat grant system, or requiring each district to impose no more and no less than the specified minimum property tax rate to obtain base level support. The latter can be done either by making the minimum tax a statewide tax or by requiring that all excess proceeds from the minimum tax be turned over to the state.

Raise the base program to a true "minimum adequate" level. Since inequality arises out of the efforts of unequally endowed districts to supplement the base program, a higher base, which would reduce districts' needs or desires to supplement, would tend to reduce financial disparities.

Discourage or limit supplementation. For the same reason, any change that reduced local supplementation would tend to reduce inequality. One possibility would be to raise the property tax rate associated with the base program. That would tend to discourage local districts from imposing still higher rates for supplementation. A more direct approach would be to set upper bounds on either supplementary tax rates or permissible levels of supplementary support.

Redefine the local tax base to reduce interdistrict disparities in ability to raise supplementary funds. This could involve either a shift away from the property tax base to a tax base less unevenly distributed among districts (for example, personal income) or narrowing of the definition of taxable property (for example, by allowing districts to levy supplementary taxes only on residential property).[23]

Allocate state aid in a manner that compensates for differences in ability to raise supplemental funds. As we shall show, this implies a shift to the variable matching principle of distributing the state portion of public school support.

It will become evident in the discussion of specific reform proposals that combinations of these five approaches underlie all the major alternatives. Whether a specific strategy is necessary, sufficient, or relevant in a particular instance depends on the chosen equalization goal. The next section of this chapter will attempt to relate the various strategies and equalization doctrines. First, however, existing systems that include variable matching, which may well be the most powerful mechanism available for carrying out the equalization mandate, will be examined.

Percentage Equalization, Guaranteed Valuation, and the Variable-Matching Principle

During the school year 1968-69, the states of Iowa, Massachusetts, New York, Pennsylvania, Rhode Island, Utah, and Wisconsin operated systems that contained significant elements of variable matching.[24] The distinguishing features of these systems, as the name implies, are that the state matches locally raised school revenues, and the rate of matching varies in inverse relation to district wealth. An important consequence of the first feature is that a district's aid entitlement is not a predetermined lump-sum amount but depends on the district's own fiscal decisions.[25] If two districts that are identical in wealth and all other respects tax themselves at different rates, the district that sets the higher rate will receive more support from the state. The second feature is the one that potentially provides a strong equalizing effect: by calculating appropriate matching rates for each district, it is possible for the state to let districts of varying wealth raise revenue *as if* their tax bases were identical.

The specific formula that most of the above-mentioned states have adopted is the one known as "percentage equalization." In its pure form, this plan assures every district, no matter how small its tax base, no less than a stipulated minimum yield (in dollars per pupil) per percentage point of local tax. If the actual yield of the district's local tax is less than this minimum, state aid funds are provided to make up the difference. Each district, in effect, is given the opportunity to raise revenue as if it had at least a certain minimum tax base. For that reason, this type of aid scheme is sometimes referred to as a "guaranteed valuation" formula.[26]

It is possible to write the "pure" percentage equalization formula several different ways, depending on which of its properties is to be emphasized. The fact that the state fills the gap between what the district actually raises and what it would have raised if it had the guaranteed level of ability is shown by the formula

$$S = r(V_g - V),$$

where V_g is the minimum effective tax base (valuation guaranteed to each district), and $V_g - V$ is the ability gap. (S is always greater than zero in this and the following versions.) State matching of locally raised revenue is underscored by writing the formula as

$$ S = L \left(\frac{V_g}{V} - 1 \right) , $$

where L is the amount of locally raised revenue per pupil, and the quantity in parentheses is the matching ratio. State sharing of the burden of school support with districts, but at a variable rate, is emphasized by using either of two forms

$$ S = E \left(1 - \frac{V}{V_g} \right) = E \left(1 - k \frac{V}{V_0} \right) , $$

where E is total revenue per pupil (as above), the quantities in parentheses are the fraction of a district's funds to be provided by the state, V_0 represents the statewide average tax base, and k is the fraction of support to be provided out of local funds by a district with tax base V_0. These different formulas have appeared in the literature under various names, but in fact they all are mathematically identical.[27]

Table 2-2 illustrates the equalizing effect of a hypothetical "pure" guaranteed valuation formula in which each district is given the power to raise revenue as if its tax base were $20,000 per pupil. The first two columns of the table specify the districts' revenue entitlement as a function of tax rate (the

Table 2-2. A Hypothetical Guaranteed Valuation Plan (guarantee level = $20,000 per pupil)

Tax Rate r	Revenue Entitlement per Pupil (r x $20,000)	$5000 Local Revenue	Aid	$10,000 Local Revenue	Aid	$15,000 Local Revenue	Aid
2%	$ 400	$ 100	$ 300	$ 200	$ 200	$ 300	$ 100
3	600	150	450	300	300	450	150
4	800	200	600	400	400	600	200
5	1000	250	750	500	500	750	250
6	1200	300	900	600	600	900	300
Matching ratio (state/local)		3 : 1		1 : 1		1 : 3	
State share (state/state + local)		0.75		0.50		0.25	

Actual local tax revenue and required state aid in districts with tax bases of:

revenue entitlement is the tax rate multiplied by $20,000). The other three pairs of columns show the actual proceeds of the local school tax and the amount of state aid required to bring revenue up to the guaranteed level when the actual district tax base is $5000, $10,000, and $15,000. For example, the district with $5000 AV is entitled to an $800 per pupil program if it imposes a 4 percent tax, but the actual yield from applying that rate to the district's small tax base is only $200. The remaining $600 must be provided out of state funds. For that district the state share of total revenues is 0.75 (or, what amounts to the same thing, local revenues are matched at a ratio of 3 to 1).

For the districts shown, this hypothetical formula produces perfect fiscal neutrality: total available revenue per pupil depends only on the locally chosen tax rate and not on local wealth. However, the equalizing effect breaks down when the formula is applied to very wealthy districts. A district with $25,000 AV, for example, would raise more than the amount shown in the second column of the table for any given tax rate. In order to offset that advantage the formula would have to permit negative matching. Specifically, since the hypothetical district's actual tax base is 25 percent higher than the $20,000 guaranteed level, the state would have to take away one fifth of that district's locally raised funds to limit its opportunities to those available to others. In other words, the formula equalizes perfectly only if all restrictions on the matching rate are eliminated, including the restriction that prohibits "negative matching." As normally understood, however, the term "guaranteed valuation" denotes a minimum guarantee and does not include the notion of "negative aid" to a district.

In practice, states that use variable matching formulas have all imposed restrictions that substantially dilute the equalizing effect of the formula. Only Utah has a formula that permits negative matching, and that permission applies only to a narrow range of tax rates.[28] Other state formulas not only permit districts to retain local revenues that exceed the guaranteed entitlement, but also impose other restrictions that undercut the equalizing effect of the formula. These include aid floors, limits on the amount of per pupil revenue to be shared by the state or on local revenues to be matched, and upper and lower bounds on the permissible matching rate. As examples:

1. The percentage equalization formula used by the state of New York in 1968-69 limited state sharing to the first $760 per pupil, established an aid floor of $274 per pupil, and limited the matching ratio to 90 percent.
2. The Massachusetts formula in the same year limited the state share to between 15 and 75 percent.
3. The Wisconsin system, also in 1968-69, established both aid floors and upper bounds on sharable revenues for each of several categories of districts.[29]

The effect of each of these restrictions is either to provide more aid to wealthy districts or less aid to poor districts than called for by the pure formula. Imposition of a ceiling on expenditures to be shared is an especially serious restriction because it entirely eliminates the effect of matching grants for all districts spending more than the stipulated upper bound. Thus, in New York State in 1968-69, most districts spent above the $760 per pupil ceiling. From their point of view, the state's percentage equalization formula was indistinguishable from a foundation's program formula with a $760 per pupil foundation level. If a district chose to spend more than $760, it was on its own, just as if there had been no matching aid program.

Figure 2-4 and 2-5 illustrate the opportunities available to low, average, and high tax base districts under guaranteed valuation programs with and without constraints. In Figure 2-4, which represents a pure percentage equalization formula, it has been assumed that the guaranteed valuation level has been set somewhere between the actual tax bases of the average- and high-wealth districts. The result is that the two less wealthy districts enjoy the ability to raise revenues as if they had the guaranteed tax base, V_g. It is assumed in this example that the state does not take away excess revenues raised by wealthy districts. Therefore, the high-wealth district (H), which is able to raise more than the guaranteed amount at any tax rate, retains its superior opportunities.

Figure 2-5 demonstrates the effects of two kinds of restrictions, (1) a lower bound on the matching ratio; and (2) an upper bound on the amount

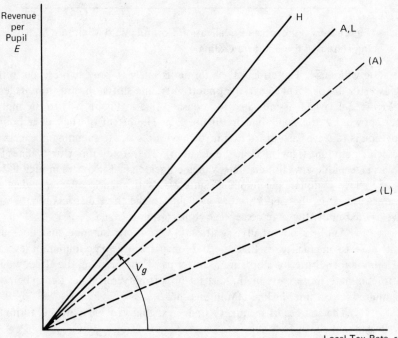

Figure 2-4. Percentage Equalization Formula, No Restrictions.

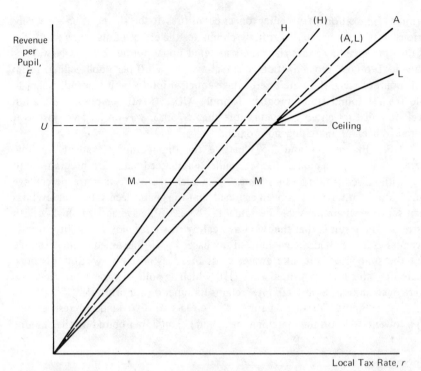

Figure 2-5. Percentage Equalization Formula with Minimum Matching Rate and Expenditure Ceiling.

the state will share. The effect of the former is solely to provide more aid to the high-wealth district. That district's opportunity line shifts upward from its level in Figure 2-4 (which is indicated by a dashed line in Figure 2-5) to the higher level shown by the solid line in Figure 2-5. The effect of the upper bound provision is to leave each district on its own with respect to spending in excess of the ceiling amount (labeled U in the diagram). Therefore, opportunity lines for the average and low wealth districts, which coincide at all tax rates in Figure 2-4, diverge above U dollars per pupil in Figure 2-5. Both changes, obviously, lead to greater spreads in the opportunities available to the three districts than would have existed under the pure percentage equalization formula.

　　　　Another potentially significant restriction, but one that does not contribute to inequality, is that the state may require some minimum level of per pupil expenditure by all districts. In terms of the diagram, the effect would be to eliminate those parts of the district opportunity schedules falling below a minimum revenue line, such as MM in Figure 2-5.

　　　　The sources of inequality under existing variable matching formulas can be summarized as follows:

1. If there were no constraints on the operation of the formula, a percentage equalization or guaranteed valuation system would establish fiscal neutrality among all districts with tax bases equal to or less than the guaranteed level. That is, per pupil support in those districts would depend on the locally chosen tax rate only, not on an individual district's tax base.
2. The prohibition of negative state aid under existing systems gives districts whose tax bases exceed the guaranteed level superior opportunities to finance their schools. The higher the guaranteed level, the fewer the districts that fall into this advantaged category. To achieve full fiscal neutrality for all districts, the state would have to *take away* excess locally raised revenues from districts with more than the guaranteed level of wealth.[30]
3. The effect of adding constraints to the formula is to strengthen the relationship between financial opportunities and wealth. Aid floors and lower bounds on matching rates create special advantages for wealthy districts. Aid ceilings and upper bounds on matching rates assure inferior opportunities for low-tax-base jurisdictions.

The implication for reform is that interdistrict disparities in financial opportunities can potentially be eliminated by switching from flat grant or foundation program systems to those based on the variable matching principle. However, improvement is certain only if the variable matching program is substantially free of side conditions and constraints. Otherwise, the degree of improvement, if any, will depend on specific values of the formula parameters. It is possible, for example, that financial outcomes could be more equal under a system that simply gave each district a large flat grant than under a system that nominally featured variable matching while sharply restricting the matching rate or the per pupil amount of aid. Those states that already operate variable matching programs can approach full fiscal neutrality to any desired degree by eliminating or relaxing provisions of law that restrict the equalizing effect of the variable matching formula.

ALTERNATIVE POST-SERRANO SYSTEMS

The equal protection litigation of the last few years has stimulated a heavy flow of interpretive, analytical, and polemical writing, much of it on the question of how post-*Serrano* school finance systems should be structured. Several major proposals for new financing systems have been developed and publicized. Some of these have been endorsed by official state and federal advisory bodies and incorporated into school finance bills placed before state legislatures. The discussion of alternatives, in other words, is well advanced and has already had a significant impact on policymaking.

Despite all this activity, however, it is difficult to come away from the post-*Serrano* literature with either a comprehensive view of the array of available alternatives or a good grasp of the considerations that might lead a policymaker to prefer one plan over another. There are two principal reasons for this gap in communications: one is that writers have not explicitly pointed out that there are different interpretations of financial equality and that different interpretations lead to different financing formulas. The second is that there has been undue emphasis on proposals that embody the uniform provision doctrine—full state funding—and the fiscal neutrality doctrine—district power equalizing—and corresponding neglect of intermediate possibilities and formulas designed to meet less rigorous equalization standards. In the discussion that follows, we attempt to show that full state funding and district power equalizing are merely special cases of a more general class of funding formulas, and that other alternatives and combinations have at least equal claims for consideration as means of achieving the various equalization goals.

Full State Funding and District Power Equalizing as Special Cases

The current debate over school finance reform revolves about full state funding and district power equalizing to such an extent that it is almost mandatory to make them the point of departure. We first describe the general characteristics of each plan and then show how they fit into a larger family of alternatives. Detailed examples of formulas based on the full state funding and district power equalizing concepts will be provided later in this section.

Full state funding. This term embraces the class of school finance systems in which the state government raises all school revenues and distributes funds according to the number of pupils in each district and other educationally relevant factors. All fiscal decisions are centralized at the state level. Local jurisdictions retain the right to control their funds and manage their programs, but they have no taxing power or authority to determine the overall level of support for their schools.

Full state funding is a radical alternative in the sense that it abolishes the local role in school finance. However, it does not, as some critics have claimed, necessarily lead to the simplistic expenditure equalization policy of "one scholar, one dollar." In fact, the formula for allocating funds among districts could be very complex under full state funding, but the complexity would have to do with the many local characteristics that a state might want to take into account, rather than with relationships between school support and local fiscal ability and effort. The only respect in which full state funding would truly be simple is that there would be one school tax rate for all.

District power equalizing. This class of alternatives became well known originally through the writings of J. Coons and his colleagues, who were instrumental in developing the plaintiff's case in *Serrano*.[31] The concept was developed specifically to implement the fiscal neutrality doctrine while leaving each district free to determine its own level of school support. Thus, it provides the answer to those who contend that equalization necessarily means uniformity, centralization, and neglect of local feelings about the importance of schooling.

Basically, district power equalizing calls for the state to establish a single support-versus-effort schedule applicable to every district. Each district would be free to choose its own level of fiscal effort, thereby determining the level of per pupil support to which it is entitled according to the state schedule. Transfers of funds between the state and the districts would make up for the difference (positive or negative) between the amount of that entitlement and the actual proceeds of the local levy.

It is apparent that a percentage equalization formula such as was discussed earlier would be one form of district power equalizing, provided there were no side conditions or restrictions, including no prohibition of negative matching. Each district would be entitled to no more and no less than its own chosen property-tax rate would bring in when applied to a standard, statewide, computational tax base. All districts choosing the same property-tax rate would receive the same per pupil support. But the power equalizing concept also allows for other possibilities: for one thing, it is not necessary that effort be measured by the property-tax rate. Effort could be defined relative to community personal income or some other measure of local income or wealth. Second, it is not necessary that there be a proportional schedule relating per pupil support to effort, nor even that the schedule be linear. Third, the definition of support could be modified by inclusion of various need and cost factors, just as under full state funding.

One thing that is essential to the district power equalizing concept, however, is that a wealthy district's aid entitlement be allowed to become negative, requiring the district to turn over some of its locally raised revenue to the state. There is no other way to implement the principle of "equal support for equal effort" without bringing every district up to the spending level attainable by the state's wealthiest district—a practical impossibility in most cases. In this respect, district power equalizing joins full state funding under the heading of "radical" alternatives, since it breaks with the tradition that the proceeds from locally levied property taxes "belong" to the levying jurisdiction.

A broader family of alternatives. There has been so much discussion of full state funding and district power equalizing as rival proposals that many have been led to believe they are the only alternatives that will satisfy decisions of the *Serrano* type, and that they are diametrically opposed plans. The first belief arises from focusing exclusively on the strictest interpretations of the various court rulings while neglecting other possibilities, and is therefore probably incorrect. The second belief is correct with respect to pure forms of full state funding and district power equalizing, but wrong with respect to versions of the two formulas that have actually been proposed or that can be considered serious candidates for adoption. For realistic proposals, the opposite would be closer to the truth: formulas based on the full state funding and district power equalizing concepts are indistinguishable.

The key to this apparent contradiction is that neither full state funding nor district power equalizing is usually recommended in its pure form. Advocates of power equalizing would generally agree to inclusion of an expenditure floor, a corresponding minimum statewide tax rate, and, perhaps, an upper limit on spending in their formulas. Most proponents of full state funding seem willing to consider some limited leeway for local supplementation of the statewide program, especially if access to supplemental support is "power equalized."

Taking those modifications into account, if can be seen that the two formulas offer support in the same general form—a uniform base program throughout the state plus a supplementary amount added at local discretion and under conditions that assure a desired degree of equalization. In the case of modified full state funding, the base program is the amount of the nominal statewide program, which the districts are free to supplement. In the case of modified power equalizing, the base program is the expenditure floor, above which districts are free to choose from the prescribed support-versus-effort schedule. The real choice, therefore, is not between a strictly uniform program on one hand, and unrestricted choice from an open-ended expenditure versus tax rate schedule on the other. Those are extreme cases that occur when one component of the more general formula is set at zero. In other cases, differences among proposals primarily reflect different answers to the following two questions about funding magnitudes:

1. What should be the level of the statewide base program and how should that program be financed?
2. To what degree and under what equalization scheme should local jurisdictions be permitted to tax themselves to obtain supplementary support?

The justification for the assertion that there is a large family of alternatives becomes clear as we consider the variety of possible answers to these two questions. With respect to the base program, alternatives can be generated by varying (1) the base level of support; (2) the kinds of need and cost factors used to modify the base program and their respective magnitudes; and (3) the mix of taxes used to finance the base program. With respect to supplementation the policy parameters that can be varied include (1) the tax source that localities are permitted to tap for the purpose of supplementation; (2) provisions for state matching of local supplementary revenues (including applicable limits on matching rates or amounts of aid); (3) need and cost factors applicable to supplementary support; and (4) upper bounds on per pupil support or local fiscal effort. All together, then, there are at least seven dimensions along which alternative financing systems can be differentiated.

The discussion that follows is concerned with specific formulas that can be generated by varying those parameters. For this purpose, formulas are grouped according to the degree of equalization to be achieved. The discussion begins with the goals of uniform provision and fiscal neutrality, for which the possibilities are relatively clear-cut; then examines the larger array of alternatives that can be used to achieve limited variation; and, finally, indicates the plans that are relevant if only a minimum provision of schooling is required.

Financing Uniform Educational Provision

So long as there are districts with different tax bases or different tastes for education, statewide uniformity of support can be achieved only through full state funding. Under that plan, there is no local financial opportunity schedule, and hence no need for a diagram to depict expenditure and tax rate possibilities. Nevertheless, three sets of parameters need to be set to specify a complete full state funding formula: (1) the base level of support; (2) need and cost factors; and (3) the proportions in which different taxes are used to finance the program. The following discussion of considerations that apply to these choices also applies to decisions about the base program portions of other funding alternatives.

The level of the base program. The uniform base level of support may be specified as a number of dollars per pupil in an average district (or a number of dollars per pupil of a certain type, if various categories of pupils are distinguished). In comparing reform alternatives, however, it may be more informative to specify the level in relative terms—for example, as a percentile of the existing distribution of support. Thus, rival proposals might call for establishment of a base program at the existing state median (50th percentile) level, or for "equalization up" to, say, the 60th percentile level. An advantage of describing the level in relative terms is that it permits different proposals to be compared across states even where states vary considerably in absolute levels of support.

The main consequences that need to be considered in setting the base program level are the total cost to the state, and the redistributive effects on individual districts. The latter is particularly critical because a district that receives less money for schools under full state funding than it received previously has no way of recouping through its own efforts. Political considerations make it certain, therefore, that a state would set the base level so that only a minority of districts and a small fraction of schoolchildren faced cutbacks in support; that is, the base level would have to be well above the existing state average level of per pupil spending.

In its report calling for full state funding in New York, the Fleischmann Commission recommended equalization up to the 65th pupil percentile *plus* distribution of a considerable additional sum through the operation of a compensatory need factor.[32] This would have made most districts as well off under the new plan as under the old (at the cost, obviously, of a substantial increase in total statewide spending for public schools). But apparently this was not considered a sufficient cushion against the political shock of redistribution. In addition, a long transition period was proposed during which high-spending districts would be permitted to retain their superior programs (at state expense) while waiting for the other districts to "catch up."[33] Although political difficulties may not be as severe elsewhere, the fact that full state funding will force some districts to spend less than they are spending now is a drawback that needs to be taken into account in assessing the merits of the proposal.

Need and cost adjustments. Assuming that fund apportionments to different classes of districts are adjusted to reflect presumed variations in resource costs, and also assuming that the weighted pupil method is used to compute each district's relative need, the expenditure level for each type of district under full state funding would be given by

$$E_i = Bc_i \ (w_1 \frac{A_1}{A} + w_2 \frac{A_2}{A} + \ldots + w_n \frac{A_n}{A}),$$

where

E_i = per pupil expenditure for a district of type i,

B = the statewide base level of expenditure per pupil of category 1 for a district with average resource costs,

c_i = the cost adjustment factor applicable to districts of type i,

A_j/A = the proportion of pupils in the district who fall into category j,[34]

w_j = the weight assigned to a pupil in category j for the purpose of allocating funds (relative to a weight of 1 assigned to pupils in category 1).

To illustrate the effect of this adjustment scheme, suppose that there are only two kinds of pupils—regular and disadvantaged—assigned weights of 1.0 and 1.5, and that there are two kinds of districts—urban and other—assigned cost factors of 1.1 and 1.0. The combined effect of the two adjustment factors is shown in Figure 2-6. A nonurban district with no disadvantaged pupils receives

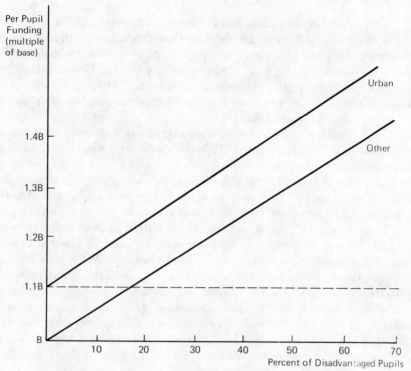

Figure 2-6. Hypothetical Need and Cost Adjustments.

the base amount of support, B, per pupil. An urban district with no disadvan-taged pupils receives 10 percent more (1.1B), as shown. Support for either type of district increases with the fraction of pupils in the district who are disadvantaged. A district with 40 percent disadvantaged pupils, for example, receives 20 percent more support per pupil than a district with none. If that district were urban, its total allotment would be 32 percent more per pupil (1.2 X 1.1) than the base amount.

The two major policy questions a state would have to resolve in specifying its formula are: (1) For what categories of districts and pupils should costs and needs be differentiated? (2) What should be the magnitude of the cost adjustment factors and pupil weights? Regarding costs, it is unlikely that any state has data that could be used to construct objective cost factors for various classes of districts, taking proper account of resource quality variations. The use of crude cost data (for example, actual salaries paid) without quality adjust-ments could actually result in perverse reallocations from high- to low-cost districts.[35] For the time being, then, the decision on whether to provide extra money to urban or other allegedly high-cost districts must be almost entirely subjective, taking account of prevailing beliefs about the magnitude of cost disparities. This applies, of course, to cost differentials for any type of formula, not only full state funding.

As to needs, certain kinds of differential pupil weighting are already widely accepted, and there are more or less established weights reflecting conventional practice (for example, high school pupils often appear to receive about 25 percent greater weight than elementary pupils). Certain other categories of pupils also receive incremental funds through categorical programs. It would not be difficult to retain these distinctions as elements of a general weighted-pupil allocation scheme.[36]

The real political issue concerns weighting for various categories of the educationally disadvantaged: What should those categories be and how large a compensatory factor should be provided? Existing federal and state compensatory programs have tended to concentrate, as much for administrative convenience as for any other reason, on pupils from poverty backgrounds (AFDC recipients or children from low-income families). An alternative approach would base compensation on more direct educational criteria, such as scores on initial aptitude and achievement tests. There are some technical problems in connection with the statewide testing that would be required, but a shift from an approach that is widely perceived as ethnic- and class-oriented might ultimately generate more support for the compensatory equalization principle. The question of the magnitude of the adjustment remains one for subjective educational and political judgment. Proposals seem to center on a 50 percent differential or a $300 lump-sum increment.[37] There is very little data that could be used to develop a scientific opinion regarding the "proper" amount.

The mix of taxes.   The uniform statewide program can be financed out of general state revenues (sales, income, business taxes), a statewide property tax (on all property, business property only, and so on), or some other earmarked education tax. Decisions on the mix of taxes to be used have important potential effects on the distribution of school tax burdens among localities and individuals (see Chapter 4).

One substantive point worth noting is that the statewide property tax is an important potential funding source. The rate of that tax could conceivably be the same as the average statewide property tax rate under the existing system. This means that reform—even of the most drastic kind—would not necessarily result in a net shift away from property taxation.[38]

In an analysis of alternatives other than full state funding, the proportion of support derived from a statewide property tax is a variable that can have important effects on patterns of local school spending. We return to the tax mix issue again in discussing other fiscal alternatives.

Formulas for Achieving Fiscal Neutrality
The fiscal neutrality criterion is satisfied by any two-part formula that provides (1) a uniform base program financed out of taxes levied at uniform statewide rates and (2) a single support-versus-effort schedule according to which

districts can obtain supplementary funds if they choose to levy supplementary taxes. This class of formulas can be described as "base program plus power equalized supplementation." All the remarks made about financing the base program in the context of full state funding apply equally to the base program portions of these alternatives. Assuming, then, that the design of the base program has been settled, the remaining issues have to do with definitions of "effort" and "support" and the shape of the schedule relating the two.

Alternative supplementation schedules. The simplest alternative is one that provides supplementary support in direct proportion to a locally chosen supplementary property tax rate. Suppose, for example, that the base program is set at $600, the statewide property tax associated with the base program at 2 percent, and the "slope" of the supplementary support schedule at $200 per percentage point of tax, which corresponds to an effective tax base of $20,000 per pupil. The total support available to a district would be

$$E = \$600 + (r - .02) \cdot \$20,000 ,$$

or, more generally,

$$E = B + (r - r_0) V_0 ,$$

where B is the base program, r_0 is the statewide property tax rate, V_0 is the effective tax base, and r is the tax rate chosen by the district. If one compares this with the equation for a conventional foundation program given earlier, it can be seen that the two are identical except that supplementary support is proportional to the standard computational tax base, V_0, instead of the district's actual tax base, V. In other words, this formula produces exactly the result that a foundation program formula would if every district had exactly the same tax base.

Figure 2-7a illustrates the financial opportunities made available by the proportional supplementation formula, and Figures 2-7b through 2-7e illustrate the effects of some alternative schedules. In Figure 2-7b, the formula is the same as in 2-7a except that it is assumed that there is no statewide property tax, the base program being supported entirely out of general state taxes. In effect, each district receives a flat grant plus the opportunity to supplement according to the proportional schedule. Figure 2-7c illustrates the same program as Figure 2-7a, but with an upper bound on supplementary support. More complicated schedules are also feasible. Figure 2-7d depicts a piecewise-linear supplementation schedule that provides support at one rate up to a certain level, E_1, and at a lower rate thereafter. Figure 2-7e shows that it would even be possible to have a curvilinear schedule relating support to effort.

As was pointed out earlier, strict fiscal neutrality can be achieved

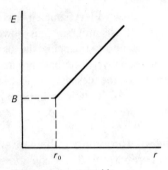

a. Base program, statewide property tax, proportional supplementation.

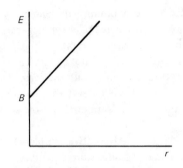

b. No statewide property tax.

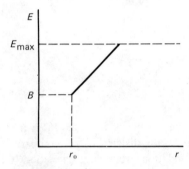

c. Upper bound on supplementation.

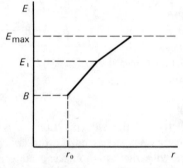
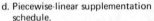

d. Piecewise-linear supplementation schedule.

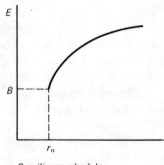

e. Curvilinear schedule.

Figure 2-7. Base Program plus Power-Equalized Supplementation: Formula Variations.

only if high-wealth districts receive negative aid: each district with a tax base higher than the effective tax base in the formula ($20,000 per pupil in our example) would have to turn over a fraction of the proceeds of its supplementary levy to the state. To illustrate the kinds of transactions that might be involved, we have constructed an example, presented in Table 2-3, corresponding to the piecewise-linear formula shown in Figure 2-7d. The first two columns of the table make up the expenditure versus tax rate schedule. It has been assumed that the state allows each district to select any tax rate between 2 and 6 percent and to obtain per pupil support ranging from $600 to $1300. Between 2 and 4 percent, each percentage-point increase in tax rate brings in an additional $200 per pupil; after 4 percent, each percentage point brings in $150 per pupil.

The remaining columns show how much aid a district with a given tax base would be entitled to as a function of its chosen tax rate or level of support. These amounts are determined by comparing the level of support indicated in the second column with the amount obtained by applying the corresponding tax rate to the district's assessed valuation. For example, suppose that a district with $12,000 AV chooses the combination of an $800 per pupil program and a 3 percent tax rate. The 3 percent rate applied to the district's actual $12,000 tax base brings in only $360, which means that the state must supply the remaining $440, as shown in the table.

If the district is sufficiently wealthy its aid entitlement can become negative, but whether aid is negative or positive may depend on the tax rate the district chooses. As examples, the district with $30,000 AV must always turn over a portion of its supplementary revenues to the state ("negative aid"); the district with $24,000 AV receives positive aid up to a point, but the amount diminishes as a function of tax rate and eventually becomes negative. Aid for the

Table 2-3. State Aid to Local Districts Under a Hypothetical Power Equalizing Formula

Tax Rate	Support per Pupil	State aid per pupil when district assessed value per pupil is:				
		$6000	$12,000	$18,000	$24,000	$30,000
2.0% (min)	$ 600	$ 480	$ 360	$ 240	$ 120	$ 0
2.5	700	550	400	250	100	−50
3.0	800	620	440	260	80	−100
3.5	900	690	480	270	60	−150
4.0	1000	760	520	280	40	−200
4.5	1075	805	535	265	−5	−275
5.0	1150	850	550	250	−50	−350
5.5	1225	895	565	235	−95	−425
6.0 (max)	1300	940	580	220	−140	−500

district with $18,000 AV increases with tax rate up to a point but declines thereafter. Part of each revenue increment after the peak is, in effect, recovered by the state. In general—and this applies to districts with all levels of wealth—the state matching rate is not a constant under these formulas but varies continuously with the locally chosen tax rate.

Policy parameters. The main parameter values that need to be set under these formulas are the level of the base program, the level of the statewide property tax, and the slope(s) of the supplementation schedule. If the schedule is linear, only one slope must be specified (the level of the upper bound, if any, must also be stated). If it is piecewise-linear, a slope must be chosen for each segment. The functional form must be specified if the schedule is curvilinear.

The base level program, in this case, represents the amount needed to support a "minimum adequate" program. (It is subject, of course, to modification by relative need and cost factors.) One approach to quantification is to relate the base to actual spending under the existing system—that is, to set the base at some percentile of the existing distribution that can be agreed on as adequate, given the average wealth of the state. A second approach is to derive a base program by "costing out" a standard set of school inputs (for example, one teacher for every twenty-seven pupils, one supervisor for every ten teachers, certain allotments of materials per pupil, and so on).[39] Both approaches are essentially arbitrary. Nothing better can be done, given the lack of quantitative knowledge of connections between expenditure levels and educational results.

Two kinds of considerations are relevant to the decision on the level of the statewide property tax. First, there are the distributional considerations, which are the same as those relevant to full state funding. Second, it is necessary to take into account the effect of the statewide property tax rate on local supplementation. If the statewide property tax rate is set at about the median local rate under the existing system, then the average district is likely to be deterred from supplementing to any appreciable extent. Districts that previously paid higher rates, or enjoyed levels of support higher than the new base, would still have incentives to add-on support; but, in general, spending would be constrained. If the state's goal is to prevent aggregate costs of public education from rising sharply as a by-product of equalization, then a high statewide tax may be a useful policy tool. But there is a potential conflict between the goal of property-tax relief, which points toward a low, or even zero, statewide tax, and the goal of holding down aggregate school spending, which would be advanced by a high statewide rate.

The most important influence on local propensities to supplement, and therefore on aggregate spending, will be the slope of the supplementation schedule. An increase in the slope reduces the effective price of education to each district, making additional supplementation more attractive. Consider, for example, the situation of a district with a $10,000 tax base facing alternative schedules with slopes of $100 and $200 per percentage point of tax rate. If the slope is $100, there is no matching of the district's supplementary levies. The district raises precisely the amount it is entitled to from local taxpayers, who pay the full cost of supplementary support. If the slope is raised to $200, the district becomes entitled to $100 in state matching funds for every $100 raised locally. This has the effect of a 50 percent discount on education. Supplementation becomes more attractive, and a higher level of spending is encouraged. A steeper schedule also means more state funding. Each increase in the slope shifts additional districts from the negative to positive aid category and raises the matching rate for districts already receiving aid.

It is conceivable that with the standard tax base set somewhere around the tax base of the average district, the entire supplementation system could be run with no net input of state funds. Excess revenues from wealthy districts would balance off aid payments to poorer districts. But when the standard tax is set higher, a deficit is created. Therefore, if a state government desires either to hold down aggregate spending or to minimize the state contribution, a gently sloping schedule is the indicated solution. On the other hand, the lower the slope, the more districts would fall into the negative aid category. The unpopularity of that status is likely to be such that there will be a politically determined lower bound to the slope of the schedule.

Viewed in this light, formulas that taper off the supplementation schedule (for example, those represented in Figures 2-7d and 2-7e), or that impose upper bounds on per pupil spending, are compromise solutions. Up to a certain point they allow districts to express their tastes for education under the same favorable conditions as would be available to a district of above-average wealth. But after that point, the state's desire to limit expenditures takes precedence. The supplementation schedule becomes less favorable, making the price too high for all but the most education-oriented districts. In the extreme case, an absolute upper bound is set on spending.

Another purpose served by setting upper and lower bounds on per pupil spending is reduction of absolute expenditure and tax rate disparities. This is not an automatic consequence of fiscal neutrality. With a fiscally neutral formula like the one represented in Table 2-3, for example, some districts could spend twice as much as others. It would not be inconsistent for a state to adhere to fiscal neutrality but also to strive within the framework of that principle to reduce absolute disparities in educational support. A high base level of support, an expenditure ceiling, and a tapering supplementation schedule are all means to achieving that end.

Alternative tax sources and definitions of effort. Nothing about the concept of fiscal neutrality says that local support must come from property taxation or that effort must be measured by the tax rate on property. Other possibilities for which arguments can be made on equity grounds include shifting to a more broadly based tax, such as an income tax; shifting to an income-based definition of effort; and introducing progressivity into the support-versus-effort schedule.

The argument for a shift to an income tax is that two districts, or two individuals, may be paying the same property tax rate but not bearing equal burdens in a more fundamental sense. This is possible because the ratio of residential property to income varies among individuals and jurisdictions. Jurisdictions or individuals with higher income-to-property ratios pay lower percentages of their income for education even though tax rates are the same. For example, suppose that a professional family with an annual income of $20,000 and an elderly couple with a retirement income of $5000 each occupy houses worth $40,000. A 1 percent tax on the full value of the property would take $400 from each—2 percent of the family's income but 8 percent of the retired couple's. An income tax would come much closer to taxing the two households in proportion to ability to pay.[40]

Similar comparisons may be made across districts. For a number of reasons, communities with the same average income may differ in the average assessed value of homes.[41] In all such cases, equal rates of property taxation will be reflected in unequal fractions of income taxed away to support schools. A shift to a locally levied income tax as the source of supplementary school support would tend to eliminate those disparities.

Even if property taxation is retained, the property tax rate does not have to be used as the measure of a district's fiscal effort. It would still be possible to define effort as the amount of locally raised supplementary funds relative to community personal income. This would tend to eliminate distortions caused by interdistrict variations in income-to-property ratios. Unlike a switch to income taxation, however, this change would not do anything to compensate for horizontal inequities among individuals within each jurisdiction.

An argument for a progressive supplementation schedule arises from the observation that a given percentage tax represents more sacrifice when applied to the income of a household making $5000 a year than one making $25,000. For the sacrifice to be equal, the tax would have to be progressive. If an income-based measure of effort is used, this means that the effort required to obtain a given level of support should be an increasing function of district income. It is not clear whether the argument also applies when the property tax rate is used as the measure of effort, because residents of districts with large amounts of taxable wealth do not necessarily have high personal incomes. It would be unreasonable, certainly, to make someone pay a higher tax rate on his house because he happens to live in a district with large amounts of industrial and commercial property. An alternative possibility would be to base a progressive system on the amount of *residential* property per capita, or per pupil, in a district. Residential property values do correlate fairly well, in general, with personal incomes, and essentially the same effect would be produced as by relating the progressive schedule to income.

Formulas for Limiting Variation in Support

The doctrine of limited variation is the least well-defined equalization standard because it depends on a judgment as to how much variation is excessive. No attempt will be made here to resolve that question. From the kinds of federal and state legislation that have been proposed, it does appear that the answer is likely to be a "small" fraction of the average level of support—a standard deviation of per pupil spending on the order of 10 percent of the mean, rather than, say, 30 or 40 percent.

Since this equalization standard is essentially negative, one could construct innumerable formulas to meet it, but most of those would have no educational or political rationales. We will focus on only two categories of alternatives: (1) formulas that provide "nearly uniform" support; and (2) formulas that guarantee fiscal "near neutrality." As these titles suggest, we have in mind plans that deviate only slightly from the strict versions of full state funding and district power equalizing discussed above. Those plans can be considered serious candidates for adoption by state authorities because they equalize to a very substantial degree, while they avoid some of the more radical features of the purer formulas.

Limited supplementation of a high base program. Figure 2-8a represents a system that permits each local district to raise a limited amount of revenue to supplement a high statewide base program. The supplementary revenues are unmatched, which means that the proceeds of each percentage point of supplementary tax are proportional to local wealth. Since the schedules representing opportunities of low-, average-, and high-wealth districts diverge rapidly, it would be necessary to limit supplementation to a small fraction of the base program to prevent disparities from becoming excessive. As shown in the diagram, each district would be free to increase per pupil support only in the narrow range from B to E_{max}.

To illustrate numerically, suppose that the base program were set at $1000 and the statewide tax rate at 3 percent. An unmatched local supplement of $100 would require 2, 1, and 0.5 percent increments in tax rate from districts with $5000, $10,000, and $20,000 tax bases. As a consequence of supplementing the base program by only 10 percent, in other words, substantial tax rate disparities would be created. It would not be possible to allow much greater leeway without producing a clearly unacceptable range of variation.

The guaranteed valuation approach to local supplementation makes it possible to allow much more local choice without excessive spreads in tax rates. Such a plan is depicted in Figure 2-8b. All districts whose actual tax bases are less than the guaranteed amount, V_g, would have the proceeds of their supplementary local levies matched by the state. High-wealth districts like the one shown in the diagram would not receive aid, but would be permitted to retain the full proceeds of their own supplementary levies. The formula for supplementary matching would look exactly the same as the percentage equalization formulas described earlier.

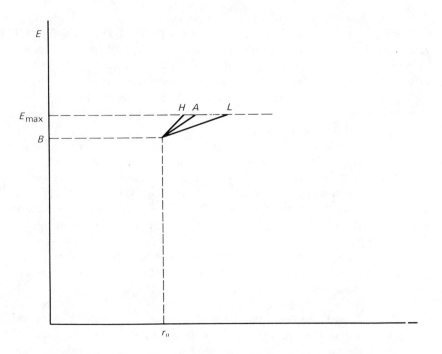

Figure 2-8a.   High Base Program plus Limited, Unmatched Supplementation.

Taking the same example as before, and assuming equalization up to a $15,000 per pupil effective tax base, districts with $5000 and $20,000 tax bases would have to pay 2 percent and 1.5 percent rates, respectively, to supplement their programs by $300 per pupil. Considerable supplementation could be permitted without developing unacceptable tax rate differentials. The range from B to E_{max} is therefore shown to be much larger in Figure 2-8b than in Figure 2-8a.

The reason that a state legislature might prefer such a plan to a base program plus power equalized supplementation is that the guaranteed valuation approach does not require the state to take funds away from wealthy districts. Thus, if the courts do not insist on a very strict interpretation of fiscal neutrality, a program of this kind might be much more acceptable politically.

Power equalizing up to a point. Another set of limited variation formulas reflects the proposition that access to school support should be fully equalized up to a certain level, but beyond that level localities should be free to raise additional funds on their own. A possible rationale for this position is that there is an upper bound on the level of schooling that is vital in terms of equal

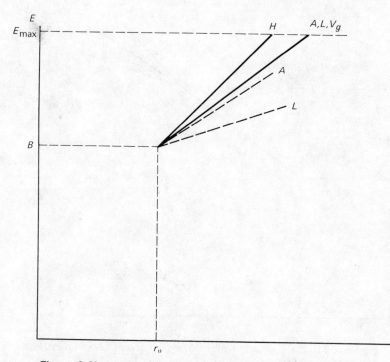

Figure 2-8b. High Base Program plus Limited, Guaranteed Valuation Supplementary Schedule.

economic, political, and social opportunities of the kind emphasized in *Serrano*.[42] Once that level has been reached, it can be argued, additional school support should be construed as a luxury or private consumption good for the pupils of a particular district. The state, it would follow, is under no more compulsion to make that luxury equally available to everyone than it would be to equalize all other local services. A secondary reason is that by permitting districts to supplement beyond the range of the power equalization schedule, the state would be able to control its own school aid budget without imposing a fixed upper bound on per pupil spending. That feature has obvious political attractions.

    Figure 2-9a depicts a system that consists of a base program plus power equalized supplementation plus additional supplementation at local expense. If the end of the power equalization schedule, E_1, were set sufficiently high, only districts that valued education very strongly would be motivated to go beyond that point. Departures from fiscal neutrality could be kept very small.

    Figure 2-9b shows a more complicated hybrid system in which the funding formula has four stages: (1) the base program; (2) a power equalized schedule; (3) a guaranteed valuation schedule; and (4) unmatched supplementa-

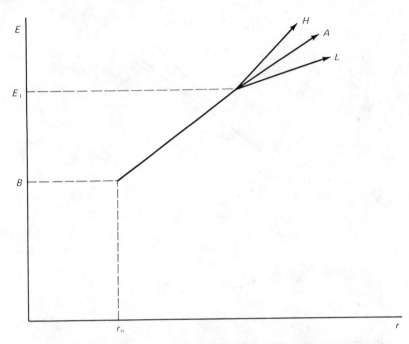

Figure 2-9a. Base Program plus Power Equalized Supplementation plus Unmatched Supplementation.

tion. The rationale for shifting at a certain point from a power equalized schedule to a guaranteed valuation schedule is essentially what was stated above: it may not be considered proper to "tax" districts because they choose to provide comforts and conveniences to their school children once equal access to basic educational opportunities has been assured for all districts. The difference between this formula and the previous one is that the state subsidizes poorer districts in the expenditure range from E_1 to E_2 to assure that interdistrict variations do not exceed acceptable limits.

Obviously, other hybrid formulas can be imagined, but those discussed here seem to represent the most reasonable possibilities. By setting appropriate values of the parameters of the alternative formulas shown here, it should be possible to produce any desired degree of financial equalization while still responding to demands for local choice, legislative desires for cost control, and other relevant concerns.

Alternatives that reduce tax base disparities. All formulas discussed thus far have one thing in common: they are aimed at reducing expenditure and tax rate disparities among districts with unequal taxable wealth, *taking those*

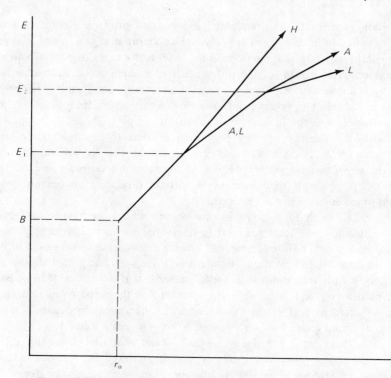

Figure 2-9b. Base Program plus Power Equalized Supplementation plus Guaranteed Valuation Supplementation plus Unmatched Supplementation.

wealth inequalities as given. An alternative approach, which we now consider, is to reduce financial disparities by changing local tax bases, making them less unequal than they are at present.

This possibility was not discussed earlier because it was not relevant to the stricter equalization doctrines. Under full state funding, variation in local tax bases makes no difference because local taxation is not allowed. Under the fiscal neutrality doctrine, tax base disparities make little difference because they are compensated for by state matching. But if limited variation is to be the standard and formulas that do not fully equalize opportunities are to be allowed, then measures aimed at tax base inequality become more interesting.

Three potential approaches to reducing tax base disparities are to allow districts to tax residential property only; to switch to a nonproperty tax base, such as income, that is less unevenly distributed among districts than taxable property; and to reorganize districts into units that are more nearly equal with respect to taxable wealth.

Residential property per pupil is probably more evenly distributed among school districts than residential and business property combined. The range of variation in the former is likely to be no more than two to one, except for a few special cases, and the range in the latter is five or six to one or more in many states. The reason for the difference is that commercial and industrial property is distributed very unevenly. An otherwise ordinary town that happens to have an oil refinery, power plant, or major factory within its boundaries can look extremely wealthy in terms of its ability to support schools.[43] It follows that narrowing the tax base by permitting districts to tax only residential property would make tax bases more equal. It would then become possible for states to give districts greater freedom to supplement their programs and to retain the proceeds of their local taxes without producing an unacceptable amount of expenditure or tax rate inequality.

A switch to personal income as the school tax base would have similar distributional effects as a shift to residential property. The range of tax base variation would be comparable, and, for the most part, districts would be in about the same relative positions. In addition, there would be potential gains in tax equity for the reason discussed earlier—namely, that the income tax rate is a better measure of local "sacrifice" for education than the property-tax rate, and hence a better guide for state matching. Also, horizontal inequities among individuals within each school district would be significantly reduced.

There are some doubts about the administrative feasibility of a school income tax. They can probably best be resolved by studying actual experience in Maryland and Wisconsin, for example, where some form of local-option income tax for education has been in effect.

Theoretically, the entire problem of inequality in school finance could be solved by reorganizing districts into units with equal per pupil wealth. The effect would be the same as pure district power equalizing. Every district would have exactly the same ability to support schools, and expenditure variations would arise only out of differences in the value that different localities place on education. So drastic a reorganization is not practical for two reasons. First, it would be necessary to construct large, ungainly districts, combining cities, suburbs, and rural areas. Second, boundaries would have to be changed constantly as tax bases in different areas grew at different rates. Moreover, the reorganization would undercut the rationale for local fiscal autonomy, which is based on the notion of relatively homogeneous communities expressing their disparate preferences for education. Nevertheless, less extreme forms of reorganization could do a great deal to equalize financial opportunities and would be especially potent in combination with other reforms.

It is difficult to generalize about the prospects for reorganization because states vary so greatly in the degree to which they have consolidated and rationalized their districts.[44] States that already operate countywide and large city districts can probably accomplish little more through reorganization.[45] California, however, operates hundreds of small districts, some of which represent the extremes of the distribution of taxable wealth. There and in other states, further consolidation could do much to reduce tax base inequalities.

An attempt to reduce inequality by redrawing boundaries will probably require changes in state laws governing school district organization. Existing laws often provide for approval of mergers by voters in the district concerned. But existing financing systems give high-wealth districts strong incentives to remain independent even where larger size might be more efficient. Those laws are just as much a part of the pattern of state action that produced existing inequities as those that authorize existing school finance formulas.

As financing formulas are reformed, resistance to reorganization is likely to decrease since it will be less important to "protect" a high tax base. On the other hand, reorganization will make it possible to reform formulas in a less drastic manner than would otherwise be necessary. In that sense, district reorganization and shifts to more equalizing formulas are mutually reinforcing, "synergistic" reform measures.

The Minimum Provision Alternative

The choices that must be made to carry out the minimum provision alternative, the least restrictive equalization doctrine, are identical to those needed to implement the most restrictive alternative, full state funding. Values of the same three parameters must be chosen: the level of support, need and cost factors, and proportions of revenue to be raised from each tax source. The difference, of course, is that local supplementation is prohibited under full state funding. Under the minimum provision doctrine, local supplementation is permitted and, by definition, is neither matched nor controlled by the state.

Given that there is no objective method for determining either the "correct" level of minimum support or the most desirable mix of taxes, decisions on both must emerge from political bargaining (subject to whatever constraints are set by the courts). The lineup of districts with different tax bases, income levels, and preferences for education on the issue would seem to be as follows:

1. Districts with high tax bases *or* low preferences for education (other things being equal) would be likely to prefer a low base level of support. This would be true for the former because they would be relieved of the responsibility of supporting high base programs for others, while retaining the ability to support generous programs for themselves. It would be true for the latter because they want to retain the option of using their funds for purposes other than education.
2. Districts with low tax bases *and* high preferences for education would be likely to prefer a high base program, since that would permit them to provide quality education despite their limited ability to raise local funds.
3. Given the base level, districts with *low incomes* would tend to prefer that the

base program be supported out of *progressive* state taxes. That would shift much of the burden of support to others.

4. Given the base level, districts with *high incomes* would tend to favor reliance on *regressive* state taxes for base program support.
5. There is also likely to be an interaction effect: the lower the tax base relative to income, the more likely a district is to prefer a statewide property tax to more broadly based taxes.

Noting the "or" in statement 1, as opposed to the "and" in statement 2, it is easy to see how a coalition of districts with above-average wealth and below-average interest in education could be assembled in favor of keeping the base level low relative to the prevailing level of support. Of course, "high" and "low" are relative, and some states with strong preferences for education support even their poorer districts very generously by national standards. Yet, if this analysis is correct, it underscores the important role of an outside agency, such as the courts or the federal government, in bringing about intrastate equalization, which is equivalent in this context to assuring a truly adequate base level of support.

LOCAL RESPONSES AND EXPENDITURE DETERMINATION

Although a considerable amount can be learned about the equalization effects of alternative formulas by analyzing the financial opportunities they provide, that method does not reveal the whole story. It is also necessary to ask how districts will respond. What tax rates and levels of spending will they choose when given access to more or less favorable opportunities than they enjoyed in the past? Under every alternative but full state funding, aggregate levels of state spending and distributions of taxes and school support will depend, ultimately, on those local choices. Where matching is involved, the cost to the state will also depend on the tax rates that districts select. To appreciate the consequences of different formulas, therefore, it is necessary to assess possible local responses and to compare the positions that districts are likely to choose with their initial positions under existing systems.

Fiscal Responses of Individual Districts

First, consider the response of an individual district whose opportunities are changed by reform. Suppose that initially a foundation program is in effect and that the district is one of low wealth whose opportunities are improved by reform. Let point *P* in Figure 2-10 represent the district's initial position, and let *XX* be its opportunity schedule. The relatively gentle slope of the schedule reflects the district's small tax base. Suppose that a new system with a base program and power equalized supplementation goes into effect and

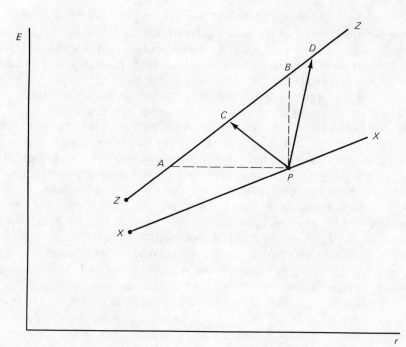

Figure 2-10. An Individual District's Response to a Shift in the Opportunity Schedule.

that the district is then able to choose a position along the superior opportunity line ZZ. The question is, what position will be chosen?

As the schedules are drawn, it can be seen that the new schedule is more favorable in two respects. First, its level is higher. At any tax rate above the indicated minimum, the district obtains more support than under the former system. Second, the new schedule is steeper. Each increment in the local tax rate produces a greater increment in support per pupil than previously. Since opportunities to raise school funds have become more favorable, it is extremely unlikely that the district would choose to spend less per pupil than before. Therefore, point A, which represents the same level of spending as point P, but at a lower tax rate, can be considered a lower bound on the district's options. If the district simply retains its preform tax rate, it will move to position B—a higher level of spending at the same rate paid previously. However, it is possible that education will seem such a bargain to local authorities because of the more favorable schedule that the district would actually choose to increase its tax rate in order to take advantage of the high incremental yield. Therefore, there is no clear-cut upper bound on the district's options. The district could select point *C*, which means that it would enjoy both an expenditure increase and a tax rate decline relative to its initial position. Or it could select point *D*, which represents an increase in both tax rate and per pupil spending.

The district's choice in this matter will depend on how strongly it values expenditure increases relative to potential tax rate reductions. It is possible to demonstrate theoretically that when the *level* of the schedule rises by a given amount (as it would, for example, if the base program were increased), the increase in local expenditure will, in general, be only a fraction as great. It is not possible, however, to place *a priori* constraints on the effect of an increase in *slope*, except to say that the effect will be positive.[46] Therefore, little more can be said from a theoretical point of view than that the change in per pupil spending due to reform will be a positive function of increases in both the level and slope of the opportunity schedule made available to each district.

There have been a number of empirical studies of determinants of local school spending, including some that have focused on local responses to changes in state aid formulas..[47] But the results of this research are useful only for predicting average statewide responses, not responses by individual districts. In particular, there have been no conclusive demonstrations of systematic differences in responses by districts with different characteristics (greater or lesser responsiveness to schedule changes by districts with high wealth, high tax rates, high initial levels of spending, and so on). Therefore, quantitative estimation of district by district responses to reform proposals and, consequently, of overall distributional effects, remains beyond the present state of the art.

Changes in Expenditure Patterns

Although it is not feasible to do quantitative simulations of local responses, we can provide a qualitative analysis of changes in expenditure and tax patterns that are likely to follow from school finance reform. The same financial opportunity diagram that we used to present alternatives can also be used to illustrate the effects on variously situated districts of shifts from one formula to another. We will consider two cases, each involving a shift from an initial foundation formula to a reformed system. The two systems considered are a full state funding program partly financed by a statewide property tax, and a formula that provides a base program plus power equalized supplementation.

Effects of a shift to full state funding. Figure 2-11 shows how levels of spending and tax rates in different districts would have to change if a state were to shift from a foundation formula to full state funding. The opportunity schedules created by the initial foundation formula are shown by dashed lines (the same set of opportunities was illustrated in Figure 2-2). The amount of per

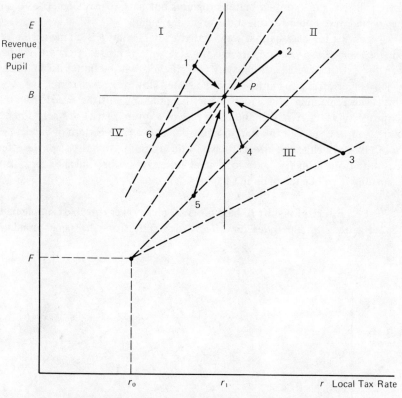

Figure 2-11. Effects of a Shift to Full State Funding.

pupil support, B, under full state funding is set at the level that a higher-than-average tax base district would reach if it levied the existing statewide average tax rate (r_1). That combination is labeled point P. The numbered points mark initial positions of some representative districts, including districts with high and low wealth and high and low preferences for education. The arrows indicate directions and relative magnitudes of the transitions that districts would have to make in shifting to the new system.

    Districts gain or lose from the change according to which of the Roman-numbered quadrants in the diagram they initially occupy. Districts in quadrant I (higher initial spending and lower tax rate than point P) are clear losers. The change forces them both to increase taxes and reduce their level of spending. Districts in quadrant III, such as the districts numbered 3 and 4 in the diagram, are clear gainers. After reform they can both spend more and pay lower taxes than initially. The districts in quadrants II and IV experience mixed results. A district like number 2 has less to spend but also pays lower taxes;

districts like 5 and 6 obtain better programs but have to pay higher taxes than they would have opted for under the original system.

If, for reasons that were stated earlier, point P is set higher than the existing average level of support and the statewide tax rate, r_1, is set no higher than the existing average, the majority of districts will be better off in terms of tradeoffs between expenditure and tax rate. However, that is not the whole story. The remaining funds to pay for the program must be raised from state nonproperty taxes. Whether the taxpayers of a given district are net gainers or losers from the shift to full state funding depends on the pattern of incidence of those taxes as well as the effects shown in the diagram. An analysis of the effects of a shift from property taxes to general state taxes is beyond the scope of this discussion; it will be taken up in Chapter 4.

Effect of a shift to base program plus power equalized supplementation. Figure 2-12 illustrates the effects of a shift from the same foundation

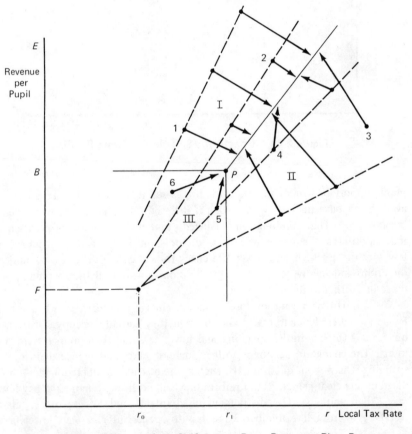

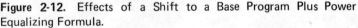

Figure 2-12. Effects of a Shift to a Base Program Plus Power Equalizing Formula.

formula as was shown in Figure 2-11 to a new formula that consists of a statewide base program plus a power equalized supplementation schedule. The combination of the base level and the required statewide property-tax rate is labeled *P*. It has been assumed that *B* is somewhat higher than an average tax-base district would have raised under the existing system at the statewide average tax rate. The slope of the supplementation schedule (the solid line in the diagram) is also assumed to be higher than the opportunity schedule of an average-wealth district under the foundation formula.

As a result of the change, every district must shift from its initial position to a point somewhere along the new schedule. Each district is given the right, however, to select the point it prefers. Therefore, in contrast to the previous example, local preferences play an important role in determining the final pattern of expenditures and tax rates.

The choices available to an individual district depend on which of the three Roman-numbered sectors it initially occupies. Sector I includes all districts that initially spent at least as much as the new base level *and* had initial positions above the new schedule. All such districts have local tax bases higher than the new common tax base established by the power equalization schedule. Therefore, all such districts will find themselves in the negative aid category after reform. They will either have to reduce their levels of spending, increase their tax rates, or both. The indicated transitions for districts 1 and 2 in Figure 2-12 illustrate the kinds of shifts that will be required.

Sector II includes all districts that initially paid tax rates higher than the new statewide rate, r_1, and had initial positions below the new schedule. All such districts have less taxable wealth than the new common tax base and therefore become recipients of positive matching aid. Those districts clearly gain from reform because they can obtain higher levels of spending, lower tax rates, or both. Some of those localities, however, may find the steep supplementation schedule so favorable that they will actually increase their tax rates to obtain higher levels of support. The district numbered 4 in the diagram represents such a case.

Sector III contains districts that are in a mixed situation. They will be influenced primarily by the base program provisions of the new system, which will force them both to spend more and to tax more for their schools. A district like 5, which is below the leftward extension of the opportunity schedule, could be considered a gainer from the change since it will be shifted to an expenditure-tax combination that was above its former opportunity line. A district like 6, however, is clearly worse off because it formerly had access to combinations better than point *P*, but rejected them to remain at its initial position.

Given our assumptions about the level and slope of the new schedule, the majority of districts will fall below the new opportunity line (and its leftward extension) and will be potential gainers. Again, however, it is not possible to determine the net effect on local taxpayers without considering the incidence of the other taxes used to finance the base program and the state's matching funds. Most districts and pupils would end up with greater quantities of resources as a result of the change, but whether they would be better off overall depends on how they value those gains relative to the additional state and local taxes to be paid.

Effects on Aggregate Spending and Taxes

Although there is nothing about any of the proposed formulas that would automatically cause aggregate expenditures to rise, political consider-ations make it very likely that distributional reform will be accompanied by significant increases in aggregate school spending. Basically, most people who have appraised the situation do not believe that a state legislature will adopt a plan that forces any appreciable number of districts to cut back sharply on their educational programs. It is even harder to believe, given today's widely expressed hostility to property taxation, that alternatives that would force up the average property tax rate in a state will be considered. Therefore, the prospect is that equalization will have to take place primarily by raising expenditures where they are now low and reducing property taxes where they are high, and that most of the necessary funds will have to be provided out of state general revenues.

The main considerations pertaining to particular kinds of alternatives are the following:

1. Alternatives that produce statewide uniformity of support, or that establish base programs and severely limit local supplementation, will have to set minimum support levels at or above the existing state average to minimize the number of forced reductions in high-spending districts.
2. Alternatives that feature power equalized supplementation will either have to make the effective tax base considerably greater than the state average tax base or include a high base program to avoid placing large numbers of districts in the negative aid category. Either option would tend to raise total spending.
3. Alternatives based on the guaranteed valuation principle would raise ex-penditures in present low-spending districts while permitting wealthy dis-tricts to retain their better-financed programs, thereby producing an aggre-gate increase.
4. Alternatives based on the minimum support principle would have to set base programs substantially higher than actual levels of spending in poor districts to attain reasonable standards of adequacy; wealthier districts would still be free to spend large amounts, as at present.

All of the above point to substantial increases in spending levels as a by-product of reform. A number of devices that could be employed to limit increases have been mentioned, such as upper bounds on local add-ons, high statewide tax rates, tapered supplementation schedules, and redefinitions that would narrow the local tax base. However, given the basic need to avoid widespread forced reductions in service, all those measures can not be expected to provide more than a partial offset to a general upward trend.

NOTES

1. *Robinson v. Cahill*, 118 N.J. Super. 223, 287 A.2d 187 (1972).

2. President Nixon, in his January 1972 State of the Union Address and subsequent statements, sketched out a plan that would provide substantial federal funds for schools on the condition that states ceased to rely on taxation of residential property for public school support. As an example of congressional proposals for reform, a 1973 bill by Congressman Perkins (H.R. 16) would make federal aid conditional on states' reducing the range of interdistrict inequality in per pupil spending to 10 percent. See *Education Daily* 6 (January 11, 1973).

3. For example, during 1972 and 1973, Minnesota and California made their school finance systems substantially more equalizing. But reform efforts were defeated in Michigan, New Jersey, and several other states.

4. Measurement problems do arise if capital as well as current expenses are to be included. It then becomes necessary to impute values to services provided by school buildings and other facilities. Additional problems arise in connection with fixed financial obligations such as bond debt payments and contributions to teacher retirement funds. The question there has to do with handling of current expenses incurred in order to pay for past services.

5. The major references on this point are F. Mosteller and D.P. Moynihan, eds., *On Equality of Educational Opportunity* (New York: Random House, 1972); and C. Jencks, et al., *Inequality: A Reassessment of the Effect of Family and Schooling in America* (New York: Basic Books, 1972).

6. For example, the report of the Fleischmann Commission in New York State calls for an additional weighting of 0.5 for pupils exhibiting defined "special educational needs." See *Report of the New York State Commission on the Quality, Cost, and Financing of Elementary and Secondary Education*, Vol. 1 (New York, 1972).

7. In California, for example, such central-city districts as San Francisco and Oakland spend relatively large amounts per pupil and appear wealthy in terms of the per pupil tax base. At the same time, they have educationally disadvantaged populations of substantial proportions whose needs are apparently not being met with existing resources. Yet those districts would have to make do on reduced budgets if a simple policy of dollar leveling were adopted. Joel Berke, among others, has shown that central cities in general would tend to lose financially from simple dollar equalization. See House Committee on Education and Labor, "Inequities in School Finance: Implications of the School Finance Cases and Proposed Federal Revenue Sharing Programs," in *Financing of Elementary and Secondary Education*, Washington, D.C., 1972.

8. "Educational need" was dismissed by a federal court as a judicially unworkable standard in *McInnis v. Ogilvie*, 394 U.S. 322 (1969). The ruling was affirmed without opinion by the Supreme Court. A similar result was obtained in *Burrus v. Willkerson*, 310 F. Supp. 572 (W.D. Va. 1969), affirmed 397 U.S. 46 (1970).

9. This view has been argued, in particular, by Arthur Wise of the University of Chicago.

10. *Rodriguez v. San Antonio Independent School District*, 337 F. Supp. 280 (W.D. Tex. 1971).

11. Note, for example, the California court's summary of parent plaintiffs' complaint: "the parents allege that . . . they are required to pay taxes at a higher rate than taxpayers in many other districts to secure for their children the same or lesser educational opportunities"; also, the linking of "educational opportunities" with "revenue available for education" in *Serrano*, 5 Cal. 3d 584, 487, p. 2d 1341 (1971).

12. This interpretation has been discussed in R. Reischauer and R. Hartman, *Reforming School Finance*, Washington, D.C.: The Brookings Institution, 1973.

13. This analogy is brought out in Chapter 4.

14. The national studies are (1) the report of the National Educational Finance Project (NEFP), published in five volumes with individual titles (see especially, R.L. Johns, K. Alexander, and D.H. Stollar, eds., *Status and Impact of Educational Finance Programs*, Gainesville, Florida: NEFP, 1971); and (2) *Report to the President's Commission on School Finance* (Washington, D.C., 1971).

15. The federal contribution, which has amounted to 6-8 percent of national support for elementary and secondary education in recent years, will be ignored in the remainder of this chapter. Terms like "per pupil spending," "expenditures," "revenues," and so on, should be understood as pertaining to state and local funds only.

16. Duane O. Moore, "Local Nonproperty Taxes for Schools," in R.L. Johns et al., *Status and Impact . . .*, pp. 209 ff.

17. A number of formulas that we include in the lump-sum category do contain the requirement that a district must levy a stipulated minimum tax rate in order to be eligible for state aid. We still call that a lump-sum grant since the amount of aid cannot be affected by marginal district tax rate or expenditure decisions.

18. R.L. Johns and R.G. Salmon, "The Financial Equalization of Public School Support Programs in the United States for the School Year 1968-69," in R.L. Johns et al., *Status and Impact . . .*, p. 122.

19. Ibid.

20. Under most state formulas, the foundation amount varies by type of pupil. For example, foundation amounts for a California unified school district in 1971-72 were $405 per pupil in grades 1-3, $375 per pupil in grades K and 4-8, and $508 per pupil in grades 9-12 (*Handbook for Computing Apportionments to California School Districts, 1971-72,* Sacramento: California State Department of Education, 1971). The single foundation amount referred

to in the discussion of alternative formulas should be interpreted as a weighted average of the amounts provided for different types of pupils.

21. The hypothetical assessed valuations per pupil are typical of California, where property is assessed at about 22 percent of full value. The statewide average assessed valuation in California in 1970-71 was about $24,000.

22. The flat grant amount also varies by type of pupil (see fn. 20, above).

23. Nonresidential property is generally believed to be less evenly distributed among districts than residential property. Recent unpublished work by J. Stucker of The Rand Corporation suggests, however, that the difference may be less than expected. The data in each state would have to be examined before this line of reform is pursued.

24. See Johns and Salmon, fn. 18, above. For further details on state formulas, see *Public School Finance Formulas, 1968-69*, Office of Education, U.S. Department of Health, Education, and Welfare, (Washington, D.C., 1969).

25. In practice, state formulas may relate a district's aid entitlement in the current year to effort or spending in the previous year, which means that from a one-year perspective the amount of aid is predetermined. In the longer run, however, a district is able to determine its own level of spending and the corresponding level of matching aid.

26. "Guaranteed valuation" is a more general term than "percentage equalization" because the latter refers specifically to a formula that makes per pupil support *proportional* to the local tax rate. A guaranteed valuation formula need not be proportional, nor even linear. All that is necessary is that a certain minimum increment in per pupil support is guaranteed for each increment in the local tax rate.

27. By definition, $E = S + rV$ and $L = E - S$. Therefore,

$$S = r(V_g - V) = \frac{E - S}{V}(V_g - V) = \frac{L}{V}(V_g - V) = L\left(\frac{V_g}{V} - 1\right),$$

which is the second formula given in the text. The relationship

$$S = \frac{E - S}{V}(V_g - V) = (E - S)\left(\frac{V_g}{V} - 1\right),$$

when solved for S, yields

$$S = E\left(1 - \frac{V}{V_g}\right).$$

For a district with tax base V_0 aid is

$$E\left(1 - \frac{V_0}{V_g}\right),$$

the quantity in parentheses being the state share. The local share is V_0/V_g, which we denote by k. Therefore $V_g = V_0/k$ and

$$S = E(1 - \frac{V}{V_g}) = E(1 - k\frac{V}{V_0}).$$

28. *Public School Finance Programs. 1968-69* (the Utah plan is described in pp. 284 ff.).

29. Ibid., pp. 206, 134, and 319.

30. The only other possibility is for the state to set the guaranteed level so high that no district is wealthy enough to generate excess revenue. But in most states that would necessitate a guarantee level many times greater than the state average tax base, and an unreasonably high level of state funding would be required.

31. For a full exposition of district power equalizing, see J.E. Coons, W.H. Clune III, and S.D. Sugarman, *Private Wealth and Public Education* (Cambridge: Harvard University Press, 1970).

32. *Report of the New York State Commission . . .* , pp. 2.14-2.15.

33. Ibid., p. 2.16. The effect of this bow to "political realism" is that wealthy districts in New York State would enjoy state-financed property tax relief while still being permitted to offer programs superior to those in other districts levying the same rates. Exactly when the other districts would catch up depends on whether high-spending districts would be held to fixed dollar ceilings or permitted to adjust those ceilings for increased costs. If the former, the catch-up period would be relatively short; if the latter, and if the cost adjustments were not done very rigorously, the poorer districts might not catch up for 10 or 20 years, possibly never.

34. For this purpose, categories might include pupils at different grade levels; pupils in different programs (e.g., vocational vs. college preparatory); pupils with designated "exceptionalities" (handicapped, retarded, gifted, etc.); and pupils assigned to various educational need categories on the basis of family background, test scores, or other evidence.

35. For example, a proposed equalization plan for the state of Michigan would have established regional salary indexes on the basis of current salaries paid, and allowed extra funds to districts that paid higher average salaries because their teachers had more training or experience. The first provision entirely neglects the possibility that regional differences in salary may be correlated with regional differences in teacher quality. The second provision would give extra funds to districts that employed higher quality teachers in the past, thereby permitting them to retain their advantages in the future. See Bureau of Programs and Budget, *School Finance Reform in Michigan* (Lansing, April 1972).

36. A problem that arises when categorical programs are brought into the general financing formula is that of *targeting*. How does one assure that funds given to a district because it has children with special needs and problems will actually be used to benefit those children? This has proved to be a major

problem in connection with federal compensatory education programs, where so-called "comparability" guidelines intended to control targeting have been poorly enforced (See "Title I Comparability: A Preliminary Evaluation," The Lawyer's Committee for Civil Rights Under Law, Washington, D.C., September 1972). The same problem exists for other categorical programs whether or not funds are allocated separately. However, combining all funds in one large pot might make it even more difficult to assure the intended allocations.

37. The 50 percent factor, as we have noted, was used in the recommendations of the Fleischmann Commission; the $300 figure is the amount that the U.S. Office of Education has cited, on occasion, as the increment sufficient to "make a difference" in raising achievement of disadvantaged children.

38. There would, of course, be major shifts in the distribution of property-tax burdens among districts. Those with lower-than-average initial rates would pay more; those with high initial rates (mainly poorer districts) would pay less. However, that is not the whole story. There are good reasons to believe that property values themselves would be altered through capitalization of the tax rate increases or decreases (see Reischauer and Hartman, *Reforming School Finance*). Thus, a more complicated series of adjustments would have to take place.

39. This approach was pursued in a California study carried out for the State Board of Education.

40. There is a continuing controversy in public finance about the best measure of "ability to pay." Ideally, one would want a comprehensive measure that takes account of income over an extended period ("permanent" income) and of wealth. Neither current income nor property value is really satisfactory. Of the two, however, income seems preferable, especially when it is realized that residential property value is the value of the home one occupies, not one's equity or net worth in that property.

41. Sources of variations in the ratio of home values to incomes include locational factors (e.g., differences in land values as a function of distance from the city), environmental differences (e.g., effects of polluting industries on prices of homes), and differences in tastes for housing associated with such variables as age and family size.

42. The *Serrano* decision elaborated on a number of consequences of schooling that make education a "fundamental interest." The question is, what level of school support must be guaranteed before those interests are fully protected? Or is the *relative* level of support the critical factor?

43. California examples include the districts of Huntington Beach and El Segundo, both of which appear property-rich because of their oil installations; but they would otherwise be districts of very ordinary wealth.

44. Statistics on the size distribution and number of districts in each state are provided in the annual *Digest of Educational Statistics*, Office of Education, Department of Health, Education and Welfare, Washington, D.C. In 1970, for example, the number of operating districts was about 18,000 (down from nearly 100,000 in 1949), but Nebraska, Illinois, Texas, and California each operated over 1000 districts.

45. Recently, however, the question of "metropolitan consolidation" has emerged as a major issue, even where existing districts are already relatively large (e.g., Virginia). The central issue is racial desegregation, but there are also some important financial considerations.

46. A discussion of the theory is presented in S.M. Barro, *Theoretical Models of School District Expenditure Determination and the Impact of Grants-in-Aid*, Santa Monica: The Rand Corporation, 1972. The discussion is couched in terms of effects of lump-sum grants and changes in the "price" of schooling, which can be translated into a formulation in terms of level and slope.

47. See, e.g., David Stern, "Effects of Alternatives State Aid Formulas on the Distribution of Public School Expenditures in Massachusetts," *Review of Economics and Statistics* 55 (February 1973).

Chapter Three

School Finance Reform and the Courts after Rodriguez

R. Stephen Browning and David C. Long
Lawyers' Committee for Civil Rights Under Law

During the past few years the American public has been awakened to the gross inequities in the funding of public education in most of the fifty states. As a result, reforms in both the allocation of educational benefits and tax burdens are now being seriously considered by legislatures,[1] courts[2] and study groups[3] across the country.

This activity continues despite the United States Supreme Court's recent pronouncement, in *San Antonio Independent School District v. Rodriguez*, that these inequities are not repugnant to the United States Constitution.[4] The issue now is whether the school finance reform movement will continue at its earlier pace. That is, what effect will the *Rodriguez* decision have on courts, legislatures and study commissions that have been involved in the effort to reform the collection and distribution of public funds for education? More specifically, does *Rodriguez* signal the end of court involvement in issues pertaining to the inequities in school finance systems? In short, to what extent did the decision dissipate the momentum that had been building up in state legislature over the past several years?

Rodriguez has clearly shifted the focus of school finance reform away from the federal courts. However, it seems unlikely that state courts and state legislatures will now simply ignore the great disparities in educational services and facilities that exist among school districts in most states. A legal tradition of concern over inequalities, particularly those in educational opportunities, has developed that transcends the narrow defeat of an active federal court role in eliminating this injustice. Certain state courts will likely continue a more active role, for the Supreme Court in no way foreclosed state courts from redressing disparities in educational opportunities on state constitutional grounds. Moreover, the obligations to provide elementary and secondary education, which most state constitutions impose, afford a sound legal basis for state courts to judge these educational inequities, a basis that is independent of the federal Constitution interpreted in *Rodriguez*. Moreover, *Rodriguez* and the many similar suits that have been filed have dramatized the injustice of permitting educational resources to be allocated on such irrational criteria as the amount of taxable wealth located within a school district. As a result, much of the momentum for reform of the financing of public education is likely to continue in state legislatures irrespective of prodding by the courts.

But there are good reasons to believe that state courts will continue to be active in school finance issues. And, indeed, the last word with respect to the role of federal courts in this area has probably not yet been spoken.

EQUAL EDUCATIONAL OPPORTUNITY—A BRIEF HISTORY OF REFORM

What Is Equal Educational Opportunity?

Equal educational opportunity in America's elementary and secondary schools is a cherished national ideal that has long received the attention of the executive, legislative, and judicial branches of government at both the state and federal levels. Though few would quarrel with the ideal, there is much confusion about its meaning, either as an educational or a legal concept (the latter being the primary focus of this chapter). What is equal educational opportunity, and how do you measure it? In the minds of the public it means many different things. Some have thought of it in terms of equal educational inputs—for example, facilities, teachers' salaries and other tangible or intangible resources. Others have viewed it in terms of equal educational ouputs, such as student performance as measured by standardized tests or even career achievements. Still others have identified it with inequalities stemming from racial or economic discrimination.

The judicial and legislative meaning of equal educational opportunity is still evolving, and it mirrors these different views. In the federal courts, concepts of educational equality have been forged primarily in cases interpreting the Equal Protection Clause of the Fourteenth Amendment to the United States Constitution: "No state shall . . . deny to any person within its jurisdiction the equal protection of the laws." The law has, to date, dealt with the following kinds of educational inequalities:

1. Equal services and facilities among racial groups (e.g., in school plant, per-pupil expenditures, teacher experience);
2. Equal intangible factors among racial groups (e.g., morale, prestige, expectations in the school);
3. Equal or balanced racial compositions of the school;

4. Equal consequences of the school for individuals from rich and poor backgrounds;
5. Equal public resources to the schools regardless of the wealth or poverty of the school district.

Equal services and facilities. The case of *Plessy v. Ferguson* provides a historic starting point for a discussion of the legal meaning of equality of educational opportunity. In this 1896 decision the Supreme Court held that public facilities could be racially segregated, provided that the separate facilities were of equal quality.[5] This rule, known as "separate but equal," guided the federal courts for nearly sixty years. For about fifty of these years courts professed that they were requiring segregated schools to be equal, but the rule was honored more in the breach.[6] It was not until about 1950 that courts began to look with any care at the various aspects of educational equality in segregated school facilities—pupil/teacher ratios, teacher experience, per pupil expenditures, the age of buildings, and so on.[7]

Equal intangible factors. By this time the Supreme Court began to see that racially separate schools lacked certain intangible educational advantages even when their services and physical facilities were equal to those of white schools. Among these less tangible factors were the school's prestige,[8] reputation among its alumni,[9] and learning atmosphere.[10] Such inequalities could not be corrected simply by spending more money, at least not in the short run. The focus of these cases was at the university level, and the remedy was admission of the black plaintiff to the white school with the intangible advantages.

Racial equality. In 1954, judicial examination of educational opportunities suddenly took a different course, but one whose direction had been set by the earlier cases. The Supreme Court, in its historic 1954 decision *Brown v. Board of Education*, held that racially separate schools were inherently unequal.[11] Because of this inherent inequality the Court determined that it would no longer permit segregated schools and no longer require a showing that black schools were unequal in tangible or intangible educational factors before ordering integration. Thus a third dimension of equal educational opportunity— racially balanced and integrated schools—became constitutionally required, at least insofar as the schools had been previously segregated by law.

Equal consequences. During the 1960s it became apparent that the *Brown* decision would have no effect on the educational opportunities available to the many minority students who would never sit in integrated classrooms. In addition, the War on Poverty focused public attention on the plight of the poor, and the poor included whites as well as minorities. There was sufficient concern about the disproportionately low academic achievement of students from impoverished and minority backgrounds to produce legislative activity directed toward changing this.

Thus, in the mid-1960s, new approaches to equality of educational opportunity were taken, primarily through legislation. Compensatory education programs were developed at federal and state levels to eliminate the effects on school children of racial isolation and economic and cultural deprivation. The new programs, funded primarily by the federal government, set a goal of equal achievement regardless of background, and sought to diminish the effect that differences in individual abilities could otherwise have had on educational success. The most significant of the federal education programs were those created by the Economic Opportunity Act of 1964[12] and the Elementary and Secondary Education Act of 1965.[13] Title I of the latter act authorized billions of dollars to be used to bring the achievement levels of educationally disadvantaged children up to that of children from different economic and cultural circumstances.

McInnis v. Ogilvie: The courts can't guarantee equal consequences. By the late 1960s educators and students of constitutional law expressed an increasing awareness of the inequities in state school finance systems and the great gap between the ideal of "equal educational opportunity" and its fulfillment in terms of any of its dimensions, especially for racial minorities and the poor. Their articles focused upon the needs of educationally disadvantaged youngsters who, because of socioeconomic background, could not effectively compete with more advantaged students.[14] These scholars noted that these disadvantaged students typically received fewer educational resources than other students; yet, because of the greater educational needs of the disadvantaged, they required more educational resources than their well-to-do peers.

These articles were in no small part responsible for a series of law suits filed in the late 1960s challenging the constitutionality of state systems of financing schools. The suits, brought on behalf of poor children, complained that existing state school finance systems unconstitutionally denied equal educational opportunities because educational funds were not allocated on the basis of children's educational needs.[15]

The most publicized of the "educational needs" suits, *McInnis v. Ogilvie*, was quickly dismissed by a three-judge federal court with the pronouncement that the plaintiffs had provided no standards for measuring "educational needs" and that it was therefore an unworkable directive for the courts, although perhaps a worthy guide for legislative policymakers.[16] The Supreme Court summarily affirmed this decision without opinion.[17]

These suits were ahead of current constitutional doctrine. The courts at that point had given the concept "equal educational opportunity" constitutional meaning only in the context of racial discrimination. Indeed, the courts had not determined that educationally disadvantaged children, regardless of their race, were constitutionally entitled to *equal* educational resources. Yet, the plaintiffs in *McInnis* asserted that, because of their greater educational needs, they were entitled to *more* resources than other children.

Fiscal Neutrality: A New Judicial Strategy to Achieve Equal Educational Opportunities for the Poor

It was apparent, after *McInnis*, that if the concept of equal educational opportunity was to have constitutional meaning outside of the racial context, new constitutional theories had to be developed. It was equally clear that any constitutional standard in this area would have to be readily understood and easily administered by the courts. At about this time certain legal scholars were studying how unequal local property-tax bases cause great educational expenditure inequalities among school districts.[18] They were particularly struck by the arbitrary effect school district wealth had on the educational quality offered by poor school districts, which, even at far higher local tax rates than tax-rich districts, cannot offer the quality of education that rich districts provide with less effort.

Earlier in this century, state aid formulas had been designed to compensate for such disparities. But at that time the better public schools were primarily in the central cities, and the state legislatures were frequently motivated by the desire to bring rural and small-town schools closer to the level of the "lighthouse" schools of the big cities.

Population and wealth shifts have rendered these early reforms obsolete; instead of equalization, the formulas created by these statutes now often tend to reinforce inequities between rich and poor school districts.[19] Moreover, state aid programs have come to benefit the property-rich suburbs at a time when, because of population shifts and reapportionment, their political power in state legislatures has increased significantly. In short, the legislative situation today with respect to reform of state school finance systems is one of inertia resulting from (1) the power of wealthy school districts; (2) the insecurity of districts of average wealth that reform might not significantly benefit them; and (3) the poor districts' lack of influence in the absence of help from the districts of average wealth.[20]

This failure of the states to eliminate the growing inequities in the finance systems they created became the object of constitutional scrutiny by legal scholars, who suggested that these inequities violated the Equal Protection Clause of the Fourteenth Amendment. Coons, Clune, and Sugarman argued that the Constitution, with respect to the funding of public education, requires "fiscal neutrality," which means that the "quality of public education may not be a function of wealth, other than the wealth of the state as a whole."[21]

The fiscal neutrality standard measures "wealth" by the value of a school district's tax base per pupil. And, since the property tax is the only tax the school districts in most states can levy, such wealth is usually measured in terms of a district's assessed property valuation per pupil. Thus, the fiscal neutrality theory, which measures wealth as local tax base per pupil available for education, was designed to challenge the unequal educational resources available to tax-poor districts.

This district-wealth standard is quite different from the standard of personal wealth and educational need articulated in *McInnis*. School district wealth is not always correlated with personal wealth—that is, poor people sometimes live in rich districts and vice versa. Furthermore, the fiscal neutrality theory does not mandate *any* particular educational policy. It does not require, but would certainly permit, more educational resources to be provided for poor or educationally deprived children. It does assume, however, that the quality of public education is related to the amount of dollars spent. But the standard essentially proscribes a current evil without prescribing any particular educational policy. The elimination of local taxable wealth as a determinant of a school district's expenditures is all it requires.

Serrano v. Priest—A first victory for fiscal neutrality. The persuasiveness of the Coons, Clune, and Sugarman analysis, and the utility of their proposed fiscal neutrality standard, were immediately apparent to a number of attorneys who had school finance cases pending when *McInnis* was decided adversely. Although one view was that *McInnis* signaled an early demise to school finance reform litigation, these attorneys incorporated fiscal neutrality in their pleadings and made it their central constitutional theory.

The California Supreme Court's August 1971 decision in *Serrano v. Priest* emerged as the first judicial pronouncement on fiscal neutrality as a constitutional principle. It held that the plaintiffs in *Serrano* had stated a claim that, if proved, would result in the California system for funding public schools being declared unconstitutional under both the United States and California constitutions.[22] In the words of the court:

> We have determined that [the California] funding scheme invidiously discriminates against the poor because it makes the quality of a child's education a function of the wealth of his parents and neighbors.[23]

The announcement of the *Serrano* decision was accompanied by much confusion about what the California Supreme Court had prohibited or required. One mistaken belief was that it held the local property tax unconstitutional; another was that it required equal dollars per pupil. Actually it did neither of these things. In fact, it did much less than most people believed. It merely held unconstitutional those disparities in educational quality between school districts that result from unequal school district property tax bases.

The *Serrano* decision was the subject of enormous national publicity. The reason for such a response was quite simple. The California system of funding schools, with its substantial reliance on local property taxes, was similar to systems operating in every state in the Union. If the California system violated the fiscal neutrality standard, the other state systems probably did also.

What fiscal neutrality would require has been described in Chapter 2. It is important to understand that most state school finance systems probably would not have conformed to the standard—more for what such systems fail to do, than for what they do. That is, it is largely what states permit school districts to do that creates the problem. The "Final Report to the California Senate Select Committee on School District Finance" points out how states have created school finance systems characterized by the inequities condemned in *Serrano* and subsequent cases:

> (1) The state permits local school districts to exist, (2) the state gives each district the power to raise money through a local property tax on property physically located within the district's border, (3) the state permits each district to keep the money it raises, knowing that from district to district the ability to raise money for schools varies widely because of the dramatically uneven distribution of property wealth about the state, and (4) the state fails to equalize these wealth differences through "state aid"[24]

In sum, the combination of facts (3) and (4) above is what condemned the California school finance system. Even though state aid had some equalizing effect, it failed to eliminate the effect that differences in taxable wealth per pupil among school districts had on educational expenditures. Thus, so long as local districts can and do exploit local wealth advantages, a state school finance system would not pass the *Serrano* test.

Post-Serrano decisions. Following the announcement of the *Serrano* decision, a groundswell of school finance litigation emerged across the country with more than thirty suits being filed in state and federal courts. Within eighteen months, eight other state or federal courts from as many states had spoken to the issue of interdistrict school finance inequities.[25] Lower federal courts in Minnesota and Texas declared unconstitutional the methods for financing education in those states. State courts in Arizona, Kansas, Michigan, and New Jersey did likewise. The Wyoming Supreme Court rejected a school district consolidation plan because of the inequalities in taxable wealth per pupil between districts that would result from its implementation. Most adopted legal reasoning similar to that employed by the California court in *Serrano*, holding that statewide school finance schemes that permitted educational resources to vary between districts according to the taxable wealth of each school district violated the equal protection provisions of the federal or state constitutions. However, the Arizona and New Jersey cases were decided on different grounds.

The state court in Arizona found that state's system unconstitutional under the equal protection provisions of both the Arizona and United States constitutions and, like *Serrano*, required fiscal neutrality. However, unlike the other courts the Arizona court provided relief exclusively for the harm to taxpayers in tax-poor school districts. These taxpayers had to pay higher property taxes than those in wealthier districts to obtain the same educational resources for their school children. The Arizona court held that since education is a fundamental interest of the state, such discrimination against taxpayers in its funding is unconstitutional.

The New Jersey decision, unlike the others, was not based on state or federal equal protection provisions. The constitution of the state of New Jersey requires the state legislature to provide a "thorough and efficient" system of public education, and the trial court in New Jersey found that the statewide system of funding schools resulted in the children in certain districts receiving an education that was less than "thorough."

SAN ANTONIO INDEPENDENT SCHOOL DISTRICT V. RODRIGUEZ: THE SUPREME COURT SLOWS THE PACE

With the large number of active school finance cases working their way through the courts after *Serrano*, one was certain to reach the United States Supreme Court soon. The first to do so was an appeal from a decision of a three-judge federal court, which had held the Texas school finance system unconstitutional in *Rodriguez v. San Antonio Independent School District*.

There was great uncertainty concerning how the Supreme Court would decide such a case. Lower federal and state courts alike had relied on the Equal Protection Clause of the Fourteenth Amendment to the Constitution to strike down state school finance laws. However, the United States Supreme Court, the ultimate arbiter of the meaning of that federal constitution, had never addressed this issue. Thus, other courts considering the constitutionality of inequities between school districts in educational resources looked to analogous areas for precedent. Two lines of cases are particularly important. First, for the constitutional importance of education and a proscription of discrimination in how it is provided, they looked to the Supreme Court's decision holding racially segregated schools unconstitutional. Second, cases ensuring impoverished defendants substantially equal treatment in the criminal process to that available to more affluent defendants formed the basis for finding that discrimination based on wealth is constitutionally "suspect."[26] In its decision of March 21, 1973, in *San Antonio Independent District v. Rodriguez*, the United States Supreme Court rejected this use of past precedent, and in a five-to-four decision upheld the Texas school financing scheme, which causes substantial inequalities between districts in the allocation of education funds.

Mr. Justice Powell, writing for the five-member majority, held that the educational interests at stake in *Rodriguez* were not constitutionally "fundamental," nor was the discrimination among school districts in the amounts of taxable wealth available for support of the public school districts constitutionally "suspect." Consequently the Court refused to apply what has been called the "strict scrutiny test." Where discrimination affects constitutionally fundamental interests (e.g., equal access to the electoral process or the right to travel),[27] or is based on suspect classifications (e.g., race), it has usually been strictly scrutinized with the state being required to sustain a heavy burden to justify such discrimination. The burden, which has often been referred to as the state having to show a "compelling state interest" for the discrimination, is difficult to carry. Indeed, the state of Texas conceded that if this test were applied, its financing system would fall.[28]

Refusing to apply the strict scrutiny test, the Court held that the heavy reliance of the Texas school finance scheme on unequalized local property tax bases and the resulting discrimination against children in poor districts had only to be justified as *reasonably* related to some legitimate state objective. To sustain the inequalities on this basis the Court accepted the argument of the state of Texas that the present system fostered "local control," and that it provided an adequate minimum educational offering in every school in the state. Conceding that poor districts probably had little local control because of their inability to raise significant extra funds from local taxation, the Court held that Texas did not have to adopt the system that most successfully furthered local control. Thus, even though the Court recognized the need for reform of school finance systems that have relied too heavily on the local property tax, it did not see its role as encompassing the consideration and initiation of such reforms.

Three dissenting opinions, written by Justices Brennan, White, and Marshall, were filed. The latter two are especially noteworthy because they contain strong challenges to the reasoning employed by the majority opinion and deal with issues that are sure to arise in any subsequent school finance litigation.

The dissenting opinion of Mr. Justice White argued that the state of Texas had offered no rational basis for sustaining such discrimination based on the educationally irrelevant factor of school district wealth. He agreed with the majority that local control was a legitimate objective for a state to pursue in its funding of public education. However, he saw no rational relationship between the *means* chosen by Texas for supporting the schools—which effectively prevent parents in poor districts from augmenting school district revenues from local taxes—and the states professed *end*—local control. According to Mr. Justice White the majority's equal protection analysis, which condoned gross discrimination in the Texas system, was nothing more than an "empty gesture."

The lengthy dissent of Mr. Justice Marshall took the majority opinion to task on virtually every point. He rejected the majority's suggestion that the effect of spending variations on educational achievement was an issue relevant to the resolution of the case. Thus, the court needed to look only at what the state provides children and not what they are able to do with what they receive. And the state should bear the burden of justifying any discrimination among children in the *opportunity* to learn.

Moreover, Mr. Justice Marshall attacked the Court's rigid two-step equal protection analysis, which separates all rights into two classes to determine the appropriate standard of constitutional review: (1) those rights explicitly or implicitly protected by the constitution; and (2) those that are not. He found this arbitrary categorization to be inconsistent with past decisions of the Supreme Court. Such decisions, he argued, had adopted a more flexible case-by-case approach for judging the constitutionality of discrimination where the court has weighed the character of the classification, the relative importance to the individuals discriminated against of the governmental benefits they do not receive, and the interests of the state in support of the classification.

The Significance of Poverty under
the Federal Constitution

The plaintiffs in *Rodriguez* sought to have the adverse effect that a wealth-based school finance system has on property-poor school districts declared to be in violation of the Equal Protection Clause of the United States Constitution. Plaintiffs also sought to show that, in Texas, children from poor families resided disproportionately in tax-poor school districts. Thus, the case presented the issues of the constitutional significance of educational expenditure differences related to both *district poverty* and *personal poverty*.

In discussing the poverty-related discrimination alleged in *Rodriguez*, Mr. Justice Powell, writing for the majority of the Court, noted there were three possible ways of looking at the class of children discriminated against: (1) those from families whose incomes fall below some identifiable level of poverty; (2) those who are poor in comparison with others; and (3) those who, rich and poor, happen to live in poor school districts. The Court interpreted its past decisions, with respect to discrimination resulting from poverty, as protecting only those who "were completely unable to pay for some desired benefit, and as a consequence they sustained an absolute deprivation of a meaningful opportunity to enjoy that benefit."[29] For example, in its decision dealing with the rights of indigents to have a free transcript for a criminal appeal, the Court emphasized there was no "adequate substitute" for a full transcript;[30] other criminal procedure cases are described as only benefiting those who are "totally unable to pay the demand sum"; and the Court interprets one of its recent election decisions dealing with the constitutionality of large filing fees for candidates to state office as involving a situation that "effectively barred all potential candidates who were unable to pay the required fee" where there was "no reasonable alternative means of access to the ballot."[31]

In light of this analysis, the Court criticized the class of poor people in *Rodriguez* because there was no showing that the Texas system "operates to the *peculiar disadvantage* of any class fairly definable as indigent, or as composed of persons whose incomes are beneath any designated poverty level." As noted above, the Court viewed poor people as benefiting as well as being harmed by the present system. The Court also found no evidence that the "poorest people" are "concentrated" in the poorest districts.[32] Moreover, the Court noted that plaintiffs were *not denied access* to the public schools. Their claim was that their schools are inferior because of the poverty of their school district. The Court responded that "where wealth is involved the Equal Protection Clause does not require absolute equality or precisely equal advantages."[33] Furthermore the Court stated that, because of the "infinite variables" involved in this type of case, equal quality education cannot be assured except in the "most relative sense," and plaintiffs in *Rodriguez* alleged only that they received a "poorer quality education" rather than "no public education."[34] The Court also rejected "difference in per pupil expenditures" as being too simplistic a measure of equal educational opportunity.[35]

The Court indicated that if poverty resulted in a total exclusion from the educational process, a different result might obtain: if the state required tuition payments there would be a clearly defined class of poor people who could not pay the prescribed sum and who would be "absolutely precluded from receiving an education." It saw this as a more compelling case for judicial intervention.[36]

It is important to note, however, that the Court did not hold that *relative* discrimination based on personal poverty would always pass constitutional muster. It merely held that the pattern of relative discrimination in educational opportunities against poor children in Texas was not consistent enough throughout the state for the Court to decide whether such discrimination would give rise to close judicial scrutiny. The evidence in the case showed a significant correlation between individual wealth and educational expenditures in the richest and poorest districts, but showed a mixed picture for the large number of districts in between. Consequently, the Court refused to view the facts in the case as supporting the proposition that in Texas affluent children are systematically benefited and children from poor families systematically disadvantaged, and left for a future case whether *relative wealth* can be a proper basis for identifying a suspect class.

The majority opinion raised the question of whether, if a better correlation had been shown, discrimination would be proved by a "bare positive correlation or some higher degree of correlation."[37] The Court also questioned the use of median income statistics because they do not show with any precision "the status of individual families." It would have liked to have seen evidence as to average income, and the mode and concentration of poor families in each district.[38]

The Court also indicated that more than a mere correlation would be necessary to prove comparative discrimination; additionally, proof may be required that the quality of education is "dependent on personal wealth."[39] Thus the adverse effect of educational discrimination on poor people may not be enough to trigger a comparative discrimination theory; a showing that the discrimination *results* from the fact of individual poverty may also be required.[40] Since most poverty cases are based on the effect of state action or inaction on the poor, this could, in many cases, be an insurmountable barrier.

Thus *Rodriguez* does not resolve the question of whether a constitutional theory challenging educational discrimination can be based on comparative poverty. Justice Stewart, in his concurring opinion in *Rodriguez*, unequivocally rejected any comparative poverty standard. He defined indigency to mean "actual or functional indigency; it does not mean comparative poverty vis-à-vis comparative affluence."[41] However, some comparative poverty situations can be viewed as absolute deprivations, particularly if the focus is solely on the people at the lowest end of the scale. For example, if the public schools were to charge tuition or fees, both absolute and relative deprivations could result; that is, the poorest families may not be able to afford any education for their children and the less poor may be able to purchase only a small amount of education compared with the affluent. The distribution of educational resources by socioeconomic status in such a case could be shown to result in the poorest children being effectively excluded from a minimum educational opportunity.

What has been said so far concerning the Court's treatment of the plaintiffs' claim, that the Texas school finance system discriminated on the basis of wealth, has dealt primarily with the relevance of personal poverty. However, plaintiffs placed primary reliance on the theory that there was discrimination against all children who reside in poor districts irrespective of the personal income of their families. The majority of the Court held that there was nothing constitutionally suspect about discrimination against all those, both rich and poor, who happen to reside in districts with less taxable wealth than others. Thus the plaintiffs' "district wealth" theory was clearly rejected by the Court.

The Importance of Education under the Federal Constitution

The Supreme Court in *Rodriguez* refused to find that education is "fundamental" as a matter of federal constitutional law. As has been discussed, a finding of constitutional fundamentality would have set in motion close judicial scrutiny of any impairment of the interest so considered and required the state to show some compelling state interest to justify such discrimination. The Court rejected the notion of education's fundamentality as a basis for deciding the Texas case, on the ground that a right to education is neither explicitly nor implicitly guaranteed by the Constitution.[41] Plaintiffs in *Rodriguez* had argued that the right to education is at least implied in the Constitution because of its relation of other constitutional guarantees such as free speech and the franchise. While the Court considered the possibility that "some identifiable quantum of education is a constitutionally protected prerequisite to the meaningful exercise" of the right to speak and to vote, it asserted that "no charge fairly could be made that the [Texas] system fails to provide each child with an *opportunity to acquire the basic minimal skills* necessary for the enjoyment of the rights of speech and a full participation in the political process."[42] No explanation was given as to why "no charge" could be fairly made.

Thus, the Court appeared to leave open the possibility that the federal Constitution, through the federal courts, may be responsive to children who are excluded from the educational process or who are not given an opportunity to acquire sufficient education to carry out the responsibilities of citizenship. At the same time it assumed that the Texas school finance system did not disadvantage children in this way.

In its 1973-74 term, the Supreme Court will have another opportunity to address the issues of educational adequacy and exclusion from the educational process. In *Lau v. Nichols*, non-English-speaking Chinese students claim that they have been effectively excluded from an education by the failure of the San Francisco Unified School District to provide any instruction that would enable them to benefit from their classes, which are taught in the English language. The United States Court of Appeals for the Ninth Circuit, attaching no legal significance to the fact that the Chinese students could not comprehend what was going on in the classroom, held that their constitutional rights to equal protection were not violated since they received the same instruction as all other students. The major issue in the case is whether the effective exclusion of these Chinese students from the educational process by the school district's failure to do anything to overcome their language disability is a violation of the Fourteenth Amendment's Equal Protection Clause. The Supreme Court has agreed to hear the case and a decision is likely in 1974.

Additionally, there are a number of cases that have been decided by or are pending in federal district courts throughout the country, challenging the exclusion by school districts of children with various mental and physical handicaps.[43] These suits differ from *Lau* in that they involve students for whom no instruction is provided—that is, they are not permitted to attend classes—rather than being effectively excluded by language from participating, as in *Lau*. These suits on behalf of handicapped children are significant because it is common for school districts to provide no instruction whatsoever for many such students; in addition, educational strategies are not available that can provide handicapped students with the skills and understanding to live useful lives. It is likely that at least one of these "exclusion cases" will be heard by the Supreme Court within the next several years.

The exclusion cases will probably not play a direct role with respect to reform of school finance systems. Of course, if plaintiffs win, additional educational costs will have to be assumed by someone—in the first instance probably by school districts, who will then put pressure on their legislatures to increase state assistance for the education of non-English-speaking and handicapped students. Since state and federal categorical assistance for the education of such students is already well established, it is likely that a state's response to a court order is more likely to take the form of the creating or the increased funding of categorical programs rather than a reassessment of the relationship between educational funding and taxable wealth.

These cases may, however, tell us whether *Rodriguez* was intended to post the whole area of education and related finance issues as off-limits to the federal courts, or whether the Supreme Court was largely concerned about magnitude of the upheaval that it believed an affirmance in *Rodriguez* would cause, but did not intend to say that such issues can never give rise to a constitutional claim on which relief may be granted.

Inequities Resulting from the Property Tax under the Federal Constitution

The Supreme Court in *Rodriguez* clearly held that the federal Constitution does not prohibit the states from creating school finance systems in which heavy reliance on local property taxes results in wealthy school districts offering high-quality education and tax-poor districts providing inferior offerings. What is the reach of the Court's opinion with respect to other tax related educational inequities?

The Court in *Rodriguez* indicated that it was not anxious to deal with matters concerning how state and local revenues are raised and disbursed. Confessing a lack of expertise and familiarity with local problems it thought necessary for making wise decisions with respect to the raising and disposition of public revenues, and noting that all taxes inherently contain some discriminatory effect, the Court said that it will not impose "too rigorous a standard of scrutiny" on local fiscal schemes.[44] Thus, most challenges to inequities caused by state and local tax provisions are likely to receive a chilly reception in the federal courts.

However, one property-tax related education finance problem to which the *Rodriguez* majority opinion specifically refers and did not foreclose federal relief in was that presented in *Hargrave v. Kirk*.[45] In that case Florida's statutory limitations on local property-tax rates for schools support were rolled back to low levels, thereby effectively barring school districts with low assessed valuations per pupil from ever providing their children with the educational resources that richer districts could provide by taxing at or below the maximum rate. Plaintiffs in *Hargrave* won before a three-judge federal court. The Supreme Court in 1971 reversed and remanded because it believed the federal court should have abstained from reaching a decision until the effect of the new school finance system, of which the millage rollback law was a part, had been fully considered in a convenient state court proceeding. Thus, the Supreme Court has never reached the merits of the district tax rate limit issue.

It is possible that the federal courts may still hold unconstitutional such tax rate limits on school districts that seriously and permanently discriminate against children in poorer school districts—that is, the rate limits are not just part of a millage rollback accompanying a plan for greater state aid to education. The basis for this view is the importance the Supreme Court, in *Rodriguez*, placed on local control of educational finance. The state of Texas had relied on this justification to defend its finance system, and the Supreme Court accepted this, noting that there had been no showing that the poorer districts in Texas were *precluded* by law from increasing their educational expenditures, as were the districts in *Hargrave*.[46]

A rate limit suit, while of potential benefit to school children, does nothing to eliminate property-tax inequities. Indeed, the unfairness to taxpayers of present school finance systems would be increased. This would result from the fact that increasing the school tax rate in a tax-poor district could dramatically increase the burdens on the district's taxpayers with little to show in terms of increased per pupil expenditures. For example, if a district with $5,000 assessed valuation per pupil increases its tax rate by $1 per $100 of assessed valuation, it will increase the educational expenditures in the district by only $50 per pupil. The same tax rate increase in a district with $50,000 assessed valuation per pupil will raise $500 additional for each pupil in the wealthier district. Thus, taxpayers in the poorer district, to raise $500 additional per child, would have to pay ten times the tax rate of the richer district.

The Supreme Court displayed marked indifference to the effect of another situation that remains the subject of litigation in *Fort Worth Independent School District v. Edgar*, now pending in the federal district court in Texas.[47] This was thought to be a suit with some potential for bringing about school finance and property tax reform in those states that have no adequate statewide program for equalizing local assessments or do not use equalized assessment data for distribution of state school aid. The case was filed by the three large school districts of Fort Worth, Houston, and Dallas against the Superintendent of Public Instruction, among others. State school aid in Texas is apportioned by use of a county economic index, one part of which consists of assessed property valuation per pupil. Unequalized assessed valuation as reported by local assessors is taken as correct in making up the index. Since the three Texas cities assess at a much higher percentage of market value than many other areas in Texas, these cities look richer than they are and consequently get less state aid than they would otherwise be entitled to.

Unfortunately, Mr. Justice Powell's opinion in *Rodriguez*, while not considering whether an equalizing aid scheme that relies on unequalized assessed valuation is constitutional, showed great insensitivity to its irrationality, and there are statements in the opinion that arguably appear to condone this Texas practice.[48]

The Effect of Rodriguez on School Finance Suits in State Courts

The *Rodriguez* decision and the reasoning that underlies it is not binding on state court school finance suits based on state constitutional claims. The United States Supreme Court is the final authority as to the meaning and application of the federal Constitution, and the *Rodriguez* case was a challenge based on the Equal Protection Clause of the Fourteenth Amendment to that Constitution. No state constitutional issues were raised in *Rodriguez*.

At the time the *Rodriguez* decision was announced, more than thirty-five school finance suits, pending in federal and state courts, were based in whole or in part on the federal Constitution. To the extent that these suits were so based, they were probably disposed of by *Rodriguez*. However, just as many, or perhaps more, suits that relied upon state constitutional arguments that are entirely independent of the United States Constitution were then pending in state courts. These suits were not disposed of by *Rodriguez*, for state supreme courts, and not the Supreme Court of the United States, are the final arbiters of the meaning and application of state constitutional provisions.

Thus, the *Rodriguez* decision, rather than rendering a unified national ruling interpreting the federal Constitution as demanding equality of educational opportunity, by deferring explicitly and repeatedly to the principles of federalism,[49] has signaled state judicial and constitutional supremacy and finality on the issue of whether there may be interdistrict discrimination in state school finance systems. It is now up to the states to evaluate for themselves the nature, function, and importance of public education and the legality, under state constitutions, of discrimination in how it is provided.[50]

It is important to note that the reasoning used by the Court in *Rodriguez* and by Mr. Justice Stewart is supportive of state courts taking a much closer look at these educational inequities than the Supreme Court did. The Supreme Court found that education is not a "fundamental interest" under the federal Constitution, which meant that the Court would not strictly scrutinize the discrimination resulting from the Texas finance system. The Court determined that education is not "fundamental," in large part, because a right to an education is neither implicit nor explicit under the United States Constitution. Moreover, the federal government has not undertaken to provide education to all children. In contrast, the states have undertaken this obligation; indeed, they are compelled by their state constitution to do so. Every state constitution requires the state to maintain a system of free public schools, which many constitutions require to be "thorough and efficient" or "general and uniform" or to meet similar standards.[51] If such language appeared in the federal Constitution, it can be said on the basis of *Rodriguez* that education probably would have been considered fundamental. Thus, even if state courts decide in interpreting their state constitutions to apply the reasoning used by the Supreme Court, education should be considered fundamental as a matter of state law.

THREE IMPORTANT SCHOOL FINANCE CHALLENGES BASED ON STATE CONSTITUTIONAL PROVISIONS: SERRANO, MILLIKEN, AND ROBINSON

This reasoning process, to find education fundamental under state constitutions for purposes of analysis of state equal protection guarantees, was explicitly used by the Michigan Supreme Court to invalidate the Michigan school finance system on the basis of state law.[52] It was implicit in the California Supreme Court's decision in *Serrano v. Priest*,[53] and was rejected by the New Jersey Supreme Court, which held New Jersey's school finance laws unconstitutional on other state grounds.[54] These three cases, the judicial and legislative sequels within those states, and the acceptance of their grounds for decision by the courts of other states, appear to hold the key to the future of school finance litigation.

Serrano v. Priest

In *Serrano v. Priest*, as noted above, the Supreme Court of California held the state's school finance laws unconstitutional on the basis of facts alleged in the plaintiffs' complaint, which had been dismissed by the trial court. The Court said that it was a violation of both the federal and state constitutions to make the quality of a child's education depend on the wealth of his parents and neighbors. The case was then remanded for trial, since the court's decision had assumed that the facts the plaintiffs alleged were true. The trial, which lasted for five months, was completed in May 1973.

Since there was little disagreement between plaintiffs and defendants about disparities between school districts in assessed valuations per pupil, tax rates, and educational expenditures, the *Serrano* trial has focused primarily on the issues of (1) whether expenditure inequalities injure children in poor districts; and (2) whether a bill recently passed by the California Assembly sufficiently eliminates the inequities complained of. For the first time in school finance litigation there was a full airing of the "cost-achievement" issue—the relationship of educational inputs (and especially operating or total costs) to educational outputs as measured by achievement on standardized tests. The issue had been previously raised and some evidence on either side of the issue heard in other cases, but no case other than *Serrano* has explored so thoroughly both the factual contentions on both sides and the legal relevance (or irrelevance) of the issue.

Defendants in *Serrano* contended that the plaintiffs had to prove a positive relationship between cost and achievement (holding socioeconomic status constant); furthermore, defendants sought to show that there was no such relationship. Plaintiffs took the position that the cost-achievement issue is not relevant since all plaintiffs seek is that the state provide them with the same *opportunity* to benefit from a public education, and are not asking the state to guarantee results. Furthermore, the school finance system has been structured by the state on the premise that money makes a difference, and it ill behooves the state and wealthy school districts, which benefit from its inequities, to defend this maldistribution of resources on the basis that it makes no difference; indeed, if it does not, wealthy districts have no basis for defending the rationality of their own expenditures. Plaintiffs also argued that achievement scores on standardized reading and math tests measure only a small part of what education is all about. Additionally, plaintiffs challenged the research upon which defendants relied, pointing out that educational research is still at a primitive stage; that most of it does not deal with the effect of additional educational inputs received by given children on their achievement (most research has not measured the effect of providing particular children with increased educational resources); and that there are studies other than those on which defendants rely that show a significant relationship between cost and achievement.

The trial court's decision in *Serrano* is expected in 1974. Whatever the court decides, the decision is certain to be appealed again to the California Supreme Court. Since the first *Serrano* decision relied on both the federal Constitution and the equal protection provision of the California Constitution, the California Supreme Court could reach the same result as its earlier ruling, irrespective of *Rodriguez.**

Milliken v. Green

Another state in which the Supreme Court has held its school finance provisions to be in violation of the state constitution is Michigan. The judgment in *Milliken v. Green* was handed down while *Rodriguez* was awaiting decision in the United States Supreme Court.[55] The Michigan court held that education is a fundamental interest under the Michigan Constitution. It also determined that the cost-achievement issue was irrelevant as a matter of law to its constitutional analysis since the Michigan Constitution requires the legislature to "maintain and support" a system of free public schools; thus the only question the court had to decide was "whether or not the legislature's action maintains and supports free public schools equally or, if not equally, with valid classification."[56] Based on the fundamentality of education and the suspectness of wealth as a basis for classification, the court held that there was no compelling interest served by the educational disparities stemming from taxable wealth differences among districts. Further, the court found no rational basis for the discrimination. Both holdings were based on the equal protection provision of the Michigan Constitution.

---

*Editor's Note: On April 6, 1974 the trial court issued a 106 page decision in which it declared the California School Finance System unconstitutional and gave the state six years to correct the inequalities.

The status of this decision is uncertain, since a motion for rehearing was granted in February 1973 by the Michigan Supreme Court and two members of the court have retired, one each from the majority and dissenting opinions in what was a four-to-three decision. Also, on August 14, 1973, Michigan enacted a new statewide school finance program that purports to satisfy the standards set out in *Milliken v. Green.* *

Robinson v. Cahill

A third state supreme court, in a most interesting decision, has held its school finance system unconstitutional, but on different grounds and with different results from the other two. The New Jersey court, in *Robinson v. Cahill*, found that the present method of financing schools violates the state constitutional provision pertaining to education, which requires that

> The legislature shall provide for the maintenance and support of a thorough and efficient system of free public schools for the instruction of all the children in the state between the ages of five and eighteen years.[57]

The court said an education that is thorough and efficient "must be understood to embrace that educational opportunity which is needed in the contemporary setting to equip a child for his role as a citizen and as a competitor in the labor market."[58] This much of the opinion sounds like an output standard, and the trial court below had found that both educational inputs and outputs were inadequate in certain New Jersey school districts.[59] However, the New Jersey Supreme Court goes on to say that it finds the constitutional demand not met "on the basis of discrepancies in dollar input per pupil." It thus appears that the court had both inputs and outputs in mind when it wrote its opinion. The court viewed the "thorough and efficient" requirement as mandating "an equal educational opportunity for children,"[60] and further found that the existing finance scheme was not "visibly geared to the mandate that there be a 'thorough and efficient system of free public schools,' " and "has no apparent relation to the mandate for equal educational opportunity."[61]

The key to harmonizing these statements appears to be the court's finding that "the state has never spelled out the content of the educational opportunity the constitution requires."[62] Thus, a major aspect of the constitutional violation appears to. be the failure of the state to take its constitutional obligations seriously in funding public education and, indeed, in not establishing input and output criteria for judging whether a thorough and efficient education is being provided.

The *Robinson* case is also interesting on the taxpayers' side. The trial court had ruled that the New Jersey school finance provisions were unconstitutional for the reason, among others, that taxpayers in poorer districts are forced to pay higher property taxes for education than taxpayers in wealthier districts;

---

*Editor's Note: On December 14, 1973, the Michigan Supreme Court vacated its earlier decision.

the lower court found that this violated the tax uniformity provision of the New Jersey Constitution as well as the state's equal protection guarantee.[63] Although the local district would normally be considered the jurisdiction within which local property-tax rates would have to be uniform, the judge believed the state was the relevant jurisdiction for purposes of uniformity when the revenues raised served "common state educational purposes."[64]

The New Jersey Supreme Court rejected the trial court's view of the state constitution's tax uniformity provision. It held that education is a state function, but when the state delegates the fiscal responsibility for education to local districts, the property tax raised by local districts is a local and not a state tax; thus, uniformity of rate is required only within each school district.[65]

The New Jersey Supreme Court diverged significantly from the equal protection analysis used by the highest courts of California and Michigan. The trial court in *Robinson*, in part relying on *Serrano*, had found that under New Jersey and federal equal protection provisions the inequities to children and taxpayers should be subject to strict scrutiny because education is a fundamental interest of the state and classifications based on wealth are disfavored; and it could find no compelling justification for sustaining a finance system that discriminated in this manner. The New Jersey Supreme Court was reluctant to rest its decision on state equal protection grounds, because it confessed an inability to determine what services were "constitutionally fundamental."[66] Additionally, although the court viewed certain discrimination based on individual wealth as arbitrary and thus unlawful, it did not see differences in benefits and tax burdens resulting from unequal local tax bases as constituting a suspect wealth classification. The court expressed fear that the differences in educational expenditures that resulted from such district wealth differences could not be distinguished from differences in the provision of other services, and that a ruling based on a *Serrano*-type equal protection wealth analysis would change the state's political structure.[67]

Perhaps the New Jersey Supreme Court has created a straw man when it asserts that for the purpose of an equal protection analysis it would not be able to confine a decision, regarding the provision of educational services, to both the "fundamentality" of education and the "suspectness" of district wealth. Courts are expert at drawing such lines. Indeed, the specific state constitutional obligation to provide education, which the court does enforce, belies education's indistinguishability from other services. In any event, the New Jersey decision clearly separates, at least for purposes of state constitutional analysis, the inequalities among children and among taxpayers under the state's current school finance system. The court says that the state, if it chooses to assign its education obligation to local government, "must *compel* the local school districts to raise the money necessary."[68] Thus the New Jersey court requires only that children be treated fairly.

This difference between the New Jersey decision and those from

California and Michigan may not be so significant with respect to reform alternatives that are politically viable to state legislatures. This is because the New Jersey legislature, in developing a school finance program to comply with the court's order, is likely to be just as concerned with its effect on local taxpayers as on children, even though, unlike California and Michigan, it need only be concerned with children.

State Court School Finance Litigation: Where Else Besides California, Michigan, and New Jersey?

The discussion to this point has focused upon the opinion of the Supreme Court of the United States in *Rodriguez* and the emerging state constitutional law pertaining to the inequities produced by present statewide systems of school finance. Little has been said about the likelihood of numerous state courts across the nation declaring their finance systems unconstitutional, and for good reasons: the *Rodriguez* decision is too recent for its effect on state courts' interpretations of their own constitutions to be known. More time must pass and more work must be done before prediction in that regard would be anything more than speculation. Much research on state law and constitutional history remains to be done.

One thing is clear, however—the momentum for reform of the inequitable allocation of educational resources and tax burdens that has accelerated since the *Serrano* decision was not stopped by *Rodriguez*. It has been undoubtedly slowed since federal courts will not be prodding legislatures to action. However, many legislative bodies are already in action. Florida, Kansas, Maine, Michigan, Minnesota, Utah, and several other states have passed significant reform legislation. Nearly every state has a school finance commission at work. The legislative reform efforts under way demonstrate that equity in the allocation of educational resources is workable and politically viable, thereby diminishing the fear of untried alternatives currently paralyzing some state legislatures.[69]

The movement for reform of school finance programs now underway in many legislatures has great relevance to the course of school finance litigation in state courts. It is likely that the pace of litigation will slow significantly in the next few years, in large part to see whether legislatures, absent court orders, will come to grips with the inequities in their school finance systems. To the extent that they do, the need for litigation will be obviated.

There are also other reasons for believing that future litigation in this area will proceed more slowly than in the past. After *Serrano* there were those who believed that a school finance case could be won by submitting to a court a single exhibit that showed on a per pupil basis the assessed valuation of school districts in the state, their property-tax rates, and educational expenditures. As attorneys on both sides of these cases have become increasingly knowledgeable about the issues, the complexity of these cases has multiplied. More preparation than in the past will have to be done prior to filing future school finance cases, and these cases will take longer to get to trial after filing. The future decisions of the California courts in *Serrano* and of the Michigan Supreme Court in *Milliken* may provide guidance as to what issues are relevant. The Supreme Courts of other states may also in the near future render decisions in already filed school finance cases.

As is readily apparent, this is an area of judicial and legislative activity that is in great flux. The United States Supreme Court, by ordering the federal courts to avoid school finance inequity issues, has shifted the forum to state courts—it has by no means precluded state courts from playing a major role in making educational finance rational, or in breaking the link between the amount of assessed property valuation a school district has and the resources it can devote to public education.

NOTES

1. During 1972-1973 the *Legislative Review*, published by the Education Commission of the States, has maintained a continuing commentary on the progress of school finance proposals in state legislatures. See also A.C. Staufer, "Major School Finance Changes in 1973" (preliminary paper) (Denver: Education Commission of the States, 1973).

2. For a listing of school finance suits pending prior to the Supreme Court decision in *Rodriguez*, see U.S. Commission on Civil Rights *Inequality in School Financing: The Role of the Law* (Washington, D.C., 1972), pp. 52-77.

3. Pipho, *Survey of School Finance Study Commissions and Committees: A Report of the Education Commission of the States* (Denver, May 1972).

4. *San Antonio Independent School District v. Rodriguez*, 36 L. Ed. 2d 16, 93 S. Ct. 1278 (1973).

5. *Plessy v. Ferguson*, 163 U.S. 537 (1896).

6. See, e.g., *Cumming v. County Board of Education*, 175 U.S. 528 (1899); *State ex rel. Weaver v. Board of Trustees of Ohio University*, 126 Ohio 290, 185 N.E. 196 (1933); *Williams v. Zimmerman*, 172 Md. 563, 192 A. 533 (1937).

7. See, e.g., *Blue v. Durham Public School District*, 95 F. Supp. 441 (M.D. N.C., 1951); *Davis v. County School Board*, 103 F. Supp. 337 (E.D. Va., 1952).

8. *Sweatt v. Painter*, 339 U.S. 629 (1950).

9. Ibid.

10. *McLaurin v. Oklahoma State Regents*, 339 U.S. 637 (1950).

11. 347 U.S. 483 (1954).

12. 42 U.S. C. §2701 et seq.

13. 20 U.S. C. §241 et seq.

14. See, e.g., Horowitz, *Unseparate but Unequal—The Emerging Fourteenth Amendment Issue in Public School Education*, 13 U.C.L.A. L. Rev.

1147 (1966); Kirp, *The Poor, the Schools, and Equal Protection*, 38 Harv. Education Rev. 635 (1968).

15. These cases are cited and discussed at some length in Silard and White, *Intrastate Inequalities in Public Education: The Case for Judicial Relief Under the Equal Protection Clause*, 1970 Wisc. L. Rev. 9.

16. *McInnis v. Shapiro*, 293 F. Supp. 327 (N.D. Ill., 1968).

17. *McInnis v. Olgilvie*, 394 U.S. 322 (1969).

18. See A. Wise, *Rich Schools, Poor Schools* (Chicago: University of Chicago Press, 1967); Coons, Clune, and Sugarman, *Educational Opportunity: A Workable Constitutional Test for State Finance Structures*, 57 Cal. L. Rev. 305, 311 (1969).

19. See J. Coons et al., *Private Wealth and Public Education*, (Cambridge: Harvard University Press, 1970).

20. Ibid., p. 293.

21. Coons, Clune, and Sugarman, 57 Cal. L. Rev. at 311 (1969).

22. 96 Cal. Rptr. 601, 487 P.2d at 1241 (1971).

23. 96 Cal. Rptr. at 604, 487 P.2d at 1244.

24. "Final Report to the California Senate Select Committee on School District Finance," Vol. I (1972), p. 9.

25. *Hollins v. Shofstall*, No. C-253652, Super. Ct., Maricopa Co., Ariz. (decided June 1, 1972); *Caldwell v. Kansas*, No. 50616 (D.C. Johnson County, decided August 30, 1972); *Milliken v. Green*, 203 N.W. 2d 457 (Mich. Sup. Ct., 1972); *Van Dusartz v. Hatfield*, 334 F. Supp. 870 (D. Minn. 1971); *Robinson v. Cahill*, 118 N.J. Super. 223, 287 A.2d 187 (1972); *Spano v. Board of Education of Lakeland School District No. 1*, 328 N.Y.S. 2d 229 (Sup. Ct. Westchester County 1972); *Rodriguez v. San Antonio Independent School District*, 337 F. Supp. 280 (W.D. Tex. 1971); *Sweetwater County Planning Comm. v. Hinkle*, 491 P.2d 1234 (Wyo. 1971) and 493 P.2d 1050 (Wyo. 1972).

26. See, e.g., *Griffin v. Illinois*, 351 U.S. 12 (1956); *Douglas v. California*, 372 U.S. 353 (1963).

27. See, e.g., *Harper v. Virginia Bd. of Elections*, 383 U.S. 663 (1966) (access to the electoral process); *Shapiro v. Thompson* 394 U.S. 618 (1969) (right to travel).

28. 36 L. Ed. 2d at 33.

29. Ibid., at 35.

30. Ibid., at 36.

31. Ibid.

32. Ibid., at 36-37.

33. Ibid., at 37.

34. Ibid.

35. Ibid., at 37, n. 56.

36. Ibid., at 38, n. 60.

37. Ibid., at 38.

38. Ibid., at 38, n. 61.

39. Ibid., at 38.

40. Ibid., at 38-39, n. 62.

41. Ibid., at 59, n. 6.

42. Ibid., at 45.

43. See, e.g., *Mills v. Board of Education*, 348 F. Supp. 866 (D.C. D. C. 1972); *Harrison v. Michigan*, Civ. No. 38357 (D.C. E. D. Mich., October 30, 1972).

44. 36 L. Ed. 2d at 48.

45. 313 F. Supp. 944 (M.D. Fla. 1970); vacated, 401 U.S. 479 (1971).

46. 36 L. Ed. 2d at 53, n. 107.

47. Civ. No. 4-1405 (D.C. N. D. Tex.).

48. The Court says the amount Alamo Heights (a wealthy district) and Edgewood (a poor district) must pay into the state education fund reflects a "rough approximation of the relative taxpaying potential of each" (36 L. Ed. 2d at 32). The Court also notes that it has been suggested that the formula be altered "to promote a more accurate reflection of local taxpaying ability, especially of urban school districts" (Ibid. at 32, n. 37). Justice Marshall, in dissent, quotes a published criticism of the Economic Index that in "evaluating local ability [it] offers a little better measure than sheer chance but not much." (36 L. Ed. 2d at 69).

49. 36 L. Ed. 2d at 47, 49, 57.

50. In his dissenting opinion, Justice Marshall put it this way: "Of course, nothing in the Court's decision today should inhibit further review of state educational funding schemes under state constitutional provisions." 36 L. Ed. 2d at 101, n. 100.

51. More modern state constitutions have even more explicit language pertaining to the state's obligation to provide public education. The 1970 Illinois Constitution requires the state to "provide for an efficient system of high-quality public educational institutions and services," and mandates that the state shall have "primary responsibility for financing the system of public education." Illinois Constitution, Art. X, Sec. 1. The Montana Constitution, adopted in 1972, states that "[e]quality of educational opportunity is guaranteed to each person of the state" (Art X, Sec. 1).

52. *Milliken v. Green*, 203 N.W. 2d 457 (1972).

53. 96 Cal. Rptr. 601, 487 P.2d 1241 (1971).

54. *Robinson v. Cahill*, 62 N.J. 473, 303 A.2d 273 (1973); relief considered, 63 N.J. 196, 306 A.2d 65 (1973).

55. 203 N.W. 2d 457 (Dec. 29, 1972).

56. 203 N.W. 2d at 460.

57. 62 N.J. 473, 303 A.2d 273 (1973).

58. 303 A.2d at 295.

59. *Robinson v. Cahill*, 118 N.J. Super. 223, 287 A.2d 187 (1972).

60. 303 A.2d at 294.

61. Ibid. at 295-296.

62. Ibid. at 295.

63. 287 A.2d at 215-216.

64. Ibid.

65. 303 A.2d at 287-294.

66. Ibid., at 282-286.

67. Ibid. at 283.

68. Ibid. at 297.

69. This fear may have influenced the Supreme Court's decision in *Rodriguez*. See 36 L. Ed. 2d at 48, n. 85.

Chapter Four

The Effect of Reform in School Finance on the Level and Distribution of Tax Burdens

Robert W. Hartman and Robert D. Reischauer

The Brookings Institution

Legal and political challenges to the existing methods of financing elementary and secondary education promise to change not only patterns of school expenditures but also educational tax burdens. In all likelihood, school finance reform will bring both increased aggregate educational tax collections and shifts in the distribution of tax burdens among school districts and individuals.

This chapter explores some of the many tax-burden changes that could occur. To place them in perspective, the first section briefly describes the current situation. The second section reviews the methods of finance that seem to comply with the edicts of the lower courts and the implications of these rulings for the aggregate level of school taxes. An analysis follows of the various mixes of taxes that could be used to support such new schemes and the burden these taxes would place on various households and jurisdictions. The final section of this chapter touches on some little-discussed consequences that may result from shifts in educational tax burdens.

WHO PAYS FOR PUBLIC SCHOOLS TODAY?

The aggregate burden of supporting public schools varies tremendously among the states and school districts of the nation. School revenues amounted to over 7 percent of the personal income of New Mexico, while in Rhode Island the figure

This study was supported in part by a grant from the Edna McConnell Clark Foundation. The views expressed are solely those of the authors, and should not be attributed to the trustees, officers, or other staff members of the Brookings Institution or to the Edna McConnell Clark Foundation.

was just over 4 percent (see Table 4-1). In absolute terms, per capita school revenues were $278 in New York but less than half as much in Alabama. Variation in the amounts of revenues raised per pupil is not the only factor reflected in these wide differences; the considerable variation in the fraction of the total population enrolled in public schools also plays an important part in determining aggregate school tax burdens. This is especially true at the school district level, where the fraction of the population enrolled in public schools may be as low as 15 percent in some central cities and as high as 35 percent in nearby suburban jurisdictions.[1]

It is no easy task to determine who ultimately bears the burden for supporting the public schools of any state or locality. The answer depends not only upon the total level of resources devoted to education, but also upon the level of government providing these resources, the mix of taxes used to generate these monies, and the numerous circumstances affecting the incidence of these taxes. Nationally the federal government provides 7 percent of the revenues for education, states contribute 41 percent, and the balance is derived from local sources. But as Table 4-2 indicates, these national averages do not convey an accurate picture of the situation existing in many states. Nor do statewide averages accurately describe the relative importance of the various sources of revenues for many school districts within a state. As Table 4-3 reveals, individual districts may rely on very different levels of government for their revenues, even when the amounts expended per pupil do not vary greatly.

Federal grants account for 22.6 percent of the total school revenues in Wyoming, but just over 2.1 percent in Connecticut. On a per pupil basis, the difference is from $214 in Wyoming to $27 in Connecticut. The variation is due almost entirely to the fraction of the student body that is eligible for the various federal educational aid programs (Title I, Impacted Areas Aid, Vocational Aid, and so on); thus a state or school district can do little to increase its allotment of federal aid.

Federal school aid is drawn from general revenues, which in turn come overwhelmingly from individual and corporate income tax collections. Although the incidence of the corporate income tax is a matter of debate among economists, and loopholes abound in the personal income tax, it is generally conceded that overall the federal tax system is relatively progressive—that is, the tax burden as measured by the fraction of one's income paid in taxes is greater for the rich than for the poor.[2] As opposed to state or local taxes, federal levies are uniform throughout the nation. No matter where an individual lives, his federal tax burden will be the same. Therefore it is fairly safe to conclude that the 7 percent of school revenues derived from federal sources comes disproportionately from wealthier taxpayers, or from the states and school districts in which such persons are located.

State revenues account for as much as 90 percent of total educational revenues in Hawaii and as little as 10 percent in New Hampshire. Similar variations occur among the school districts of any one state. In general, state funds are a relatively more important source of revenue for low- than for high-spending school districts, and for districts with little property wealth. Overall, little correlation can be seen between the burden of state education taxes (state school taxes as a percent of personal income) and the income of the state (see Table 4-4).

A handful of states earmark specific revenue sources for state educational aid. For example, the revenue of the statewide property tax on utilities and railroads; a point or two from the sales tax; or the profits from state run lotteries, gambling enterprises, or liquor stores may be statutorily set aside for school aid. But most state educational support derives from state general revenues. Each state raises such revenues in different ways. Oregon, New York, and Maryland rely heavily on state personal or corporate income taxes, but a number of other states do not even have such levies. General sales taxes are the mainstay of other state revenue systems, and selected sales taxes are important in still others (see Table 4-5).

If it is difficult to draw generalizations about the source of state school revenues, it is even harder to make inferences about the incidence of these taxes. Although state personal income taxes are in general mildly progressive and fall overwhelmingly on the particular state's residents, some state income taxes are closer to proportional than progressive, and others (New Jersey and New Hampshire) are taxes imposed solely on nonresident workers in the state. Depending upon the theory of incidence one accepts, a state's corporate income taxes are paid either by stockholders, by all recipients of property income, or by consumers; for most corporations the vast majority of such persons do not reside in the state imposing the tax. State general and specific sales taxes are usually regressive or, at best, proportional, and are borne mainly by residents. In Nevada, the District of Columbia, and Hawaii, however, a major portion of such taxes may be paid by out-of-state tourists or commuters. Similarly, Massachusetts residents may pay a significant fraction of the New Hampshire tobacco and liquor taxes.

In summary, the state share of school finance revenues is raised primarily from the residents of the state through taxing systems that are probably close to proportional in their incidence. Significant variations in incidence patterns do occur from state to state, as the estimates shown in Table 4-6 make clear.

Although the burden of federal taxes is the same throughout the nation, and state educational taxes are uniform throughout the school districts of any state, the local educational tax burden facing a family depends very much upon the particular school district in which it lives. This variation stems from differences in the amounts of local revenues raised for education, in the size of the local tax base, and in the particular taxing instruments that are used.

Property taxes are the mainstay of most school districts' revenue

Table 4-1. School Revenue Burdens, 1969, and Percent of Population Enrolled in Public Schools, 1969-70

	Revenue as a Percent of Personal Income	Local/State Revenues as a Percent of Personal Income	Per Capita Revenue	Percent of Population Enrolled in School
Alabama	4.7%	4.0%	$ 128.6	23.3%
Alaska	6.9	5.0	311.7	26.0
Arizona	6.3	5.8	227.2	24.7
Arkansas	5.0	4.1	144.6	24.1
California	4.6	4.3	194.2	23.6
Colorado	5.7	5.3	215.1	24.9
Connecticut	5.4	5.3	264.6	21.3
Delaware	6.1	5.7	273.0	24.2
Florida	5.1	4.6	181.0	21.0
Georgia	4.5	4.1	155.0	24.4
Hawaii	6.2	5.6	272.5	23.9
Idaho	5.1	4.7	161.8	25.6
Illinois	5.0	4.7	242.5	21.2
Indiana	4.6	4.3	182.0	23.7
Iowa	5.6	5.4	207.7	23.5
Kansas	5.6	5.3	219.8	22.8
Kentucky	5.0	4.3	155.8	22.1
Lousiana	5.7	5.0	176.3	23.1
Maine	5.8	5.4	185.7	24.3
Maryland	5.6	5.2	244.8	23.2
Massachusetts	4.4	4.1	194.2	20.7
Michigan	4.9	4.7	211.3	24.6
Minnesota	6.1	5.8	232.5	24.4
Mississippi	6.0	4.7	144.1	24.1

Missouri	4.7	4.3	184.3	22.2
Montana	6.5	6.0	221.3	25.2
Nebraska	4.5	4.3	164.7	22.2
Nevada	5.2	4.7	242.7	26.1
New Hampshire	4.6	4.3	174.2	21.5
New Jersey	5.2	4.9	239.9	20.7
New Mexico	7.2	5.9	217.5	28.1
New York	5.6	5.3	278.5	19.1
North Carolina	5.2	4.4	166.4	23.4
North Dakota	6.0	5.4	185.9	23.8
Ohio	4.5	4.3	184.5	22.8
Oklahoma	4.3	3.8	151.3	25.0
Oregon	6.3	5.9	241.0	23.0
Pennsylvania	5.2	4.9	206.2	20.0
Rhode Island	4.3	4.0	183.6	19.8
South Carolina	6.0	5.1	173.8	24.9
South Dakota	5.6	4.9	173.3	25.0
Tennessee	4.8	4.2	146.3	22.9
Texas	4.6	4.2	167.7	24.1
Utah	6.8	6.3	213.2	28.7
Vermont	6.7	6.5	248.2	25.3
Virginia	5.4	4.8	191.9	23.2
Washington	5.7	5.3	233.8	24.0
West Virginia	5.9	5.2	172.2	22.9
Wisconsin	5.8	5.7	228.4	22.5
Wyoming	7.0	5.6	240.8	26.2

Sources: National Education Association, Research Division, *Rankings of the States, 1971*, Tables 15, 81, 82, and 83; population data from U.S. Bureau of the Census, *Statistical Abstract of the United States, 1971*, p. 14.

Table 4-2. Sources of Revenues

	Percent of Revenue *Receipts by Source*		
Region and State	*Federal*	*State*	*Local and Other*
50 States and D.C.	7.1%	40.9%	52.0%
New England	4.6	23.5	71.8
Connecticut	3.1	23.1	73.8
Maine	7.3	32.1	60.6
Massachusetts[a]	4.7	21.7	73.6
New Hampshire	5.0	5.3	89.7
Rhode Island	7.8	37.2	55.0
Vermont	6.1	33.0	60.9
Mideast	5.4	43.0	51.5
Delaware	7.1	69.4	23.5
Maryland	7.1	43.3	49.7
New Jersey	4.3	25.1	70.5
New York[a]	5.4	47.4	47.2
Pennsylvania	4.9	48.7	46.4
Dist. of Columbia	14.1	...	85.9
Southeast	13.3	52.6	34.1
Alabama	18.3	62.0	19.7
Arkansas	17.3	46.1	36.6
Florida	9.7	54.3	36.0
Georgia	10.8	52.7	36.5
Kentucky	16.5	53.5	30.0
Louisiana	12.5	57.0	30.5
Mississippi	26.0	49.8	24.2
North Carolina	11.7	68.7	19.6
South Carolina	16.5	57.4	26.1
Tennessee	13.3	45.4	41.3
Virginia	10.6	34.2	55.1
West Virginia	12.6	49.9	37.7
Great Lakes	4.8	36.1	59.1
Illinois	4.9	36.3	58.8
Indiana	5.4	32.8	61.8
Michigan	3.8	44.5	51.7
Ohio	6.2	30.5	63.3
Wisconsin	3.1	31.6	65.3

Table 4-2. (cont.)

Region and State	Percent of Revenue Receipts by Source		
	Federal	State	Local and Other
Plains	5.3	35.6	59.0
Iowa	2.5	24.0	73.5
Kansas	6.8	29.9	63.3
Minnesota	4.5	54.5	41.1
Missouri	6.8	35.9	57.2
Nebraska	6.4	17.3	76.3
North Dakota	10.0	28.8	61.3
South Dakota	10.0	15.5	74.5
Southwest	9.5	47.6	42.9
Arizona	8.4	43.0	48.6
New Mexico	18.5	62.3	19.2
Oklahoma	11.6	40.7	47.7
Texas	8.5	48.1	43.4
Rocky Mountains	8.8	34.3	56.9
Colorado	8.5	28.3	63.2
Idaho	12.2	39.8	48.0
Montana	8.5	23.9	67.7
Utah	7.9	53.2	38.9
Wyoming	7.6	30.8	61.6
Far West	6.2	36.0	57.9
California[a]	6.1	34.8	59.1
Nevada	5.9	42.0	52.1
Oregon	4.5	19.9	75.6
Washington	7.7	51.0	41.3
Alaska	17.4	70.8	11.8
Hawaii[a]	8.4	88.7	2.9

[a]Estimates by NEA Research Division.

Source: National Education Association, Research Division, *Estimates of School Statistics, 1971-72*, Table 10, p. 35.

systems. However, almost half of the states permit some or all of their school districts to levy nonproperty taxes of one sort or another. For example, several of New York's counties impose countywide educational sales taxes, the receipts from which are divided among the school districts of the county. Similarly, in Pennsylvania and Maryland, local income tax receipts are used to support

Table 4-3.   Local, State, and Federal Revenue Receipts per Pupil, Selected California School Districts, 1968-69 School Year

School District	Local		State		Federal	
	Percent	*Amount*	*Percent*	*Amount*	*Percent*	*Amount*
California						
Beverly Hills	86.7%	$1,112	11.4%	$145	2.0%	$25
Lake Tahoe	79.2	766	18.0	174	2.8	26
Dixon	74.0	541	21.6	157	4.4	32
Los Angeles	62.3	451	30.8	223	6.9	49
San Diego	46.5	370	42.3	337	11.2	89
Ceres	27.4	204	53.6	400	19.1	142
State average	59.9	480	34.3	275	5.9	47

Source: *Review of Existing State School Finance Programs*, Vol. 2: *Documentation of Disparities in the Financing of Public Elementary and Secondary School Systems—By State*, A Commission Staff Report submitted to the President's Commission on School Finance (1972), p. 37; and USOE, *Digest of Educational Statistics 1969.*

Table 4-4.   State and Local Education Tax Burdens, 1970

State	Per Capita Personal Income	State School Taxes as Percentage of Personal Income	Local School Taxes as Percentage of Personal Income
Alabama	$ 2,853	2.8%	1.0%
Alaska	4,592	6.7	1.0
Arizona	3,591	2.7	3.0
Arkansas	2,791	2.1	1.8
California	4.426	1.7	2.8
Colorado	3.816	1.8	3.8
Connecticut	4,856	1.4	4.4
Delaware	4,324	4.6	1.4
Dist. of Columbia	5,466	–	3.8
Florida	3,642	2.8	1.7
Georgia	3,332	2.4	1.5
Hawaii	4,527	5.3	0.2
Idaho	3,240	2.3	2.9
Illinois	4,502	1.9	3.4
Indiana	3,781	1.9	3.8
Iowa	3,688	1.7	4.3
Kansas	3,823	1.6	3.4

Table 4-4. (cont.)

State	Per Capita Personal Income	State School Taxes as Percentage of Personal Income	Local School Taxes as Percentage of Personal Income
Kentucky	3,073	2.7	1.5
Louisiana	3,049	3.6	1.9
Maine	3,257	1.9	3.6
Maryland	4,255	2.3	3.9
Massachusetts	4,360	1.2	3.4
Michigan	4,059	2.5	3.3
Minnesota	3,824	3.0	3.2
Mississippi	2,575	3.0	1.5
Missouri	3,704	1.5	2.8
Montana	3,379	1.5	4.3
Nebraska	3,751	0.8	3.1
Nevada	4,562	1.9	2.8
New Hampshire	3,590	0.5	4.1
New Jersey	4,598	1.4	3.7
New Mexico	3,131	4.3	1.5
New York	4,769	2.8	2.8
North Carolina	3,207	3.5	1.0
North Dakota	2,995	1.8	3.9
Ohio	3,972	1.3	3.1
Oklahoma	3,312	2.0	2.4
Oregon	3,705	1.2	4.7
Pennsylvania	3,927	2.4	2.8
Rhode Island	3,902	1.6	2.7
South Carolina	2,936	3.4	1.6
South Dakota	3,165	0.9	4.5
Tennessee	3,085	2.2	2.1
Texas	3,531	2.7	2.4
Utah	3,213	3.5	2.6
Vermont	3,465	2.6	4.8
Virginia	3,607	1.9	3.1
Washington	3,993	3.0	2.4
West Virginia	3,021	2.6	2.0
Wisconsin	3,693	1.8	3.9
Wyoming	3,556	2.2	3.8
U.S. Total	3,933	2.2	2.9

Sources: Income from *Survey of Current Business*, August 1971. Revenues from NEA, *Estimates of School Statistics, 1971-72* (1971-R13), Table 9, p. 34.

Table 4-5. Sources of State Tax Revenues (In Percent of Total Revenues)

State	General Sales or Gross Receipts	Individual Income	Corporation Net Income	Selected Sales and Gross Receipts, Total	Total License Taxes	Property	Other Taxes[a]
United States	29.6%	19.1%	7.8%	27.3%	9.6%	2.3%	4.4%
Alabama	32.3	12.9	4.7	38.0	7.8	3.5	.8
Alaska	–	37.8	6.2	23.7	17.1	–	15.2
Arizona	36.6	13.7	4.4	23.9	6.2	14.3	.9
Arkansas	30.9	12.1	7.5	35.3	11.5	.3	2.4
California	32.0	20.9	10.7	22.8	6.5	4.2	2.9
Colorado	29.3	27.5	7.1	23.7	9.3	.2	2.7
Connecticut	34.9	.7	16.1	34.8	7.8	–	5.7
Delaware	–	35.0	6.9	21.9	32.2	.2	4.0
Florida	46.3	–	–	34.5	12.4	2.4	4.3
Georgia	35.7	19.6	9.0	29.2	5.4	.3	.7
Hawaii	47.8	30.8	4.3	15.0	1.2	–	.8
Idaho	26.7	23.5	7.1	25.0	16.4	.5	.7
Illinois	35.1	20.1	4.9	27.8	9.7	.1	2.3
Indiana	38.0	21.6	.9	27.6	8.2	2.3	1.5
Iowa	35.6	17.9	3.9	24.8	14.3	.7	2.8

Kansas	33.7	18.2	4.5	28.7	10.7	2.4	1.8
Kentucky	38.1	17.3	5.6	27.0	6.4	3.8	1.9
Louisiana	49.8	5.7	4.1	27.9	8.4	3.2	30.7
Maine	40.1	9.1	4.0	31.6	11.0	1.8	2.4
Maryland	21.9	38.2	5.6	23.4	6.4	3.2	1.4
Massachusetts	12.1	37.2	15.7	25.6	6.1	..	3.4
Michigan	35.3	17.7	8.3	20.8	13.1	3.5	1.2
Minnesota	19.2	33.9	7.8	26.2	8.3	.6	4.2
Mississippi	46.9	9.1	4.1	29.2	6.5	.8	3.3
Missouri	42.0	15.8	2.6	24.2	13.6	.3	1.5
Montana	—	30.2	7.5	37.4	11.6	6.3	6.9
Nebraska	28.7	17.0	3.3	36.8	12.7	.8	.8
Nevada	36.7	—	—	49.5	10.3	2.9	.6
New Hampshire	—	3.7	—	66.2	20.3	3.7	6.2
New Jersey	26.7	1.3	12.7	34.1	16.5	3.7	4.9
New Mexico	31.3	13.1	3.0	25.7	8.1	5.3	13.5
New York	16.5	41.0	11.3	19.2	5.3	.2	6.5
North Carolina	22.2	22.8	9.4	32.2	9.8	2.0	1.6
North Dakota	35.3	12.7	2.5	28.0	17.1	1.2	3.3

Table 4-5. (cont.)

State	General Sales or Gross Receipts	Individual Income	Corporation Net Income	Selected Sales and Gross Receipts, Total	Total License Taxes	Property	Other Taxes[a]
Ohio	38.7	–	–	38.8	18.0	3.4	1.1
Oklahoma	18.7	10.1	5.5	36.5	16.1	–	13.2
Oregon	–	49.5	9.3	20.9	16.0	.7	3.7
Pennsylvania	34.1	–	19.1	29.4	11.6	1.2	4.7
Rhode Island	34.2	8.1	10.1	34.6	9.0	–	3.9
South Carolina	35.4	17.5	7.8	32.0	5.8	.3	1.1
South Dakota	42.3	–	.7	42.0	13.3	–	1.8
Tennessee	35.1	1.8	8.7	33.9	16.9	–	3.6
Texas	28.0	–	–	33.5	15.3	3.2	15.0
Utah	36.2	24.4	4.7	20.5	6.2	5.1	2.9
Vermont	12.6	32.3	4.3	36.1	11.3	.1	3.1
Virginia	22.0	29.6	7.1	29.5	8.3	1.3	2.3
Washington	53.1	–	–	26.1	7.2	11.0	2.6
West Virginia	47.2	10.4	1.0	30.8	8.9	.1	1.7
Wisconsin	20.5	36.8	7.9	20.1	6.9	5.4	2.5
Wyoming	36.7	–	–	26.2	18.7	12.8	5.8

[a]Death and gift, document, stock transfer, and other taxes.

Source: Advisory Commission on Intergovernmental Relations, *State-Local Finances: Significant Features and Suggested Legislation* (The Commission, 1972), Table 9, pp. 23-24.

Table 4-6. State Taxes for Public Elementary and Secondary Education as Percent of Money Income, Urban and Rural Areas (1968-1969)[a]

States	$2000-2999	$3000-3999	$4000-4999	$5000-5999	$6000-7499	$7500-9999	$10,000-14,999	$15,000 and over
Hawaii	4.3%	4.4%	4.0%	3.9%	4.0%	4.0%	4.1%	4.2%
Delaware	1.3	1.5	1.5	1.5	1.7	1.9	2.2	3.2
North Carolina	1.7	1.7	1.8	1.9	2.1	2.2	2.4	3.5
Washington	3.1	3.1	2.7	2.6	2.5	2.4	1.9	1.6
California	1.6	1.7	1.6	1.6	1.7	1.5	1.8	2.5
Michigan[b]	2.3	2.3	2.1	2.2	2.1	2.2	2.3	1.7
New York	1.4	1.8	1.8	1.8	1.8	1.9	2.0	3.1
Colorado	0.9	1.1	1.0	1.0	1.1	1.2	1.2	1.3
New Hampshire	0.6	0.5	0.5	0.5	0.5	0.4	0.4	0.4

[a]Proportion of state general revenue taxes (and in some states, earmarked taxes) allocated for public elementary and secondary education. Income excludes imputed rental payments on owner-occupied residences and also excludes federal income tax offsets.

[b]There may be some discrepancies in the Michigan analysis, since state income tax data were available in a form that could not be readily adapted to the methodology used in computing tax burdens for the other states in this study.

Source: Betsy Levin et al., *Public School Finance: Present Disparities and Fiscal Alternatives,* (Washington, D.C.: The Urban Institute, July 1972).

schools. But even in these states, local revenue for schools derives mainly from property-tax receipts.

In most states, school property-tax rates vary tremendously from district to district. Generally these tax rates are lowest in rural areas (Table 4-7) because rural school districts raise very little in the way of local revenue. Large cities also commonly have low school property-tax rates. In New York State, for example, the six largest cities all have lower school tax rates than the statewide average.[3] This situation arises not because cities raise small sums of local revenues per pupil or because per capita tax bases of cities are large, but rather because these jurisdictions have relatively small fractions of their population enrolled in public schools. Although suburbs generally have larger per capita tax bases than cities, they have the highest tax rates. This reflects both the large amount of locally raised school revenue per pupil and the high fraction of the suburban population enrolled in public schools.

Showing which districts have the highest property-tax rates provides little insight into who actually bears the burden of such taxes. This depends upon the incidence of the tax in the particular jurisdiction involved; there is little agreement among economists on this issue. Some regard the property tax on improvements as a form of excise tax borne by the final consumers of the

Table 4-7. Effective Local School Property Tax Rates by Type of District Relative to Statewide Average[a]

State	Large Cities	Slow-Growing Suburbs	Fast-Growing Suburbs	Small Cities	Rural
Delaware	135	102	149	112	45
North Carolina	122	–	–	111	84
Washington	109	167	128	104	93
California	96	109	101	102	85
Michigan	98	121	131	108	82
New York	91	123	145	103	110
Colorado	103	118	122	90	78
New Hampshire	81	127	–	103	113

[a]State average = 100.

Source: Betsy Levin et al., *Public School Finance: Present Disparities and Fiscal Alternatives* (Washington: The Urban Institute, July 1972).

services of the property that is taxed.[4] Under this view, the property tax on rented dwelling units is shifted to the occupants in the form of higher rents, the tax on commercial and industrial property is shifted to consumers in the form of higher prices, and the tax on owner-occupied homes is borne by homeowners. The incidence of a tax that is shifted in this manner will depend upon the relative consumption of housing and consumer goods by families in various income classes. Since housing expenditures and outlays for consumer goods tend to absorb a much larger fraction of *current* incomes of the poor than of the rich, such a tax would appear to be highly regressive. However, when longer-term indexes of ability to pay are used, the case for regressiveness becomes much weaker. One of the major reasons that housing expenditures and other major consumer durables take up a large share of the resources of families with low current income is that in the low-income class there is a disproportionate number of families who are very young, or very old, or suffering from temporary spells of unemployment. These households have set their housing and consumption standards on the basis of their long-run ("normal") income, which exceeds their current income. Some recent studies of homeowners have shown that families with higher normal incomes tend to own homes that are more valuable in relation to income than lower-income families.[5] Thus, the property tax, for homeowners, may be progressive when measured against longer-term indexes of ability to pay.

For renters the situation is more complex. Even if rental payments absorb a larger fraction of the long-run incomes of poor than of wealthy renters, property taxes are levied against the value of the property, not rent. Because rental properties that house the poor tend to be older and more costly to operate, to be in neighborhoods offering little prospect for capital appreciation, and to involve higher risk, the ratio of value-to-rent for these structures is probably far lower than that for buildings housing wealthier tenants. If so, the property tax, even if fully shifted to the tenant in the form of higher rental payments, may be far less regressive than a comparison of rent to income ratios would suggest.[6]

Economists have increasingly come to challenge the view that the property tax is completely shifted onto consumers. The argument runs as follows. Initially the owners pay a property tax that is levied on their houses, buildings, and factories. Since this added cost reduces the profitability of real estate and other taxable property as a form of investment, it is likely to divert capital into untaxed or more lightly taxed sectors of the economy. Such a movement of capital will lower the profitability of capital in the untaxed sectors until a point is reached at which owners of all kinds of capital receive an equivalent rate of return after deductions and taxes. At this point, the question arises as to how new investment responds to the lower rate of return on capital.

One possibility is that there will be a reduction in the aggregate flow of new investment. If this happens, the property tax will become a burden on consumers as well as on owners of capital. As new construction and investment in capital goods proceeds at a lower level than would have occurred without the property tax, the aggregate supply of housing will be less than it would have been. Competition by consumers will drive up rents, and part of the burden of the property tax will be shifted to consumers.[7]

The other possibility is that investment may not change appreciably when the rate of return on capital drops. The basis for this view is that the flow of investment is limited by the aggregate amount of saving in the economy. Most studies have shown that aggregate saving is not sensitive to changes in interest rates or the profitability of capital. Thus, the imposition of a property tax would not affect the aggregate supply of homes, apartments, or commercial and industrial buildings; and the tax could not be shifted to tenants and consumers. Instead, according to this theory, the burden of the property tax ultimately falls on all owners of capital whose after-tax profits are reduced by the tax.

If the property tax is a tax on capital, it will be borne by individuals roughly in proportion to the value of their capital assets; the burden will be greatest for those whose holdings of capital are disproportionately large in relation to their incomes. One group with this characteristic is the elderly, but high-income groups also tend to have large asset holdings in relation to their incomes.

In summary, although politicians and the public may have been persuaded that the property tax is a regressive tax on housing expenditures, it is still an issue that is very much up in the air. On the one hand it may be a tax borne by owners of capital, in which case its incidence is at least mildly progressive. On the other hand it may be an excise tax that is shifted to consumers and tenants. In that case, when measured against current income, the incidence of the tax is probably regressive, but when measured against normal income, it is probably close to proportional.

To these conclusions about the inherent incidence of the property tax must be added the other administrative and operational factors that affect the ultimate incidence of the tax. First, many taxing jurisdictions tend to assess properties housing low-income families at a higher fraction of market value than those housing the wealthy. This administrative practice biases the tax in a regressive direction. Second, state and federal income tax provisions that permit families to deduct property taxes from their taxable incomes have a similar effect. Homeowners who itemize their deductions benefit from these provisions in that they are able to shift part of their property-tax bill onto the state and federal governments through a reduction in their income tax liabilities. Since, on the whole, such taxpayers have higher than average incomes, the effect is regressive. Third, the distribution of families with differing incomes among the thousands of local jurisdictions—each with a different property tax rate—may also influence the actual amounts paid by the various income classes. A progressive influence should be exerted by the fact that a disproportionate fraction of the nation's low-income population lives in the South and in rural areas where property tax rates are relatively low. Fourth, a good deal of the local property tax may be borne by those living outside the particular school district imposing the tax. For example, whether the tax on commercial and industrial property is borne by consumers or by capitalists, most of it will fall on those living in different school districts.

In summary, the ultimate burden of the local share of school revenues cannot be derived simply from observing the pattern of variation of revenues among school districts. Just where this burden falls will depend upon the type of tax used (property, income or sales), the incidence of that tax (does the property tax fall on consumers or capitalists?), and the peculiar circumstances of the local tax base (the fraction that is commercial and industrial).

THE DISTRIBUTION OF TAX BURDENS BY
DISTRICT UNDER REFORM PLANS

A careful reading of several studies that address themselves to reforms in school finance in response to the recent court cases discloses two school finance methods that seem in principle to satisfy the courts' mandates. When political reality is combined with principle, these two alternatives shrink to one. This section will first describe this single solution and delineate the policy parameters that must be set under it, and then assess the tax-burden implications for various types of school districts under different versions of these policies. Finally, the impossibility of predicting tax-burden changes for particular existing districts will be discussed.

Two Alternatives

California and New York span the breadth not only of the nation but also of the two most frequently cited models of school finance reform. The Fleischmann Commission recommended "that the State of New York undertake full funding of educational costs." In California, the Consultant Staff to the Senate Select Committee on School District Finance, after an exhaustive review of alternatives, recommended a program for district power equalizing.[8]

In its simplest form, district power equalizing (DPE) would leave each and every school district with the choices depicted as line *OA* in Figure 4-1. Each district may choose its property tax rate, and, once that choice is made, its per student expenditure level is set by line *OA*, which is determined by the state.[9] If local revenue (at the chosen tax rate) is insufficient to fund the expenditure level shown on line *OA*, the state grants the district the necessary difference for each enrolled public school pupil. On the other hand, if local revenues exceed the permissible expenditure level, the district must remit the excess funds to the state. In principle, the system can be set up so that all necessary subsidies are raised from the surplus funds contributed by wealthy communities.

No one is seriously advocating a pure DPE program, for several reasons. First, to meet one interpretation of the legal requirements it may be

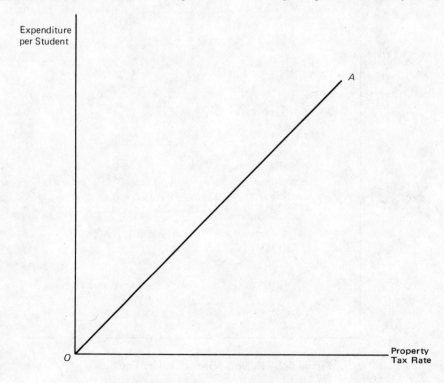

Figure 4-1. Pure District Power Equalizing.

necessary to impose a minimum expenditure level in each district. This would ensure that no district chooses such a low tax rate and per student expenditure level that indigent members of the community would be deprived of constitutional guarantees of minimally acceptable public education. (The wealthier members of the community could presumably send their children to private schools, and that is why they might vote for low taxes and low expenditures.)

Second, if a minimum expenditure level is set under DPE, the state must raise enough money to finance that minimum. To avoid windfall gains to property owners, it is likely that part of the financing package will be a uniform statewide property tax or a minimum local property tax. Thus, in the real world of DPE there will be both a minimum expenditure level and a minimum property tax.

Third, above the minimum expenditure level, a linear DPE schedule, as shown in Figure 4-2, could apply, in principle, to all possible expenditure levels. In the real world, such is not likely to be the case. If the schedule is set to have a very flat slope, wealthy districts (measured in property value per student) will be taxed much more than a dollar for each extra dollar they are allowed to spend on education. Political resistance to such a formulation would be formidable.[10] Yet, if the DPE schedule were set with a very steep slope, the

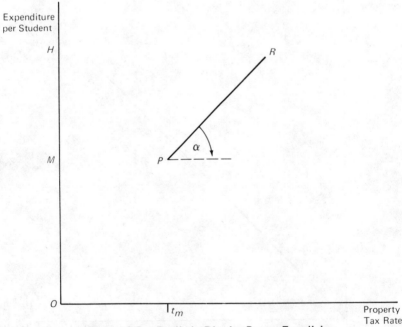

Figure 4-2. Realistic District Power Equalizing.

state would have to provide large subsidies. The stronger the response of school districts to the cheap education implicit in a steep DPE curve, the greater the raid on the state treasury. Therefore, many advocates of DPE propose a steep DPE schedule for a range of expenditures above the minimum expenditure level, and a flat schedule at high expenditure levels to discourage heavy drains on the state treasury. In the limit, the flat schedule could be made horizontal—that is, a ceiling on per pupil expenditure would be imposed.[11]

When all these amendments to a pure DPE plan are introduced, the options open to all school districts would look like those shown as line segment *PR* in Figure 4-2. The key policy variables in a realistic DPE plan are the following.

OM = the state-mandated minimum expenditure per pupil.

t_m = the uniform property tax rate imposed on each district to finance, partly or fully, the minimum expenditure level.[12]

α = the angle whose tangent measures the dollar increase in expenditures per student in each district for each additional unit increase in the property tax rate above the state-set minimum property tax.

$\dfrac{OH}{OM}$ = the level of spending (measured as a percent addition to the minimum) beyond which the state schedule discourages expenditures.

"State assumption," the major competitor to DPE, encompasses financing programs in which the state undertakes to raise "substantially all" the funds for education, allowing districts to make only limited add-ons to the state allocation to each district. In its most restrictive form, state assumption would not allow any district to add its own funds to the state allocation. In this extreme case, all districts would face an opportunity diagram with one point on it (say, *P*, Figure 4-2). The state would set two policy parameters, OM, the expenditure level for each district,[13] and the statewide property tax, t_m.

Few people support the extreme case of full state assumption,[14] because of the inevitable conflict between political reality and budget constraints. If no district is allowed to supplement the state allocation, the size of OM becomes the major educational finance issue. If OM is set below the level of spending previously enjoyed by a significant number of districts, these districts will have to curtail their expenditures, which is politically unacceptable. Conversely, if OM is set so high that almost no district is forced to cut back expenditures, the state's education budget, in most cases, would rise enormously (see Table 4-8, below). A compromise solution, appealing to legislators, would set OM at a fairly high level, but would allow at least those districts whose current spending exceeds OM to supplement OM with local funds.

At this point state assumption with a local add-on would leave the various districts of a state in the position depicted by Figure 4-3. Rich districts

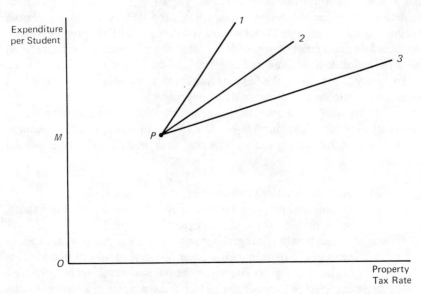

Figure 4-3. State Assumption with Unlimited Add-ons.

could spend according to line *P1*, poor districts according to line *P3*. However, we cannot lose sight of the fact that the court decisions of 1971-72 inveighed against systems of educational finance in which wealth played a major role in determining educational expenditures. State assumption with unlimited add-ons based on local wealth may not conform to legal requirements. The financing scheme could conform more closely to court orders if there were a ceiling on expenditures or equalization of districts' ability to supplement expenditures.

Imposing a ceiling on expenditures without equalizing the ability of districts to spend between *P* and the ceiling is of questionable constitutional validity. The courts have never made clear whether a small amount of wealth-related expenditures would be acceptable—for example, if the ceiling were 10 percent above the minimum. In any event, the courts would certainly allow a larger gap between the minimum and the ceiling if districts' abilities to spend in this range were equalized. Moreover, influential wealthy districts, we believe, would opt for a higher ceiling with equalized add-ons rather than a lower ceiling financed out of their own funds.[15]

One Program of Reform

If these predictions about state legislative behavior are correct, then as pointed out in Chapter 2, both DPE and state assumption boil down to the same "policy," namely the choice of the four parameters listed previously (OM, t_m, α, OH/OM). Plans leaning toward DPE as a guiding philosophy are more likely to choose a lower OM, a higher ratio of OH/OM, and perhaps a lower state property tax rate compared with state assumption plans. But this is not a discrete pair of alternatives; it is a variety of policies that a state can turn to. Therefore it is sufficient to analyze the effect of various choices made in each of the four policy parameters without labeling the entire plan as state assumption or district power equalizing.

Tax Burden Effects of State-Established
Minimum Expenditure Levels

An essential part of state reform of elementary and secondary education funding is the establishment of minimum per student expenditure levels throughout the state. All states have established minimum expenditure levels for their school districts, so that "reform" means raising these minimum levels above their present amounts. Establishing the statewide minimum expenditure level is sure to be a major political battleground, for the minimum level will be the only "assured" number in the entire reform package. For the same reason, a great deal of attention will be paid to the tax-burden implications of the state-level revenues required to finance the minimum expenditure requirements. These revenue sources will be discussed in the next section. We first turn to the various ways that a minimum could be established and how it could be adjusted over time.

The function of a state-imposed minimum expenditure level is to ensure that no student falls below some socially agreed-upon level of resources devoted to his education. In a world where policymakers knew the level of educational outputs that constituted a socially acceptable minimum and what resources were required to produce that minimum, the job of setting a minimum level would be easy. One would find the resource use level that satisfied the output requirements (reading scores, level of social adjustment, citizenship understanding), find the associated inputs (teacher hours, books, and equipment), "cost out" the inputs, and establish the results of the exercise as the minimum expenditure level. Needless to say, current knowledge does not permit this kind of calculation, so the states will have to settle for some less objective way to determine minimum expenditures. The most practical way is to look at existing expenditure levels in the various school districts of the state.

One technique is to arrange school districts in order of increasing expenditures and focus on a specific district's expenditure level as a target for minimum expenditure. For example, a state could establish the expenditure level of the 70th percentile district in some base year as the minimum for the first year of a reform program. Naturally, the 70th percentile district by no means implies that 70 percent of the students receive fewer dollars of education. Indeed, in most states for which data are available, the lowest spending districts tend to have small enrollments. Thus, to guarantee that a substantial number of students would receive increased expenditures on their behalf under state minimum programs, a relatively high district percentile would have to be used as a target.

A more direct method of taking into account variation in district size is to peg the state minimum to a pupil percentile. Under this framework, enrollments are arranged in ascending order of their district's spending level, and the target is set as a given student percentile. For example, a state may undertake to fix its minimum at the 70th percentile student.

Although setting the minimum with reference to a student percentile target makes much more sense to economists—it is, after all, the students whose welfare is of chief interest here—the district target has a role to play in the politics of school reform. Many of the data presented to the courts on inequality were based on district-to-district differences, without any weighting for the size of districts. In the *Rodriguez* case, for example, the evidence presented to show the inverse correlation of wealth and district spending did not at all indicate the relative size of the districts at the extremes of the range of wealth or spending; yet the lower courts found this evidence persuasive.[16] State legislators will likely be very interested in how many districts profit by any reform proposals. Probably no proposed minimum level of spending will be considered seriously unless at least half the districts in the state could be shown to "benefit" (that is, the minimum level exceeds their current spending) from the program.[17]

We have experimented with a number of alternative student percentile targets to ascertain whether 50 percent of the districts in each state would benefit under a program that guarantees minimum expenditure levels. In 1969-70, states would have had to equalize up to the 70th percentile student in order to ensure that at least half of the districts in each state would benefit. In some states, raising expenditure to the 70th percentile student would benefit well over half the districts, but in no state would half the districts fail to be better off.

As a rough approximation, then, we might expect most states to impose a minimum expenditure level at about the 70th percentile student level. Naturally, some states would shoot for a higher, others a lower, level, and we mean only to stress the 70th percentile student as a rough nationally applicable minimum expenditure level.

Table 4-8 shows the extra revenues that would have been required in each state in 1969-70 to raise expenditures in all districts to the state's 70th percentile student level. Nationally, such a leveling up of expenditures would have imposed additional revenue requirements of some $3 billion, or about $60 per public school student. In the absence of a federal program to assist states in meeting this cost, additional revenues would have to be raised at the state level. To put the required revenues in perspective we have expressed the costs in each state in terms of:

Table 4-8. Costs and Tax Burdens of Raising District Expenditures to the 70th Percentile Level

| | Cost of Leveling-up per Pupil Spending to 70th Percentile (millions) | Leveling-up Costs as Percent of: | | | |
| | | State Aid to Education | Personal Income | Revenue Sharing | Untapped Fiscal Capacity |
State	1969-70	1969-70	1969	1972	1969-70
Alabama	$ 20.1	7.4	0.2	22.2	3.0
Alaska	4.5	9.7	0.4	68.2	10.0
Arizona	48.8	29.2	0.8	97.2	16.2
Arkansas	18.1	16.4	0.4	33.2	3.7
California	267.7	18.8	0.3	47.8	8.9
Colorado	50.1	41.7	0.7	91.9	11.1
Connecticut	71.8	38.6	0.5	106.8	12.6
Delaware	5.8	5.6	0.3	36.1	4.4
Florida	92.4	14.7	0.4	63.0	4.4
Georgia	31.1	8.2	0.2	28.6	3.3
Hawaii[a]	–	–	–	–	–
Idaho	16.1	39.1	0.8	75.6	12.2
Illinois	342.5	41.4	0.7	125.0	17.3
Indiana	84.7	24.6	0.4	74.4	9.0
Iowa	36.3	23.5	0.4	48.1	7.6
Kansas	20.2	14.3	0.2	38.5	3.4
Kentucky	36.0	14.0	0.4	41.4	5.5
Louisiana	22.2	6.6	0.2	18.1	2.7
Maine	12.4	22.0	0.4	39.9	12.9
Maryland	33.4	11.1	0.2	31.2	6.8
Massachusetts	81.8	40.9	0.4	44.2	20.4
Michigan	150.2	19.5	0.4	66.9	9.4
Minnesota	67.5	17.8	0.5	63.4	17.0
Mississippi	25.3	7.6	0.5	28.6	8.3
Missouri	73.1	28.8	0.5	74.4	6.3
Montana	22.8	63.3	1.0	111.3	14.9
Nebraska	14.7	35.9	0.7	37.7	4.1
Nevada	1.4	3.6	0.1	12.2	0.6
New Hampshire	9.3	9.5	0.4	56.1	4.3
New Jersey	126.9	12.0	0.4	76.2	10.1
New Mexico	5.8	4.5	0.2	17.6	2.8
New York	331.2	15.6	0.4	56.2	0
North Carolina	43.2	8.4	0.3	31.1	4.6
North Dakota	9.6	33.7	0.5	43.3	11.8

Table 4-8. (cont.)

State	Cost of Leveling-up per Pupil Spending to 70th Percentile (millions) 1969-70	Leveling-up Costs as Percent of:			
		State Aid to Education 1969-70	Personal Income 1969	Revenue Sharing 1972	Untapped Fiscal Capacity 1969-70
Ohio	211.3	41.1	0.5	98.8	7.9
Oklahoma	27.9	18.8	0.4	47.4	3.3
Oregon	22.7	23.9	0.3	42.8	5.0
Pennsylvania	210.2	20.2	0.5	75.6	13.5
Rhode Island	15.4	28.9	0.4	63.7	18.4
South Carolina	16.9	6.8	0.2	23.4	4.7
South Dakota	7.0	48.3	0.3	29.0	8.6
Tennessee	61.8	24.1	0.6	62.6	7.5
Texas	113.2	14.4	0.3	45.7	3.4
Utah	6.8	6.0	0.2	22.2	4.5
Vermont	14.0	39.2	1.0	95.2	72.9
Virginia	78.9	26.1	0.5	74.2	8.5
Washington	65.9	15.6	0.5	84.5	11.0
West Virginia	13.9	10.3	0.2	26.8	4.8
Wisconsin	43.6	15.4	0.3	32.7	42.5
Wyoming	9.4	50.8	0.9	94.3	6.9
U.S. Total	3,095.9	19.8	0.4	–	8.9

aHawaii is a state-run system that financially is a single district.

Sources: Advisory Committee on Intergovernmental Relations, costs of leveling up: Table 4; personal income: Table 5. State aid: NEA, *Estimates of School Statistics*, 1970-71, 1970, R-15, Table 9; revenue sharing: *Department of Treasury News*, Dec. 8, 1972; untapped tax capacity: ACIR, Table 9: defined as the revenues a state would raise if it exerted a tax effort equal to that of the highest effort state, i.e., New York.

1. State aid to elementary and secondary education in 1969-70. This measure gives some idea of how great an expansion of existing commitments to education will be needed to finance a minimum level program.
2. Personal income (1969). This measure indicates the burden on state taxpayers in relation to their aggregate ability to pay.
3. Revenue sharing (1972). This measure shows the fraction of the total revenue sharing grant given to the state and its localities that would be required to finance a minimum expenditure program in each state.
4. ACIR's index of each state's untapped fiscal capacity. This measure shows what fraction of a state's untapped tax potential (defined in terms of the tax effort made by New York State) would be used up in financing leveling up to the 70th percentile student.

As is clear from the table, there would be a wide variation in the additional tax burdens necessary to level expenditures up to each state's 70th percentile student level. Although it would take only 0.1 percent of the personal income in Nevada, ten times that fraction would be needed in Montana. In areas where existing state aid was limited, leveling up would imply a massive increase in the state's educational role. In Wyoming and Montana an increase of over 50 percent is implied. However, when looked at in terms of either the amount of revenue sharing money the states are receiving under the State and Local Fiscal Assistance Act of 1972 or the size of the untapped fiscal capacity of the states, the added burden of equalization does not appear to be too great.[18] In a few states, it is probably unrealistic to expect attainment of the target level in a single year, without considerable dislocation.

Most probably, when a state legislature establishes new minimum expenditure levels for education, it will want to build into the system a formula for growth in the minimum. Without such a growth provision, over time the minimum level will become outdated, and expenditure disparities will increase as has happened in the past.

Two kinds of growth formulas have been suggested for minimum level programs, each of which has different implications for taxpayer burdens. The first would link the growth of the minimum expenditure level to some index of *educational costs*. That is, the base year minimum would be adjusted annually by the change in enrollments and a measure of per pupil costs, based, presumably, on current statewide teacher salaries and other input cost adjustments. The second growth formula would base annual increases on enrollment growth and an adjustment for increases in the *general price level.* Either of these formulas will increase tax burdens to the extent that they allow minimum expenditure levels to grow relative to personal income. The growth in minimum expenditures will depend on enrollment growth and on the cost factor used in the formula—educational costs or general prices.

Nationally, public school enrollment is decreasing. In the 1960s, public school enrollments grew faster than the population in general, but now most projections show an absolute decline in public school enrollments in the coming decade. Even nonpublic schools enroll a smaller percentage of the school-age group than at present, public enrollment growth will be much slower than in the past. In any case, enrollments will grow about as fast or slower than the growth in the population in general.[19]

In the absence of outside intervention there is a tendency for the secular trend of educational costs to be in excess of the general price level. This relationship arises mainly because education is a low-productivity industry; so long as wages in education keep pace with wages in general, there will be an inevitable trend for unit costs in education to rise. In the coming decade, however, the interplay of two shorter-term phenomena may overshadow the secular trend. First, there is a teacher glut, and it gives little sign of abating. If wages of teachers were to respond to this glut—by rising slower than the average wage—then the rise in educational costs might be held down to something like the general price level. Second, with growing unionization and a move toward statewide bargaining for teacher salaries, there is likely to be a short-term bulge in teacher wages. In the long run, statewide bargaining may eliminate the practice of competitive jacking up of salaries among school districts, even if unionization increases. In the short run, however, creation of statewide bargaining means, almost inevitably, that there will be an attempt to raise salaries of teachers in low-paying areas to create a single standard throughout the state. Thus, the near-term outlook is for costs of educational services to rise faster than costs in general. Against this background, we can now turn to an examination of how a minimum expenditure formula based on education costs is likely to affect school-tax burdens, defined as public outlays for the program divided by personal income.

It can be shown that tax burdens will increase only if the sum of the rate of growth in enrollments over the growth in population plus the excess of the growth in educational costs over general prices exceeds the real per capita growth of income. Judging by historical trends, real per capita income should rise by about 3 percent per year over the next decade. As noted previously, enrollment will at most grow at the same rate as the general population in the coming decade, and it may grow more slowly. Thus, tax burdens will rise if, and only if, educational costs outrun costs in general by more than 3 percent per year. So long as statewide bargaining does not result in such an inflation of educational costs, which seems likely, a growth formula based on educational costs will *not* cause the minimum expenditure program to raise tax burdens in the future.

A growth formula based on enrollment and the general price level is sure to reduce tax burdens over time. Limiting the increase in minimum expenditure per student to the rise in general price level implies a reduction in real educational resources per student, so long as educational costs continue to exceed costs in general. Even if the introduction of such a formula forces increases in educational costs down to that of prices in general, in which case real resources per student would be constant over time, tax burdens would still fall as a result of growing productivity in the economy in general.

If state legislatures are looking for some way to allow a minimum expenditure level program to adjust to changing times without causing a built-in bias toward increasing taxpayer burdens, a growth formula based on educational costs should suffice. Under it, taxpayer burdens will rise only if educational costs rise excessively; so vigilance in salary negotiations, particularly, will be required. The alternative formula, basing increases in minimum per student expenditures on the general price level, contains a built-in bias toward reduced educational tax burdens, so it is far from "neutral."

To review our analysis to this point: for several reasons states will probably introduce minimum expenditure programs at a fairly high level. Taken in isolation, such an education reform will impose substantial new burdens on state-level taxpayers. But the increase is well within the bounds of what states can afford when a high-effort state constitutes the standard of comparison or when new sources of revenue such as general revenue sharing are taken into account. This is a one-shot rise in tax burdens; it is not likely to be repeated over the coming decade, even with relatively generous growth provisions written into state minimum plans.

Tax Burdens of the Combination of Minimum and Add-On Segments

Although all educational finance reform packages will include a minimum level program and a common tax base add-on plan, many combinations of these two policy parameters are possible. To narrow the field, in this section we discuss the tax burden implications of combinations of the two policy parameters under a state-level budget constraint. That is, we will analyze the implications for a state that must choose between a generous minimum program combined with a low common tax base add-on or a less generous minimum program combined with an add-on program in which the common tax base is high.

We can best understand the effects on aggregate tax burdens of shifts between minimum expenditure level support and changes in the guaranteed tax base of the add-on program by looking at each part of a two-step change. First, we analyze the determinants of the effect of an increase in the guaranteed tax base on total expenditure (total tax burden). Second, we analyze the factors that explain how districts would react to the reduction in the state-supported minimum expenditure level necessitated by the requirement that we keep the state budget fixed throughout our discussion.

Increase in the common tax base. Suppose we start with the situation in a state that has already instituted financial reforms. For simplicity, suppose that the state finances a minimum expenditure program out of nonproperty revenues and that each district is allowed to add on to the minimum level according to a common tax base. Figure 4-4 depicts this kind of school finance program showing, along line *MP*, the choice of expenditure and tax rate faced by each school district in the state. Various school districts have chosen such points as 1, 2, and 3 at which to operate their school systems. Those school districts whose own tax base exceeds the state guarantee level implied by *MP* will be paying into a state equalization fund; school districts with tax bases lower than the common tax base will be receiving a state supplement.

Now let the state increase the common tax base that it allows each district to use in computing its educational resources. On Figure 4-4, this change is shown as a steeper opportunity line, *MP'*. How would we expect districts to react to such a change? The district that initially was operating at point 2 might

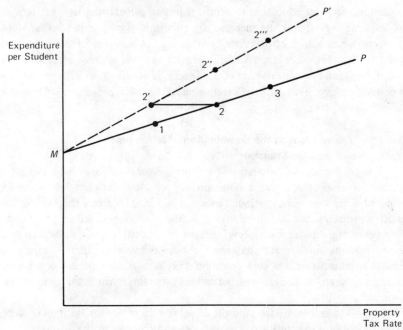

Figure 4-4. Opportunity Locus When Common Tax Base Is Increased.

be expected to react to the increase in the common tax base by selecting a point on MP'' to the right of point $2'$. Choice of a point near $2'$ means that the district chooses to react to a lower tax price of education by substituting state funds for local funds, without any appreciable increase in expenditures on education; such a district exhibits "low price sensitivity." At the opposite extreme, a district might react to the raising of the common tax base by moving from point 2 to a position such as $2''$ or $2'''$ in Figure 4-4. The district choosing $2''$ would maintain its tax rate and, in effect, use all of the newly available state funds to expand its educational offerings. Districts choosing $2'''$ react so strongly to the lowering of the tax price of education that they raise their tax rate, thereby substituting education for some of the noneducational services that they previously consumed. Districts choosing points near or to the right of $2''$ exhibit "high price sensitivity."

Most districts initially operating at point 2 would probably choose some point along MP' between $2'$ and $2''$, thereby substituting state for local funds, in part but increasing expenditures on education. The greater the price sensitivity of districts, as defined above, the greater will be the expenditure increase from any given increment in the common tax base. If price sensitivity is positively correlated with the original expenditure levels, moreover, the disparities in expenditure would widen under a regime of an increased common tax base.

State budgets must increase if the common tax base is raised. To see this, observe that the common tax base add-on program is equivalent to a state matching grant to each district.[20] When the common tax base is increased, the matching ratio in each district is increased. Since all districts can be expected to raise expenditures at least slightly, the combination of an increased matching rate and increased expenditures ensures that state budget outlays will rise. (In the special case where the add-on program was initially self-financing, the increased common tax base means that the wealthiest taxed districts will pay less, some districts will switch from taxed to grant receiving status, and all grant-receiving districts will get more than they did previously.) Given the average rate of price responsiveness of districts, state outlays will rise more (1) the greater the concentration of large expenditure increases in districts with low per student wealth; and (2) the higher is the initial expenditure level in high wealth districts.[21]

Lowering the minimum expenditure level to compensate. A state-imposed increase in the common tax base will, in any event, increase the state budget for education. Suppose the state raises the funds necessary to meet the greater costs in the add-on program by reducing minimum support grants to each district. In this case, the state-level budget "for education" will be unchanged.

We can illustrate the effects of a reduction in minimum expenditure levels by a parallel shift in the expenditure-tax line. In Figure 4-5, MP' is the expenditure-tax line when the minimum expenditure level is M. Points 1, 2, and 3 represent the combination chosen by three districts. Now suppose the minimum expenditure is reduced to M'.[22] The school district initially operating at point 2 will have to choose among the expenditure-tax options on line $M'P''$.

The district might respond to the lowered minimum grant level by raising its own tax rate and moving to point $2''$. In this case, the district reacts to a reduction in its income, occasioned by the lower minimum grant, by reducing only noneducational expenditures. Since the income reduction has no effect on education in this case, we label such a district as a "low income effect" district. At the other extreme is a district that responds to the reduction in the minimum grant by lowering its expenditures by the amount that the minimum grant declines (see point $2'$). In effect, such a district reacts to a reduction in its income by maintaining its consumption of all other goods and services and letting the entire income effect be borne by its education sector. This is a "high income effect" district.

Most districts will, naturally, respond somewhere in between $2'$ and $2''$, allowing both education and other goods and services to decline in response to a reduction in the minimum expenditure level. Local property tax rates will increase as the district restores to education some of the funds that would have been removed had they simply cut education by the amount of the reduction in the minimum grant.

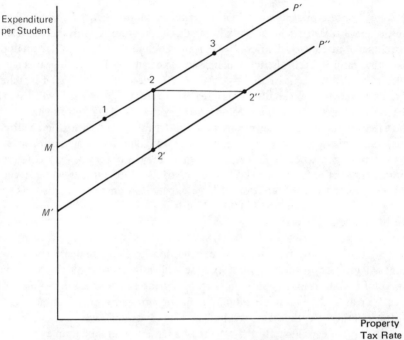

Figure 4-5. Opportunity Locus When Minimum Expenditure Is Reduced.

The combined effect. On purely theoretical grounds, for a fixed state education budget a shift in the mix of state outlays away from support of the minimum program toward support of the add-on program may increase, decrease, or leave unchanged total expenditures (tax burdens) of education in the state. However, with a few reasonable assumptions, we can show that under most circumstances such a shift in policy will result in increased aggregate tax burdens and expenditures, with the expenditure increases concentrated among the high-spending districts.

Figure 4-6 shows the increase in the common tax base of the add-on program with a compensating reduction in the minimum level program. MP is the original expenditure-tax line, and $M'P'$ is the new one. The three zones identified in the diagram represent districts whose choice of expenditure originally was less than R (zone I); exactly R (zone II); or greater than R (zone III). For districts in each zone we can identify the conditions under which their expenditures will increase or decrease when the opportunity line shifts from MP to $M'P'$.

Zone II districts. A zone II district can consume exactly the same amount of education and other goods at point X under both MP and $M'P'$.

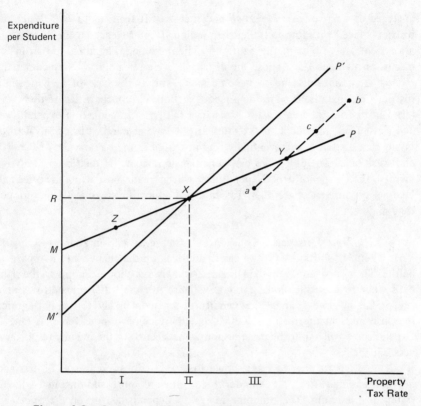

Figure 4-6. Combined Effect of Lower Minimum Expenditure and Higher Common Tax Base.

Under *MP* it chose *X* over all other points on *MP*. The zone II district, after *M'P'* is introduced, will therefore never choose a point to the left of *X*: Every point on *MP* to the left of *X* is superior to corresponding points on *M'P'*, and since *X* was originally chosen over other points on *MP*, a zone II district would be irrational to choose a point to the left of *X* on *M'P'*.[23] A zone II district will therefore never reduce its expenditure in moving to *M'P'* from *MP*. Only if its price responsiveness is nil will such a district spend only *X*. The higher the price responsiveness of zone II districts, the more will their expenditures rise under the change being discussed. Zone II districts will always raise their property tax rates.

Zone III districts. Consider a district that initially chose point *Y* in zone III. The change in such a district's fortunes when *MP* shifts to *M'P'* can be most readily explained by breaking that shift into two parts. Draw a line segment *ab* through *Y* parallel to *M'P'*. The behavior of district *Y* can then be analyzed as a move from *MP* to *ab* and then a shift from *ab* to *M'P'*. When the district is faced with line *ab* rather than in line *MP*, it is clear that the district will always choose a point to the right of *Y*. The reasoning is identical to that in our discussion of zone II. Suppose the district had chosen point *c*. Now comes the second step: *ab* shifts up to become *M'P'*. This is the case of a change in a district's income discussed in the previous section. We concluded there that a fall (rise) in district income always leads to a fall (rise) in education expenditures and a rise (fall) in education tax rates. In the case at hand, this is equivalent to saying that district *Y* will eventually find its equilibrium at a point on *M'P'* north and west of *c*. Therefore, we can conclude that zone III districts will always increase their expenditures. Expenditures will increase most when the price and income responsiveness are high. Tax rates for education in zone III may rise or they may fall.

       Zone I districts. Consider a district such as *Z* in zone I (see Figure 4-6). When *MP* shifts to *M'P'* we can again break up the change into two parts as before. The conclusions are: (1) District *Z* will always choose a point to the right of *Z*; that is, the educational tax rate will rise in zone I; (2) expenditures may rise or fall in zone I; and (3) expenditures are most likely to rise if the price responsiveness in the districts is high and the income responsiveness is *low*.[24] Expenditures will fall if the price responsiveness is low or the income responsiveness is high.

       Up to now we have shown that total educational expenditures and tax burdens may rise or fall under a shift toward more add-ons and a lower statewide minimum. The outcome in reality depends heavily on the price and income responsiveness in the three zones we have identified. These results are summarized in Table 4-9. Total tax burdens (expenditures) will increase most if price responsiveness is high and if high income responsiveness is positively correlated with the initial level of school expenditures. Expenditure disparities will increase if high price and income responsiveness are positively correlated with initial spending levels. Finally, local tax rate increases will be concentrated in

Table 4-9. Expenditure and Tax Changes Resulting from Shift to Higher Common Tax Base for Add-on Program and Reduction in Minimum Expenditure Level

	Zone I	Zone II	Zone III
Expenditure Change	Higher or lower	Higher	Higher
School Tax Rate Change	Higher	Higher	Higher or lower
Expenditure Increase Maximized if	High price responsiveness	High price responsiveness	High price responsiveness
	Low income responsiveness		High income responsiveness

low-spending districts if those districts exhibit the lowest price and income responsiveness.

Although it is not possible to predict with certainty the income and price responsiveness characteristics of school districts in a post-reform world, it is likely that high-expenditure (zone III) districts will exhibit higher price responsiveness than low expenditure (zone I) districts. We base this expectation on the observation that high-expenditure districts probably would be providing many "nonessential" (for example, music lessons) services through the schools. Since there are many nonschool substitutes available for such services, districts would be sensitive to price changes. For low-spending districts, providing mainly essential services, small changes in the marginal tax price are less likely to induce expenditure changes since there are fewer substitutes available for such services. If high price responsiveness is correlated with initial spending levels as just posited, a shift in the state budget from the minimum level program to the add-on program would be accompanied by higher total tax burdens[25] (and expenditures) and greater expenditure disparities among school districts.

A shift in state policy, under a fixed education budget, toward a more generous program of supplementation and less support of minimum expenditure levels, has mixed results in terms of the policy results usually valued in the school finance area. The plus factor is the overall increase in education expenditures, and a minus factor is the likely increase in expenditure disparities among districts.

Two ameliorative policies suggest themselves for consideration by a state attempting to attain the benefits of a shift to greater add-ons without the social costs. First, imposing an upper limit on expenditures would reduce disparities in education spending by choking off expenditures of the highest-spending districts. Second, the notion of maintaining a "fixed education budget" for the state level requires careful examination with the kind of financial reform under discussion. Suppose a state wishes to encourage education in a way that emphasizes free choice and fairness. Then, as seen before, it will raise the common tax base, thereby reducing each district's tax price for education. The state can pay for the larger state outlays thereby incurred with taxes on property, income, or sales, or even a head tax. "Balancing the state budget for education" requires imposing a head tax on school children, which, analytically, is the same as a reduction in state grants for minimum support levels. All forms of general state taxation can be expected to discourage spending on education, whether they be income taxes or head taxes on children, because education is a normal good whose consumption is reduced when disposable income shrinks. The difference between a head tax on school children and, say, an increased income tax is mainly one of who pays the tax, not one of which affects "education" more. Therefore, for a state interested in raising education expenditures without increasing disparities between the rich and the poor, the key elements in a rational program are the reduction of the tax price of education through an increase in the common tax base,[26] and an increase in taxes (or a reduction in subsidies) whose incidence is mainly on wealthy persons. A reduction in state grants for minimum expenditures is merely a disguised way of paying for the increased supplementation program by taxing in a most regressive manner.

Comparison of Post-Reform Program to
Existing Tax Burdens by School District

Much interest attaches to *What Will Happen to Taxes in New York City* (substitute your favorite school district) if school finance reform comes to New York State. It is instructive to take stock of what we have learned so far toward answering this question. School finance reform will entail dropping the local property tax as it is now constituted, the creation of a state-based minimum expenditure level financed in whole or part by a state property tax, and the opportunity for districts to impose property taxes on themselves (up to a point) under a power equalized schedule. Therefore, What will Happen to New York City's Taxes depends on

1. The elimination of the local school property tax as we now know it. The key question here is who really pays New York City's educational property tax.
2. The incidence of the taxes used to finance the state minimum grant program. How is New York City affected by state-level taxes on income, sales, or property?
3. What level of expenditure and taxes will New York City choose under the common tax base add-on program?

The first two factors affecting the tax burden of any existing school district constitute the subject of the next section, where we deal with the incidence of various kinds of taxes. The answer to the last question should now be clear: New York City (or any other place) will impose on itself a relatively high local property tax, and enjoy the maximum allowable add-on if it has a strong preference for education, if its residents view the property tax as being paid by outsiders, or if the composition of the populace changes in the direction of people who more strongly desire education.

None of these attributes of particular places is known. We can observe how existing school districts have chosen to tax and spend on education in the past, but education finance reform promises such a dramatic shift in the opportunities open to any district that we doubt whether any inferences about preference functions derived from past behavior means much for the future. Similarly, popular conceptions of who really bears the burden of property taxes will probably undergo a major change in the near future as attention is focused more on the incidence of that tax. What economists will conclude, much less what the taxpaying public will believe, is at present unpredictable. Finally, as our last section will indicate, one of the truly long-term effects of school finance reform may be to change the incentive structure that currently motivates people to live where they do. Thus, even if we knew the true preference functions of today's New York City population, the chances are that by the time the second act of education finance reform began, the cast of actors would change.

All this is by way of apology for not being able to supply the reader with the definitive answer on what will happen to any particular district's taxes under school tax reform. At the most, we can indicate the pattern of tax incidence for various state-level taxes among school districts and families.

THE EFFECTS OF STATE TAXES ON
DISTRICTS AND FAMILIES

States undertaking to pay for an expanded program of support for education can choose from a variety of potential tax sources. The most prominent among these are state income, sales, and property taxes. Determining what mix of taxes "best" suits any particular state depends on local conditions as well as on more basic tax characteristics, such as responsiveness to economic growth, ease of administration, and neutrality of the tax on economic activity. A large part of the decision, however, will be, and should be, based on the distribution of the various taxes on families and among jurisdictions.

The nature of the change in tax burdens among individuals and communities would, of course, depend upon which state taxes were raised, the incidence of these taxes, and the extent to which new revenue sources were used to substitute for local property taxes rather than to add new revenue to the system. The incidence of the property tax about which debate continues would also be important.

Certain types of tax changes could relieve some groups entirely from the responsibility of supporting public education. For example, replacement of the local educational property tax with increased state sales or personal income taxes would provide a windfall to the owners of commercial and industrial property if their property taxes fell without any commensurate increase in other taxes they pay.[27] Nonresident property owners would be another group that would stand to gain from any reduction in property taxes. In some vacation areas, such as New England and the mid-Atlantic seashore, a small but significant fraction of the real property consists of summer houses owned by persons living in different states. Property taxes have been a convenient method for residents of such areas to tax these high-income persons. Sales taxes might recoup some of the lost tax from nonresidents, but income taxes would not.

If new or higher corporate income taxes replaced local school property taxes, just the opposite type of change could occur. Industry or consumers would suddenly have their educational tax burden increased, while homeowners (and possibly tenants) would experience a net reduction in their tax burdens. In some states, other changes besides increasing corporate taxes may be suggested that could result in an exportation of a good deal of school taxes to the residents of other areas. For example, raising Nevada's entertainment tax, or taxes on hotels and lodging in New York, Florida, Hawaii, or the District of Columbia, would have such an effect. But overall such taxes—including corporate income taxes—are not capable of generating the large amounts of money needed for school finance reforms.

A new revenue source that has received a considerable amount of attention is the statewide property tax. A number of school finance reform proposals have advocated such a tax as part of a move toward full state assumption or a greatly expanded state financial role in school finance.[28] Such a tax could generate a large amount of revenue. However, the burden it would place on various communities and their residents would be very different from that imposed by the existing school property taxes. In effect, since the tax rate would be the same throughout the state, communities would contribute in proportion to the equalized value of their property. If such a state tax were set so as to generate the same amount of revenue as now produced by local school property taxes, many rural communities would experience substantial increases in property tax rates because farmland tends to be underassessed[29] and tax rates in rural areas are generally extremely low. Large cities would often experience a similar increase in school property levies for the reasons discussed in the first section of this chapter. The state property tax proposed by the Fleischmann Commission would have resulted in higher property levies in that state's six largest cities, while many of the wealthiest communities in the state would have experienced a reduction in their property tax levies. But such generalizations do not hold everywhere, as can be seen from Table 4-10, which shows the percentage increase or decrease in school tax rates that would occur if New Jersey established a statewide property tax that generated the same amount of revenue as local school property taxes now produce. Six of the state's large cities would experience tax increases, but in ten cities tax rates would decline. Similarly, a mixed pattern occurs in suburbs as well as in nonmetropolitan areas.

A similar type of analysis can be applied to other sources of increased state revenues. Table 4-11 illustrates the burden alternative tax sources would place on a number of counties in New York if statewide taxes were levied in such a way as to raise the same aggregate amount now produced by local school property taxes. A comparison of the burdens of various taxes shown in the first four columns with the last column provides a rough estimate of how each area would fare if the state were to distribute its receipts on the basis of enrollment. New York City and Westchester and Nassau Counties would be better off under the existing system under which they keep all of the money raised through the local system of property taxes. On the other hand, in rural Madison and St. Laurence counties, a shift to statewide taxation would generate about $2 of receipts for every $1 extracted from the community in state taxes.[30]

Table 4-10. Percent Increase or Decrease in Tax Rates in New Jersey Implied by Statewide Property Tax Set to Yield the Same Aggregate Amount as Local School Property Tax

Cities Over 50,000 Population

Atlantic	58.7%	Bayonne	20.9%
Camden	−10.3	Jersey City	−16.1
Bridgeton	−19.0	Union City	−20.1
Millville	−21.2	Trenton	−24.0
Vineland	−14.6	Clifton	78.8
Bloomfield	12.4	Passaic	4.9
East Orange	−19.3	Patterson	−4.3
Irvington	10.4	Elizabeth	6.2
Newark	−61.8		

Metropolitan Counties Exclusive of Large Cities

Atlantic County	9.9%	Gloucester	−26.8%
Bergen County	17.6	Mercer	7.1
Burlington	−19.1	Morris	−8.7
Camden	11.4	Passaic	9.4
Cumberland	−14.2	Salem	−13.7
Essex	2.9	Union	−15.4
Hudson	38.0	Warren	−0.4

Nonmetropolitan Counties

Cape May	120.9%	Ocean	2.4%
Huterdon	−11.4	Somerset	−6.2
Middlesex	−10.2	Sussex	−13.7
Monmouth	12.6		

Source: New Jersey Chamber of Commerce, *1972 Property Tax Data*.

Of the three potential sources of state revenue, New York City's (and other large commercial centers') tax burden increases more under a state property tax than under income or sales taxes. Wealthy suburbs—for example, Westchester and Nassau Counties—have most to lose under a state income tax, and poorer rural areas suffer most by retail sales taxes.

Although the preceding discussion shows how different jurisdictions are affected by various types of state revenues, it says little about the incidence of such taxes for individuals. Low-income homeowners living in high property tax districts stand to gain under any shift in tax sources, while high-income homeowners residing in tax havens would pay more under a shift to state revenue sources. But beyond these groups, the effects of a shift in tax sources on various classes of individuals are difficult to predict. New or increased state income taxes would, of course, hit the rich much more than an increase in sales

Table 4-11.   Per Capita Burden of Local School Property Taxes in Selected New York Jurisdictions, Various Alternative State Taxes Capable of Raising the Same Revenue, and Distribution on the Basis of Enrollment, Various Years, 1968-1970

Government	Local School Property Tax 1969[a]	State Property Tax[b]	State Income Tax[c]	State Sales Tax[d]	Distribution Based on Enrollment[a]
New York State	$103	$103	$103	$103	$103
New York City	90	105	97	97	78
Westchester County	170	142	207	129	104
Nassau County	189	139	169	136	128
Suffolk County	142	104	76	105	140
Madison County	72	68	52	78	149
Sullivan County	146	142	54	193	118
St. Laurence County	66	72	40	87	132

[a]Financial Data for School Districts, Year Ending June 30, 1969, State of New York, Department of Audit and Control, 1970, Tables 1 and 3.

[b]Based on the 1968 distribution of full valuations of real property taxable for county purposes. *New York State Statistical Yearbook, 1970*, Table H-25, New York State Division of the Budget.

[c]Based on the 1969 distribution of New York State personal income tax liability by county of resident. *New York State Statistical Yearbook, 1971*, Table H-9.

[d]Based on the distribution of state sales taxes collected in 1970-71 (unpublished estimates of the New York State Department of Taxation and Finance).

taxes. But the effect of any corresponding reduction in local property taxes would depend upon the incidence of this tax. If this tax now falls largely on capitalists rather than consumers and renters, any substitution of sales or income taxes for existing property levies would hurt renters and consumers.

The previous analysis suggested that local school districts, even in a reformed system, will be allowed to supplement the basic allotment they receive from the state. This add-on need not be raised from the existing local property tax base. In fact, a number of arguments can be made for adopting school finance reform plans that call for shifting to some other local tax base. If such a change did occur, it would profoundly affect the local school tax burdens facing many families.

One suggestion that has been made is to move toward a tax with a broader base than property. Local income or sales taxes would fill this prescription. In many states (though not in all)[31] such a shift would reduce the range of per pupil tax base discrepancies among school districts; thus, the problem of establishing a fair and politically feasible common tax base would be eased. Use of a broader tax base would also result in a system with more horizontal equity, because income or total consumption expenditures are generally regarded as better indexes of ability to pay than is the value of one's residence. The situation in which neighbors with identical incomes but different tastes in housing pay different fractions of their income for school property taxes would be eliminated.

Shifting to local income or sales taxes as a source of local school support could be fairly simple from an administrative standpoint. The local tax could "piggy back" on a state sales or income levy, as is already done in a number of states, such as Maryland. The main drawback of such a shift is that although residential property is a fairly immobile tax base, consumer expenditures and personal income are not. Thus, if local sales or income tax rates were to differ significantly among school districts, shopping patterns and residential location decisions could be significantly affected. For example, reliance on local sales taxes for school support may result in "shopping plaza enclaves" developing, just as "industrial enclaves" have been induced by existing tax systems.

It is important to note that if local income or sales taxes replaced property taxes as the source of locally raised school revenues, the relative rankings of districts could change appreciably. What were "wealthy" districts could become "poor." For example, industrial enclaves housing low-income families would be transformed in this manner. Movement to an income tax, moreover, would eliminate the possibility of shifting part of the local tax onto nonresidents.

A less drastic change than completely abandoning the property tax as the source of local educational revenues is to redefine the local property tax base. One suggestion that has received considerable support would be to restrict local districts to taxing residential property alone. Commercial and industrial property could be subjected to a uniform statewide tax. Since nonresidential property is distributed extremely unevenly among school districts, such a change would tend to reduce the range of variation in the per pupil property tax bases of school districts. Most residential property is owned by the residents of the jurisdiction, and therefore little of the tax could be exported to others living outside the specific school district. A by-product of the change to taxing only residential property at the local level would be a greater rationality in the taxation of business. Business, rather than facing very different school property tax rates in different districts, would be subject to the same property tax rate in all districts. The tendencies of business to cluster in tax havens would be eliminated.

SECONDARY EFFECTS OF SCHOOL FINANCE REFORM

Changes in revenue sources and the aggregate level of school taxes may have a number of secondary effects that have not been analyzed in any great detail. Foremost among these is the possibility that any reduction in the local property tax or any shift to statewide property taxation could result in major changes in property values. At present, the value of taxable property to some extent reflects the amount of tax that must be paid each year by the owner, as well as expectations about possible changes in future tax levels. The abolition of all property taxes would bring about an increase in real property values relative to other asset prices because the ownership of real property would no longer entail the payment of an annual tax. Unless owners of rental and commercial property were forced to pass on their savings to tenants and consumers, their apartments and factories would appreciate, because the after-tax flow of income generated by these properties would rise; owner-occupied housing would appreciate for analogous reasons. If a 2 percent property tax were fully capitalized into current real estate values, its removal could cause prices of homes and buildings to appreciate by about 20 percent. Those owning real estate, under such a change, would see their wealth positions enhanced relative to those holding other forms of assets. In general, the richer and older segments of society would be benefited, and the unequal distribution of wealth would be exacerbated.

The spectre of this occurring has been one of the factors leading many observers to the conclusion that a statewide property tax is a necessary component of any school reform package that calls for a reduction in local school taxes. Yet a statewide tax—even if it generated the same amount of money as now produced by local taxes—would result in major changes in real estate prices among communities. Property values now reflect a tax advantage in school districts that are able to generate a great deal of school revenue with low tax rates; these values should fall with a statewide tax. On the other hand, in poorer jurisdictions the property values should rise.

Much the same situation would arise under a DPE plan. The relative tax advantage of wealthy communities would disappear. If property values now reflect these advantages, such values could be expected to fall. On the other hand, in poorer districts the amount of local expenditure generated by any level of taxes would rise under a DPE plan, and one would expect that property values would increase to reflect this improvement.

Another major secondary effect that could result from changing the system of taxes that support education deals with residence and job patterns. One factor influencing the location of industry is local taxes, although there is little evidence to show that its effect is strong. Any move toward state financing of education would reduce the relevance of this factor. Industrial enclaves might be expected to lose much of their appeal, and central cities and other high-tax jurisdictions would gain in attractiveness. Under a DPE form of financing, industry could be expected to be drawn to communities that have exhibited a low preference for educational spending.

Residential location decisions also could be affected by new forms of raising school revenues. If states became the principal units of government that raise revenues and disperse money, wealthy families would no longer have as

great an incentive to isolate themselves in separate communities. Neither school
tax burdens nor per pupil expenditures would be appreciably affected by their
choice of school district.[32] Under a DPE system, families can reduce their tax
burdens, but only by moving to districts that have shown little interest in school
spending.

To the extent that a DPE plan or increased state responsibility for
raising school revenues results in a move toward an equalization of educational
quality and a reduction in tax differences among school districts, the high-tax or
low-expenditure districts of today may become relatively more attractive places
to live. Families with school-age children may be less anxious to flee central
cities. The battle of upper-middle-class families for entrance into the few
exclusive suburbs may subside.

NOTES

1. See Robert D. Reischauer and Robert W. Hartman, with the
assistance of Daniel J. Sullivan, *Reforming School Finance* (Washington: The
Brookings Institution, 1973), Chapter 2.

2. See Joseph A. Pechman, *Federal Tax Policy* (rev. ed.; Washington: The Brookings Institution, 1971).

3. *Report of the New York State Commission on the Quality, Cost
and Financing of Elementary and Secondary Education* (Albany, 1972), Vol. 1,
p. 2.33.

4. Most economists agree that the tax on the value of land is borne
by the owner of this fixed resource. Land values represent 40 percent of the
value of real taxable property.

5. For a summary of these studies, see Frank de Leeuw, "The
Demand for Housing: A Review of Cross-Section Evidence," *Review of Economics and Statistics* 53 (February 1971): 1-10.

6. If the incidence of a fully shifted property tax is defined as T/Y,
where T is the tax and Y is the tenant's income, then

$$\frac{T}{Y} = \frac{tM}{Y} = t \ \frac{R}{Y} \ \frac{M}{R} \ ,$$

where t is the effective tax rate on the market value, M, of the unit, and R is the
rent. The tax would be progressive,

$$\frac{d\left(\frac{T}{Y}\right)}{dY} > 0,$$

if the tendency for R/Y to be lower among richer persons was more than offset
by a rise in the ratio of value-to-rent, M/R, caused by the factors mentioned in
the text. These points are based on the work of George E. Peterson, as reported

in "The Regressivity of the Residential Property Tax," Working Paper 1207-10 (Washington: The Urban Institute, November 8, 1972) (mimeo.).

7. Of course, even if new investment fell, a number of obstacles would impede the complete or immediate shifting of property taxes. For example, since new investment represents only a tiny fraction of the housing stock in any year, it may take many years for the supply to adjust to a new or increased property tax.

For an elaboration of the obstacles, see Peter Mieszkowski, "The Property Tax: An Excise Tax or a Profits Tax?" *Journal of Public Economics* 1 (April 1972): 76-96; M. Mason Gaffney, "The Property Tax Is a Progressive Tax," in National Tax Association, *1971 Proceedings of the Sixty-fourth Annual Conference on Taxation*, (1972), pp. 408-426. A careful summary of the more traditional view is contained in Dick Netzer, *Economics of the Property Tax* (Washington: The Brookings Institution, 1966), Chapter 3.

8. The Fleischmann Commission Report is cited in Footnote 3 above. Charles S. Benson, *Final Report to the Senate Select Committee on School District Finance*, submitted by the Consultant Staff (Sacramento: The Committee, 1972), Volume 1, Chapter 4.

9. DPE could, in principle, be established with *income* per student as the measure of wealth, with districts choosing different income tax surcharges and school expenditure levels. This possibility is discussed in Reischauer and Hartman, *Reforming School Finance*, Chapter 4.

10. Setting a flat slope for a DPE schedule means that, at least on the margin, wealthy school districts pay a tax on each unit of education consumed. To defend the efficiency of such a sumptuary tax, one would have to argue either that education in wealthy communities creates *negative* social benefits or that residents of rich communities that spend a lot on education enjoy a disproportionate share of the gains from educating children in low-wealth school districts. It is not enough to argue that high-wealth communities can afford taxes. The principle of ability to pay justifies taxes based on wealth *but not taxes based on education expenditures.* Only by appealing to a new principle of fiscal equity under which the yield of a local tax "belongs to the state" can one defend a flat DPE over a substantial spending range. See Chapter 2 in this volume for a discussion of this issue.

11. See Chapter 2 for an extended discussion of different types of school expenditure schedules.

12. t_m is a choice variable, given OM, in that the state need not impose a uniform property tax to fully finance the minimum expenditure level. The next section discusses the implications of alternative state-level taxes.

13. OM need not be the same for every district under DPE or state assumption. Factors such as age-mix of pupils or cost-factors could be built into a state plan. For discussion, see Chapter 2.

14. For a notable exception, see the Fleischmann Report.

15. Once capacities are equalized there will be a ceiling for the same reasons that DPE will result in a ceiling—to avoid an uncontrollable state budget for education.

16. The Texas case: *Rodriguez v. San Antonio Independent School District*, Civil Action 68-175-SA, U.S. District Court, Western District of Texas, San Antonio Division (1971).

17. Naturally a district can benefit, even if the minimum level is set below its previous per student expenditure, if the schedule for supplementary expenditures is sufficiently generous. But there is a principle of politics and mass communication that always seems to focus on a number rather than a schedule, as was recently illustrated by public discussion of demogrants and negative income taxes.

18. One-third of the revenue-sharing fund is paid to state governments and may be used for education. Two-thirds of the amount goes to local governments, who are precluded from using the money for non-capital education expenditures. However, if local governments used their grants to reduce local taxes, the state or school districts could adopt a program of educational equalization without increasing the aggregate state and local tax burden.

19. See Reischauer and Hartman, *Reforming School Finance*, Chapter 3.

20. Add-on expenditures per student under a common tax base program are defined by the relation $E_i = t_i B$, where

E_i = the expenditure level per student in excess of the minimum in district i.
t_i = the chosen tax rate in district i.
B = the common base per student.

The state grant (S_i) to district i is then

$$S_i = t_i (B - B_i),$$

indicating that the state makes up enough money to the district (or taxes the district enough) to give it the equivalent of the common base, B. It thus follows that

$$S_i = (1 - \frac{B_i}{B}) E_i,$$

which is a state matching formula under which the state pays or taxes total expenditure at the rate $(1 - B_i/B)$.

21. State outlays to district i in period t are equal to

$$S_{i,t} = (1 - \frac{B_i}{B}) E_{i,t}.$$

Letting M stand for the matching ratio, the change in $S_{i,t}$ between two time periods during which M and E change can be approximated by

$$\Delta S_i = M(\Delta E_i) + (\Delta M) E_{i,t}$$

Since M is inversely related to district wealth, statement one is implied by the first term of this equation. Since ΔM will rise by a larger amount in rich districts than in poor districts for any given change in B ($\partial M/\partial B = B_i/B^2$), the second term implies statement two.

22. The reduction in M required to balance the state education budget is not simply the deficit incurred when the add-on program is liberalized. As we shall see, the lowering of M induces changes in tax rates and expenditures of districts, thereby changing the deficit in the equalization fund. The text assumes that several iterations have taken place and that M' is indeed the state education budget balancing level of minimum expenditure.

23. Two warnings to the reader. One, "a superior point" on the diagram means that for a given tax rate the expenditure is higher at the superior point. Two, when we say "irrational," we are using the conventional economics of *individual* choice applied to school-district decisions. We are aware of the hazards of this application, but cannot think of anything better.

24. A low-income responsiveness here implies that districts will not reduce education expenditures much when their income falls. If the income responsiveness is low, a high price responsiveness may be sufficient to raise expenditures.

25. This conclusion implicitly assumes that high income responsiveness is not highly correlated with initial low spending levels.

26. Or an increase in minimum grants if the state wishes particularly to raise education levels in low spending districts.

27. To compensate for such a possibility, Governor Cahill in New Jersey proposed an "excess gains tax" as part of his school finance reform package. This tax would capture the gains resulting from the net reduction in the property tax liability of business and industry.

28. For example, The Fleischmann Commission (New York); Governor Cahill, *A Master Plan for Tax Reform* (New Jersey); *Final Report to the Senate Select Committee on School District Finance* (California), pp. 27-28.

29. Allen D. Manvel, "Trends in the Value of Real Estate and Land, 1956 to 1966," in *Three Land Research Studies*, prepared for the Consideration of the National Commission on Urban Problems, Research Report 12, Washington, D.C., 1968, p. 6.

30. Three cautions must be observed in the interpretation of these estimates. First, other distributions of state funds are possible. If extra weight were given for children from disadvantaged homes or for low achievers, the large cities and rural areas would receive considerably more than they do under a flat per-pupil grant, while the suburban counties would receive less. Second, Table 4-4 shows only the substitution of state taxes for the current level of local property taxes, and ignores the increased level of funding that will be necessary under reform as well as the reactions of school districts to any add-on programs. Third, patterns of residence may be affected by significant changes in public school financing. For example, the number of families that leave large cities for the suburbs when their children reach school age might be reduced; if this happened, state aid would increase along with school enrollment in the cities.

31. See Reischauer and Hartman, *Reforming School Finance*, Chapter 4.

32. Of course, the major incentive may not have much to do with taxes or expenditure, but instead may be a desire to have one's children go to school with "their own kind."

Chapter Five

The Transition to a New School Finance System

Charles S. Benson
University of California, Berkeley

In most state governments, compliance with the *Serrano* dictum that the "quality of public education shall not be a function of local wealth" will entail notable transformations in the financial relationships of their most expensive services—the elementary-secondary schools. This chapter considers major problems of transition to a *Serrano*-pure system of finance, insofar as those transitional problems can be identified at the present time. I shall concentrate attention on the following: (1) the possible effect of *Serrano* in forcing rich households to abandon public schools for private; (2) the difficulties, at least in district power equalizing schemes, of preserving a more or less uniform definition of public educational expenditures; (3) under *Serrano*-induced adjustments in property tax rates, the possible damage done to poor households in property-rich districts; and (4) the apparent inconsistency between statewide fiscal reform in education and the goal of improving the financial position of large cities. At the end of the chapter, I will try to indicate how these problems may be moderated by certain "phasing-in" techniques.

TWO REFORM PROPOSALS

To assist in understanding the transitional problems, it will be helpful to sketch the outlines of two different reform plans recently presented, both of which apparently satisfy the *Serrano* criterion. One is the full state funding (FSF) proposal of the Fleischmann Commission, and the other is the district power equalizing (DPE) plan prepared by a group of consultants for the California Senate Select Committee on School District Finance.[1]

Full state funding. In full state funding, the state government becomes the single source of nonfederal school revenues.[2] In the New York plan, the low-spending districts are brought up to the 65th percentile of operating expenditures per student per year. To make such a proposal definite, it is necessary, of course, to rank districts in terms of their operating outlay per student, and in doing so it is prudent to exclude certain kinds of expenditures that vary a great deal from one district to the next.[3] In the case of New York, these excluded items, which henceforth would be fully funded as categorical aids, are student transport, school lunch, expenditures for services of regional educational authorities, and debt service.[4]

High-spending districts are charged to maintain their given outlays per student, but are not allowed to increase them until such time as the statewide basic level of funding (established initially at the 65th percentile) reaches their own level, at which point the higher spending places would begin to move ahead in step with the rest of the districts in the state. (It is anticipated that the state will gradually increase the basic level of funding to provide for improvements in quality and to recognize inflationary rises in costs.) The districts that are "saved harmless" (that is, are continued at their present levels of expenditure per student), are fully supported from state revenues. Moreover, costs of new construction of schools and all past debt service are taken over by the state.

The basic idea of full state funding as expounded by the Fleischmann Commission is the following: "The State shall determine a defensible basis of distributing money to the school districts. Equal sums of money shall be made available for each student, *unless a valid educational reason can be found for spending some different amount*" (italics in original).[5] Note that the statements go beyond conventional interpretations of what is required to "satisfy *Serrano*," for, on one hand, the state becomes the chief and single decision agency with respect to major educational resource allocations, and, on the other hand, the state is enjoined to make equal distribution per student except where educational criteria (for example, differences in characteristics of students, differences in prices of educational services) indicate an alternative course. Not only is local wealth barred from influencing educational resource allocations but so are tastes of residents of different school districts.

From the beginning of its existence, the Fleischmann Commission was concerned with the problem of educational failure. Therefore, it included in its full state funding recommendation the proposal that low-achieving students receive extra grants; specifically, it is stated that such students be weighted at 1.5 for grant computation purposes, as compared with a weight of 1.0 in the general case.[6]

On the revenue side, although the commission recommended the abolition of all local taxation for schools, it proposed that a statewide school property tax be instituted. It held that the rate should be set to yield approximately what had formerly been collected in the aggregate by local authorities for schools. Such a rate is $2.04 per $100 of full value assessment. Also, the commission recommended that the state adopt a "circuit-breaker" property tax relief measure. The proposal reads as follows:

> For relief of grossly overburdened homeowners, the Commission recommends the tax credit approach ... [to permit] any family paying more than 10 percent of state taxable income in property taxes for schools to credit the excess against their state income tax bill. In cases where the family pays no income tax, or less income tax than is due the taxpayer from overpayment on the state property tax for education, the State would reimburse the taxpayer for the overpayment. .... A special procedure is required for granting relief for apartment dwellers. We urge that 20 percent of individual rents be considered state property taxes, and that anyone for which this 20 percent figure exceeds the specified percent of gross income be permitted to credit the excess against income taxes.[7]

In summary, the revenue recommendations argued not for abandonment of property taxation for schools, but for its improvement through elimination of interdistrict inequities and through establishing income-specific relief for householders. In general, both measures should reduce the regressivity of the tax with regard to low- to middle-income households.

District power equalizing. In three respects the plan prepared for the California Senate Select Committee on School District Finance is similar to the Fleischmann proposals. First, the plan specifies greater use of fully funded categorical aids such as school construction, transport, regional centers, and so on. Second, the plan is designed to include extra support for low-achieving students (in the case of California, low-income as well). Third, the plan includes a circuit-breaker feature that offers property tax relief to low-income householders, regardless of whether they are homeowners or renters.[8] However, with regard to the main recommendation on collection and distribution of noncategorical school funds, there is a fundamental difference between the two plans. In California the *Serrano* criterion of divorcing the level of local educational spending from district wealth is met by establishing a precise schedule of local tax rates and school expenditures per student, such that any two districts having the same local school tax rate have available the same amount of noncategorical dollars per student.

There were several reasons for choosing district power equalizing in California, two of which are especially important. First, it was deemed important in California to maintain the power in the local school districts to balance their own budgets, which is to say that the consultant's group, of which I was a member, became convinced of the case for local control, as applied to *district* financial affairs.

Second, there was what has been called the "rural problem." *Serrano* drew attention to the anomaly that certain school districts have low school tax rates and high school expenditures, whereas others have high tax rates and low expenditures. In rural areas, on the other hand, one frequently finds large numbers of small districts that have low tax rates *and* low school expenditures per student. We were warned that a high mandatory statewide school property tax would drive marginal farmers from their chosen occupation, and that we should not propose such a nonneutral fiscal device. DPE allows the state to use a small minimum school property tax, but at the cost of associating low school expenditures with low local tax rates—the state, that is, permits students in rural areas to be meagerly provided for. In California, this seemed the lesser evil. Full state funding, contrarily, implies a fairly high statewide property tax rate, unless one can assume that the state budget will absorb revenues formerly raised by property taxation into increased yield from broad-based state levies, such as income and sales taxes. In the present economic climate, we held that such an assumption was unrealistic. In any case, money not to be raised by property tax is in competition with the financing of new and improved programs for disadvantaged students, and these latter grants are especially helpful in dealing with the financial problems of the large cities. Thus, the rural problem stands in some conflict with the metropolitan problem. DPE, more than full state funding, allows the use of a minimum property tax rate that is compatible with the conventional interests of rural communities.

There is, however, a danger that an open-ended DPE schedule will pose too great a threat to the state budget. Under the sharing arrangement, large numbers of districts might spend irresponsibly and pass along to the state an unmanageably high bill for matching shares. To forestall this possibility, we adopted a nonlinear DPE schedule, under which districts are provided financial inducement to spend up to a "normal amount" per student, and above that amount the financial inducement is lessened. The particular schedule we selected as our first recommendation is shown in Figure 5-1.

Problems of Transition

Each of these two plans—and I believe these two plans and their variants represent the field of post-*Serrano* options—entails major shifts in the financing of California's largest state-local public service—elementary-secondary education. Hence, we can reasonably expect to encounter problems of transition.

Private, nonsectarian education traditionally has been small in the United States.[9] Sectarian enrollment itself is relatively small, and serves all classes. It follows that wealthy households customarily send their children to public elementary and secondary schools, even though they have the means to do otherwise. We need not be troubled about *Serrano* harming the children of the rich, for wealthy households, in general, know how to take care of

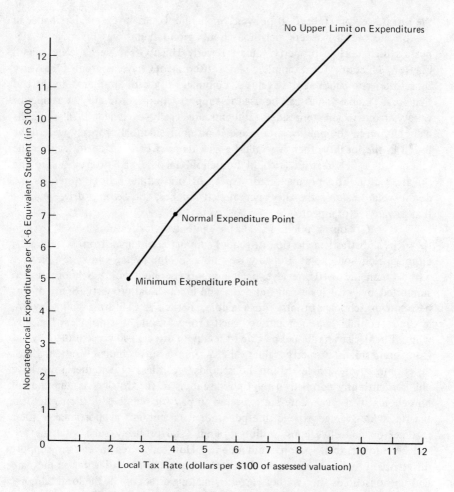

Figure 5-1. Proposed DPE Schedule in California.

themselves. The problem centers on what might happen to the public school system if the rich depart in wholesale numbers to use private institutions.

In the United States we have had at best a "semipublic" educational system. In Carl Shoup's terminology, education in the first instance is a group-consumption good.[10] Further, discrimination among consumers is easily practiced. The child in Baldwin Park is no more able to attend schools in Beverly Hills than if the Beverly Hills schools were financed and administered strictly in the private sector. (Indeed, if he were bright, he would have a greater chance in the private sector.) Where rich households group themselves in enclaves that possess high taxable property values (Beverly Hills; Great Neck, Long Island; Clayton, Missouri, for example), state governments have consented to leave those property values at the exclusive command of district residents, to the end that local taxable values can be used to support schools, ordinarily of a superior variety, from which nonresident students are legally excluded. If all residents had children in the public schools and if no nonresidential property were to be found in the locality, then it would be an almost effortless step to transfer the schools of a rich district (rich in household income and property) into the private sector. The private sector aspect of our public school system is, no doubt, what has held the allegiance of rich families, and *Serrano* drives right at that private sector aspect.

Of course, public schools have public sector features as well. Even in the richest districts, a portion of school support is obtained from state grants, although rich households probably pay more, on the average, in state taxes for schools than the district receives back in grants (per household). Schools are also supported by local levies on industrial and commercial property. Some of our best-known school districts—for example, Berkeley, California and Clayton, Missouri—contain large amounts of such property, and it is not clear logically why affluent districts should be able to retain, in effect, 100 percent of the yield from nonresident property values, the *Serrano* issue completely aside. Local taxes, moreover, are levied on households regardless of whether they have children currently enrolled in the public schools of the district. Assume that all households of a given state are expected to pay for public education priced at the statewide average expenditure per student in amounts proportional to their incomes on collective consumption grounds (and probably such payments *are* roughly proportional to household income). How can the extra levies to support differentially high expenditures in rich districts be justified, insofar as they are laid on households that are not currently making direct use of the local schools? Not, surely, on collective consumption grounds. For parents who have previously had children enrolled in the schools or who will in the future, the levies are a means of spreading the differential cost over one's working life. A long-term bank loan, tied in with school support based on user charges, would yield approximately the same results. However, for households that are childless or that will make exclusive use of private institutions, there is an obvious interest in seeing school tax bills reduced, and the so-called "lighthouse school districts," with their wealthy, middle-aged pattern of residence, include many such voters. Even for active parents, the shift to privately administered schools has attractive features: simple residence in the district would not entitle a child to membership in the school (one feature of "publicness"); hence, schools could be more socially selective in admissions. Also, private institutions possess greater flexibility in hiring staff than public.

The burden of these remarks is that allegiance of upper-middle-income families to the public educational system is tenuous; so much so, in fact, that *Serrano* may deal it a fatal blow. Why should anyone care? What would such a shift mean for the educational system as a whole? There appear to be three causes for concern.

First, this country has avoided developing any important class-based hierarchy of elementary-secondary schools, by type. Nonsecular private institutions have sufficiently small total enrollment as to be counted as quite special cases, and secular institutions stand in some isolation nowadays from the mainstream of American life. Admittedly, some public schools are better than others, but for present argument, this is beside the point. What is important is that when a public high school graduate from a low-income family applies for college admission, say, he is subject to no systematic bias on grounds that he attended a public school; after all, this same type of school is used in full measure by high-income families, even though they have the means to choose private institutions. In many other countries public schools are thought to be basically inferior to privately managed ones, and this attitude is a barrier to social mobility, and dilutes the effectiveness of the screening—or "talent search"—function of the educational system.

Second, rich families hold political power disproportionately to their numbers. Up until now, many of them have been advocates of public school spending. My observation indicates that well-to-do families display greater interest in seeing legislative appropriations for schools raised to higher levels than do poor families. Should the rich shift to private education, they might not be so keen to press state legislators for larger appropriations.

Finally, there is the "lighthouse school district" argument, holding that income-rich, property-rich districts, such as Scarsdale and Shaker Heights, provide necessary leadership in displaying the attributes of superior educational services. This argument is used by the rich to defend the privileged status of their schools within the public sector, but it retains a certain validity in assuring that public schools are not as rule-bound and bureaucratic as they might otherwise be.

FSF and DPE appear to deal quite differently with high-expenditure districts. Under the Fleischmann (New York State) version of FSF, high-spending districts are frozen at their existing levels of expenditure per student. In exchange for such loss of power—that is, to balance the district budget from local taxable resources—most high-spending districts receive school property tax reductions. The proposed statewide school tax rate of $2.04 per $100 of full value assessment would produce the tax reductions in selected Nassau and Westchester County districts, as shown in Table 5-1. Note that the districts shown are all relatively rich in taxable property, yet they receive tax reductions under *Serrano* reform.[11]

Offsetting the reduction in school property taxes would be increases

Table 5-1.   Tax Reductions, High-Wealth Suburban Districts, under Full State Funding, New York State, 1970-71

District	Full Value Assessed Valuation per Student	Change in School Tax Rate ($s per $100 of Full Value Assessment)
Glen Cove	$44,938	−$0.415
Hempstead	70,454	−0.255
Great Neck	85,476	−0.750
Oyster Bay	78,374	−0.220
Mount Kisco	68,957	−0.305
Bronxville	88,480	−0.020
Briarcliff Manor	49,235	−1.615
Scarsdale	67,427	−0.545
State Average	$36,996	$0.0

in broad-based state taxes, such as income and sales taxes. The total bill for Fleischmann educational changes is $1 billion, a 20 percent rise in public elementary-secondary expenditures. Since the incidence of the property tax is U-shaped with respect to household income, a shift toward state income and sales taxation might be seen by rich households as a good step in any case.[12]

In the version of DPE presented to the California Senate Select Committee, rich districts retain the power to set whatever level of school budget they wish, but they are obliged to move their school tax rates up quite far if their spending is to be in any way unusual. Our preferred response function shows changes in Beverly Hills and Carmel, as indicated in Table 5-2.[13] Beverly Hills has an 82.5 percent rise in school tax to maintain a program costing $368 less per student than its 1970-71 level; in Carmel, the tax rate goes up 46 percent to defend a budget showing a $162 per student decline.

Our general approach to the rich district problem in California was along the following line. Suppose a household with one child in public school lives in a house with a market value of $60,000. Assessed value, 25 percent of market, is $15,000. Twelve hundred dollars of noncategorical spending per K-6

Table 5-2.   Financial Effects of District Power Equalizing on Two Rich California Districts, 1970-71

District	1970-71 Status		DPE Plan	
	Expenditure per Pupil	School Tax Rate	Expenditure per Pupil	School Tax Rate
Beverly Hills	$1770	$3.164	$1402	$5.773
Carmel	1240	2.996	1078	4.375

equivalent student (approximately) equals Beverly Hills' $1,770 in resources per pupil in 1970-71. Minimum statewide school property tax is set at $2.50 (see Figure 5-1 above). Incremental tax rate to provide $1,200 of noncategorical funds per student is $4 for $700 (normal expenditure point), plus 5 times $1 ($1 in tax rate for each $100 rise in spending above $700), equals $9, minus $2.50 statutory minimum, equals $6.50. On the property assessed at $15,000, this is an incremental tax bill of $975. Hence, the household could continue to enjoy a program similar to that of Beverly Hills at an optional school tax bill of less than the, say, $1,400 a year a good private school would charge in fees. However, the private school option becomes more attractive as house value rises, though the breakeven point obviously depends on how many children of school age the family has. And, until the legal status of tax credits and tax deductions for tuition fees is clarified, only the public school contribution offers real benefits to the household or payer of federal income tax.

Under reform of education finance, the state presents wealthy householders who live in property-rich districts two quite distinct alternatives. These alternatives, indeed, may be regarded as mutually exclusive. In the first instance, the state would take action to stabilize school property tax rates in such districts (possibly after giving local taxpayers an initial reduction); at the same time the state would demand that these districts accept state control over the level of *district* expenditures per student. Under the second alternative the state would allow residents of rich districts to retain control of school budgets, while requiring them to make substantial contributions through additional local property taxes to pay for educational programs in poorer districts. It probably does not make sense to ask which option the rich would prefer; for one thing, they are not likely to be of a single mind, and, for another, much might depend on the details of a given version of FSF or DPE. And surely opinions would shift over time.

Within the framework of alternative responses to *Serrano*, what actions are wealthy households likely to take? As for Fleischmann's version of FSF, I suggest that they will do the following: (1) plead for the modification of the plan to include an optional local add-on. If the add-on is unlimited in absolute amount, or unlimited as a percentage of a benchmark per-student figure, it would probably violate Proposition I of *Serrano*. If limited, a *de minimus* argument might prevail. To conform with *Serrano*, any substantial add-on should be power equalized. (2) Urge the state to increase the size of its educational budget. Sooner or later, new money would flow to rich districts and, although the new money might not do much to preserve their relative position over other districts, it would allow them to provide salary increases to their (presumably) superior teachers who had loyally remained in their employ. (3) Begin to employ tutors for private after-school instruction. (4) If none of the above satisfied, use private institutions exclusively.

My own assessment is that none of the first three actions would be especially damaging to the fabric of the public education system. Indeed, action 3, purchase of supplementary educational services, could be beneficial in the long run. Basic study would occur during the ordinary school day, and supplementary programs would cater to the individual student's special tastes and talents. It would be a form of de-schooling, paid for by those who could afford it in the form of user charges. If the idea of supplementary education programs caught on in the suburbs, it should be possible to extend such programs into central cities on a voluntary enrollment basis, but there the programs, I believe, should be provided mainly free of charge. This general approach would give the consumer a greater degree of choice in the public sector.

As for DPE, wealthy households would be likely to urge the legislature to increase the slope of the DPE schedule in order to produce more dollars of spending in the school district for any given increase in district tax rate. Unfortunately, this action makes it very tempting for low-wealth districts to raise their expenditures to high levels. The consequences for the state budget are costly in the extreme, but the situation is not so bad as if the large cities are low-wealth districts; on the contrary, most large cities are middle- to high-wealth places.

To succor the state budget under a "soft" district power equalizing schedule, the smaller high-wealth districts might press for increases in the statewide minimum school property levy. There are two problems here: one is that some cities might be caught in a larger property tax contribution than they wish to make; another is that rural districts, often characterized by low expenditures *and* low tax rates, would almost surely be adversely affected, meaning that marginal farmers would give up cultivation.

Thus, DPE seems to offer less room for the public-private com-promise of FSF to be worked out (under which richer parents would use the public schools for basics and purchase supplementary services in the private market), because even to supply suitable basic programs in the public schools would call for substantial local tax rate increases. The choice is between high local taxes for schools plus fees for private supplements as against opting for the minimum permissible tax rate and use of private institutions for all educational services. Given the general appeal, as I see it, of private institutions for rich households, I suspect the latter choice would come to be the preferred one over time. DPE, then, requires the rich to engage in more effective manipulation of statewide educational policy to protect themselves than does FSF; for with the latter, even if statewide actions fail, the public-private compromise remains financially feasible. Residents of Scarsdale and Great Neck could simply convert their school tax reductions under FSF into private purchase of supplementary services.

It can be argued, of course, that rich households would find FSF the easier plan to cope with because expenditures per student are maintained at their existing levels in all high-expenditure districts. This might be described as a peculiar and possibly undesirable feature of the Fleischmann proposals. If, indeed, the "save harmless" feature was to be dropped, the required statewide school property tax rate could be reduced by 10 percent (approximately). Fleischmann assumed it would be much more important to citizens of high-expenditure districts to keep their programs in place than to have a slightly lower statewide tax rate. Furthermore, the Fleischmann Commission did not think it appropriate that the state order districts to cut their expenditures drastically—in a number of cases the cuts would have been in the order of 50 percent—because contractual relationships on one hand, and layout of physical plant on the other, make such adjustments extremely difficult to carry out. The commission assumed that if its proposals came under court scrutiny, the "save harmless" feature would be permitted to stand under the argument that the state, by freezing expenditures in high expenditure districts while allowing rates of spending in all other places gradually to move upward, had demonstrated intent to comply with criteria of equity within a reasonable space of time.

Three general observations seem to apply to responses of rich householders to *Serrano*, somewhat independently of the nature of the reform plan imposed. First, the rich are more likely to remain in the public system if the state share of educational expenditures is large. Second, provision of optional educational services by public regional authorities, satisfying the demands of students who have strong tastes for educational programs, will likewise help to retain the allegiance of the wealthy. Regional programs funded on any sensible basis will meet *Serrano* criteria, optional enrollments notwithstanding, and through economies of scale, regional authorities *could* offer higher quality and greater diversity in courses than almost any fulltime private institution, all at no great burden to the taxpayer. Third, allegiance of rich households to the public education sector could be seriously damaged if tax credits or even tax deductions for education fees are generally accepted. The primary advocates of such measures are leaders of private secular educational establishments who are facing great financial problems of their own. However, the primary beneficiaries, given *Serrano*, might be the nonsecular private institutions.

The Definition of Public Educational Expenditures

In district power equalizing schemes, local government have strong incentives to shift service responsibilities among different local agencies. The roots of the problem, of course, are (1) that something called "school expenditures" is power equalized, and other local services, even though subject to various forms of state subsidy, are generally not; and (2) that there is considerable overlap in services provided by different local agencies (both school and library departments offer library services, both school and health departments offer health services to young people, and so on).

In the main, one would expect all districts in which the schedule of school expenditures to local school tax rates is steeper than the state's DPE schedule (property-rich districts) would seek to shift expenditures out of the school department into other agencies. Districts whose own school-expenditure to tax-rate schedule is flatter than the state's DPE contract would try to push expenditures into the school department and away from other agencies. *Serrano*-pure DPE school finance is definitely nonneutral with respect to the distribution of responsibilities among local governments[14] (see Figure 5-2).

Interdepartmental shifts in property-rich districts are probably

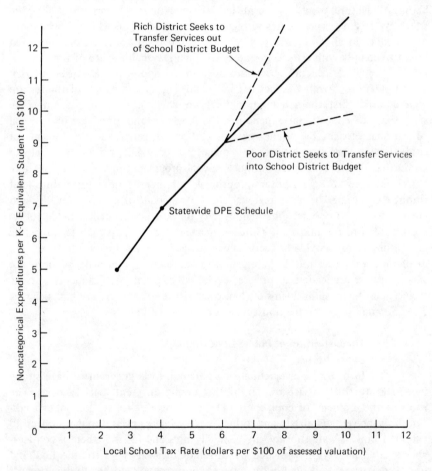

Figure 5-2. Effect of DPE on Administrative Allocations of Related Services.

impossible to regulate closely. School services in all such districts in their various components are likely to be above statewide standards. Suppose, then, in Beverly Hills the school department and the library department reach agreement that henceforth library expansion will take place primarily in the budget of the library department, with due attention to making department services available to school children. On what grounds could such action be held improper? And how could intent to evade the affects of DPE on a rich district be proved? Similar shifts could occur between the school department and the health and recreation departments. However, in the case of property-rich districts, I see little reason for concern about damage to young people. The shifting, probably inevitable, is one means that the well-to-do will use to protect themselves from *Serrano* and can slow down their departure from the public school system.

In property-poor districts, the problem is both more serious and more complex. Assume that many such districts are inhabited by households of low income and that the schools in these districts have disproportionate numbers of students who are performing poorly. The effect of *Serrano*-style DPE is to reduce the "price," measured as incremental tax rates relative to incremental expenditures per head, of services managed by the school department compared with the "prices" of services managed by other local departments. By operation of substitution effects, one can expect the size of school department operations to grow relative to the scale of activities elsewhere in the local public sector.

If the school department, because of its preferred budgetary position, takes on health services for young people of equal or improved caliber to those previously offered by the health department, then the *Serrano* reform may have caused no damage, at least. It seems likely, however, that there will be a shift away from nonschool services toward conventional educational expenditures within the whole local government structure. That is, although the school department takes on *some* services that formerly were supplied by the health department, most of its newfound income will be devoted to conventional educational activities. Other local departments, meanwhile, are forced to contract or, at the least, to expand less than they would have, because of their unfavorable price position relative to educational services.

Yet to shift resource allocations toward the educational services and away from other local social services may be precisely the wrong kind of tradeoff to improve the lot of low-income students—specifically, to help them raise their school performance.

> Equality of opportunity cannot be provided by the schools alone; its disadvantaged young student is too much affected by his home and neighborhood environment. . . . If housing conditions, open green spaces, libraries, youth centers, cultural programs and cheap, clean urban public transport, as well as good teachers and attractive schools, are important to provide equality of opportunity, then we must recognize . . . responsibility . . . to respect the interrelatedness

of home, workplace, shops, recreational facilities, and means of transport.[15]

More recently, Henry M. Levin has written that

> it is probable that the law of diminishing marginal returns is applicable to the (capital embodiment) investment function such that concentration on any single source of investment will be wasteful or at least less optimal than dividing investment over all the requisite inputs. A second assumed property . . . is that the effect of any additional input through one source of investment will probably depend upon the levels of investment from other sources. For example, a child with inadequate nutrition or medical care (e.g., untreated vision problems) will likely have a much greater difficulty in learning for any level of instructional inputs than a child who has received higher levels of investment in nutrition and medical care. . . . Both of these properties suggest that if equality must be brought about through educational policy alone, then educational services must include far more than *instructional services.*[16]

Since budgets of local education departments are concentrated traditionally on *instructional services*, there is a danger that *Serrano*, as a partial solution to the whole problem of local government finance, will hinder the progress of low-income students in property-poor districts by directing resources into the formal educational sector at the expense of services more productive at the margin: nutrition, medical care, nonschool libraries, youth centers, housing renovation, and the like. The problem is made worse in such states as California, which have restrictive education codes under which school districts are forbidden to undertake any action not expressly allowed to them by law. In contrast, some states, such as Minnesota, grant powers to school districts to vote funds for any service not expressly forbidden to their control. The Minneapolis school district operates a residential summer camp over 200 miles from the city. In Berkeley, the summer music camp attended by children in the Berkeley public schools is run by the city recreation department. It is not at all clear whether the Berkeley Unified School District could take over the operation of Cazadero Music Camp.

To some extent, these same problems are to be found in FSF. For example, educational improvements in districts being leveled up to statewide expenditure standards might be siphoned off as cities and towns sought to move programs now handled by other municipal departments into the school budget. In summary, *Serrano* poses a major problem for allocation of public resources in property-poor districts—districts that once were thought to be the primary beneficiaries of the *Serrano* dicta.

Poor Households in Property-Rich Districts

The argument of *Serrano* is that state governments have allowed property-rich districts to retain undue advantages in financing educational services. It follows that reform must penalize rich districts by some means, at least in the sense of removing their favored position with regard to property-poor districts. Under DPE, it is reasonable to expect that all or practically all property-rich districts will find it necessary to increase their school tax rates. Yet, substantial numbers of very poor households live in property-rich school districts. Some indication of the magnitude of the problem is shown in Table 5-3, which shows the distribution of the lowest quartile of single-family homeholders (assessed value of house less than $4376) in an eight-county California sample, by change in tax rate required under the recommended version of DPE. Of these low value homes, 48 percent would be subject to a tax increase, and 15 percent would have an increase of more than $2.50 (per $100 of assessed valuation) at a time when the average school tax rate in California is slightly less than $5.

It might appear that full state funding is free of the problem, for as noted in Table 5-1, property-rich districts in, for example, New York, generally

Table 5-3. Distribution of Lowest-Quartile Single-Family Houses (Assessed Value Less Than $4,376) by Amount of Change in School District Tax Rate Due to Ordinary DPE[a]

Increase in Tax Rate	Number of Homes	Percent of Homes	Mean Assessed Value
More than $3.00	71	0	$3,528
$2.50 to 3.00	30,512	15	3,812
2.00 to 2.50	374	0	3,130
1.50 to 2.00	2,443	1	2,866
1.00 to 1.50	8,286	4	3,863
0.50 to 1.00	12,126	6	2,511
0 to 0.50	46,759	22	3,605
−0.05 to 0	40,572	19	3,378
−1.00 to −0.50	35,251	17	3,729
−1.50 to −1.00	33,884	16	3,830
−2.00 to −1.50	202	0	4,316
−2.50 to −2.00	0	0	−
−3.00 to −2.50	0	0	−
less than −3.00	0	0	−

[a]Relates to residential property in the following counties of California: Alameda, Contra Costa, Kern, Marin, San Francisco, San Mateo, Santa Barbara, and Santa Clara.

Source: Charles S. Benson et al., *Final Report to the Senate Select Committee on School District Finance* (Sacramento: Senate Education Committee, 1972), p. 83.

receive local tax reductions. However, Table 5-2 refers to suburban "lighthouse" districts. In New York, large cities are property-rich in school finance terms, mainly because of their heavy parochial school enrollments. Large cities are usually demanded to raise school tax rates under the Fleischmann proposals, with the required increase in Buffalo being especially great. Aside from depressed rural areas, most poor people live in large cities, so FSF also presents problems. It would be ironic in the extreme if the chief short-term effect of *Serrano* were to raise the amount of local taxes collected from the very poorest part of our population.

In my opinion, a property tax circuit-breaker is the proper way to handle this transitional problem. Our proposal in California would modify an existing Senior Citizen Property Tax Relief Act as follows.

1. Removal of the age restriction currently set at age 62.
2. Provision for relief to renters and owners of cooperatives and multiple-family units.
3. Redefinition of relief ceiling.
4. Redefinition of methods of claiming relief.

"Claimant" means an individual who has filed a claim under this plan, is a member of a household and was a resident of California on or before the first day of January preceding the end of the fiscal year for which a claim for assistance is filed. "Income" is defined as the sum for all members of the household of adjusted gross income as used for purposes of the California Personal Income Tax Laws.

The proportion of property taxes to be reimbursed by the state is based on the claimant's household income, as shown in Table IV [5-4]. For the purpose of this plan, "property taxes accrued" is defined for homeowners as current property taxes (exclusive of interest, penalties, principal payments on improvements, bonds, and charges for service) levied against a claimant's homestead by any taxing agency. Assistance is equal to the applicable percentage applied to "property taxes accrued" of an amount up to and including $600. No assistance is allowed on that portion of the tax bill in excess of $600. The $600 ceiling on the relief plan is based on the median full value of dwellings in California in 1971, which was approximately $23,000. Assuming an average tax rate of $10 per $100 of assessed valuation (25 percent of full value), the average tax payment on median dwellings is $575, rounded to $600.

For owners of cooperatives or owners of a homestead where such homestead is an integral part of a large unit such as a farm or a multipurpose or multidwelling building, "property tax accrued" is that percentage of the total property taxes accrued as the value of the homestead is of the total value. In no case is assistance allowed for property taxes paid in excess of $600.

For renters, "property taxes accrued" is defined as a representative

Table 5-4. Percentage of Property Tax to be Reimbursed by the State, Depending on Household Income

If the total household income is not more than	The percentage of the first $600 of levied property taxes to be reimbursed or credited is:
$1,000	96%
1,500	92
2,000	92
2,500	88
3,000	80
3,500	70
4,000	60
4,500	52
5,000	45
5,500	38
6,000	32
6,600	26
7,000	21
7,500	16
8,000	12
8,500	8
9,000	6
9,500	5
10,000	4

amount equal to 4 percent of income. This figure assumes that, on average, gross rent is about 25 percent of income and property taxes about 20 percent of gross rent. Thus property taxes on average would represent 5 percent of income. But allowing all renters to claim property taxes equal to 5 percent of income would overstate the tax paid by some renters. Therefore it seems preferable to let any renter claim a standard allowance for imputed property taxes equal to 4 percent, without having to submit any evidence of the actual amount of rent paid. A household that really did pay more than 20 percent of its income for rent could claim imputed property taxes equal to 20 percent of actual rent paid, but it would also be required to furnish documentation of actual rent paid. This procedure gives renters the same kind of choice between standard or itemized deductions in claiming property tax relief that is now provided for anyone filing an income tax return. The amount of relief shall equal the applicable percentage from Table IV [5-4] applied to the imputed amount of property tax up to and including $600.

The procedure for claiming relief would use the administrative

machinery of the state income tax. Regardless of actual income tax
liability, each California resident desiring property tax relief would
file an income statement with the Franchise Tax Board between
January 1 and April 15. Prior to but no later than the following
November 1, the Franchise Tax Board would return to eligible
homeowners a statement verifying the amount of adjusted gross
income reported. Property tax bills mailed the first week in November would include instructions for claiming relief. The taxpayer
would calculate his property tax liability using the enclosed income
table and return the Franchise Tax Board verification with his check.
    . . . A renter claiming relief would simply submit a regular income
statement, which would have a place to check whether this renter
chose to count imputed property taxes as 4 percent of income or 20
percent of actual rent paid. The board would calculate his relief,
credit it against his state income tax liability and refund any excess
to the renter.
    A special problem arises for welfare recipients. Federal regulations
require reducing welfare payments by an amount equivalent to cash
income received. . . . A solution to this problem is available by
directing individual relief to Welfare Offices with the stipulation that
it be added to the individual's shelter allowance for "unmet shelter
needs."[17]

    The relief for poor households would apply to the total tax rate.
Hence, cities could improve services through local taxation free of concern that
too harsh a burden was being placed on low-income families, including retirees
who live in rented quarters. In earlier years in California, large cities were able to
export a portion of their municipal overburden by overassessing industrial and
commercial properties relative to residential. This is no longer permitted. The
circuit-breaker, however, opens the way to heavier taxation than at present of
nonresidential holdings and of residential properties enjoyed by rich householders. It is the intention, of course, that local losses in revenue occasioned by
poor taxpayers claiming relief would be made up by the state from general
revenue sources.
    There are other ways to take care of poor householders in the face
of *Serrano* reform. One possibility is to use average household income as the
measure of local taxable capacity in education funding schemes, instead of
assessed valuation per student. In industrial tax havens, this procedure would
offer unusual tax benefits to owners of nonresidential property and, indeed,
defeat the intent of *Serrano* to bring such holdings up to paying their fair share
(by statewide standards) of educational costs. This consideration leads to the
proposal that nonresidential property be taxed at a statewide rate. But for what
services? If for education, why not all local? Yet it may be important to retain
some incentives in local governments to strengthen their fiscal position by

attracting industry to their sites. Splitting the tax rate, moreover, runs afoul of constitutional tax provisions in some states, including, possibly, California. It seems probable that such fundamental changes in the state-local fiscal structure as the one now being discussed should not be initiated simply to shore up an inequitable revenue structure for a single local service, even the most expensive one, but should come about through a general overhaul of the state's financial system.

A yet stronger district-wide measure is to use household income as the measure of local fiscal capacity, at the same time introducing a progressive DPE schedule, under which richer districts would be entitled to smaller increments in expenditures per student for any given local tax rise than poor districts.[18] As one would expect, such a measure does not offer as much protection as the circuit-breaker to low-income households in wealthy districts, since progressive DPE is bound to give rougher treatment to rich districts than ordinary DPE does. However, it is reasonable to say that the circuit-breaker is a more precise instrument than progressive DPE. Average household income in most large cities, after all, does not depart far from the statewide average, and the relief afforded by progressive DPE is attuned to that fact.

Financial Requirements of Large Cities

It is a commonplace of social-policy thought in America that large cities are in serious financial difficulty. Pressed by newly militant public employees' unions, faced with problems of crime, violence, air pollution, deteriorating neighborhoods, drug abuse, poorly functioning schools, racial antagonisms that forestall attempts to achieve a more rational allocation of public resources, inadequacies of public transport, and so on, cities see that even federal revenue sharing on the scale now planned is utterly insufficient to meet their needs. The concern is then expressed that compliance with *Serrano* dicta will somehow make the financial difficulties of the cities even more serious. Why should it?

Here we reach an anomaly. By conventional standards of measuring local capacity to support educational services, many cities appear to be rich, not poor. Assessed valuation per student commonly stands above state average and, in some cases—for example, New York and San Francisco—quite far above. The reason is partly that cities have, almost by definition, large amounts of taxable, nonresidential property, and office buildings send no children to the schools. Second, cities frequently have an unusually large population of children enrolled in private schools, especially the secular schools, and when wealth is measured in relation to public school attendance only, cities are made to appear to be richer than they actually are, for the private school students do represent an educational cost. Third, measurement of local wealth is frequently based on attendance, and this penalizes the cities, given their high rates of truancy and within-year dropouts.

If cities fall into the category of high-wealth districts, then compliance with Proposition I of *Serrano* may demand that they raise their school tax rates. The Fleischmann full state funding recommendations require school tax increases in eleven of the twenty-one districts in New York having more than 12,500 public school enrollments (1970-1971 figures), and this includes all of the five largest (see Table 5-5). These changes should be viewed in comparison with statewide average tax rates of $2.04. This is the price demanded of large cities in New York to buy their way into a statewide system of educational finance.

City authorities naturally would prefer to avoid such school tax increases. They point out that the cities have high nonschool expenditures; they therefore claim that the share of local tax base available for schools is smaller in cities than in suburbs. This argument leads easily to the proposal that differentials in necessary costs of nonschool services be capitalized out of the given city's tax base in computing a kind of nominal school tax rate. The difficulty with this approach is determining criteria for necessary costs; also, one may question whether the burden of correction for deficiencies in finance of the general range of municipal services should fall on the education grant structure alone. Cities are not uniformly afflicted with municipal overburden, and the attempt to deal with noneducational finance questions through education grants might well be too blunt an instrument to make the proper distinctions among different concentrations of population.[19]

On the other hand, cities have exceptional necessary costs within the educational sector itself. These fall into two categories: (1) high prices to be paid for educational resources (land, buildings and their maintenance, possibly teachers' salaries, and so on); and (2) extra services required to meet educational needs of urban youth (services for handicapped children, for the non-English-speaking, and the like).[20] These costs are recognized by Fleischmann by an extra weighting in the main full state funding proposal for students whose achievement scores are low; by new and enlarged categorical aid programs outside the main formula; and by shifting provision of a number of high-cost

Table 5-5. School Tax Increases, 1970-71, Associated with Full State Funding of Public Education, New York State, Five Largest Districts

District	Tax Rate Increase, $s per $100 of Full Value Assessment
Buffalo	+ $0.60
Rochester	+ .33
New York City	+ .15
Syracuse	+ .39
Yonkers	+ .30

programs (certain vocational, handicapped, construction, and so on) to regional authorities, to be financed by broad-based tax instruments.

Full state funding proposals have advantages for the cities once the transition to the new school tax rate is accomplished. First, cities would thereafter be protected from having to make local tax increases to meet increases in urban educational costs; this becomes especially important in light of expected declines in the size of parochial school enrollments.[21] Second, cities are thereafter freed from the stigma of being high-wealth districts able to meet their exceptional educational needs from their own resources. Cities would be able to make a clear case for extra state school funds to meet their high necessary costs. Third, FSF implies statewide collective bargaining, and it is probable that statewide bargaining would moderate the rise in big-city teacher costs.[22]

In the California version of DPE, major cities, except San Francisco, fare well so long as compensatory education grants (priced at $500 million annually) are combined with the noncategorical grant scheme.[23] It is my opinion that when the circuit-breaker proposal is added in, even San Francisco becomes a winner, but I cannot offer a final statement on this point until we are able to use household income data by school districts, from the 1970 *Census of Population*. In short, the transition process is easier on cities under DPE in California than it is under FSF in New York. The reason is not mainly attributable to the difference in funding mechanisms; it is rather that California compensatory education proposals are more closely geared to the needs of large cities; and, because of small parochial school populations, California cities do not have as differentially high assessed valuations per student (except San Francisco).[24]

In California, protection of the cities rests on the compensatory education proposals (primarily) and on the circuit-breaker (secondarily). What if these two features of the total package were to be stricken by the governor's item veto? If this is judged a strong possibility, then I would opt for (1) decentralization of large city school districts; and (2) DPE based on household income (as the measure of local fiscal capacity). However, to maximize the inflow of state funds to urban areas under such procedures requires maximizing social stratification of newly decentralized districts. As is often the case, one would face a tradeoff of social values.

ALTERNATIVE PHASING-IN TECHNIQUE

It is the general view that the public responds badly to sudden change and that transitional problems are eased if legislation required gradual shifts only.[25] Accordingly, plans developed in response to *Serrano* allow a certain amount of time to occur before full implementation is obtained. The phasing-in techniques of Fleischmann FSF and California Senate Select Committee Report DPE and a very slow form of phasing-in for the DPE that has been considered in Connecticut will now be discussed.

Fleischmann full state funding. On the expenditure side, the leveling up of districts to the 65th percentile and the weighting of low-achieving students at 1.5 for calculation of grants are intended to take place immediately at a cost to the state budget of approximately $590 million. Achievement of equality in basic expenditures per student will take a considerable period of years, according to plan, and will occur as inflationary forces push the statewide normal expenditure level upward (as stated, set initially at the 65th percentile of district average spending per student). If the state does not find it necessary to allow the "save harmless" districts relief (from time to time) with respect to their absolute budgetary spending limit (per student)—and this is a big if—I estimate that about twelve years would be required to achieve approximate equality in basic normal expenditures per student across the state.

On the revenue side, the circuit-breaker is intended to go into effect immediately at a cost to the state in forgone property tax revenues of approximately $125 million. The change to the statewide school property tax rate ($2.04 per $100 of full value assessment) is to occur in equal increments over a five-year period. That is, districts now taxing themselves at higher than $2.04 will receive equal decrements toward that rate for five years; those now undertaxing themselves would come up to the $2.04 in "five easy steps."

District power equalizing as proposed to California Senate Select Committee. This plan provided for a short phasing-in period—three years only. The technique can best be understood by referring back to Figure 5-1. In any year of the DPE plan, a district may choose any expenditure level above the minimum grant of $500 per K-6 equivalent. A district can go up to the normal expenditure level of $700 per K-6 equivalent by raising its tax rate from the $2.50 minimum to $4. These rates, it should be noted, apply to unified districts (elementary and secondary combined) only. Rates for other types of districts are shown in the main report.

In the first year of DPE a district can raise additional funds above $700 per K-6 equivalent based on local wealth. In the second year the wealth equalized range is extended to $1 per K-6 equivalent; that is, each additional $100 of expenditure per K-6 equivalent up to $1000 requires (in a unified district) a $1 increase in the tax rate. In the second year of DPE, districts would still support noncategorical expenditures above $1000 per K-6 equivalent by taxes on local wealth. Finally, from the third year on, all expenditures are fully wealth equalized. A district can obtain any expenditure level above $700 per K-6 equivalent by raising its tax rate $1 (in a unified district) for each additional $100 per K-6 equivalent.

Connecticut DPE plan. The Connecticut Governor's Commission on Tax Reform has considered a linear DPE plan that provides an extremely gradual phasing-in period. In this respect, it stands in marked contrast to the California plan. In Connecticut DPE, each school district would have its own DPE schedule. Initially, this is nothing more than its locally raised operating revenue per student, stated in relation to its own set of property tax rates. Phasing-in would occur as the state claimed all local school revenues attributable to increases in local valuations and redistributed them to the districts. About half of the yield from increments in value of taxable property would be used to increase the fictional yield of school property taxation in all districts equally, and this part of the distribution is intended to allow rich, high-spending districts, among others, to meet inflationary pressures. The other part of the state distribution would go only to the poorest half of the districts in Connecticut (as measured by property valuation per student) and in proportion to their lack of wealth. The statewide average school tax yield would be recomputed each year to help determine the amount of extra "taxing power" each of the poorest half districts is to receive.

It is estimated that in ten to fifteen years after the start of the program about 90 percent of the districts would have power equalized schedules that would differ from each other by no more than 10 percent. The plan apparently never would produce identical schedules for all districts—at least not in this century. The Connecticut plan does not force changes in expenditures or tax rates; hence, it is relatively free, one would say, of transitional problems. However, the question of whether so mild an implementation process meets Proposition I of *Serrano* remains open. Resolutions of that kind of question may remain for the courts to determine.

NOTES

1. See *Report of the New York State Commission on the Quality, Cost, and Financing of Elementary and Secondary Education* (Manly Fleischmann, Chairman), Vol. I (New York: Viking Press, 1973), hereafter referred to as the *Fleischmann Report*; and Charles Benson et al., *Final Report to the Senate Select Committee on School District Finance*, (Sacramento: California Senate Education Committee, 1972).

2. Some full state funding proposals, such as the one laid out by the President's Commission on School Finance, *Schools, People, and Money* (Washington, 1972), pp. 33-37, allow local districts to make limited supplements to their school budgets. The Fleischmann proposal does not, on the grounds that local supplements would lead to a re-creation of the present inequitable system.

3. While it would have been more exact to make the ranking of annual expenditures in terms of students rather than in terms of districts, the use of the districts as the unit gave the commission a proposal that was easier to explain to the public.

4. For technical reasons, tuition payments were also excluded, as were state payments for "urban aid."

5. *Fleischmann Report*, p. 2.12. Of course, as is now clear, it was not seen possible to bring about such equalization of expenditures immediately. The commission did not wish to propose that any district be required to reduce its expenditures, and state budgetary constraints ruled out raising all districts to the expenditure level of the highest—hence, the recommendation for "leveling up" to the 65th percentile only.

6. In its full report, the commission suggested other categorical grants and weightings too numerous to mention.

7. *Fleischmann Report*, p. 2.36. "State taxable income" in New York is income net of deductions for dependents and standard exemptions.

8. Because terms of reference of the California project were confined to financial matters, and the Fleischmann staff had to deal with the whole range of educational concerns, such recommendations were worked up in greater detail in California than in New York.

9. In the eastern United States, relatively greater use than elsewhere is made of private nonsectarian institutions. Yet, in 1969-70 in New York State, such institutions enrolled only 1.3 percent of the total K-12 school population. See Louis R. Gary et al., *The Collapse of Non-public Education: Rumor or Reality?* (a report prepared for the New York State Commission on Quality, Cost, and Financing of Elementary and Secondary Education, 1971), Vol. I, pp. I-5, I-6.

10. Carl S. Shoup, *Public Finance* (Chicago: Aldine Publishing Company, 1969), pp. 66-74.

11. This situation is generally characteristic of the school districts in Nassau, Westchester, Suffolk, and Rockland counties—the New York City suburban ring. It occurs as districts are both relatively rich (for New York State) and very high spending. But the *Serrano* argument does not apply in New York because the local tax rates in rich districts, though high by state standards, by no means justify their extraordinary levels of expenditure.

12. Charles L. Schultze et al., *Setting National Priorities: The 1973 Budget* (Washington: The Brookings Institution, 1972), p. 444.

13. The "preferred response function" represents the assumption that school districts under DPE will act so that the cost to the state of implementing the plan will lie between the maximum and minimum of possible costs. Maximum cost to the state would occur as wealthy school districts chose low local tax rates—say the rates prevailing when the plan was introduced—and poor districts chose high local rates—higher, say, than those required to maintain their existing levels of expenditure per student. Minimum cost to the state predicts just the opposite kind of actions in rich and poor districts. The "preferred response function" assumes a set of tax rates that gives a middle range estimate of how much DPE would cost the state.

14. On the other hand, there is some evidence that local governments are slow to respond to such fiscal incentives. Rhode Island has had a decade's experience with DPE, and the local government codes are reasonably permissive about the question of which units of local government can do what.

Yet, when James Kelly and I studied the operation of the Rhode Island plan in 1966, we could find little indication, for example, that school authorities had moved into new areas of service. There is a "lack of clear evidence that the opportunity provided by the open-ended matching grant to extend school services into relatively neglected, but socially crucial, areas has been seized." Special Commission to Study the Entire Field of Education, *The Rhode Island Comprehensive Foundation and Enhancement State Aid Program for Education* (Providence, 1966), p. 17. This begs the question, of course, of shifts in scale of particular services among local departments.

15. Charles S. Benson, *The Cheerful Prospect* (Boston: Houghton Mifflin, 1965), pp. 54-55.

16. Henry M. Levin, "Equal Educational Opportunity and the Distribution of Educational Expenditures," *Education and Urban Society* (February 1973), p. 161 (emphasis added).

17. Benson et al., *Final Report to the Senate Select Committee . . . ,* pp. 14-16. In preparing this proposal, we judged that administrative convenience was served by having homeowners claim their relief in their property tax bills while requiring renters to obtain their tax offsets or cash rebates through the state personal income tax machinery. Others may prefer that both sets of claimants obtain relief through state personal income tax submissions.

18. In the study for the California Senate outlined above, David S. Stern was chiefly responsible for the work on progressive DPE.

19. Harvey Brazer, *Fiscal Needs and Resources* (a report to the New York State Commission on the quality, cost and financing of elementary and secondary education, Albany, 1971), Chapter 4.

20. Cities have unusually large numbers of handicapped children for the very reason that they provide services for them, whereas many suburban communities do not. The cities are able to help in this way because of economies of scale, but, even so, cost per student remains high.

21. See Gary, *The Collapse of Non-public Education*, pp. II-3 to II-9.

22. When local authorities bargain with teachers, they bargain in part with the state's money. Increases in contract awards do not fall strictly on the local taxpayers. In statewide bargaining, big contract awards would be translated immediately into increases in state tax rates on sales and income, and political pressure against such increases is strong. Also, less "whipsawing" of bargaining units would be possible.

23. Benson et al., *Final Report to the Senate Select Committee . . . ,* pp. 82-83.

24. Both DPE and FSF were simulated in the California *Report*; hence, the statement is based on evidence, assuming the validity of our response functions.

25. On the other hand, the Watson initiative, which was defeated on the November 1972 ballot in California, was based on just the opposite idea.

Chapter Six

Effects of Expenditure Increases on Educational Resource Allocation and Effectiveness

Henry M. Levin
Stanford University

Can court-mandated edicts change deeply-rooted social and political behavior? Such a question must surely haunt the historian who would review the record of school segregation following the 1954 *Brown* decision. In 1972 the schools of the nation were more highly stratified racially than in 1954, despite almost twenty years of litigation, moral suasion, and social agitation over the issue. In this chapter it will be argued that *Serrano* and similar suits aimed at equalizing educational opportunity will result in a similar fate with little change in the educational fortunes of those students for whom the equal protection "victories" were allegedly intended. Unless a redistribution of expenditures is accompanied by a substantial redistribution of decisionmaking authority, the educational outcomes and life chances of those who are the ostensible recipients of higher expenditures will hardly be affected. In short, without massive changes in the political structure of our society, the *Serrano* decision has all of the earmarks of a bold and humanitarian gesture that will not produce the ultimate result that the court had in mind.[1]

For the last seventy years or so the schools have relied heavily on the local property tax for a major share of their support. Differences in the local property tax bases among geographic entities have resulted in substantially lower financial support for schools in some areas than others, and even assistance from state treasuries has not come close to equalizing expenditures among school districts. The result is that children who reside in property-tax-poor school districts have substantially less spent upon their schooling than those in richer districts; and paradoxically, the tax rates are often higher in the poor communities.[2] In essence, the California Supreme Court attacked this pattern in the *Serrano* decision by declaring that "this funding scheme invidiously discriminates against the poor because it makes the quality of a child's education a function of the wealth of his parents and neighbors."[3]

It is important to note that the court was concerned with the "quality of a child's education" and not expenditures per se. That is, the court operated on the tacit belief that a fairer system of educational support would lead to a more equal distribution of educational opportunities and outcomes. Thus *Serrano* and similar decisions can be approached at two levels: First, what kind of funding arrangement is consistent with the assertion of the court that the educational expenditures on a child should not be a function of the wealth of his parents and neighbors? And, second, what kind of administrative arrangement will translate increases in educational expenditures into concomitant improvements in the educational welfare of the intended beneficiaries?

Most of the responses to *Serrano* deal only with the first issue, equity in the distribution of expenditures and in the school tax system.[4] But *Serrano* and similar cases are ultimately concerned with a redistribution of educational opportunities among children, not just the redistribution of dollars among school districts. Accordingly, one should ask how the additional monies will be transformed into school services that will improve the educational and social outcomes for the target groups.

This chapter describes these linkages and scrutinizes their implications for increases in educational expenditures. First, I suggest what must be done to improve educational outcomes. Second, I review how the present structure for providing well educational services satisfies those requirements. Third, I explore a decision model and empirical evidence relating increased funding from higher levels of government to educational operations and outcomes. Finally, I describe policy conclusions from this analysis.

LINKING DOLLARS AND SCHOOLING OUTCOMES

The necessary and sufficient conditions for school budgets to be transformed into improved educational results are indicated in Figure 6-1, a simple flow diagram of the stages by which budgets are established and converted into educational resources and outcomes.[5] First, the polity determines through its governmental processes what budget will be provided for school purposes. In practice these decisions are made by the federal and state governments, and the thousands of local school districts or educational agencies that are responsible for existing funding arrangements. This diagram ignores such complexities by aggregating all of these decisions under the heading of a general polity.

Budgetary resources represent funding available for the general support of school services, but the monies themselves must be translated into specific resources that can be used in the schooling process. Thus, at the next stage the budget is used to pay for personnel services, facilities, instructional materials, and other educational resources. The marketplaces supply specific

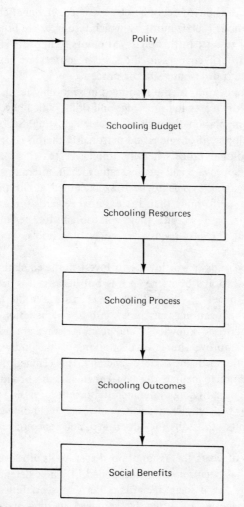

Figure 6-1. Translating Expenditures into Educational Outcomes and Social Benefits.

inputs—for teachers, administrators, special personnel, building and construction, and so on. Often these decisions are made in consultation with or through direct negotiations with the major personnel organizations; acting in behalf of their constituencies to influence employment levels, salaries, employee mobility, and other personnel policies.

The selected resources are combined into the schooling process to produce such outcomes as changes in attitudes, knowledge, reading and numerical proficiencies, values, and other aspects of student development. This process refers to the organization of schools, classes, and personnel configurations, as well as to the methods (curriculum) by which resources are brought together to obtain educational results. In this phase, attempts to improve schooling productivity are made through changes in the ways resources are used as well as by increasing the amount of resources in the process.

The application of the resources in schooling results in a variety of outcomes, notably increases in knowledge and skills, which have been the object of extensive documentation through achievement testing. Schools also have an effect on the development of values and personality factors. For example, in our society the educational process heavily emphasizes extrinsic rewards, such as gold stars, social approval, and grades rather than internal satisfaction. The process socializes young people to be less concerned about the nature of the work that they are performing than the external rewards (grades, status, wages, pensions, vacations, and so on) they will obtain for performing it.[6] Such outcomes represent the less-discussed aspects of schools, but they represent outcomes nevertheless.

Society finds it worthwhile to invest in the educational process, not because of the educational outcomes per se but because it is believed that these results yield social benefits.[7] Accordingly, the last stage of the transformation is the translation of educational outcomes into social benefits. Outputs of the schools such as increased knowledge and reading scores are useful only to the degree that they improve the level of welfare of the individuals who have achieved these results or of the society generally. It is claimed that the schooling sector increases national income through enhancing the productivity of workers,[8] improving the functioning of democratic society by raising political literacy and understanding of complex issues,[9] increasing technological advance and cultural attainments through the discovery and encouragement of latent talent,[10] and so on.

In recent years the assumption that schools produce this wide range of social benefits has been seriously questioned.[11] The existence of the schools is justified on the basis of social benefits rather than schooling outcomes per se. Since the social benefits are often far removed in time and space from the schooling outcomes, it is difficult to evaluate the role of different school policies on them. Thus, our evaluations often analyze the observable effects of schools on immediately measurable outcomes, such as achievement tests, and we assume that these outcomes are ultimately translated into social benefits. The analysis that follows is also handicapped by the lack of knowledge on ultimate social effects, so I limit my scrutiny of budgetary effectiveness to schooling outcomes rather than their ultimate social benefits.

In summary, the schema suggests that additional funding will affect schooling outcomes by providing more or different resources that will enter the schooling process, and that these additional resources will result in improvements in schooling outcomes. Thus, an analysis of the effects of higher spending should raise at least three questions: (1) How will additional budget dollars be allocated? (2) What changes will these allocations make in the schooling process? (3) What changes in schooling outcomes will take place? Any effort to enhance school outcomes should be reflected in the responses to these questions.

Under what conditions are additional monies likely to be transformed into improved school outcomes? In the past it has always been assumed that school decisionmakers would make financial decisions that would normally improve the effectiveness of their educational programs, but recent research and evaluation on the subject have not upheld this assumption.[12] Since efforts to equalize the finances available to school districts would necessarily provide considerably more dollar support for low-wealth and high-cost jurisdictions, one might ask how this money will be allocated. More specifically, what assumptions are necessary for the state to expect that additional financial support will have a powerful effect on educational results?

The conditions under which educational expenditures will translate into improved educational outcomes are fairly stringent. First, there must be substantial agreement on which outcomes are important; second, there must be knowledge of how added resources can be used to improve those outcomes; and third, those who are responsible for the educational process must have incentives to maximize the socially desirable outcomes. In each case, the actual situation seems to contrast with the assumptions that are necessary for added dollars to improve educational results.[13]

There are many divergent views on what constitutes good education. While there is general agreement that basic skills such as reading and arithmetic are important, some citizens view the primary role of schools as that of providing discipline and order in the lives of children, stimulating competition, and increasing respect for authority in order to prepare youngsters for the world of work. Still other groups view the role of the schools as helping children to become aware of their values and needs, to learn how to learn, and to increase interactions with viewpoints and persons with whom they would normally not have contact in a society that is highly segregated, both socially and racially. To the degree that these goals are in conflict, decisions must be made that will favor one set of objectives over another.

Even if agreement could be reached on goals, there is no body of knowledge that would guide decisionmakers in converting additional resources into improved outcomes. For example, it is asserted that most supplementary educational funding for children from low-income families is applied to improving academic performances of such children, a view that will be challenged below.[14] Yet, even if we accept the improvement of reading scores as one of the prime objectives, there is no body of literature that can describe with any reliability how changes in the amounts and organizations of inputs will raise reading levels. There is not even evidence to support the contention that reducing class size will improve such outcomes, even though that is the most common application of additional schooling dollars.[15]

Finally, it is difficult to see any direct relationship between the incentives provided to those responsible for the educational process and such educational outcomes as improved reading scores. Personnel in schools that fail to teach basic skills or motivate their students are not penalized in any way. They receive salary increases and seniority according to their longevity in the system rather than according to their accomplishments. Accordingly they have little incentive to conform to the aims of external school constituencies. Indeed, the lack of incentives for improving schooling outcomes also explains why schools are reluctant to innovate and experiment to discover new approaches that are more effective than the older ones.

THE ACTUAL DECISIONMAKING FRAMEWORK

There is no agreement on educational priorities, no body of knowledge that can predict the effects of different school policies on educational outcomes, and no relation between staff incentives and the rhetorical goals of schools. This all suggests that school budgets are not likely to be translated efficiently into improved educational outcomes. Rather, the actual application of the increased support is likely to be determined by the power and interests of the decision-makers themselves, and the factors determining these outcomes may be completely devoid of the educational concerns cited above.

It is useful, then, to review the decisionmaking scenario of the local educational agency (school district) with respect to the allocation of funds from higher levels of government. To see if the model we posit has good explanatory value, it is important to be able to apply it to an existing source of data. Accordingly, the following analysis refers to a model of decisionmaking that can be applied specifically to the experience derived from Title I allocations under the Elementary and Secondary Education Act of 1965.[16] Under this Act appropriations were distributed to the states to provide supplemental educational support for the schooling of children from low-income backgrounds. The applications from local educational agencies for these funds, as well as the subsequent audits and evaluations, provide reasonably good knowledge of how the money was allocated and which groups benefited.

The Model

The following model is designed to explain how local educational agencies spend money provided to them by state and federal governments. In this example, they are provided with an additional sum of money from state and federal sources to improve educational outcomes for disadvantaged children. We wish to raise several questions: Who are the major constituencies at the local level that have a strong interest in how the money is allocated? What are the goals of each of these constituencies? What is the relative power of each group, and what kinds of coalitions seem probable? Finally, what is the likely outcome of this scenario? That is, which goals are actually attained and which are sacrificed?[17]

Table 6-1 attempts to provide a heuristic approach to answering these questions. Six major constituencies are denoted, and their goals, relative power, and abilities to form coalitions are posited. In each case, constituency refers to a group with a common interest. This does not mean that every member of a group shares this interest—that is, there are many diverse views represented within a particular constituency—but if that group exhibits a consistent behavior that obscures these underlying diversities, then we assume that the consistencies adequately summarize the behavior of the group.

Constituencies, Goals, and Power

The six major constituencies in our model include: (1) local taxpayers; (2) parents of disadvantaged students; (3) disadvantaged students; (4) the school board; (5) teachers; and (6) administrators (see Table 6-1). Each of these groups has a legitimate interest in the allocation of revenues designated for the schooling of disadvantaged students.

1. Local taxpayers. The local taxpayers have an interest in transforming to higher levels of government as much support as possible for a function that might otherwise be provided, partly or fully, by local revenue sources. In particular, it is in the interest of local taxpayers to reduce or minimize the local tax burden for any particular level of educational services. To the degree that state and federal monies might be used for services that would otherwise be supported by the local taxpayers, this goal can be satisfied. For example, if funds for the education of the disadvantaged simply supplant funds that would have been allocated to such students, then the burden of the local taxpayer for supporting such services has been reduced. This goal has become especially important in recent years in light of highly visible and substantial rises in property tax burdens, the major source of local school support.

Although the goal of local taxpayers can be viewed reasonably as that of minimizing their tax burden, their power to effect that outcome is only

Table 6-1. Local Constituencies and the Decision for Allocating Increased Revenues from State or Federal Government

Constituency	Goal	Power	Coalition	Outcome
1 Local taxpayer	Minimize local burden	Moderate	With 4	Substitution of outside money for local
2 Disadvantaged parent	Improve educational outcomes for disadvantaged children	Low	No	No change
3 Disadvantaged student	Improve educational environment	Low	No	No change
4 School board	Minimize conflict	High	With 1 and 6	Low conflict
5 Teachers	Increase employment and job benefits	High	With 6	More employment
6 Administrators	Increase employment and minimize conflict	High	With 4 and 5	More employment low conflict

moderate in the sense that they are not a direct party to the allocation decision. Instead, the elected or appointed school board must do their bidding. Not only is the taxpayer somewhat removed from the actual decision negotiations but the sanction of electing different school board members or recalling the present ones is not very powerful because taxes are just one of many issues in school-board elections.

2. Disadvantaged parents. Parents of disadvantaged students represent a second constituency that has a direct interest in the allocation of state and federal funds for schooling disadvantaged youngsters. It seems reasonable to assume that their principal concerns are addressed to improving educational outcomes for their children, particularly proficiencies on standardized tests, and reducing the probabilities that their children will drop out. This goal derives from the widespread belief that these educational outcomes are related to economic and social success in the world at large; and if disadvantaged students are to raise their status, they must improve their educational attainments.

But the parents of disadvantaged students are themselves disadvantaged with regard to political and economic power; and they are not a first party to the allocation decision either. If taxpayers as a group lack substantial power in the allocation decision, the disadvantaged parent constituency is almost outside of the influence arena completely. They are not highly organized; they usually represent only a minority of the population; and for a variety of reasons (of which one is their own low educational attainment) their vote is disproportionately small even in relation to their numbers. Often they are represented by school boards who are elected at large, and they are very unlikely to win a majority of proponents under such conditions. Accordingly, they have little if any power to affect the allocation decision.

3. Disadvantaged student. The disadvantaged student is central—in theory—to the decision to allocate increased revenues to his education. Although his parents are more likely concerned with the end results of the educational process, he is likely to be more concerned with the process itself. Silberman characterized the schools as "grim joyless places. . . . How oppressive and petty are the rules by which they are governed, how intellectually sterile and esthetically barren the atmosphere, what an appalling lack of civility obtains on the part of teachers and principals, what contempt they unconsciously display for children as children."[18] Although Silberman viewed this description as characterizing most schools, its most poignant aspects seem to be especially applicable to schools attended by youngsters from low-income families, especially those drawn from minority backgrounds. For many, if not most, of these children, schools are just not very enjoyable places to be, and this fact is reflected in the lower attendance rates for such children as well as higher dropout statistics.

What power do disadvantaged students have to get funds channeled toward improving the educational environment? In most respects they are in the same relatively powerless position as their parents, only they are disenfranchised as well. Indeed, their only sanctions are those of cutting school, dropping out, disruption, and vandalism; and these actions can often lead to greater repression in the schools' never-ending quest to maintain control.

4. School board. In theory it is the school board that is responsible for making the decision for allocating increased revenues from state and federal governments to the schooling of disadvantaged youngsters. That is, the school board represents the legally sanctioned arm of the state for governing the local school district. But school boards are beset by many conflicting pressures and a substantial amount of administrative trivia without the resources and information to perceive clearly the educational implications of their decisions.[19] The immediate pressures are on the resolution of existing conflicts and claims among a variety of parent groups, taxpayer groups, employee groups, and various educational agencies, while they attempt to ameliorate future conflicts. Indeed, it appears that the principal goal of the school board is to minimize conflict, because the avoidance of obvious clashes implies a high degree of control and competence in guiding the rudder of school policy.[20]

The school board has a substantial amount of power to avoid or minimize conflict on allocation matters. It can limit the items that appear on the agenda; it can refer potential problems to the bureaucracy to resolve; it can fail to provide information on school performance to the public when such information is likely to spur a controversy; it can be "selective" in determining whether parent complainants truly represent the interests of the segments of the community that they claim to;[21] and most of all it can ratify agreements worked out between the other two powerful constituencies—the teachers and administrators.

In addition, the school board is a first party to the allocation decision and can insulate its pronouncements from public criticism by claiming special expertise on the budgetary questions (even though most school boards are completely dependent on the school administrators for "interpretations," "explanations," and "rationale" for budgetary allocations).

5. Teachers. The teachers represent both the easiest and most difficult constituency to characterize. They are easy to characterize because their priorities have been asserted loudly and consistently over time in both their public pronouncements and in their negotiations with the school boards. Specifically, the goal of the teacher organizations has been to increase the employment and job benefits of teachers through reductions in average class size, increases in remedial specialists, extra pay for planning time, narrowing the scope of normal duties to increase the number of tasks that require extra remuneration, and so on.[22] These concessions represent top priorities in the bargaining packages of teacher organizations, and they also represent the crucial portions of the recommendations for "educational quality" that are advocated by the state and national teacher associations and unions.

The goal of the teachers appears to be to allocate increased revenues for the schooling of disadvantaged children to increased employment and job benefits for teachers. Of course, such strategies are couched in the terminology of raising educational quality, but this claim requires supportive empirical evidence rather than rhetorical justification.

Teachers' interests are not always easy to characterize. Probably no other group shares such a wide diversity of individual viewpoints about how the schooling of the disadvantaged might be improved. Certainly, informal discussions with individual teachers indicate that many thoughtful teachers do not feel increases in personnel and benefits per se will make much difference in educational outcomes for children.[23] But as long as teacher organizations push so hard for the "teacher benefits" solution to spending additional money, this diversity of viewpoints is obscured by the overall behavior of the group.

The teacher group has a powerful influence on the decision for allocating additional revenues for the schooling of the disadvantaged. First, they represent a first party to the decision by virtue of their ability to negotiate directly with the school board on how additional funds will be spent. Second, they have many sanctions at their disposal including subtle acts of noncooperation; the refusal to perform what they might define arbitrarily as duties that require additional remuneration; and the ultimate sanction, the strike. They also have heavy support for their position at the state levels where legislatures have shown a willingness to support the special pleadings of the educational professionals for laws that require added personnel.[24]

6. Administrators.   The last constituency in the model is the school administrators. In theory, they serve the role of carrying out the policies established by the school board. Conceptually the school board sets educational policy, and the administrators manage the schools in a manner consistent with those guidelines. In fact, studies of school boards and administrators have suggested that the reverse is often the case—the school board is charged with processing minutia while the administrators set policy by their daily actions.[25]

Administrators appear to have two goals with regard to the expenditure of additional state and federal revenues for schooling disadvantaged children. First, the school board has the authority to reward and sanction administrators, meaning that there will be a desire to pursue the school board's objective of minimizing conflict. To the degree that administrators can defuse potential conflict situations that might arise in allocating additional funding, they have spared the school board such anguish, and school boards will look favorably on administrators who prevent such conflicts from emerging at the school board level. Second, administrator status and mobility is closely tied to the size and financial magnitude of the organization that he is administering. In large measure, the remuneration of principals, superintendents, and other administrators is linked to the number of employees whom they supervise and the salaries of their subordinates. Increases in the numbers and salaries of teachers and other employees will tend to push up the salaries of administrators.

Accordingly it is reasonable to believe that administrators would wish to allocate such compensatory funds to increasing employment and job benefits for school district employees generally, while attempting to minimize conflict over the decision. School administrators, too, appear to be in an especially powerful position to effect their goals. They are a first party to the allocation decision by virtue of their role as the bargaining agent for the school board, and they can make recommendations that favor their own interests under the guise of "professional" negotiations. That is, like the teachers, they can clothe their own motives in the rhetoric of educational improvement, and the school board and second-party constituencies have neither the resources, the information, nor the professional status to challenge them.

Coalitions and Outcomes

Obviously, policy outcomes cannot be predicted from this information unless the possibilities of coalitions among constituencies are considered. The most likely coalitions appear to be the following. The school board has an interest in keeping the local taxpayer quiescent while minimizing conflict. Any change in tax burdens is highly visible, and taxpayers tend to be a very vocal group, so the school board will wish to maintain the existing tax burden or even be prone to using "outside" money to support services that would otherwise be provided by local funds so as not to increase the strain on local taxpayers. Likewise the school board and the administrators have common interests in minimizing conflict. Accordingly, the school board would appear to coalesce most closely with the administrators and the local taxpayers.

Teachers' and administrators' goals often overlap. Both groups benefit from increased employment and higher job benefits. The traditional view is that teachers and administrators sit on opposite sides of the bargaining table; but both have a common set of incentives on the major issue of how to allocate additional school revenues, and the administrators are constrained in their concessions only by the requirement of minimizing conflict (which means that they must avoid increases in the tax burden if at all possible).[26] No possible coalitions appear to exist for disadvantaged parents and students, either with each other or with other constituencies.

The policy outcomes predicted by this model are straightforward. There would be a tendency to use state and federal funds to supplant local tax support for the provision of school services. That is, outside money would be used, in part, to reduce the local tax burden for school programs that would have been offered even in the absence of such external funding.

Because the administrator-teacher coalition is strong, almost all the external funding would be devoted to benefits for teachers and administrators rather than to disadvantaged children. The revenues would be devoted to increased employment and job benefits for educational professionals, and the decision would be one based on their interests. That is, there would be little evidence that this decision derived from a thoughtful and extensive plan to improve the education of disadvantaged youngsters, even though these allocations would be rationalized on their alleged contribution to the welfare of disadvantaged children rather than to advantaged adults.

This solution would also satisfy the school board's need to minimize conflict. The generous treatment of the local taxpayer would keep him quiescent, while the decision would be closed off effectively to other "outside" constituencies. Finally, the model suggests that it is unlikely that the educational environment or educational outcomes for disadvantaged children will improve unless the increases in employment and employee benefits can themselves effect such changes. As we noted above, this possibility is subject to empirical verification, and we should not assume, a priori, that benefits that improve the status of professional educators are necessarily the same as those that improve the status of disadvantaged youngsters.

In summary, the following groups would be most likely to benefit from additional state and federal revenues for schooling the disadvantaged: teachers, administrators, school boards, and local taxpayers. The groups that would not appear to benefit are the disadvantaged students and their parents.

Is the Model Predictive?

The model presented here can be compared with the actual experience encountered under Title I or the Elementary and Secondary Education Act of 1965. Under this legislation the federal government has been providing about $1.1 billion a year to the states to distribute to school districts to provide additional educational services for children from low-income families. In applying for the money, local school districts were required to state the purposes and design of their Title I programs, and they were required to evaluate the results of their efforts. Thus, we can assume that the school districts understood well the focus of the program, and we can accept at face value the goals that they claimed they were attempting to achieve: for example, increasing reading proficiencies.

During the last seven years, approximately $8 billion has been allocated to Title I programs, and the results of these programs have been summarized in the form of local, state, and national evaluations as well as "special" studies on specific aspects of the Title I experience.[27] Accordingly, there is substantial information that can be drawn upon for testing the predictive power of our model for describing local expenditure allocations of Title I funds. A review of that literature suggests: (1) Title I funds were commonly used to supplant the use of local monies rather than to supplement them as the law intended; (2) most of the Title I funds went toward larger and better paid staffs; (3) there was very little conflict over the local utilization of Title I monies since the information dissemination and community participation provisions of the law were consistently violated by local educational agencies, and the decisions were made by the professionals themselves; and (4) extensive evaluations of Title I programs have found that on the average there were no changes in educational outcomes for disadvantaged children. The next paragraphs take up these points one by one.

1. An extensive analysis and audit of Title I expenditures found that Title I revenues have been commonly used by local school districts to supplant state and locally raised revenues so that the latter could be reallocated to nondisadvantaged children or to tax relief.[28] Although such use violates the guidelines for the Title I program, the infractions were so common that in 1970 the U.S. Department of Health, Education and Welfare convened a task force whose efforts were devoted largely to setting out a monitoring and enforcement system that would prevent such supplantation. Even with the advent of a new reporting system and threats to cut off Title I aid if such funds were substituted for state and local support, there is every indication that supplantation continues to be a serious problem.[29]

   2. The available data suggest that about 90 percent of Title I funds spent in recent years have been allotted to personnel benefits.[30] The principal expenditure strategies have been those of reductions in class size; the hiring of more supervisory and remedial specialists; the employment of more administrators, evaluators, curriculum specialists, teaching aides, and consultants; and the provision of extra pay for "planning" time and other duties that are considered to be a part of the program. The schools allocated almost as much Title I support to truant officers and other attendance services as they did to health services for disadvantaged children, even though children from low-income backgrounds are likely to suffer from a large variety of untreated health problems that will surely affect their educational proficiencies.[31]

   3. Very little overt conflict emerged over the allocation of Title I funds. Spending decisions were generally made in a closed setting among the educational personnel and school boards without the involvement of groups from the communities whose schools were allegedly to be the recipients of Title I expenditures. Again, the enacting legislation and Title I regulations were violated; since they stipulated that "to encourage intelligent involvement, regulations require that terms and provisions of each project be made available for public inspection"; that appropriate vehicles for community involvement be established by school systems, such as Title I advisory committees; and that at least half of the members on such committees be representatives of the poor community.[32] In contrast, The National Advisory Council on the Education of Disadvantaged Children found that out of 116 programs observed by its consultants, only 2 reflected an attempt to involve parents.[33] In the extensive study of Title I carried out by the Washington Research Project, the authors reported:

> Most school officials whom we interviewed indicated that decisions concerning the needs of children and the allocation of funds were made by a few school personnel with little or no consultation with poor white, black, or brown people.[34]

   Even where such advisory committees existed it was found that they were often improperly constituted and in some cases were composed entirely of school personnel.[35] Moreover, they were normally used to "rubber stamp" the proposals drawn up by school officials.[36] Finally, it was found that many parents and community leaders were unaware of the Title I projects in their schools and that citizen requests for information were commonly denied.[37] In short, school boards and administrators have tended to minimize conflict over the allocation of Title I monies by closing off the decision and withholding information about Title I from persons outside of their closely guarded province.[38]

Such behavior on the part of the school boards and administrators is in violation of the law, but enforcement of both the spirit and the letter of this regulation is very difficult. The Title I Task Force that was convened by the Department of Health, Education and Welfare in 1970 placed a top priority on increasing the community involvement component of Title I. Unfortunately, it appears that these regulations continue to be violated.

4. Extensive evaluations of Title I programs have found that on the average there were no changes in cognitive educational outcomes for disadvantaged children. Title I regulations require that all projects be evaluated at the end of each school year, and the results of such evaluations are to be sent to the state. The states are required to review these evaluations for their annual reports, and the Office of Education then studies both the state reports and selected reports from school districts (particularly those districts who report "substantial successes" and the very large school districts). In addition, several overall evaluations have been undertaken by the U.S. Office of Education in order to characterize the national performance of Title I programs and to select exemplary programs.

Unfortunately, the sum total of all of these evaluations seems to be that few of the benefits of Title I expenditures are received by disadvantaged children. Since most of the programs concentrated on reading skills, it is useful to examine the effect of Title I funds on that outcome. In evaluating the 1966-67 and 1967-68 reading programs funded under the Act, the U.S. Office of Education concluded that on the basis of reading test scores, "a child who participated in a Title I project had only a 19 percent chance of a significant achievement gain, a 13 percent chance of a significant achievement loss, and a 68 percent chance of no change at all (relative to the national norms)."[39] Further, the projects included in the investigation were "most likely to be representative of projects in which there was a higher than average investment in resources. Therefore, more significant achievement gains should be found here than in a more representative sample of Title I projects."[40]

The inability of Title I funds to create even a nominal direct effect on reading test scores for children appears to be endemic. Among many thousands of Title I project evaluations and a few other compensatory programs, the U.S. Office of Education selected the 1000 most promising for purposes of further scrutiny by an independent research contractor. Of these, only 21 seemed to have shown sufficient evidence of significant pupil achievement gains in language or numerical skills.[41] Not only are these results discouraging in themselves, but they also reflect the evaluation bias evident in reports on compensatory education when the persons who are responsible for the program are asked to evaluate their own results. The evaluation claims are rarely supported by the evidence.

The U.S. Office of Education recently commissioned a study that reviewed all the representative data on educational effects of Title I as well as compensatory education projects that had been identified as "exemplary."[42] Based on the data obtained from Title I projects through 1970, this study could find no evidence that states were closing the achievement gap between advantaged and disadvantaged children.[43] Yet, because some individual projects had reported such successes, an attempt was made to scrutinize more closely the specific evaluations of those projects. Of some 1750 projects that were identified as appearing to meet the criteria of success in improving the cognitive functioning of disadvantaged children, only 41 (or 2.3 percent) were found to be successful when evaluated in a systematic way.[44] Of these, only half appeared to be supported by Title I funds; yet each year about 11,000 school districts have been receiving money under the program.

In summary, although there is a great deal of evidence that Title I money has helped the local taxpayer and school-district employees, there is little evidence that it has substantially improved the educational outcomes for disadvantaged children. Moreover, the political model used to explain the allocation decision suggests that without substantial realignments of political constituencies and decisionmaking structures, the same outcomes can be predicted for the future. Stated more strongly, educational personnel will *always* benefit from the expenditure of additional money on the schooling of disadvantaged youngsters, but only *rarely* will the children themselves benefit.

Serrano and the Effects of Increased Funds

In the preceding section a model of local allocation of state and federal revenues for schooling the disadvantaged was posited, and applied to the evidence provided by the Title I experience. But how applicable is this model of local decisionmaking to increases in school-district expenditures generated by the *Serrano* decision? Since the proposed fiscal responses to *Serrano* and similar decisions would have their major effects on increasing spending in the most impoverished school districts and those educating high proportions of disadvantaged students, the previous analysis is directly applicable to the *Serrano* situation.[45]

As long as the present governing structures and political alignments prevail at the local level, increases in spending are unlikely to have much of an effect on improving the relative educational standing of children residing in the districts that will receive increased allocations from the state. In contrast, the additional funds will have a powerful effect on employment and benefits for school-district personnel. In both cases the educational interests of disadvantaged children will be forced to compete with the employment and financial interests of middle-class educational professionals, and the latter group will prevail. Paradoxically, a social reform carried out in the name of increasing opportunity for the poor will have its principal effect in improving the opportunities of middle-class educators.

Although this conclusion is consistent with that of statistical studies that find little or no relationship between resource inputs and educational outcomes, there is a distinct difference in the implications that arise. The statistical studies suggest that educational outcomes for disadvantaged children have not been shown to be sensitive to variations in resources;[46] therefore, increasing expenditures on the schooling of disadvantaged children is not likely to raise educational proficiencies. Unfortunately, the methodology underlying these studies assumes tacitly that school districts are attempting to maximize the educational performances of disadvantaged youngsters, but regardless of their efforts the effects are minimal.[47] In contrast, the theory propounded here suggests that school districts are not attempting to maximize the educational status of disadvantaged students; rather, the resources that are allotted for such purposes are being used to maximize the status and employment of educational personnel while being packaged in the rhetoric of helping children.[48]

In short, the failure of additional funding to improve educational outcomes is not a technical failure of the schooling process as much as it is a technical by-product of the political process. This diagnosis is consistent with the view that so-called compensatory education has not failed; it has never been tried. Nor is it likely to be tried. Only a movement at the state level to change the governing structure of school districts so that the parents of the educationally disadvantaged and the students themselves will have a greater share of decisionmaking power is likely to move funds in an educationally productive direction for lower-class students.[49] But increasing the relative power of the less-advantaged groups of our society has never been a high-priority item in the political arena, particularly when such an action would conflict with the interests of a well-organized middle-class cadre.[50]

The power of the educational professionals can be illustrated by the fact that it took four years of effort for the California legislature to pass a rather timid enabling act to permit an OEO experiment for testing educational vouchers within the state. That is, one of the reasons for rejecting even a modest experiment financed by federal funds has been the implication that it will improve the relative power of the disadvantaged in making decisions about their schooling.[51] Moreover, the ability of the organizations representing the educational personnel to influence legislation is reflected in the December 1972 passage in California of Senate Bill (SB) 90, which would double minimum expenditure levels guaranteed by the state with no changes in the mechanism by which local allocation decisions would be made. (SB 90 raises the guaranteed support from $355 to $765 for each child in elementary grades and from $488 to $950 per student in high schools.) SB 90 was known as the educational lobby's version of school finance reform, and no attempt was made to exact a quid pro quo that might assure children educational benefits from the expenditure increases.

The power of the school personnel lobby to write its own legislative ticket is likely to rise over time. Although in the late 1960s the power of the educators seemed to be at an ebb, there was an enormous resurgence of political energy and success in 1972 as the educational organizations adopted a new political style. Although "teachers tended to be discreet in their political action avoiding overt electoral activities and maintaining their independence from political parties and action groups," times have changed.[52] In the 1972 elections the political arm of the California Teachers Association (The Association for Better Citizenship or ABC) gave campaign contributions to fifty-four Assembly candidates and seventeen State Senate candidates.[53] More surprising is that thirty of the seventy-one candidates received contributions of between $500 and $8000, very hefty amounts in state electoral races. Also surprising was that apparently the ABC was the most generous contributor among all of the political interest groups. In fact, the group that appeared to be second in its generosity, the real estate interests, showed average contributions only half the size of those of the ABC.

A Personal Postscript

The model and data presented in this chapter suggest that spending increases will have a much greater effect on the economic status and employment of educational professionals than they will have on the educational proficiencies of children. Although a fairer distribution of educational expenditures among school districts is a necessary condition for a fairer distribution of educational outcomes among children, it is not a sufficient condition. The sufficient condition requires that the additional revenues be devoted to the needs of children rather than those of school-district employees, and that condition is violated by the present political institutions.

Yet I have supported the *Serrano* principle, and I will continue to do so for two reasons. First, although *Serrano*-generated spending increases are not likely, on balance, to improve the relative educational standing of the children for whom they were intended, they will have a positive effect in a few isolated instances; specifically, the most impoverished districts may be able in some degree to improve the quality of the school environment in a way that will at least make their schools more pleasant places to be. Second, it seems absurd to refuse to more nearly equalize the educational investment allocated to disadvantaged children simply because they and their families lack the power to assure that such funds will be allocated to improving their educational status. On moral grounds I believe we would be derelict to use the political model as grounds for systematically providing less educational support for the disadvantaged than for the advantaged. Thus I feel obligated to support the *Serrano* principle, even though I am not optimistic about the educational or social outcomes.

Perhaps it is useful once again to draw a parallel with the 1954 *Brown* decision. Even though it has not produced the extensive school desegregation that many of its proponents hoped for, it is still based upon a loftier principle than the "separate but equal doctrine" of *Plessy vs. Ferguson*.[54] With all of the disappointments of the *Brown* aftermath, I still think it was the correct path. Today we stand at another crossroad. The *Serrano* decision is also based upon a sound moral principle; and even if it fails to deliver the goods, it is important to support the tenet for its own sake rather than the doctrine represented by the existing methods of financing the schools.[55]

NOTES

1. For a discussion of the limits of the courts, see Alexander M. Bickel, *The Supreme Court and the Idea of Progress* (New York: Harper and Row, 1970); and Philip B. Kurland, "Equal Educational Opportunity, or the Limits of Constitutional Jurisprudence Undefined," in Charles U. Daly, ed., *The Quality of Inequality: Urban and Suburban Public Schools* (Chicago: University of Chicago Press, 1968), pp. 47-72.

2. See John E. Coons, William H. Clune III, and Stephen D. Sugarman, *Private Wealth and Public Education* (Cambridge: Belknap Press, 1970).

3. *Serrano v. Priest*, 5 Cal. 3d 584, 487 P. 2d 1241 (1971).

4. For example, see Citizens Commission of Maryland Government, "A Responsible Plan for the Financing, Governance and Evaluation of Maryland's Schools" (Baltimore, 1971); *Report of the New York State Commission on the Quality, Cost and Financing of Elementary and Secondary Education* (New York, 1972), Vol. I, Chapter 2; and Charles S. Benson et al., *Final Report to the [California] Senate Select Committee on School District Finance*, Vol. 1 (Sacramento, 1972).

5. This process is described in greater detail in Henry M. Levin, "The Effect of Different Levels of Expenditure on Educational Output," in R.L. Johns et al., *Economic Factors Affecting the Financing of Education* (Gainesville, Florida: National Educational Finance Project, 1971), Chapter 6.

6. See Herbert Gintis, "Education, Technology and the Characteristics of Worker Productivity," *American Economic Review* 61 (May 1971): 266-279.

7. I refer to education in an industrialized and Western context. In other cultures education is considered a way of life. See Carlos Castañeda, *The Teachings of Don Juan* (New York: Ballantine, 1968).

8. Gary S. Becker, *Human Capital* (New York: Columbia University Press, 1964).

9. For an example, see Angus Campbell, Phillip Converse, Warren Miller, and Donald Stokes, *The American Voter* (New York: Wiley, 1960), p. 491.

10. Howard R. Bowen, "Finance and the Aims of American Higher Education," in M.D. Orweg, ed., *Financing Higher Education: Alternatives for the Federal Government* (Iowa City: American College Testing Service, 1971), pp. 155-170.

11. Compare the criticisms in Ivan Illich, *Deschooling Society* (New York: Harper and Row, 1971); Herbert Gintis, "Toward a Political Economy of Education," *Harvard Educational Review* 42 (February 1972): 70-96; and

Christopher Jencks et al., *Inequality: A Reassessment of the Effect of Family Schooling in America* (New York: Basic Books, 1972).

12. See the recent review in Harvey Averch, Stephen Carroll, Theodore Donaldson, Herbert Kiesling, and John Pincus, *How Effective Is Schooling? A Critical Review and Synthesis of Research Findings* (R-956-PCSF; Santa Monica: The Rand Corporation, 1972).

13. An extensive exploration of these issues is found in Henry M. Levin, "Concepts of Economic Efficiency and Educational Production," paper presented at the Conference on Education as an Industry, National Bureau of Economic Research, June 1971. These contradictions are also evident in the movement for "educational accountability." See Henry M. Levin, "A Conceptual Framework for Accountability in Education," A Report Prepared for the Task Force on Accountability and Performance Reporting of the National Academy of Education, Occasional Paper in the Economics and Politics of Education 72-10, School of Education, Stanford University, September 1972.

14. See the summary of data in Michael J. Wargo, Kasten Tallmadge, Debbra D. Michaels, Dewey Lipe, and Sarah J. Morris, "ESEA Title I: A Re-Analysis and Synthesis of Evaluation Data from Fiscal Year 1965 through 1970" (Palo Alto: American Institutes for Research, March 1972), pp. 144-164.

15. Refer to the critical survey of school effectiveness in Averch et al., *How Effective Is Schooling?*

16. For a critical survey of the act, see Stephen K. Bailey and Edith K. Mosher, *ESEA: The Office of Education Administers a Law* (Syracuse: Syracuse University Press, 1968).

17. A more general analysis of the political relationships is found in Frederich M. Wirt and Michael W. Kirst, *The Political Web of American Schools* (Boston: Little, Brown, 1972).

18. Charles Silberman, *Crisis in the Classroom* (New York: Random House, 1970), p. 10.

19. See David Minar, "Educational Decision Making in Suburban Communities," in M.W. Kirst, ed., *The Politics of Education* (Berkeley: McCutchan Publishing Co., 1970), pp. 167-183.

20. See M. Kent Jennings and Harmon Zeigler, "Interest Representation in School Governance," paper delivered at the 1970 meetings of the American Political Science Association, Los Angeles, 1970; and Wirt and Kirst, *Political Web of American Schools*, pp. 79-84.

21. Robert F. Lyke, "Representation and Urban School Boards," in H.M. Levin, ed., *Community Control of Schools* (Washington: The Brookings Institution, 1970), pp. 138-168.

22. For example, the program that has been heavily promoted by the American Federation of Teachers, the so-called More Effective Schools (MES), would drastically decrease class size and provide backup teachers and additional professionals. In New York City the MES program translates into a doubling or more of "normal" per pupil expenditures.

23. That is, it is likely that strategies to improve educational outcomes for disadvantaged children would necessitate the hiring of additional personnel. Yet, in that case, it is the planning and program that would emerge first and the personnel needs that would follow. In the present instance it

appears that the personnel demands emerge first, and the program always seems to be an afterthought that is asserted in order to rationalize the higher employment and benefits.

24. James Koerner, *Who Controls American Education?* (Boston: Beacon Press, 1968).

25. Wirt and Kirst, *Political Web of American Schools*, pp. 85-88.

26. And the school board is often willing to legitimate the agreement to avoid further conflict. For a provocative view, see Norman D. Kerr, "The School Board as an Agency of Legitimation," *Sociology of Education* 38 (1964): 34-59.

27. The U.S. Department of Health, Education and Welfare issues an annual report on Title I, and the state departments of education publish annual state reports. For special studies, see Wargo et al., "ESEA Title I"; and Ruby Martin and Phyllis McClure, *Title I of ESEA: Is It Helping Poor Children?* (Washington: Washington Research Project and NAACP Legal Defense and Educational Fund, Inc., 1969).

28. Martin and McClure, *Title I of ESEA*, Chapter 3.

29. Lawyers' Committee for Civil Rights Under Law, *Title I Comparability: A Preliminary Evaluation* (Washington, September 1972); U.S. Department of Health, Education and Welfare, "Comparability Task Force Analysis of Fiscal Year 1973 Comparability Reports and Corrective Action Plans for a Nationally Stratified Random Sample of Local Educational Agencies," November 6, 1972 (draft); Joel S. Berke, Stephen K. Bailey, Alan K. Campbell, and Seymour Sacks, *Federal Aid to Public Education: Who Benefits?* (Syracuse: Syracuse University Research Corporation, 1971).

30. Based upon calculations in M. Wargo et al., "ESEA Title I," Table 6.2, p. 121. Exact breakdowns of personnel allocations are not available. Accordingly, they were estimated from the budgetary components presented in the Title I summaries. The budgetary categories are not necessarily descriptive of their functions. For example, the category "fixed charges" in the Title I allocations is almost exclusively devoted to employee retirement expenses, a personnel allotment.

31. This is another example of expenditures being allocated to functions that help teachers and administrators rather than students. The implications for educational opportunity are explored in Henry M. Levin, "Equal Educational Opportunity and the Distribution of Educational Expenditures," *Education and Urban Society* 5 (February 1973): 149-176.

32. See the documents cited in M. Wargo et al., "ESEA Title I," pp. 51-52.

33. Cited in Martin and McClure, *Title I of ESEA*, p. 69.

34. Ibid., p. 70.

35. Ibid., p. 73.

36. Ibid.

37. Ibid., pp. 75-79.

38. Michael Kirst has pointed out to me that in recent years there has been an increasing tendency for a portion of Title I to be allocated to teacher aides and other personnel hired from the community. This strategy reduces the concern of the community regarding the larger set of allocations and

educational effects of the program by rewarding a small number of potentially vocal elements of the poor community with "paraprofessional" employment. This not only ameliorates criticism cheaply but also implicates the community in any educational failures of the programs. The total employment effect for poor communities is miniscule relative to the magnitudes of the school expenditures.

39. Harry Picariello, "Evaluation of Title I" (Washington: U.S. Office of Education, Office of Program Planning and Evaluation, 1969), p. 1 (mimeo).

40. Ibid.

41. David G. Hawkridge, Albert B. Chalupsky, and A. Oscar H. Roberts, "A Study of Selected Exemplary Programs for the Education of Disadvantaged Children," Parts I and II, Final Report, Project No. 08-9013 for the U.S. Office of Education (Palo Alto: American Institutes for Research, 1968).

42. M. Wargo et al., "ESEA Title I."

43. Ibid., pp. 174-179.

44. Ibid., pp. 179-180.

45. See, for example, Benson et al., *Final Report . . .* ; and *Report of the New York State Commission.*

46. Averch et al., *How Effective Is Schooling?*

47. Such an assumption has no factual basis, but it follows from the "theory of the firm" of conventional neoclassical economics in combination with a liberal ideology. See Levin, "Concepts of Economic Efficiency," for a discussion of the maximization principle in education. See William Behn, "Social Reality and Education," Occasional Paper in the Economics and Politics of Education (Stanford University, 1973), for a discussion of ideology and its crucial role in determining the acceptability of assumptions about the world.

48. An outstanding discussion of the conceptual approach to evaluating the "true" resources being allocated toward such educational objectives as academic achievement is found in Stephan Michelson, "The Association of Teacher Resources with Children's Characteristics," in *Do Teachers Make a Difference?* (Washington: U.S. Office of Education, OE-58042, 1970), Chapter 6.

49. See, for example, Henry M. Levin and Robert Singleton, "Equalizing Educational Opportunity and the Legislative Response to Serrano," unpublished, 1972; and Henry M. Levin, ed., *Community Control of Schools* (Washington: The Brookings Institution, 1970).

50. In this sense the present power alignment is functional and corresponds to the larger economic, social, and political system of which it is a part. See Martin Carnoy, ed., *Schooling in a Corporate Society* (New York: David McKay, 1972), particularly Samuel Bowles, "Unequal Education and the Reproduction of the Social Division of Labor."

51. For a description of the experiment, see Center for the Study of Public Policy, *Education Vouchers: A Report on Financing Elementary Education by Grants to Parents* (Cambridge, December 1970). The authorizing legislation as finally passed in 1973 provides for a district-level teacher organization veto over the participation of private schools in any voucher experiment.

52. Robert D. Hess and Michael W. Kirst, "Political Orientations and

Behavior Patterns: Linkages Between Teachers and Children," *Education and Urban Society* (August 1971), pp. 453-477.

53. Doug Willis, "Teacher, Realtors, Insurance Firms Spend Big to Get Their Men Elected," Palo Alto *Times*, October 21, 1972, p. 1.

54. Surely the *Brown* decision did have an effect on the patterns of school enrollment in the South, and this should not be ignored. See F. Wirt and M. Kirst, *Political Web of American Schools*, Chapter 9.

55. As long as the present provision of unequal educational attainments by race and social class corresponds to the social control hierarchy, the educational system is truly functional. Since there is no contradiction between the educational subsystem and the larger social system, it is unlikely that any court mandate can produce a more equal effect with regard to educational outcomes that ultimately relate to the larger social outcomes. See H. Gintis, "Toward a Political Economy of Education."

Chapter Seven

The Governance and Political Implications of Educational Finance

Alan K. Campbell and Dennis A. Gilbert
Syracuse University

Only recently have scholars begun asking, "Who governs education?"[1] Although the resulting research has not yet produced any definitive answers, there is a foundation for piecing together a fragile framework of speculation about the possible effect of recent state and lower federal court decisions on the governance of public K-12 education.[2] These decisions find that the differences in wealth standing behind students in different school districts violate the equal protection clause of the Fourteenth Amendment or similar state constitutional provisions. Generally the courts require a system of educational finance that will equalize the resources available for educating each child, regardless of the wealth of the district in which he happens to live. Observers predict that a larger state role in educational finance will result, and it seems plausible that this will alter educational decisionmaking.

    This chapter suggests what those changes might be and how they will influence the character of education. For example, it is very commonly argued that a larger state role in financing will mean more state control of education. Does available evidence support that view? And is that even the right question to ask? The first issue discussed will be this popular dichotomy of state vs. local, but a proper understanding of the effects of changes in financing will require looking at the total political milieu of education. Although education is legally a state function, by drawing upon imprecisely defined concepts of "local control" and "keeping out of politics," it has managed to secure a unique place among governmental services, possessing a governmental and finance structure all its own. These characteristics have important implications for who governs education.

    After describing the interplay of forces in educational politics, what is changing and what is likely to remain the same, some likely impacts of the recent court decisions will be analyzed by examining three areas of education decisionmaking: finance, curriculum, and personnel.

Pressures for Increasing the State's Role

Although the court rulings are very significant, pressures for the state to assume a larger share of educational financing did not start with the recent rulings. In Maryland,[3] Michigan[4] and New York,[5] studies initiated by political and civic leaders—before any of the successful court cases—recommended a greatly increased state role in financing. In analyzing where these pressures were greatest, a staff study of the President's Commission on Education Finance found that in states with high levels of per pupil expenditure and low to moderate levels of state aid there has been heavy pressure for school finance reform. The study also suggests that heavy reliance on the property tax has caused many taxpayers to seek tax relief.[6]

Among the arguments favoring a larger state role are the believed needs to reform total state-local taxes,[7] reduce the current disparities in resources available among school districts, and correct the failure of state-aid formulas to offset these disparities. At the present time state aid tends to follow the distribution of political power rather than educational need.[8] One response to this inequity was Title I of the Federal Elementary and Secondary Education Act.[9]

Despite the importance of tax reform and greater educational equity, much of the public debate about the court decisions seems to have settled instead on the issue of state vs. local control of education. Viewing education control as a zero-sum game in which one party's gain is equal to the other party's loss, some argue that a larger state share in financing education will inevitably mean more state control of education and hence an undesirable decrease in local control. Others contend that local control need not suffer under new financing arrangements, even asserting that local control would be enhanced because local jurisdictions will be relieved of their burdensome financial responsibilities and freed to exert more influence on educational policy.[10]

The State Control Issue

Although the question, "Who governs education?" is much more complex than state vs. local control, the current emphasis on this oversimplification requires examination. It was long assumed that a larger state role in education financing meant more state control, but the proposition has only recently been seriously examined. A 1957 study found "practically no relationship between the state share in school support and the *number* of controls."[11]

Then in 1971 the Urban Institute went further by categorizing statutory controls in ten states as strong, moderate, or weak. With findings that supported the earlier evidence, they concluded that for each of eleven different decision areas and for state control in general, "the extent of state controls over local decision making has no direct relationship to the percent of state funding."[12]

What, then—if anything—helps explain the degree of state control? Apparently control is not related to the proportion of total state expenditures devoted to education (see Table 7-1), but may be related to the proportion of state education funds used for equalizing education disparities within a state (see Table 7-2). However, this must be viewed with caution since it is no simple matter to determine exactly what proportion of total aid is, in fact, equalizing.

Assuming the proportion of aid used for equalizing possesses some significance for state control, the question becomes, "What are the characteristics of states that use their aid in that way?" With per capita income used as a proxy for general socioeconomic characteristics, a significant correlation is found between high income and the proportion of aid used for equalizing (see Table 7-3). There is, however, no similar correlation between income and degree of state control (see Table 7-4). Apparently, intervening political variables play a

Table 7-1. Degree of State Control Compared with the Percentage of State Budget Devoted to Education

	Restriction[a]		Percentage of State Budget to Education[b]	
	Scores	Rank	Percent	Rank
New York	31	1	37%	7
California	30	2	30	10
Kansas	25	3	44	6
Delaware	23	4	45	5
Michigan	22	5	46	4
Colorado	21	6	47	2
South Dakota	21	6	37	7
North Carolina	21	6	52	1
Washington	19	9	47	2
New Hampshire	17	10	34	9

[a]Restriction scores are based upon Urban Institute ratings of degree of state control in each of eleven decision areas (strong = 3, moderate = 2, and weak = 1); the highest possible score is 33. (New York and North Carolina vary slightly from those reported in the study as a result of recalculation.) Source: Betsy Levin and Michael A. Cohen, assisted by Roger Calloff, *Levels of State Aid Related to State Restriction on Local School Decision Making* (Urban Institute Paper no. 727-1; Washington: Urban Institute, 1973).

[b]Source: U.S. Bureau of the Census, *State Government Finances in 1970*, Series GF 70, No. 3 (Washington, 1971).

Table 7-2.   Degree of State Control Compared with the
Percentage of State Education Funds Used to Equalize
Intrastate Differences

	Restriction[a]		State Education Funds Used to Equalize Intrastate Differences, 1966-67[b]	
	Scores	Rank	Percent	Rank
New York	31	1	99%	1
California	30	2	33	8
Kansas	25	3	88	3
Michigan	22	4	94	2
Colorado	21	5	61	6
South Dakota	21	5	73	5
Washington	19	7	82	4
New Hampshire	17	8	44	7
Rank correlation significant at 0.05				

[a]See notes to Table 7-1.

[b]Source: Charles O. Fitzwater, *State School System Development: Patterns and Trends* (Education Commission of the States, (Denver, 1968). Data are not provided for Delaware and North Carolina, two states included in the Urban Institue study.

Table 7-3.   Percentage of State Education Funds Used to Equalize
Intrastate Differences Compared with Per Capita Income

	State Education Funds Used to Equalize Intrastate Differences[a]		Ranking by Per Capita Income[b]
	Percent	Rank	
New York	99%	1	1
Michigan	94	2	3
Washington	82	4	4
California	33	8	2
Kansas	88	3	6
Colorado	61	6	5
New Hampshire	44	7	7
South Dakota	73	5	8
Rank Correlation significant at 0.05			

[a]See note b, Table 7-2.

[b]Source: U.S. Bureau of the Census, *State Government Finances in 1970*, Series GF 70, No. 3 (Washington, 1971).

Table 7-4. Degree of State Control Compared with Per Capita Income

	Restriction[a]		*Ranking by Per Capita Income*[b]
	Scores	*Rank*	
New York	31	1	1
California	30	2	2
Kansas	25	3	7
Delaware	23	4	3
Michigan	22	5	4
Colorado	21	6	6
South Dakota	21	6	9
North Carolina	21	6	10
Washington	19	9	5
New Hampshire	17	10	8
Rank correlation significant at 0.1.			

[a]See notes to Table 7-1.
[b]See notes to Table 7-3.

role, but they remain to be identified.[13] Further, these comparisons are all based on analyses of statutes. Since a great deal depends on the actual amount of control exercised in the administrative implementation of these statutes, there is no certainty that these ratings reflect the actual extent of state control.

There can be a considerable gap between statutory intent and implementation. An extensive literature in political science, public administration, and organization theory has shown that hierarchies tend to develop informal arrangements that can effectively subvert efforts by the central authority to control subordinate behavior. Education is no exception.

Nor is the extent of local control uniform from district to district even in the same state. As the court decisions have stated, richer districts have more options than poorer districts.

In sum, these findings are not very helpful in determining the relationships between state control and either fiscal or socioeconomic characteristics. More extensive and sophisticated analysis needs to be done before anything of significance can be said. The situation, in other words, is far more complex than a simple issue of state vs. local control. That complexity is best demonstrated by examining the social and political environment that engulfs the performance of the education function.

Education's Political and Governmental Environment

Local government jurisdictions are creatures of the state and subject to direct state control. Even when local prerogatives are embedded in state constitutions, courts have consistently found in favor of state power. What sets education apart from other local jurisdictions is the absence of an explicit "home rule" doctrine. Many state constitutions expressly make education a state responsibility.

The states, however, normally delegate a substantial amount of responsibility for delivering education services to local school districts. More important, legal circumstances notwithstanding, the demand for local control and the rhetoric in its behalf have evolved into a consistent and persistent belief in its advantages. The result is a paradox, created by the legal realities on one hand and by a set of strongly held beliefs on the other. One result is that whatever the reality, constant lip service is paid to the doctrine of local control. Even an increase in state power is often defended on the grounds that it will serve to enhance local control. This belief in local control is buttressed by the unique governmental characteristics of the system providing education services.

Each activity of government—police, fire, sanitation, health, and the like—operates in its own political environment. But perhaps more than any other function, education has carved out for itself a special place in the American governing system. An image of uniqueness is perpetuated both because public education is said to play a fundamental role in a democratic society, and because education deals with children. Widespread public acceptance of these ideas has helped education to become and to remain the only public function possessing its own governmental jurisdictions—not combined with other activities and administered by general government as are most other governmental functions. Related to this special status is a companion insistence that education be free of "politics."[14]

These "no politics" and independence characteristics do not mean that politics are absent but rather that they are of a special kind. In fact it may well be argued that "no politics" is a tactic used to help school people obtain greater resources. Yet it is quite possible that as the public becomes concerned about the level of taxes, education's visibility and the local setting of education tax rates will make it more difficult to obtain additional funds, and thus leave education more vulnerable than functions included in a general governance system. The matter is conjectural since there is no empirical evidence that such is the case.

It is possible to examine the fiscal effects of independence since a number of school systems in the country do have common boundaries with a general government, usually city or county, and in some cases the school board members are appointed by that government, usually by its chief executive officer. A recent study finds that the degree of independence has no influence on any educational fiscal output—whether measured as per student expenditures, per capita expenditure for education, or per capita locally raised taxes for education.[15] The independence or dependence of education may be important for educational policy, but it apparently does not affect fiscal outputs. Very likely the most important determinants of local school tax support and expenditures are the socioeconomic characteristics of the community and the amount of external aid that flows into the district.[16]

The "no politics and independence" characteristics may have important nonfiscal consequences resulting from the way the school professional views his environment. He believes, according to Wallace Sayre, that

> The community when it confronts education questions should be an unstructured audience of citizens. These citizens should not be influenced in their responses to educational questions by their structured associations or organizations. Nor as members of interest groups of any kind (save perhaps in parents groups) nor as members of a political party.[17]

This view of their political constituencies most of the time undoubtedly produces greater freedom of action for education professionals than for other professionals. At times of controversy and conflict, however, just the opposite may be the case. As David Minar learned in his research about suburban schools,

> Conflict over public school questions lacks a sustaining structure. This means that instead of there being opposition to the established order at all times just because that is how the system works, there is opposition only when there is something to oppose. Again, specific issues, sometimes ideological, tend to be the motivating force. The consequence of this situation is not only that demands are focused on specifics ... but also that the authority system is not usually accustomed to being opposed and therefore it lacks resilience. Conflict is likely to come to it as a disorganizing shock; whereas in most democratic government, structured conflict is recognized as the way the game is played. In school government it often seems to be regarded as a rude and foreign intrusion.[18]

This political characteristic of education means control usually rests with the professionals and a small group of lay people having a special interest in schools. Occasional flareups may cause the superintendent to be replaced, but on the whole the pattern is one of relative harmony interrupted by only episodic conflict. The only exception to this generalization is districts with substantial socioeconomic heterogeneity, such as large cities, where conflict is quite persistent.

Uniqueness at the State Level, Too
This environment and pattern of local educational politics is replicated in many ways at the state level: separation from general government is

supported in most states with some kind of lay board between the governor and the state department of education. Often the chief education officer is appointed by the board rather than by the governor, and the state education legislative committees normally accept the rhetoric of keeping education out of politics.

Although the legal and traditional role of the governor in education varies from state to state, gubernatorial controls over education budgets, appointments, and policies are generally weak. A survey of the chairmen of state legislature education committees showed that in their opinion the most influential individual in the state with regard to changes in state school programs was the chief state school officer (44 percent, representing 31 states) more often than the governor (24 percent, representing 20 states).[19]

The relative independence of state education administrators was recently illustrated by a study of who decides how federal aid is distributed in five states (California, Massachusetts, New York, Texas, and Virginia).[20] It was found that decisions were made almost exclusively by state education department officials. No doubt the state political process, legislative and executive, is more intimately involved in the distribution of state funds, but the federal aid example is an indication of the substantial independence of many state education departments.

Still, despite this relative independence, state education departments are generally not strong administrative units. Recent infusions of federal aid, particularly that money specifically designated for strengthening state departments, have helped, but most state education departments still have a long way to go before they will be the equal of most other state departments. A recent study of such departments found that concepts of policymaking were not clear; few state officials were familiar with developing the rules and regulations governing external administration; few agencies had well-developed program plans or knew how to develop functional program plans on an agencywide basis; and few agencies had developed and codified a body of written policies.[21]

The basic constituency of state education departments includes organizations of school board members, school administrators, teachers, and educationally interested lay groups, primarily PTAs. When these groups present a common front they are normally able to have vast influence on state educational policymaking. For many years these groups, as well as state legislatures, had a rural orientation to which state departments of education responded. A relatively harmonious set of relationships emerged at the state level, resulting in some very important innovations in the education system. State aid to rural districts increased steadily, school district consolidations were promoted, and curriculum changes were made—all changes designed to provide better education services.[22]

Now this confluence of forces is disintegrating in many states. Reapportioned state legislatures, and in some states top education officials and state education departments, are beginning to concern themselves with urban as well as rural education. Teachers' groups are finding it increasingly difficult to make common cause with other school-related organizations, particularly school administrations and school board organizations. These changes point toward increased conflict and, therefore, a more overtly political environment for education policymaking and administration.

In analyzing a number of studies, Iannaccone identified a developmental typology for educational-political linkages. That is, he found education politics in various states falling into general types that might best be described as stages, with stage two growing out of stage one, and so on. Stage one is a disparate or locally based political system. Stage two is a statewide monolith, with education interest groups developing a consensus. Stage three is a statewide fragmented system with education interest groups disagreeing more than agreeing. States described as having grown from monolithic (stage two) to fragmented systems (stage three) tend to be industrialized urban states like California, New York, and Michigan.[23] As more states acquire these characteristics and perhaps as more education interest groups—especially teacher unions—pursue their own ends, the fragmented pattern will become more prevalent.

The fragmentation appears to affect the behavior of state legislatures. For example, a study in New York found that in the area of education, legislators were far more apt to vote in the interest of their particular district than to follow the dictates of statewide education or political groups. They believed that education and noneducation groups from their own district had more influence on them than formal statewide interest groups. The legislators also indicated that the variety of interest groups provided them with many sources of information, eliminating heavy reliance on formal education groups.[24] As legislators broaden their sources of information and rely on formal organizations of educators, the influence of educational professionals is bound to decline and the relative power of the legislature increase, particularly for committees assigned responsibilities for education.

The use of this legislative independence will depend in part on the quality of staff maintained by these committees. The strong professional staff of the education committee in California manages to stay very much on top of the situation. The Texas Legislative Budget Bureau is another rather effective tool of the legislature. In many states, however, lack of staff and time, turnover among legislators, absence of expertise, failure to develop Congress' "contained specialization," and the governor's line-item veto combine to reduce the role of the state legislature in educational policymaking.

In summary, states appear to be at a point of transition in their education policymaking. The dominance of education interest groups (primarily professional educator groups or lay groups dominated by these professionals) is declining. No single interest or cluster of interests has yet replaced them, and the result to date has been growing fragmentation.

As the various forces sort themselves out, the single most important development may be the evolution of teacher unions. No longer willing to trust their welfare to other education professionals, teacher unions are increasingly willing and able to go their own way, weakening the overall position of such other education professionals. This division provides opportunities for other participants to play a large part, and this situation enhances the "brokerage role" of elected officials.

The Federal Role

Their strong role in education notwithstanding, the states have been unwilling or unable to equalize educational opportunity within their boundaries or to effectively coordinate a well-conceived statewide education effort. In spite of these problems, as well as a general acceptance of the importance of education for American society, the federal government has been slow to move massively into the field. Many other functions—transportation, urban development, housing, and welfare—received substantial federal support before education did.

The reasons usually given for this lack of federal participation are Congress' inability to solve problems associated with black-white relations, separation of church and state, and fear of federal control. For many years every piece of legislation proposing significant federal aid to education attracted desegregation amendments. Congressional division on the racial issue normally caused legislative defeat. Enactment of the 1964 Civil Rights Act went far toward removing this potential barrier. Another perennial problem was the pressure for including parochial schools in general-aid formulas in the face of constitutional requirements for the separation of church and state. The National School Lunch Act, the National Defense Education Act, and others, capped with the Elementary and Secondary Education Act, all helped reduce the scope if not the core of the problem. Whether there has been similar movement in the third problem area, fear of federal control, is problematic. However, fear alone has not been sufficient to prevent the federal role from growing, albeit to a degree that is still relatively small. The constraints that have traditionally circumscribed the federal role still influence but certainly do not control policy.

In addition to the fact that general educational aid, of whatever scope, runs headlong into these difficult problems, "there is still a healthy congressional fear that general aid would expose Congress to annual and ubiquitous grass-roots pressures (accompanied by threats of political retaliation) for additional aid."[25] The consequence has been a plethora of categorical programs that contribute to fragmentation. Even in states like California where there is strong professional and legislative control at the state level, coordination is difficult because of the strong vertical ties created by special educational needs and interests, which are reinforced by categorical programs.[26]

When the federal government has been successful in altering state education department activity patterns, as it was with Title I of ESEA, it has had to bargain with the states on the nature of the guidelines,[27] and local districts have frequently managed to use the money to meet their own agenda regardless of the requirements.[28] Although the dogma of "no politics" pervades the federal level as it does the state and local, wherever the federal role increases, political influences become more apparent. The remarkable ability of aid to federally impacted areas to resist presidential attempts to cut it back is a noteworthy case in point.

It is on this but dimly understood governance process that a basic change in the system of financing education will have its effect. To predict that effect with precision and certainty would be foolish, first because exactly what form the change will take cannot be known (after all, this outcome will be a product of these same forces), and also because even if it were known, the inadequacy of knowledge about the current system and that system's variation from community to community, state to state, and region to region would still create vast uncertainties. Nevertheless, some informed guesses are possible, and a description of possible alternative outcomes can provide some guidance to asking the right questions. The framework for undertaking this task is to discuss the possible changes by decision areas: finance, personnel, and curriculum.

Finances: Amount and Distribution

There is impressive evidence that school districts possessing extraordinary wealth will use it to provide costly educational services. Many studies have found that one of the most important determinants of the level of local support of education is the socioeconomic characteristics of school-district residents. State-aid formulas of all designs have been unable to overcome the propensity of richer districts to spend more and thus maintain their fiscal advantage over poorer districts.[29]

Full state funding of educational cost is most frequently criticized for not allowing school districts to determine their own level of educational spending. The belief is that those with the resources and desire to spend more on the education of their children should be allowed to do so. In other words, the critics object to total elimination of the inequalities the courts found unconstitutional. Meeting the court requirements will probably, although not certainly, narrow the gap between rich and poor districts, but any funding arrangement that permits local options, whether through power equalizing or local add-ons, will obviously perpetuate at least some of the inequality the courts are seeking to eliminate.

The proposal most likely to substantially reduce, if not eliminate, fiscal inequality is full state funding of education. As it is generally proposed, a local add-on of 10 percent is also to be permitted. Certainly bringing expenditures among districts to within 10 percent of each other would be a very significant change. But at what point is an undesirable degree of disparity reintroduced?—15 percent? 20 percent?—or can it be anything less than 50 percent? It is clearly a matter of opinion which can be hotly contested and not easily resolved. Not even the courts have been willing to decide this matter. The point is simply that there is a significant difference in principle between full state financing and some measure of local add-on.

The New York Fleischmann Commission noted that acceptance of even a 10 percent local add-on means forever braving a slippery slope. The commission itself rejected local add-ons because it feared that 10 percent this year would be used as a bargaining lever against the state legislature for 15 percent next year.[30] The greater proportion of discretionary income and propensity of wealthier districts to spend a good deal on education would no doubt soon find a number of districts pressed against the 10 percent ceiling, looking for other ways to maintain their erstwhile fiscal advantage.

As the school board president in Scarsdale, a wealthy New York city suburb, said about full state financing, "There's a fundamental conflict between what's good for everyone and the natural desire of individuals to do the best they can for their own children. We feel a responsibility for others, but we do want to protect the kind of quality our people have come to expect."[31] Protecting Scarsdale's "quality" means more than just a save-harmless clause that keeps expenditure levels from going down. It means continuing to have a fiscal advantage over most other districts, so that, for example, the highest-quality teachers may be attracted. One tactic might indeed be to fight for a local add-on provision and then lobby intensively to get the percentage raised over time. Another tactic might be to avoid the spirit of the equalizing efforts wherever the letter of the law allows—fattening fringe benefits, lightening workloads, building "municipal" facilities that are primarily used by the schools, and the like.

Still, local add-ons are defended on many grounds. It is argued that because innovation has been found to correlate with expenditure levels,[32] higher-spending districts are educationally necessary to act as "lighthouses" for others to follow. However, the political arguments are probably more potent. The staunchest proponents of a local option are residents of middle- and higher-income areas—particularly suburbs. Their political strength is great and growing. The continuing shift of population and legislative representation away from the central cities and rural areas to the suburbs strengthens an advantage that already exists.

More important, advocates of local add-on have many allies. A broad survey of education interests found 89 percent of its respondents favored optional supplementary programs authorized and jointly funded by state and local sources.[33] In addition, such nationwide forums as the Advisory Commission for Intergovernmental Relations and the President's Commission on School Finance have recommended a 10 percent local add-on option. Not surprisingly 87 percent of the chairmen of state legislature education committees believe it would be difficult to pass full state funding in their states.[34] It appears, therefore, that the relative advantages of wealthier districts may be decreased by court-mandated changes, but the current distribution of political power stands in the way of their total elimination.

If some variant of power equalizing is used to meet the court mandate for change, the extent to which the gap between rich and poor districts is closed will depend in part on how the local tax burden is measured. If only education is considered, central cities and heavily populated urban suburbs will be at a disadvantage, because their local tax base must provide many services in addition to education. Consequently, although the tax effort for education in these areas appears low compared with middle- and high-income suburbs, the *total* tax burden for education and noneducation services is much higher. So districts that most need financial assistance may not get it if education continues to be kept entirely apart from other governmental functions.

The degree of equity actually produced by power equalizing schemes will depend greatly on the exact provisions of the proposal. If the state simply mandates levels of per pupil expenditure and local tax effort, making up the difference between what local rates raise and the required expenditure level, the expenditure outcome will be no different from full state funding. If the local district is permitted higher rates than those mandated, with its aid still computed on the basis of the gap between the mandated rate and the per pupil expenditure rate, the outcome will resemble that permitted under a local add-on provision.

More complex power equalizing would overcome some of these characteristics. One such scheme would permit a school district to choose its level of school funding, and the state would establish a schedule of local tax rates for each expenditure level. If this rate produced less in a particular district than the expenditure level associated with that rate, the state would make up the difference. If it produced more, the state would capture the difference and use it for distribution to less affluent districts.

Making the system equitable from both an expenditure and a tax point of view would require some features not necessarily integral to the concept. (See Chapters 2, 4, and 5 of this book.)

> District power equalizing distributions of school funds (including recapture of money from high-wealth districts), income-specific property tax relief (the circuit-breaker), and improved categorical programs for low-achieving, low-income students are liberal reform measures that are ... consistent with Serrano's philosophy. This ... set would do much to right the past inequitable treatment of the poor by the public education sector.[35]

The potential political opposition to this scheme will probably be as great as that to full state funding. Again, high-income suburbs will object most strenuously. Although allowed to spend more, they would have to raise their own tax rates considerably in order to qualify for high-expenditure rates, and some of the money thus raised would be taken from them.

Almost any scheme that attempts to bring more equity to education financing will increase the total amount of resources devoted to education in the short run, because it will not be politically possible to force districts to reduce the amount they are now spending. The process will inevitably be one of leveling up rather than down.

The long-run outcome, however, is much less certain. Available evidence shows that, in substantial part, state aid tends to add to rather than replace local effort, the actual extent being determined primarily by socioeconomic characteristics of the local district.[36] Further, it has been found that dividing responsibility for fiscal support between state and local governments rather than having one or the other level carry the full or nearly full burden results in higher expenditures than would otherwise be the case.[37] In general, highest state-local expenditures are found in systems that assign expenditure responsibilities to their local governments while maintaining a large flow of aid funds from the state level to the local governments.[38] These findings suggest that if a genuine system of full state funding were adopted, in the long run expenditures for education would increase less rapidly than they would in a system combining state and local funding.

On the other hand, a full state funding system might have a dramatic effect on the distribution of educational resources. By providing opportunities for the state to pinpoint areas of educational need and apply resources to them, the outcome could be a very different distribution from what now exists. Title I of the Elementary and Secondary Act may be analogous. This program is probably more effective than any other federal effort at putting resources into the districts that need them. Although the funds have not been as carefully focused on disadvantaged children within those districts as the authors of the legislation intended, the aid at least flows to those districts with the greatest need. For example, in California the central city received $19.64 per pupil, in contrast to the suburban jurisdiction, which received $11.09. In New York the comparable figures were $53.90 for the central cities and $12.35 for outside central-city areas.[39]

In five states studied, decisions about the distribution of federal aid were made almost exclusively by state education departments. The state's political process, whether legislative or executive, exhibited little influence or involvement in the distribution of these funds. And in the cases where the departments had considerable freedom in the distribution of funds, the distribution pattern closely followed that of state aid. However, for those programs like Title I, where federal guidelines required the aid be concentrated in the areas of the disadvantaged, the guidelines did affect the distribution of funds and to some extent offset the disparities created by the flow of state aid funds.[40]

All of this suggests that the fiscal outcome of a larger role for state funding of education would vary by the character of the aid system adopted. A system that continues to allow some disparities would probably not substantially change the governance status quo.

If genuine full state funding were undertaken, with local school districts playing no role in raising resources for the support of education, the outcomes would be less certain. Full state assumption opens the possibility for an improved distribution of resources by taking into account educational need. It is possible that in the long run such a system would produce fewer total resources for education than one that divides the resource-raising responsibility between state and local units.

Effect on Curriculum

Proponents often argue that state assumption of education financing would allow local school boards to devote more time to matters of educational policy, particularly curriculum. It is assumed that school boards would welcome this opportunity to focus on educational policy rather than finance. Certainly there is considerable evidence that school boards now give the lion's share of their attention to financial issues. Tax rates, school building and expansion programs, bond issues, school budgets, and teachers' salaries tend to be their major preoccupation.[41] Two closely studied boards, for example, were found to devote 60 to 70 percent of their meeting time to finance and physical facilities, and only 10 to 13 percent was given to consideration of matters that might be defined as educational policy—and most of that small proportion of their time was devoted to listening to the superintendent report on what was being done, outlining the achievements of the school, with very little attention given to problems.[42]

Whether this devotion to financial affairs is forced on the boards against their will or is a product of their own interests and abilities is a moot point. Yet a 1972 Gallup Poll suggests that the boards are behaving in ways preferred by the citizens they represent. The educational problem identified as most important was lack of discipline, followed by financial support. Eighth on the list of topics mentioned was poor curriculum.[43]

This division of attention probably also fits into the school professionals' view of the way things ought to be. School professionals, feeling that their expertise is particularly strong in the areas of curriculum and education policy, resent intrusion into those areas by people they feel are less qualified. The author of one study reports,

> When I asked a superintendent in the larger district what he would do if a board member insisted on a change in the school program, he replied that he would implement the request "Only if I could get an agreement on an important matter." Upon further inquiry he admitted that the board had not once caused him to change a decision about the educational program during the six years of his superintendency.[44]

Two forces tend to support and reinforce the professional educators in policy matters. One is the advantage enjoyed by every bureaucratic expert.

His training, full-time attention to the field, and ability to use the cloak of professionalism all aid him in his dealings with politicians. As Max Weber observed,

> The power position of a fully developed bureaucracy is always overtowering. The "political master" finds himself in the position of the "dilettante" who stands opposite the "expert," facing the trained official who stands within management of administration.[45]

Second, this bureaucratic advantage has been nicely buttressed by the "no politics" characteristic of education. As Roscoe Martin has pointed out,

> Schoolmen feel more secure when dealing with an amorphous public than when talking to Republicans and Democrats. With such a public the school spokesmen have a better chance both of naming the subject to be discussed and of keeping the conversation on a technical level where professional considerations may be expected to prevail.[46]

It is unlikely that transferring a larger responsibility for financing to the state level would substantially alter this professional dominance of educational policymaking; however, within professional ranks it might increase the role of professionals at the state as opposed to the local level. Such a shift would apparently distress large segments of the education community. A survey of a broad cross-section of educational interests, lay and professional, at both state and local levels found 87 percent of the respondents favored local control of goals and methods.[47] A survey of state legislature education committee chairmen found 87 percent favored local control.[48]

Despite these strongly held views, the role of state education departments in educational decisionmaking is increasing, and that movement is being aided by the court decisions. The question is, what difference will this shift make? None, it could be argued, because education professionals, whether state or local, are basically drawn from the same professional stream. At the head of that stream are the university and college schools of education, which interact strongly with each other through a variety of national associations, nationwide testing, textbooks, and professional consensus. In addition to training, these schools tend to dominate professional certification, providing still more homogeneity.

Any difference among professionals is apt to come from perspectives associated with their jobs—for example, the potential for the state to better focus resources where the educational need is great. In this case the larger view taken by state education officials would result not so much in educational policy innovation as in greater attention to resource distribution and better measures of local performance.

This possible attention to performance might cause a larger state role in educational policymaking to make a major difference. The already growing state role, aided by responses to the court decisions, may increase the momentum toward statewide evaluations of the quality of educational services. Some states began such evaluations even before they were recommended by the President's Commission on Education Finance, and other states are now considering them. A public opinion survey found that 97 percent of the respondents believed that state education agencies should collect evidence regarding the effectiveness of school programs,[49] and a survey of state legislators' opinions (see Table 7-5) found they too favored evaluations.

The Michigan experience is an interesting example of how these forces may work themselves out. In 1969 Michigan began an evaluation designed to serve state rather than local needs. To obtain the cooperation of teachers and school administrators, the state department assured them that it would not release comparative statewide data. However, once the information was available, pressure from the public, state legislators, the governor, and the members of the state board of education forced its release.

The widespread interest in evaluation information indicates there is already concern about the quality of the educational system's output, and an increased state involvement in financing could mobilize that concern. It is possible that educational policy and curriculum would be affected by court-mandated changes. Whether such evaluations would lead to greater concern for variations in educational needs remains uncertain. Suburban districts with a white, middle-class constituency and students wishing to go on to college will likely demonstrate the greatest interest in evaluation. In areas where educational quality most needs improvement and where current educational policy and

Table 7-5. **State Education Committee Chairmen's Views on Achievement Testing (Percent)**

	Yes	*No*
Proper management of education programs requires pupil achievement testing.	92%	4%
For those answering yes: Achievement testing ought to be on: statewide basis	72	
school district basis	26	
Achievement results should be compared: nationwide	72	19
statewide	85	7
locally	80	12

Source: Education Testing Service and Commission Staff, "What State Legislators Think about School Finance: An Opinion Survey of State Legislature Education Committee Chairmen," a report for the President's Commission on School Finance, 1971.

curriculum are probably least relevant, it will take the professionals in cooperation with the leadership in the disadvantaged areas to use evaluations as
efficacious tools for improving the status quo. An expanded state role will
probably serve this interest better than the present system.

Personnel Practices and Pay

A larger state role in education financing will probably have uneven
effects on personnel control. Teacher certification is already largely a state
function. The Urban Institute study found that in none of the ten states
analyzed were state controls over certification weak. Half were judged strong
and half moderate.[50]

Local school districts are normally free to hire their own teachers,
but they are usually restricted to selecting from among those possessing state
certification. Occasionally large cities have certification systems of their own,
but generally their standards are more restrictive than the state's. Although the
essential aspects of certification are apt to stay at the state level, local districts
will likely enjoy some powers over hiring, whatever changes are made in the
financing system. Even in Hawaii, with its completely state-financed system,
there is a measure of local involvement in the selection of personnel.

State financing will probably have a greater effect on teacher
salaries. Increased unionization has brought the question of teacher salaries to
the forefront of education politics and is pushing education into the political
mainstream. The system is moving more and more in the direction of collective
bargaining as the means of establishing salary scales. This trend is unlikely to be
stopped, regardless of what happens to the distribution of financial responsibility.

If the power to set salaries is left to local districts, the additional
resources produced by leveling up may simply result in higher teacher compensation, especially in districts previously having low expenditure levels. In the short
run at least, improved educational quality may take a back seat to improved
salaries.

It simply is not known whether unions will be able to bargain as
effectively in a statewide system since they will then not be able to play one
school district off against another. James Allen has argued that

> another gain (for state assumption) would be in the rapidly growing
> area of collective bargaining between school employees and school
> boards. As long as the bargaining process takes place at the local
> level involving hundreds of districts, the situation is bound to be
> uncertain and confused. If the state were the only source of money
> the bargaining would take place at the state level. This would
> eliminate the possibility of maneuvering to hold salaries at a given
> level as well as by teachers to use a higher level of salaries in one
> district as a kind of whipsaw to effect increases in others. There

would be each year a greater likelihood of a reasonable and fair settlement of the rewards of teachers.[51]

General public opinion tends to oppose statewide salary setting, while those more closely associated with education (big-city school board presidents, superintendents, and state legislative committee chairmen) seem to divide rather evenly on the issue, as shown in Table 7-6. In part this issue relates to the larger question of public sector collective bargaining. As public employee unions become stronger and are better able to play one jurisdiction against another, it seems probable that government at the state level will be forced to play a larger role. Bargaining over teacher's pay is not likely to be an exception. Therefore, regardless of what action is taken in response to the issues raised by the court decisions, states will become increasingly involved in the collective bargaining process. Whether that means statewide bargaining, regional bargaining, or establishment of some kind of state guidelines is not clear, but the forces toward state involvement in the whole process of setting public-sector salaries seem overwhelming. Whatever the system adopted, increased funds made available for education will undoubtedly be absorbed in very large part by higher salary levels rather than by reduction in classroom size, adoption of special programs, or other devices designed to improve the quality of education services provided.

Summary: Uncertainty and Doubts

Unfortunately the effect of a larger state role in financing education cannot be precisely predicted. Too little is known about the facts and implications of education governance to provide an adequate base for speculation about the outcome of major changes. It depends in part on how much the system is changed. If local districts are permitted to retain significant fiscal

Table 7-6. Statewide Salary Schedule for Teachers

	Favor	*Oppose*
Cross-sectional survey[a]	26%	57%
Big city school board presidents and superintendents[b]	42	52
State legislature education committee chairmen[c]	44	46

Sources: These were reports to the President's Commission on School Finance, 1971.

[a]Russell B. Vlaanderen and Eric L. Lindman, "Intergovernmental Relations and the Governance of Education."

[b]Mark Battle Associates and Commission Staff, "Big City Schools in America: The Views of Superintendents and School Board Presidents."

[c]Educational Testing Service and Commission Staff, "What State Legislators Think about School Finance: An Opinion Survey of State Legislature Education Committee Chairmen."

autonomy, no matter what the name of the plan, disparities will persist and the effect on actual decisionmaking will be relatively small. Inequities may be reduced since that is necessitated by the very nature of the court decisions, but the advantage will remain with those school districts having greater wealth. In the division of American society into large cities, suburbs, and rural areas, the greatest advantage will still rest with the middle- and higher-income suburban jurisdictions. Local school professionals and suburban state legislators will be the chief holders of power, with state education department professionals growing in influence but responding to the suburban legislators.

A move to full state financing, accompanied by state administration of education, using not semiautonomous local districts but simply decentralized state districts, could force a more substantial change. If regional fiscal and administrative devices are placed between the state and local districts, they could be used for differentiating wage levels among regions as well as permitting some options for the provision of selective educational opportunities, particularly in areas where these are needed because of the nature of the school population.

Full state funding and a substantial state role in the performance of the educational function would make it easier to focus education resources where the greatest needs lie, designing programs with more concern for variations in the types of educational services provided and increasing control over the division of educational resources among salaries, special education programs, physical facilities, and the like. On the basis of the evidence about the determinants of the total level of funding, full state financing would probably lead to an increase in total resources allocated to education in the short run, but in the long run it might have a dampening effect. It is possible that a single-level tax system would reduce the kind of leap-frogging currently found among school districts, the outcome being fewer total resources allocated to education.

The distribution of political power over education would remain heavily in the hands of educational officials, regardless of the kind of program adopted; but if full state funding were undertaken, state legislatures would play a stronger role than they do now, as would the office of the governor and his budget division. In the education community there will undoubtedly be further fragmentation caused by teachers' unions making stronger and stronger bids for power. The consensus among educational interest groups is declining in many states, having already disappeared in some. State funding will certainly not alter this trend and, in fact, may increase it, since the fragmentation is greater at the state level than at the local.

In short, the kind of system adopted to effectuate court mandates will be important in determining who will govern and the types of policy that will result. Nonetheless, a larger state role in education finance, whatever form it takes, will probably not fundamentally alter existing broad-based trends. Although the Supreme Court ruling in *Rodriguez* may act as a breakwater on this first wave of reform (see Chapter 3 above), it is not likely to stem the tide of change.

NOTES

1. Although it does not date back many years, the literature is too extensive to list here. The following bibliographies are helpful though not exhaustive: Jean Hansen, "Readings on American School Finance," *Current History* 63 (July and August 1972); Michael Marien, *Alternative Futures for Learning: An Annotated Bibliography on Education Trends, Forecasts, and Proposals,* (Syracuse: Education Policy Research Center, May 1971); Michael Marien, *Essential Reading for Education* (Syracuse: Education Policy Research Center, Fall 1971).

2. *Serrano v. Priest,* 5 Cal. 3d 584, 96 Cal. Rptr. 601, 487 P. 2d. 1241 (1971); *Rodriguez v. San Antonio Independent School District,* 337 F. Supp. 280 (W.D. Texas 1971); *Van Dusartz v. Hatfield,* 334 F. Supp. 870 (D.Minn. 1971); *Hollins v. Shofstall,* No. C-253652 (Super. Ct. Ariz. 1972); *Robinson v. Cahill,* 118 N.J. Super. 223, 287 A. 2d 187 (1972); *Sweetwater County Planning Committee v. Hinkle,* 493 P. 2d 1050 (Wyo. 1972); *Caldwell v. Kansas,* No. 50616 (D. Kan. Aug. 30, 1972).

3. Citizens Commission of Maryland Government, "A Responsible Plan for the Financing, Governance and Evaluation of Maryland's Public Schools," Baltimore, 1971.

4. The latest version of the recommendations being considered are in the "Special Message to the Legislature on Excellence in Education," by Governor William G. Milliken, April 12, 1971.

5. New York Commission on the Quality, Cost and Financing of Elementary and Secondary Education, *Final Report* (Albany: Department of Education, 1971).

6. Thomas H. Jones, *Review of Existing State School Finance Programs,* Vol. 1, a report for the President's Commission on Education Finance, 1971.

7. Advisory Commission on Intergovernmental Relations, *State-Local Revenue Systems and Educational Finance,* a report for the President's Commission on Education Finance, 1971.

8. For a review of the research on intradistrict resource allocations, see Alan K. Campbell and Donna Shalala, "Resource Literature on Educational Revenues and Expenditures," in *Theory Into Practice,* 11 (April 1972). For two recent studies, see Ralph Andrew and Robert J. Goettel, "School-by-School Resource Allocation and Educational Need in Three Urban Districts," in Joel S. Berke, Alan K. Campbell, and Robert J. Goettel, eds., *Financing Equal Educational Opportunity: Alternatives for State Finance* (Berkeley: McCutchan, 1972).

9. For a discussion of how well this title did distribute aid, see Joel S. Berke and Michael W. Kirst, *Federal Aid to Education: Who Benefits? Who Governs?* (Lexington: D.C. Heath, 1972). See also Chapter 6 of this volume.

10. "Allen Urges Study of Proposal to Let States Finance Schools," *New York Times,* July 12, 1968.

11. John Guy Fowlkes and George E. Watson, *School Finance and Local Planning* (Chicago: The Midwest Administration Center, University of Chicago, 1957), p. 33.

12. Betsy Levin and Michael A. Cohen, assisted by Roger Colloff, *Levels of State Aid Related to State Restrictions on Local School Decision Making* (Urban Institute Paper No. 727-1; Washington: Urban Institute, 1973).

13. A rather extensive literature has developed around the question of the relative effects of socioeconomic inputs and political structures and processes on outputs. Spurred by an article by Richard Dawson and James Robinson, "Interparty Competition, Economic Variables, and Welfare Policies in the American States," *Journal of Politics* 25 (March 1963): 265-289; several articles and books have explored the factors that correlate to outputs. Some of these are Thomas P. Dye, *Politics, Economics and the Public: Policy Outcomes in the American States* (Chicago: Rand McNally, 1966); Ira Sharkansky, *Spending in the American States* (Chicago: Rand McNally, 1968); Robert E. Crew, Jr., ed., *State Politics: Readings on Political Behavior* (Belmont, California: Wadsworth Publishing, 1968); Donald P. Sprengel, ed., *Comparative State Politics* (Columbus: Charles E. Merrill, 1972); Alan K. Campbell and Seymour Sacks, *Metropolitan America: Fiscal Patterns and Governmental Systems* (New York: The Free Press, 1967).

One book deals specifically with education: Jesse Burkhead, Thomas G. Fox, and John W. Holland, *Input and Output in Large City High Schools*, Education in Large Cities Series, Alan K. Campbell, ed., (Syracuse: Syracuse University Press, 1967).

14. There is a large literature on the "no politics" characteristic of education. For a summary of it, see Roscoe Martin, *Government and the Suburban School* (Syracuse: Syracuse University Press, 1962).

15. David Ranney, *School Government and the Determinants of the Fiscal Support for Large City Education Systems*, doctoral dissertation, Syracuse University, 1966.

16. Campbell and Sacks, *Metropolitan America.* Seymour Sacks, *City Schools/Suburban Schools: A History of Fiscal Conflicts* (Syracuse: Syracuse University Press, 1972); H. Thomas James, J. Alan Thomas, and Harold J. Dyck, *Wealth Expenditures and Decision Making for Education* (Stanford School of Education, Stanford University, 1963).

17. Wallace Sayre, "Additional Observations on the Study of Administration," *Teachers College Record* 60 (November 1958): 75.

18. David Minar, "Community Politics and School Board," *The American School Board Journal* 154 (March 1967): 37.

19. Educational Testing Service and Commission Staff, "What State Legislators Think about School Finance: An Opinion Survey of State Legislature Education Committee Chairmen," a report to the President's Commission on School Finance, 1971.

Of course, the reason the total number of states adds to 51 is that most states have two education committee chairmen, and they may have had differing opinions, meaning a single state could be counted twice.

20. Joel Berke, Stephen K. Bailey, Alan K. Campbell, and Seymour Sacks, *Federal Aid to Public Education: Who Benefits?* (Syracuse University Research Corporation monograph, 1971), reprinted by the U.S. Senate Select Committee on Equal Educational Opportunity, 92nd Congress, 1st Session.

21. Dean Schweickhard, "The Role and Policy-Making Activities of State Boards of Education," National Association of State Boards of Education Special Study, 1967.

22. Colin Greer, *The Great School Legend* (New York: Basic Books, 1972).

23. Laurence Iannaccone, *Politics in Education* (New York: Center for Applied Research in Education, 1967).

24. Robert E. Jennings and Mike Milstein, "Education Policy Making in New York State with Emphasis on the Role of the State Legislature," a report for the National Center for Educational Research and Development, 1970.

25. Stephen K. Bailey and Edith Mosher, *ESEA: The Office of Education Administers a Law* (Syracuse: Syracuse University Press, 1968), p. 216.

26. Berke and Kirst, *Federal Aid to Education.*

27. Bailey and Mosher, *ESEA.*

28. David O. Porter, "The Mobilization of Federal Aid by Local Schools: A Political and Economic Analysis," working draft of a paper presented at the American Educational Research Association Annual Meeting, New York, February 4-7, 1971.

29. Campbell and Shalala, "Resource Literature on Educational Revenues."

30. New York Commission on the Quality, Cost, and Financing of . . . Education.

31. "Property Tax Reform Enthusiasm Lags," *New York Times*, December 19, 1972.

32. Levin and Cohen, *Levels of State Aid*; and William H. Pafford, "Relationships Between Innovations and Selected School Factors" (Lexington, Kentucky: Program of Educational Change, University of Kentucky, 1969).

33. Russell B. Vlaanderen and Erick L. Lindman, "Intergovernmental Relations and the Governance of Education," a report for the President's Commission on School Finance, 1971.

34. Educational Testing Service, "What State Legislators Think."

35. Charles S. Benson, "The *Serrano* Decision: Where Will the Money Go?" *Public Affairs Report* 13 (December 1972).

36. Campbell and Sacks, *Metropolitan America*; and Sacks, *City Schools/Suburban Schools.*

37. Ibid.

38. Alan K. Campbell, "National-State-Local Systems of Government and Intergovernmental Aid," Intergovernmental Relations in the United States, *The Annals* (May 1965).

39. Berke et al., *Financing Equal Educational Opportunity.*

40. Ibid.

41. Martin, *Government and the Suburban School.*

42. Norman Kerr, "The School Board as an Agency of Legitimation," in Alan Rosenthal, ed., *Governing Education* (New York: Doubleday, 1969), p. 159.

43. George Gallup, "Fourth Annual Poll of Public Attitudes Toward Education," *Phi Delta Kappan* 54 (September 1972): 33.

44. Kerr, "The School Board as an Agency of Legitimation," p. 161.

45. Max Weber, "Bureaucracy," in H.H. Gerth and C. Wright Mills, *From Max Weber* (New York: Oxford University Press, 1946), p. 232.

46. Martin, *Government and the Suburban School*, p. 99.

47. Vlaanderen and Lindman, "Intergovernmental Relations. . . ."

48. Educational Testing Service, "What State Legislators Think About School Finance."

49. Vlaanderen and Lindman, "Intergovernmental Relations. . . ."

50. Levin and Cohen, *Levels of State Aid.*

51. James E. Allen, Jr., "Perspectives on School Finance," *Perspectives on Education* (Spring 1971).

Chapter Eight

The Role of Categorical Programs in the Post-Rodriguez Period

Joel S. Berke and Robert J. Goettel
Syracuse University Research Corporation

The nation's 17,000 school districts receive support from at least three jurisdictional levels: local, state, and federal. For several thousand districts, receipts also derive from substate (intermediate) agencies and from a variety of nonpublic sources as well. Although this symptom of American federalism creates a substantial degree of complexity in itself, the fact that revenues from each of these jurisdictional levels are further subdivided into many separate accounts creates "a system that almost defies comprehension."[1] Indeed, a 1970 research project that examined local school finance practices found that "when all of the local, state, and federal sources (and any private sources) are added up, most of the school districts have over fifteen different sources of funds. Large districts may have close to one hundred sources."[2]

To date, the opinions in *Serrano*[3] and similar cases have avoided involvement in this accounting nightmare and have dealt with school finances only in terms of broad categories, such as local revenues and state aid. This approach has been not only understandable, but necessary. Any other course would have left judges and legislators wandering in a trackless wilderness of trees, rather than pointing them toward the vast forests of inequity and irrationality that characterize state school finance systems in America. Nevertheless, the development of workable remedies for redressing those inequities requires that the distinction be made between revenues provided for general operating purposes and revenues reserved for particular, specifically designated uses, such as the construction of school buildings, the transportation of pupils, or the provision of a special curricula for vocational or compensatory education. Such earmarked revenue sources, generally known as categorical aids, are a component of every state school finance system and are at present the nearly universal format for all programs of federal aid to elementary and secondary education.

Concern about the role of categorical programs in reformed systems of school finance is substantial. For example, what is the relationship between categorical aid and the principle of fiscal neutrality in which the resources available for education will not be a function of local wealth? Some categorical aid programs give no consideration to local wealth or fiscal ability. Others are clearly designated to provide more aid to districts comparatively high in wealth. But since the *Serrano* principle itself does not require that general aid formulas recognize differential cost and need levels among the school districts of a state, are categorical programs necessary to assure that categories of pupils, curricula, or regions with higher than average costs are accommodated within the overall finance system? Without such programs, won't school finance systems provide only a superficial fiscal neutrality, but in fact fail to allocate educational resources in relationship to the educational burdens that districts and taxpayers have to bear?

This chapter is addressed to those concerns. First, we examine the general purposes and distributional mechanisms of categorical grants-in-aid for education. We then turn to a discussion of how categorical aids help meet the variations in need for educational and management services among school districts. Third, we describe the content and operation of state and federal categorical programs including a brief review of proposals for school finance reform in five states. Finally, we look at the potential contribution of categorical aids within the context of the legal principles that underwrite the current school finance reform movement.

Purposes and Functions of Categorical Programs

Categorical aid is a vehicle through which higher jurisdictions respond to needs for special services that are neither equally nor randomly distributed among local school districts and thus are not directly considered in general provisions for basic school support. Such needs commonly stem from the geographic or population characteristics of the district; for example, sparsely populated areas require higher per pupil transportation costs, and school systems with higher-than-average proportions of educationally disadvantaged children need higher per pupil revenues to provide compensatory services.

Categorical aid also permits superordinate jurisdictions to influence the *types* or the *manner of performance* of services provided by school districts. For economists, the justification for this influence stems from the effects of education that spill over from the local districts to serve the needs of the state or the nation. For the student of politics, the difference in the interest of the constituencies and the groups of influentials who control policy at the state and national level may be the explanatory factor.

Under both of these analytical approaches, two functional purposes of aid programs are usually observed. The first is to encourage innovative practices in local agencies. Title III of ESEA, which is designed to promote innovative educational programs, is such an example. The second functional purpose is to provide incentives for local school districts to expand the availability of services. Cubberly's models for state support of education in the early part of the century had the expansion of educational offerings as their primary goal.[4] To improve equality of educational opportunity, Cubberly recommended categorical programs that would encourage local school districts to expand the availability of kindergartens, high school programs, foreign languages, and vocational education. Federal aid for vocational education and some state aid for early childhood programs are present-day examples.

Another administrative or legislative intent commonly observed in both state and federal categorical aid programs (and generally resented by local school districts) is that of monitoring the activities of school districts through the requirement of proposals and evaluative reports. Although the effectiveness of requirements for evaluation is open to serious question,[5] the requirement in Title I of ESEA for evaluation of the effectiveness of education supported by that provision of the legislation is a significant step in intergovernmental relations, and illustrates the increased control higher jurisdictions are able to impose over local actions through categorical programs.

The actual extent of such control may be considerably less than imagined. The ability of donor agencies to exert authority over recipient officials varies markedly according to the extent of limitation on recipient action written into the laws and regulations, and informal and customary behavior patterns. The insightful studies of David Porter and his colleagues suggest that many skillful school district administrators are able to mobilize and allocate resources according to their own priorities despite legal strictures in aid programs. His analysis of the degree to which schoolmen can make symbolic allocations of aid funds for purposes that would have been supported otherwise by local monies raises significant questions about the degree to which designers of categorical programs really get their money's worth. Further, his description of the way in which some districts draw up their own objectives, and then artfully manipulate their many sources of funding to serve those ends, suggests that many local complaints about federal or state control of their activities are grossly exaggerated.[6] Nevertheless, questions of "who controls," and the operational relationships between donor and recipient agencies, are at the heart of policy debates about categorical versus general-purpose aid grants.

Distributional Mechanisms and
Fiscal Neutrality

The fundamental issue over which categorical aid programs become important in the debate concerning the financing of public elementary and secondary schools is whether such programs must meet the requirement of fiscal neutrality that has emerged in the line of cases from *Serrano* through *Millikin* v. *Green*. [7] The courts have not sought to make a distinction between spending for instructional purposes and spending for other functions—say, school construction or aid for the handicapped. Moreover, since fiscal neutrality is a legal principle derived from a common concept of fairness, it seems highly unlikely that a strong enough consensus will develop among legal scholars, fiscal experts, or educators that would permit distinctions to be made among aid programs according to their intended functions.

We believe fiscal neutrality should apply to categorical aid programs as well as to general support education aid. Its effect would be to require that funds allocated by a state may legitimately provide different amounts to different categories of educational or management purposes, but that within the legislative categories districts with greater local wealth may not be given an advantage.

The distributional mechanism used to allocate categorical aids determines in large measure the extent to which an aid program will conform to the principle of fiscal neutrality. Categorical funds are often distributed to local school districts with a clear equalizing intent: state aid is determined in proportion to the need for the service *and* in inverse relationship to wealth. In general, such aid programs will be for such services as transportation, required by nearly every school district. Other categorical programs, however, distribute aid in patterns that run counter to the way revenues would flow under a general support formula designed to focus only on fiscal neutrality. Such a pattern would be found when the need for a particular service and higher-than-average property wealth come together in the same group of districts. High-wealth, rapid-growth suburbs may benefit more than less wealthy suburbs from school construction aid; large cities with higher property values per pupil characteristically garner much higher-than-average ESEA Title I funds.

The extent of equalizing of aid for categorical programs required in varying degrees by most districts is dependent upon the proportion of actual local costs for a function supported by state aid. If, as is the case with many general support formulas, categorical aid is a small proportion of expenditures, the aid program will not substantially equalize tax burdens among districts, even if the categorical aid were allocated in an equalizing manner, as long as it continued to be a small proportion of costs. As the state share of costs increases, even when flat grant formulas are used, the equalizing effect also increases. Total equity would be achieved when the expenditures associated with a particular educational or management function are fully supported by the state (full state assumption).

In educational programs that are needed by only a few districts or are optional to all districts, the effective degree of equalization is dependent on requirements for matching funds placed upon participating districts. Both the amount and the nature of a matching requirement can have a strong influence on the degree of equalization of a particular grant program. There are two kinds of matching requirements. On one hand, if dollars are matched—the state provides X percent of the costs and the local district Y percent—there is no way the grant program can be fiscally neutral since all districts are treated the same without regard to their fiscal capacity. If, on the other hand, the local share is a function of the relative fiscal capacity of each district, the state aid will be equalizing.

Where local districts are required to put up substantial portions of the costs of a particular optional program—say 50 percent or more—relatively poorer school districts frequently elect not to participate. The result is often that wealthy school districts avail themselves of the grant, and may receive the same per pupil amount as poor districts (no equalization), but in the aggregate receive *more* state aid because of the failure of poorer districts to participate. This describes the effect of state aid programs promoted by Cubberly. Although Cubberly's stated purpose was to expand educational opportunity by expanding educational offerings, the actual result was that the increased opportunities were enjoyed more often by pupils in wealthy school districts than by those in poor school districts.

Matching provisions can, of course, also serve other objectives. One objective may be simply to have local school districts share fiscal responsibility for the program along with the state. Matching may therefore appropriately coerce the recipient unit to furnish program resources on its own.[8]

Optional grants that do not require matching funds or local fiscal participation of a specific nature may be either open-ended or closed-ended. Local school districts may be encouraged to apply for a grant whose limit has not been determined in advance, or the limit may be determined in accordance with the general standard of need specified only within broad limits set by the legislature. Closed-end grants have preset limits for local participation.[9] Additional conditions may also be attached to grant programs that may affect the willingness of local school districts to participate in the program. In each case, the grant program will not be fiscally neutral if poorer school districts as a group cannot provide staff to develop projects capable of getting funded by a donor agency.

Special Needs and Categorical Programs

Categorical state aids can play a critical role in school finance systems designed to meet the requirements of fiscal neutrality. The need for supplements to a general aid formula arises from the following dilemma: The wrong prohibited by the equal protection clause as interpreted in *Serrano* and similar cases encompasses only one aspect of wealth-based injustice in the way public schools are financed. There is a gap between the problems that school finance systems must remedy and the solutions required by the *Serrano* principle:

Whether the judicial concept of wealth discrimination, so central to the holdings in *Serrano, Van Dusartz,* and *Rodriguez*, outlines the problems of wealth discrimination as they would be analyzed by students of economics and public finance is highly questionable. For, on the one hand, the judicial focus on school finance alone without consideration of the total expenditure responsibilities of urban areas, for example, fails to provide an appropriate comparative measure of fiscal need, and on the other hand, the failure to examine the total tax responsibilities (general municipal and educational) of various jurisdictions, provides a less than accurate criteria for judging the comparative tax effort that various jurisdictions are making. . . .

On the cost side, if the equality which the constitution protects is to be substance rather than shadow, the real costs of school services should be taken into account. Thus, if certain areas of a state have higher costs for purchasing items of similar quality, be those items teachers or blackboards, school expenditures should be deflated or inflated accordingly. Higher urban costs therefore should result in higher revenues from the state to provide for meaningful equality.

But the greatest disparity in the fiscal needs of school districts arises from the composition of their pupil populations. Higher proportions of children with learning disabilities impose massively greater resource demands if those children are to have the same chance at success in school as their more fortunate classmates. . . .

This is not to say that the judicial formulation of the problem forecloses effective remedies. On the contrary, the latitude in the requirement of fiscal neutrality leaves ample space for effective reform.[10]

Meaningful school finance reform, then, must consider differences in fiscal capacity, price levels, and, most important, the need for educational and management services that differ among school districts. One way of considering those differences is through programs of categorical aid.

Why this concern about differential levels of need? Very simply, the array of special conditions that characterize school districts are randomly distributed among districts. Table 8-1 demonstrates the marked variation in the incidence of handicapped pupils and the pupils from families receiving Aid to Families with Dependent Children (AFDC) payments among the twelve geographic regions in New York State. Although the variation in the number of both types of pupils as a percent of total population is considerable, it is even greater when one looks at public school enrollments alone. Public schools, rather than parochial and other private schools, typically bear the greatest burden of educating the handicapped and educationally disadvantaged. New York City is an extreme case, with half again as many handicapped per thousand pupils, and

Table 8-1. Handicapped and AFDC Pupils by Geographic Regions in New York State

Region	Handicapped per 1000 Pupils	Handicapped per 1000 Population	AFDC per 1000 Pupils	AFDC per 1000 Population
New York City	35	5	297	42
Long Island	23	6	43	11
Rockland-Westchester	24	5	53	11
Mid-Hudson	20	4	41	9
Capital District	18	4	41	8
Northern	16	4	67	16
Mohawk Valley	21	5	53	11
Binghampton	20	5	39	10
Syracuse	21	5	71	16
Rochester	20	4	54	12
Elmira	17	4	33	8
Buffalo	26	5	72	15
Total State	27	5	133	25

more than four times as many AFDC pupils as the closest region, but substantial variation still exists among the remaining eleven regions, even though each is below the state average of 27 handicapped students per 1,000 pupils. The Buffalo region has 60 percent more handicapped than the Northern region (26 to 16). Similarly, the Buffalo and Rochester regions have almost twice as many AFDC pupils as the mid-Hudson, Capital District, and Long Island regions. Schools in New York City have more than four times as many AFDC students per thousand pupils as even the Buffalo region.

It is generally accepted that both of these categories present special educational problems for school districts and thus necessitate additional costs. Looking at the disadvantaged alone, we see in Table 8-2 that the proportion of disadvantaged students tends to be positively related to wealth as measured by property valuation on two types of incidence. The wealthier the group of school districts in terms of property value, the greater the proportion of low-achieving pupils and AFDC pupils. More important, in each wealth category the incidence of low-achieving and AFDC pupils is considerably greater in cities than it is in suburban and rural school districts. Although the New York State pattern as illustrated in Table 8-2 is not necessarily duplicated in other states, it does serve to illustrate that the burden of educating youngsters with special educational needs falls unevenly among the individual school districts of each state and, at the very least, shows that it is highly unlikely that that burden will be directly related to low wealth when wealth is measured by property valuation per pupil.

Special needs associated with public education are also not randomly

Table 8-2. Two Educational Needs Factors for 119 New York
State School Districts: City and Noncity within Cohort
Wealth Groups, 1967-68

Full Taxable Property Value per WADA (City–Noncity)	Percent Low Achieving Pupils[a]	Percent of Pupils from Families Receiving AFDC Payments
$48,000 and above		
City – $N = 1$	34.0%	15.0%
Noncity – $N = 8$	17.8	5.6
$47,999 - 36,000		
City – $N = 4$	31.5	17.3
Noncity – $N = 8$	15.0	4.5
$35,999 - 24,000		
City – $N = 9$	27.8	12.7
Noncity – $N = 28$	15.2	2.4
$23,999 - 12,000		
City – $N = 8$	22.0	8.3
Noncity – $N = 48$	17.5	3.7
$11,999 and below		
City – $N = 0$	–	–
Noncity – $N = 5$	18.4	3.0

[a]Percent below 24th percentile on statewide reading test.
Source: Syracuse University Research Corporation.

distributed in the area of management services. It is not at all surprising that forty-five of the states provide extra help for local districts with transportation services and twenty-nine assist with the extra costs of school construction. Wealth disparities aside, it is easy to understand the need for these management services and their unequal distribution among school districts. Furthermore, it is relatively easy to measure the extent of need for both services. Once a state has determined which youngsters will be transported and how far, one need only count the number of miles traveled by school buses and the cost associated with those miles. Similarly, once the state has determined guidelines for school construction, aid for construction costs can be readily determined.

Some educational needs are also easily understood and identified. There is general agreement that the costs of educating the physically and mentally handicapped are greater than the costs associated with educating the regular pupil in elementary and secondary schools. However, the specific needs and particular remedies associated with emotionally disturbed pupils and those whom we describe as being educationally disadvantaged are less understood and far more difficult to identify. Moreover, both educational need areas are typically associated with citizens from low-status backgrounds, and their incidence is most often higher than average in urban school districts.

The importance of different levels of need for educational and management services within the context of fiscal neutrality is that a higher burden of need effectively reduces the apparent fiscal capacity of school districts. Two approaches have been used to deal with this problem. First, the manner in which pupils are counted in equalizing formulas has been modified by weighting pupils with special needs more than regular pupils. Second, categorical aid is used to account for differences in need.

STATE CATEGORICAL PROGRAMS

In this section we describe the content and operation of state aid programs to meet special educational and management needs. In addition, we review school finance reform proposals in five states.

Existing Programs

All existing and proposed school finance systems make provision for categorical aids to local school districts. At the state level in 1971-72, almost $3.3 billion in state aid—17.8 percent of all aid to local districts—was distributed under special-purpose or categorical grants. Eighty-five percent of the $3.3 billion—15 percent of total state aid—was distributed through flat grants, and the remaining $.45 billion was distributed with at least some equalizing intent. However, only twelve of the fifty states have categorical programs that use equalizing formulas.[11]

Table 8-3 shows the total amount of categorical aid, the amount of such aid that is distributed in inverse relationship to district wealth, categorical aid as a percentage of all state aid, and the percentage of state/local revenues from state sources. With the exception of Hawaii, in which all funds are distributed on a categorical basis, such aids range from a low of 0.2 percent of total state aid in Virginia to 62.2 percent in Maryland. Only Nevada and Wyoming have no categorical programs in their systems of school finance. Twelve states distribute more than 20 percent of their aid through categorical grants, but only Delaware, Pennsylvania, Georgia, and South Carolina contribute half or more of state/local revenues from state sources. Another five contribute approximately one-third from state aid. Thus, in only a relatively few states do categorical state aid grants represent a major portion of state/local revenues.

Table 8-4 lists the kinds of categorical or special-purpose aid programs found at the state level. They are grouped according to their general functional purpose. Those under the heading "Special Educational Programs" are designed to provide support for a particular kind of educational need or for students in a particular instructional program. Those in the category "Educational Support Programs" cut across specific instructional areas. The category "Administration and Management Support Programs" includes functions not directly related to the provision of instructional services.

Also included in Table 8-4 are data indicating the number of states

Table 8-3. Categorical State Aid

State	Amount of Categorical Aid[a] (millions)	Amount Equalizing[a]	Percentage of Total State Aid	Percentage of State/Local Revenue from State Sources[b]
Alabama	$ 15.9	–	6.1%	75.9%
Alaska	16.5	–	14.7	85.8
Arizona	5.6	–	3.0	47.0
Arkansas	14.0	$ 9.6	3.8	55.7
California	287.3	–	20.2	37.1
Colorado	21.2	–	13.3	30.9
Connecticut	142.3	–	0.3	23.8
Delaware	24.0	–	23.0	74.7
Florida	49.7	26.5	6.9	60.1
Georgia	85.4	–	20.0	59.0
Hawaii	222.4	–	100.0	96.9
Idaho	0.4	–	0.8	45.3
Illinois	202.8	–	21.0	38.2
Indiana	30.1	–	9.0	34.7
Iowa	25.4	–	12.0	24.6
Kansas	8.3	–	6.6	32.1
Kentucky	2.9	–	1.2	64.1
Louisiana	24.5	–	5.9	65.2
Maine	15.3	8.9	23.3	34.7
Maryland	291.0	12.6	62.2	46.5
Massachusetts	87.1	43.0	28.0	22.7
Michigan	119.8	–	14.2	46.3
Minnesota	114.8	–	18.0	57.0
Mississippi	21.9	–	12.1	67.3
Missouri	60.3	–	18.5	39.6
Montana	2.2	–	5.7	26.1
Nebraska	2.9	–	6.7	18.5
Nevada	–	–	–	44.7
New Hampshire	4.7	–	51.1	5.6
New Jersey	272.6	29.7	49.5	26.3
New Mexico	17.8	–	12.3	76.5
New York	187.3	105.1	7.4	50.1
North Carolina	47.1	–	9.5	77.8
North Dakota	1.6	–	5.0	31.9
Ohio	144.9	49.8	18.4	32.5
Oklahoma	12.5	–	0.7	46.0
Oregon	14.0	–	13.1	20.8
Pennsylvania	288.2	141.1	23.2	51.2
Rhode Island	10.6	6.1	16.1	40.3
South Carolina	48.6	–	22.4	68.7

Table 8-3. (cont.)

State	Amount of Categorical Aid[a] (millions)	Amount Equalizing[a]	Percentage of Total State Aid	Percentage of State/Local Revenue from State Sources[b]
South Dakota	0.9	–	4.8	17.2
Tennessee	21.6	–	8.8	52.3
Texas	24.0	–	2.5	52.6
Utah	23.4	0.8	18.2	57.8
Vermont	10.9	–	2.6	35.2
Virginia	47.2	–	0.2	39.3
Washington	80.2	21.0	0.3	55.3
West Virginia	8.5	–	5.5	57.0
Wisconsin	104.4	–	31.9	32.6
Wyoming	–	–	–	33.3
Total	$3,265.0	$454.2	17.8%	44.0%

[a]U.S. Department of Health, Education and Welfare, Office of Education, *Public School Finance Programs, 1971-72*, Thomas L. Johns, ed. (Washington, 1973), Table 93. The amount of categorical funds distributed in an equalizing formula (column 2) is very narrowly defined by the USOE. It includes only those aid funds that are allocated inversely to wealth but excludes those that are a very high flat grant (80-90 percent of costs) or where the state assumes full costs. For example, Maryland's full state assumption of school construction is not considered an equalizing aid, even though the results are equalizing. Similarly, some special-purpose aids are included in the general aid category if the use of the funds is not expressly restricted by the state. For example, the USOE report covering New York State includes in the general support formula transportation expense aid and building expense aid, both highly equalizing, though the amount of aid is determined directly from costs incurred for each specific function. A complete recasting of the USOE report to take such distinctions into account is beyond the scope of this chapter.

[b]National Education Association, Rankings of the States, 1972, (Washington, 1972), calculated from Table 93, p. 52.

that provide state aid to meet functional needs through categorical and general grant mechanisms. The mechanism most relevant to the concern of this chapter is found under column 1, which includes those states that provide additional state aid for each function only through categorical grants. Column 3 indicates the number of states that consider the need for additional state aid for these program areas only within the framework of the basic multipurpose or general aid formula. Such provisions typically involve the manner in which pupils are counted by weighting those pupils who fall in the appropriate category or adjusting aid formulas in some way to take such needs into account.

For example, weighting for the higher cost of educating the disadvantaged is done in California, Connecticut, Nebraska, New Jersey, Minnesota, Pennsylvania, and Washington, either by counting those enrolled in compensatory education programs or by using AFDC lists. New York State's Fleischmann Commission has recommended that disadvantaged youngsters be

Table 8-4.   Categorical Aid Programs and Provisions in State Finance Systems

	Number of States Using Only Categorical Aid for Designated Purpose (1)	Percent of Total Categorical Aid (2)	Number of States with Provisions in General Aid Formula for Designated Purpose (3)	Number of States Providing Both Categorical and Formula Aid (4)
Specific Educational Programs				
Early Childhood (includes kindergarten)	2	0.1%	24	0
Compensatory Education	11	4.1	5	2
Special Education	37	19.6	12	5
Vocational Education	38	8.3	4	9
Adult and Continuing Education	10	0.3	1	1
Driver Education	26	2.0	0	0
Educational Support Programs				
Professional and Curriculum Improvement, Innovations	11	0.4	2	1
Libraries	19	3.7	1	0
Textbooks				
Supplies and Equipment				

Administration and Management Support Programs

Transportation	24	14.2	21	1
School Construction	26	24.0	3	0
Administration and Supervision	9	4.7	16	0
Emergencies and Contingencies	N.A.	N.A.	N.A.	N.A.
Orphans	N.A.	N.A.	N.A.	N.A.
School Lunch	20	2.4	1	0
Health Service	2	0.4	1	0
District Organization	4	0.1	5	1
Municipal overburden/density	0	–	4	0
Other	41	15.7	0	0

Source: *Public School Finance Programs, 1971-72*, U.S. Department of Health, Education and Welfare, Office of Education. "Other" includes categorical aids that could not be fitted into the classification.

N.A.: Data not available or included in "other" category.

weighted 1.5 and all youngsters in special class programs for the handicapped be weighted 2.05. The Commission has also recommended that extra weighting for secondary school pupils be discontinued.[12]

Column 2 of Table 8-4 shows the percentage of all categorical state aid allocated to each of the individual programs listed. Aid for school construction is the leading functional area requiring 24 percent of total categorical aid distributed in twenty-six states. Aid for special or exceptional child educational programs is made available to local school districts through categorical grants in thirty-seven states and constitutes 19.6 percent of the total.[13] Twenty-four states have special aid programs for transportation, representing 14.2 percent of the total.[14] Column 4 of Table 8-4 indicates the number of states that have provided for needs in each program area through both categorical and multipurpose grants.

Categorical aid programs are a widely used mechanism for assisting local school districts in providing for special educational and management needs. The typical state distributes less than 20 percent of state aid through categorical grants. Almost 60 percent of all state-level grants are for transportation, school buildings, and educational programs for the handicapped. Although less than 15 percent of all categorical funds are distributed through equalizing formulas, many others have at least some equalizing effect since they represent all or a large proportion of the costs of an activity. However, a number of states do not recognize the uneven distribution of the need for high cost services among districts through either categorical grants or general support formulas. There is considerable opportunity in many states for meeting local needs for high-cost services and untying the burden of achieving such purposes from local wealth.

Proposed Revisions of Categorical Programs in Five States

In nearly every state, special school finance studies by government commissions, legislative committees, or private organizations have been completed or initiated since 1971. Comprehensive proposals for five large and important states—California, Florida, Michigan, Minnesota, and New York—have already been developed. A reform package adopted by the Minnesota state legislature is operational for the 1972-73 school year. The purpose of this section is to examine the provisions in those proposals for the principal categorical functions, with particular attention to the equalization characteristics of each proposal. Consideration will also be given to the way in which categorical provisions relate to recommendations for the general support formula.

California. At present approximately 37 percent of the revenues required to support California's elementary and secondary schools comes from state sources, with 61 percent of state revenues, including all revenues for special categorical purposes, distributed on a flat-grant basis with no consideration to local fiscal ability.[15] In June of 1972 a staff of consultants headed by Charles S. Benson submitted a final report to the California Senate Select Committee on School District Finance.[16] Although the recommendations of that report did not become law in the 1972 legislative session, its provisions seem sufficiently important to merit discussion and analysis. (See also Chapter 5 above.)

The committee report recommended that the general-purpose program distribute aid through a District Power Equalizing (DPE) mechanism. The responsibility for raising revenues for basic educational activities would continue to be shared between state and local governments, but each local school district would have equal power to generate revenues (state and local together) for local schools.

Transportation.   At present transportation is a shared responsibility. The state share is distributed essentially as a flat grant, providing each district with an amount equal to the median statewide approved expense per bus per day plus 25 percent. The Senate Select Committee report recommended that all approved transportation services be the fiscal responsibility of the state through full state assumption (FSA).

School building.   Local school districts currently must exceed 95 percent of their bonding capacity to be eligible for loans from the state based upon the state's bonding capacity. The Senate Select Committee report recommended FSA for approved site acquisition, site improvement, and construction costs to be financed from bonds issued by a state building authority. Additional costs for sites, construction, and minor capital outlay (equipment) would be financed from the local general DPE grant. Existing debt service of local school districts would be assumed in part by the state as well. High-wealth school districts would continue to meet their bonding obligations, low-wealth districts would have all obligations picked up by the state, and moderate-wealth districts would have part of their annual principal and interest payments reimbursed by the state through an equalizing formula. If adopted, this approach would be a substantial improvement in terms of fiscal neutrality.

Compensatory education.   California currently has no large-scale compensatory education program funded from state and local revenues. The Senate Select Committee report proposed a large new program of compensatory education in two parts. The first part would allocate money to a district based on the number of children who score low on learning readiness tests when they enter elementary school or on achievement tests when they enter high school. This program would provide supplementary instruction services for underachieving children, and districts would receive their allotments only after they submitted proposals to the Superintendent of Public Instruction. The second part of the compensatory education package would be based on the number of children with low socioeconomic status. These funds might be used for auxiliary services (such as breakfasts, tutors, or provision of study space) to offset some of the disadvantages that low-income children face when they go home from school. A proposal cycle comparable to that for underachievers would also be used.

Handicapped pupils. This is currently a state/local shared responsibility with the state picking up most of the excess cost over the regular program cost. Aid for handicapped pupils in the proposed Senate Select Committee report would be included in the general-purpose DPE grant, bringing local fiscal capacity directly into play. A variety of weighting factors recommended by the State Board of Education would be used to adjust the regular average daily attendance count of school districts (e.g., regular K-6 pupil, 1.00; hearing handicapped, 4.40; educable mentally retarded, 2.10).

Florida. Currently, 60 percent of state/local revenues comes from state sources in Florida. Approximately 88 percent of all state aid is distributed in an equalizing manner, primarily through a Strayer-Haig foundation formula. Slightly more than half of the approximately $50 million of special-purpose aids is also distributed on an equalizing basis. However, local districts currently are permitted to exceed the foundation program by raising revenues totally from local sources.

A Governor's Citizens' Committee on Education has made a series of recommendations,[17] calling for a basic foundation program based on an 8 mill local tax rate with a permissible 2 mill fully equalized add-on. No district may exceed the 10 mill total.

Transportation. Aid for transportation services currently is included within the state minimum foundation program and this is distributed in an equalizing manner. The Governor's Committee has recommended that transportation services approved by the state be FSA.

School building. This is currently a state/local shared responsibility with state aid distributed on an equalizing basis. The Governor's Committee has recommended that the costs of school building be provided under FSA. All existing debt obligations would be assumed by the state.

Compensatory education. There is currently no compensatory education program from state/local revenues in Florida. The recommendation is that those pupils below the Florida poverty level, less those pupils identified as Title I eligibles, be weighted 1.5 and included in the general support formula.

Handicapped. Both capital and operating expenses are currently FSA—capital by reimbursement and operating costs by allotment. The Governor's Committee has recommended that a series of weightings for the various categories of handicapped be included in the general support formula.

Michigan. Approximately 46 percent of all state and local revenues currently are contributed from state sources in Michigan. Approximately 86 percent of state aid is distributed through the general-purpose equalizing formula and the remaining 14 percent is distributed as flat grants for special categorical purposes.

The initiative for school finance reform in Michigan has come from Governor William Millikin. Governor Millikin's proposals for FSA were submitted in 1972 after a comprehensive analysis of the effect on local districts of the current system of financing schools.[18] Each local district would be permitted a 6 mill power equalized enrichment add-on beyond the FSA grant. This enrichment add-on must be approved by voters. In addition, a 4.5 mill nonequalized add-on that would not require voter approval is provided for the extra costs beyond those covered in the 47 staff per each 1,000 pupil formula included in the basic general FSA program.

Transportation. The state currently pays 75 percent of the costs of an approved transportation program. Governor Millikin has recommended that transportation be handled under FSA with local operation of transportation services.

School building. Local districts levy up to 7 mills plus 10 percent of annual costs until loan amounts are repaid. The state issues bonds to pay debt service costs beyond the revenue raised by the local millage levy in this equalizing aid program. The governor's proposals do not include changes in provisions for school building.

Compensatory education, vocational education, handicapped. Michigan currently has a compensatory program in which additional aid, not to exceed $200 per pupil, is provided to those districts with more than 15 percent of pupils in grades K-6 in need of substantial improvement in basic cognitive skills. In the area of special education, the state currently provides 75 percent of professional salaries for approved teachers with salaries not to exceed $8100 for any single position. Governor Millikin's proposal calls for a 4.5 mill add-on that does not require voter approval to cover the extra costs of providing teachers and services in these areas as regular costs are assumed to be covered within the basic support program. If the 4.5 mills were levied by local districts, high-need, low-wealth districts would be severely limited in their ability to provide additional services. However, the language of the governor's proposal leaves open the option of having either the state or the intermediate districts levy the 4.5 mills and distribute services to local districts. Such options are prerequisite to untying the provision of high-cost services to local wealth.

Minnesota. Minnesota is the only one of the five states in which school finance reform proposals have run the gauntlet of the political process. The 1972-73 school year is the first in which the results of that political effort will have an effect upon local school districts. Before that year the state contributed approximately 57 percent of state/local revenues for elementary and secondary education. The current state aid system in Minnesota is a Strayer-Haig foundation program with a local tax limit.[19]

Transportation. Transportation costs in 1972-73 are shared between state and local school districts. The state picks up approximately 80 percent of the calculated amount, and the local school district picks up the other 20 percent plus any costs above those approved.

School building. There is no change in the way in which school plant is provided. It continues to be a responsibility of local school districts, with no state participation.

Compensatory education. AFDC pupils are counted 1.5 (vs. 1.00 for regular K-6 pupils) in determining the resident-weighted average daily attendance.

Handicapped. The state pays up to $5300 for each teacher of the handicapped but no more than 60 percent of any given salary.

New York State. In New York State approximately 50 percent of state/local revenues comes from the state. State general-purpose aid is distributed through a percentage equalizing formula up to an aid ceiling of $860 per pupil, with the average per pupil expenditure for 1972-73 approximately $1350. Ninety-two percent of state aid, including more than half of the special purpose aid (7 percent of the total), is distributed in an equalizing manner.

New York's Fleischmann Commission submitted its report to Governor Rockefeller and the Board of Regents in 1972.[20] The commission report calls for FSA of all educational functions. No local add-on to the basic FSA grant would be permitted.

Transportation. The state currently pays 90 percent of approved transportation costs. The Fleischmann Commission would raise that to 100 percent.

School building. This is currently a shared state/local responsibility with state aid distributed through an equalizing formula for all approved costs. Fleischmann would create a state building authority to issue construction bonds.

Compensatory education. At present, New York has a relatively small compensatory program ($50 million out of a total $6 billion spent on elementary and secondary education) directed at about forty-five of the more urban districts. This program is similar to ESEA Title I in that funds allotted to each school district are predetermined by formula, but receipt of funds requires approval of specific compensatory projects. Fleischmann recommends that the basic general-purpose FSA formula include a weighting factor of 1.5 for all pupils scoring below a minimum competence level on a statewide achievement test.[21] The amount made available for such students would be stabilized at 15 percent of the state's base FSA expenditure level multiplied by the number of students enrolled statewide.

Handicapped and vocational. New York is currently the only state that fails to provide direct additional aid to reflect the higher cost of services to handicapped and vocational pupils. However, local districts can receive equalized aid for the costs associated with sending such pupils to Boards of Cooperative Educational Services (BOCES). Fleischmann recommends that an amount equal to 2.50 of the per pupil figure for regular students be assigned to intermediate units for delivery of such services.[22]

Summary. Table 8-5 summarizes the basic provisions in reform proposals for California, Florida, Michigan, Minnesota, and New York. There is a strong predilection in these proposals for FSA to provide for additional state aid for the handicapped, though the extent to which those provisions would, in practice, be fiscally neutral would be a function of the accuracy of estimates for weighting the excess costs of such pupils and programs. Of particular interest is the inclusion in each reform package of a strong state-level provision for compensatory education. Although compensatory aid funds tend to flow to urban districts that appear to be relatively wealthy in property value, and as such are in conflict with a simplistic notion of fiscal neutrality, they are a practical response to a more complex view of equity. Though perhaps exceedingly difficult to express in legal terms, such a view holds that a greater incidence of high-cost pupils actually reduces the effective fiscal capacity of local school districts to provide services to all pupils.

FEDERAL CATEGORICAL PROGRAMS

Purpose and Development of Federal
Categorical Programs

Although categorical programs serve to supplement the general foundation programs that predominate in state school finance systems, categori-

Table 8-5.   Summary of School Finance Proposals in Five States

State	General-Purpose Program	Transportation	School Building	Handicapped	Compensatory Education
California (Senate Select Committee Report)	District Power Equalizing	Full State Assumption	Full State Assumption	Weightings for pupil count in general purpose formula	Full State Assumption
Florida (Governor's Committee Report)	Foundation Program with power equalized add-on up to local tax limit	Full State Assumption	Full State Assumption	Weightings for pupil count in general purpose formula	Weighted 1.5 for pupil count in general purpose formula
Michigan (Governor's Recommendations)	Full State Assumption	Full State Assumption	Shared state/local with equalizing formula	"Extra" costs to be provided by 4.5 mill non-equalized add-on	"Extra" costs to be provided by 4.5 mill non-equalized add-on
Minnesota (Education Law Effective in 1972-73)	Foundation program with spending limit	State/local shared (80:20)	Local responsibility	State/local shared based on teacher salary	AFDC pupils weighted 1.5 in general purpose formula
New York (Fleischmann Commission Recommendations)	Full State Assumption	Full State Assumption	Full State Assumption	Full State Assumption with 2.05 weighting for all categories of pupils	Full State Assumption with 1.5 weighting

cal programs are the traditional and nearly universal format for intergovernmental aid at the federal level. At present, somewhere around a hundred separate educational programs of aid to elementary and secondary education are in operation.[23] Despite frequent complaints about red tape and overlap, despite the introduction of federal general aid bills, and despite the widely publicized proclivity of the current administration to transform federal programs into untied block grants to the states, categorical programs will very likely continue to be the most common form of federal aid to education during the foreseeable future. Supporting evidence for this statement lies in the Nixon administration's Special Education Revenue Sharing program. Although it has the term "revenue sharing" attached to it, it is essentially an attempt to combine thirty narrowly drawn categories into five broader programs. By the time it completes the legislative process (if it ever does), the act is far more likely to look like program consolidation than revenue sharing.

Federal aid to education has been a feature of American school finance since the earliest days of the Republic.[24] The Northwest Survey Ordinance of 1785 provided that one section in each township of federal land in the Northwest Territory be reserved for education. The start of the modern programs of intergovernmental aid, however, is probably most appropriately marked by the Smith-Hughes Vocational Education Act of 1917.

The Smith-Hughes program approach provided assistance to state and local education agencies to meet some nationally perceived need—the improvement of vocational and agricultural training—and required submission of a state plan. The same type of program was repeated in a burgeoning number of programs over the six decades since the enactment of that prototype education aid. The Depression brought free lunch and milk programs. World War II brought School Assistance in Federally Affected Areas (PL 874) to assist local communities to meet the added cost of educating children of parents working at federal installations or on military bases. In 1958, Sputnik brought the National Defense Education Act intended to upgrade American education to meet the newly perceived threat of Soviet technology. Then, in 1965, the Elementary and Secondary Education Act was passed, to improve the education of the children of the poor and to foster research and innovation in elementary and secondary education.

These watersheds in federal educational assistance illustrate the major purposes that federal aid has been designed to serve. First, federal programs are intended to cope with problems that affect only a relatively small number of school districts, even though they are national in scope. More recently, programs have been designed to meet the added costs for the education of Spanish- or Chinese-speaking immigrants to the nation, costs that tend to fall primarily on a limited number of school districts in the Southwest, Florida, and California, including such special cases as San Francisco and New York City. Similarly, children who begin life in one region—in rural areas or in the

Southeast—often move later in their schooling or early adulthood to the large cities of the nation, and migrant workers move from rural areas in one state to rural areas in another as they follow the crops. A number of federal programs are designed, therefore, to relieve individual states and school districts of these nationally induced educational costs.

Second, there are national goals that may not be perceived by the states and school districts of the nation.[25] NDEA and the School Milk and Breakfast Programs were of that nature. In these instances, the national executive and legislative branches used the resources of the nation to serve what they determined to be educational needs of the nation.

Third, some needed activities are simply beyond the resources of, or are far too inefficient for, states and school districts to undertake alone. Examples of this category would be federal aid for research and development or for the training of teachers.

Fourth, only the federal government can provide any measure of equalization among the expenditure levels of the state and regions of the nation. This purpose is implicit in the distribution formulas of a number of the key aid programs.[26]

Clearly, these purposes overlap and particular categorizations can be disputed. Yet the general perception that there are national as well as state and local interests in public education has led to the development of a broad range of federal categorical education aid programs.

The Effect of Current Programs

With the possible exception of PL 874 (impacted areas aid), federal programs are designed for special functional purposes. Overall, they constitute a relatively small, yet strategically influential, component of support for public education. They are small in that federal aid constitutes only 7 percent of total revenues for public schools, but they are influential because for certain substantive purposes and for certain types of school districts, federal aid exerts a predominant effect.

Federal programs of public school support contribute varying proportions and amounts to different states (see Table 8-6). The range among the states is extreme, from 2.5 percent to 26 percent of total revenues, and from $29 to $195 per pupil. The result of the aggregation of individual entitlement formulas in nearly one hundred different federal programs, the reasons for these disparities defy simple explanation. However, the factors that are most important in shaping the interstate patterns of allocation are state per capita income (the lower the income, the higher the entitlement in many programs) and the presence of military bases and federal installations, thus qualifying the state for PL 874 funding.

Not only do federal programs play a larger part in some states than in others, but within the states they provide different types of districts with

Table 8-6. Percentage and Dollar Amount of Total Revenues
per Pupil for Elementary and Secondary Education from the
Federal Government, by State

State	Percent Federal Revenues of Total Revenues[a]	Federal Revenues per Pupil	Total Revenues per Pupil[b]
Mississippi	26.0%	$195	$750
New Mexico	18.5	168	909
Alabama	18.3	116	637
Alaska	17.4	300	1,729
Arkansas	17.3	115	669
Kentucky	16.5	127	774
South Carolina	16.5	136	825
Tennessee	13.3	99	750
Louisiana	12.5	117	939
West Virginia	12.4	99	804
Idaho	12.2	101	830
North Carolina	11.7	94	811
Oklahoma	11.6	85	734
Georgia	10.8	78	727
Virginia	10.6	109	1,033
North Dakota	10.0	86	866
South Dakota	10.0	86	862
Florida	9.7	93	962
Colorado	8.5	92	1,092
Montana	8.5	83	977
Texas	8.5	81	959
Arizona	8.4	84	1,000
Hawaii	8.4	110	1,310
Utah	7.9	66	839
Rhode Island	7.8	79	1,014
Washington	7.7	86	1,118
Wyoming	7.6	75	990
Maine	7.3	64	877
Delaware	7.1	94	1,338
Maryland	7.1	99	1,400
Kansas	6.8	72	1,069
Missouri	6.8	65	961
Nebraska	6.4	49	770
Ohio	6.2	60	968
California	6.1	62	1,028
Vermont	6.1	79	1,307

Table 8-6. (cont.)

State	Percent Federal Revenues of Total Revenues[a]	Federal Revenues per Pupil	Total Revenues per Pupil[b]
Nevada	5.9	61	1,043
Indiana	5.4	56	1,047
New York	5.4	91	1,689
New Hampshire	5.0	47	940
Illinois	4.9	67	1,382
Pennsylvania	4.9	62	1,268
Massachusetts	4.7	61	1,307
Minnesota	4.5	51	1,145
Oregon	4.5	52	1,169
New Jersey	4.3	62	1,443
Michigan	3.8	45	1,192
Connecticut	3.1	46	1,484
Wisconsin	3.1	38	1,241
Iowa	2.5	29	1,196

[a]National Education Association, *Rankings of the States, 1972*, Washington, 1972, p. 52.
[b]Ibid., p. 49.

significantly different proportions and amounts of aid. Primarily because of the workings of Title I of ESEA (aid to the educationally disadvantaged), federal aid tends to provide proportionately more funds to school districts with:

1. central-city or rural locations;
2. higher proportions of minority pupils;
3. lower income levels; and
4. greater educational need as measured by average achievement scores.[27]

As already noted, these general statements about federal-aid distributions summarize the overall effect of a multitude of individual programs. The differences in the patterns of allocation among those programs, however, are as important to understand as are the overall trends. For example, although ESEA I tends to benefit large central cities and poor rural school districts in greater proportion than other types of school districts, a number of other programs, such as NDEA, vocational education, and Titles II and III of ESEA, tend to favor suburban and smaller urban areas.

One factor that may be operating to cause these patterns of aid distribution is the amount of state discretion over the allocation of aid funds. Title I has a relatively rigid set of regulations and guidelines requiring that states focus aid on the poor and educationally disadvantaged, but NDEA, vocational aid, and Titles II and III of ESEA (as well as dozens of smaller programs) leave states much freer to assign funds unfettered by outside constraints. In a number of instances, what frequently happens is that states follow the familiar allocation procedures that they use in their own state aid formulas. A research finding on Texas practice in this regard is illustrative:

> Wherever TEA [the Texas Education Agency] had discretion in intra-state fund allocation, actual state aid formulas or a parallel system was used. The vocational education money was merged completely with state aid formulas as was Title II of ESEA, to the extent it was appropriate. ESEA-Title III of supplementary centers were based on an earlier state media center program. NDEA-Title III followed the state aid emphasis on small and rural districts, and the formula used for rating and funding projects paralleled the state aid formula. Title I has a federally mandated formula which is not similar to any state distribution and could not be changed by TEA.[28]

Given the all-too-common failure of general state-supported formulas to recognize the special fiscal problems of urban areas or the greater need for resources of districts with higher than average proportions of high-cost pupils, the results of these decisionmaking tendencies can indeed be significant. Perhaps equally important, such patterns suggest that federal aid should be examined in terms of both fiscal and programmatic purposes within the context of variation in state and local behavior.

Despite its many alleged shortcomings, federal aid has probably achieved one of the major functional purposes of intergovernmental grant programs. Many federal programs have been the major source of constructive innovation in American public education in recent years. A study of education innovation in six major cities concluded that

> it is clear that the emerging role of the federal government through the Office of Education is an external force promoting the greatest changes in the large city school districts that have been witnessed in the course of their history.... Compensatory education was virtually nonexistent prior to federal aid. The proliferation of experimental programs can be traced directly to the influence of federal aid policies. Pre-school education is now widely accepted under "headstart" auspices.[29]

The effect of federal catalysis has clearly not been restricted to large cities. NDEA III and ESEA III funding has provided many school systems in suburban or small-city areas with the fiscal elbow room to depart from the rigidity of normal budgetary necessities.

But what about federal control over local decisionmaking? The process and mechanisms by which this federal influence has come about is far more a "creative tension" between federal, state, and local purposes than it is "federal control" through rigid categorical requirements. What seems apparent in the context of the bottomheavy nature of American educational policymaking is that federal purposes, for better *and* worse, are adapted to the objectives of local education agencies. As David Porter concluded,

> *The main finding of our research on federal aid is that factors other than the federal regulations and formulas have a greater impact on the patterns of resource allocation used by recipient agencies* [emphasis in original]. . . . Federal allocators can have only very limited control over the final disposition of their funds. . . . The ambiguity of the goals, the unsophisticated technologies, the number and characteristics of its income sources, strategies such as multi-pocket budgeting or marginal mobilizing, professionalism and the vested interests of school staffs are the primary groups of factors influencing patterns of [resource] mobilization in local school districts. Most of these factors are not easily regulated or controlled.[30]

Where these factors are considered, it is not surprising that state and locally controlled funds frequently are insensitive to the added resource needs of some kinds of pupils, particularly the disadvantaged. The way local officials use federal requirements to achieve their own objectives has been described by Mayor Moon Landrieu of New Orleans. He was discussing the differential effects of categorical programs versus general revenue sharing in an area other than education, but his remarks are equally applicable to school aid. Federal categorical programs permitted him "to play catch-up for the years of neglect in deprived neighborhoods." To do the same without categorical programs, the city would have to concentrate well over half of its resources in such areas. "And that is a very tough thing to do with local dollars that are passed on by the city council."[31]

State education agencies have recognized the same potential in federal education aid guidelines. Whether guidelines are followed explicitly or state and local officials mold federal programs to their own ends, the principle of fiscal neutrality is rarely predominant. Indeed, as is often the case with the distribution of ESEA Title I, it would be in conflict with the need to be served. In addition, and certainly more important to the substance of this chapter, the courts have not applied fiscal neutrality to federal aid. Nevertheless, when the possibility of federal educational revenue sharing is considered, the role of federal aid in relation to state-local spending and tax-burden patterns becomes increasingly important. Proposals addressed to that possibility are the subject of the next section.

Proposed Revisions of Federal Programs

Although reliance on categorical programs has always characterized federal aid to education, proposals for federal general aid have frequently, but unsuccessfully, been made.[32] Once again, however, suggestions for change in the categorical approach to educational funding are widespread in Washington. Two motives are foremost: first, the search for a new source of funds for general operating expenses to supplement inadequate state and local revenues; second, a desire to escape the requirements and red tape that accompany categorical aid. These motives, singly or in combination, have led to a variety of possible federal programs, but three generic variants may be discerned: untied block grants, general aid with qualifying state distributional criteria, and special-education revenue sharing.

An untied block grant for education to permit complete state discretion over the allocation and use of federal funds is widely reported to be the favored position of the current White House staff.[33] In effect, this is comparable to general revenue sharing with the only restriction being that the funds must be used for education. That this approach has not become part of proposed federal policy is understandable; it generates strong opposition on several grounds: economic (no recognition of the "spillover" effects of education), political (it ignores the need of congressmen and senators to point to specific accomplishments and to determine the goals of funds they appropriate), and educational (the creative efforts of categorical programs in stimulating innovation and concern with education of the disadvantaged).

The second current proposal for revising federal aid represents a compromise between the untied block grants favored by the White House on one hand, and the pressures, on the other, of the United States Office of Education and congressional allies who are interested in maintaining something close to the existing categorical structure. The compromise often referred to as special education revenue sharing is reflected in the administration's proposed "Better Schools Act of 1973." That act would consolidate thirty existing categorical programs into five broad quasi-categorical areas: compensatory education, vocational education, education of the handicapped, supplemental services, and impacted areas aid. The effects of such a program in terms of national goals, however, will be determined by the nature of the guidelines and regulations attached to each area. If, for example, compensatory education is Title I *cum* existing amendments, regulations, and guidelines, we have one kind of measure. But if the targeting requirements are lessened and states control the pattern of intrastate distribution, it will be likely that districts with high concentrations of minority pupils and poor people will fare significantly worse than they do at present.

The same considerations apply to the other educational quasi-categories in the Better Schools Act. In regard to vocational education and the programs that will make up the supplemental services area, federal policies have not been effectively directive and states have long had a considerable discretion—a form of "revenue sharing"—in the categorical clothing of vocational programs, Title II of ESEA, and the NDEA III and VA. In short, the choice posed by special-education revenue sharing is not between a rigid set of federal controls versus hands-off money for the states. Rather it is a choice between differing sets of regulations. If appropriate targeting of funds were attached to special revenue sharing to ensure a focus on areas of greatest need—fiscal and educational—such an approach to federal aid could be a significant improvement over the existing helter-skelter laws. If the converse occurs and states are permitted to distribute federal funds in the same inequitable patterns that currently characterize state/local financing, then we have taken a giant step backward in educational finance policy.

One other type of program designed to serve a specific national purpose through a general rather than a categorical aid mechanism is an approach represented by the Stevenson-Mondale Bill, the Elementary and Secondary Education Assistance Act,[34] and by a measure drafted by Senator Muskie in 1972. These bills would provide general aid contingent upon the states' revision of their own school finance policies to lessen wealth-based spending disparities—in short, to encourage fiscal neutrality. These bills operate on the lever principle and seek to employ the slender pole of federal funding as a way of shifting the larger mass of state and local revenue patterns.

None of these approaches was adopted during the 1973 session of Congress. But each will recur and gain adherents. Any of the three may serve as the focus for revising federal categorically oriented aid in the future, and educational policymakers will be well advised to think hard about the advantages and disadvantages of each approach.

Summary
Categorical aid programs are a widely used mechanism for assisting local school districts in providing for special educational and management needs. The typical state distributes less than 20 percent of state aid through categorical grants. Almost 60 percent of all state-level grants are for transportation, school buildings, and educational programs for the handicapped. Although less than 15 percent of all categorical funds are distributed through equalizing formulas, many others have at least some equalizing effect since they represent all or a large proportion of the costs of an activity. On the other hand, a number of states do not recognize the uneven distribution of the need for high-cost services among districts through either categorical grants or general support formulas. Considerable opportunity exists in many states for meeting local needs for high-cost services and untying the burden of achieving such purposes from local wealth.

CONCLUSIONS AND RECOMMENDATIONS

This overview of state and federal categorical aid has discussed the purposes and structure of existing programs and the leading proposals for change at both governmental levels. We have examined the relationship between the principle of fiscal neutrality and approaches to dealing with differences in the need of local school districts for educational and management services as well as other national- and state-level goals through categorical grants. Five conclusions emerge from our examination:

1. Categorical grant programs are useful mechanisms for states and the federal government to assist local districts that have unusual needs for high-cost services.
2. Categorical grant programs are also useful in dealing with educational conditions that have a national rather than a local focus and in providing a vehicle by which states can plan effectively to deal with statewide problems.
3. Such categorical programs tend to be in conflict with a simple conception of fiscal neutrality that treats all districts alike with the exception of differences in property tax wealth per pupil.
4. But categorical programs can and should be an integral part of financial reforms consistent with and improving upon a conception of fiscal neutrality that recognizes differences in the need for educational and management services among districts.
5. The process by which categorical aid to local districts is determined can be improved to make the availability of services totally a function of need rather than local wealth. Several programs currently existing in some states and proposals that are emerging at the state and federal levels have the potential to achieve that objective.

We also noted in this chapter that categorical grants are not the only technique for recognizing differing educational needs. The varying requirements of particular groups of students can also be recognized through weighing mechanisms applied to a general-aid formula. Significant political differences may attach to these two approaches, however. Allocating aid for a particular type, say the disadvantaged, by weighing each such pupil 2.0 times an average pupil in the general formula, probably permits more local leeway in the use of funds. At the same time, it gives greater protection to the continuity of such aid. However, establishing an aid program for the disadvantaged as a separate categorical program would probably give more control to the donor government over the allocation and utilization of resources. But it might also make such aid more vulnerable to legislative repeal or reduce the chance to have the amount of state funds allocated to the category increased incrementally along with increases in the cost of living. General-support aid programs have been relatively responsive to such needs in the past.

Categorical aid programs have traditionally played another role, one that may be inconsistent with both fiscal neutrality and educational needs, but nevertheless one that should be understood by school finance reformers. Decisions concerning state aid to local school districts as well as federal aid to education are unalterably political. They determine who gets what, when and how. Despite considerable rhetoric about equity, efficiency, and need, the success of a new state-aid package is often dependent upon who comes out ahead, or at least who does not lose. Categorical programs such as "save harmless" provisions, density and sparsity aid, municipal overburden, programs for the gifted, and a host of others have frequently been the vehicles that garnered enough votes for a more equitable, more needs-based comprehensive state-aid package to get through a legislature and to be signed by a governor. The astute school finance reformer will know how to use such programs for their political value rather than simply their fiscal or educational effect.

As we noted at the outset of this chapter, we believe that fiscal neutrality applies to categorical programs as well as to general support. This would mean that within legislative categories (transportation, compensatory education, physically handicapped), districts with greater local wealth would not be given an advantage. Such a concept would require state assumption, power equalizing, or regionalization of functions served by categorical programs. It would also appear to vitiate unequalized matching provisions that are currently found in many state formulas (but not in federal) that permit wealthy districts to participate in a program with less tax effort than poorer ones.

To merge the goals of fiscal neutrality and categorical education aid, we suggest the following four guidelines for determining funding mechanisms for categorical grant programs.

1. *When all districts provide a service and there is little variation in need among districts:* The state should include aid for such services in the general operating aid formula. Examples are driver education, libraries, textbooks, supplies and equipment, administration and supervision, and health services. Flat grants or even full state assumption of such services are inherently unequal since wealthy districts receive as much aid as poorer districts.

2. *When all districts provide a service to some degree, but there is marked variation in need for the service among districts:* The state should assume (1) the entire cost of the function (transportation, school building, education of the handicapped); *or* (2) the entire excess cost beyond what is comparable to educating a pupil in a regular instructional program (handicapped, disadvantaged). But if actual costs or excess costs are not fully (or largely) borne by the state, it is more equitable to develop a weighting scale that closely approximates relative costs, and then adjust the pupil count for general-aid formula calculations.

3. *When the need for a special service is severe for only a small number of districts:* The state should assume the full costs of the relatively

unusual service. Examples are heavy concentration of educationally disadvantaged pupils, bilingual education, and migrant education.

4. *When the functional purpose is programmatic innovation (ESEA Title III, ESEA Title VI) or expansion of new programs (kindergarten, driver education, vocational education):* The state should (1) make the local share (where one is required) directly related to wealth; and (2) assure that such projects are allocated to all types of school districts with respect to wealth, community type, size, and location. The latter objective may require the donor agency (usually the state education department) to provide extra assistance in developing project proposals to those school districts that are poor and without sufficient staff to perform such tasks. The outcome should be that the term "lighthouse school district" would no longer be associated only with wealthy districts serving upper-middle-class children. Instead, all kinds of districts would have the same opportunity with the assistance of the state aid to develop new educational strategies. The process by which this aspect of fiscal neutrality in the allocation of categorical grants is to be achieved would be administrative rather than by formula.

The legal battle over reforming the ways public schools are financed may never raise the importance of categorical aid programs to a commanding position. Nevertheless, their significance must not be neglected or undervalued. As this chapter has demonstrated, both state and federal categorical programs play an integral role in satisfying resource needs that are not adequately addressed within the provisions of most general-support formulas. If we have one simple point to stress, it is that school finance reform must focus not simply on the general-aid formula that provides the bulk of funding but also on the total mix of categorical and general support. Only in that way can the allocation of educational resources match the educational and fiscal needs of the nation.

NOTES

1. Report of the Governor's Committee on Public School Education, *The Challenge and the Chance* (Austin: Texas Education Agency, 1968), V, p. 57. For a discussion of the problems associated with coordinating federal grants, see James C. Sundquist with David Davies, *Making Federalism Work* (Washington: The Brookings Institution, 1969), pp. 1-32. For a discussion of the institution and resources available for coordination at the federal level, see Harold Seidman, *Politics, Positions, and Power* (London: Oxford University Press, 1970), pp. 136-164. For a review specific to education dealing with "delivery system" weaknesses at the federal level, difficulties in federal state relations, and the reduced effect of federal monies due to "resource mobilizing" at the local level, see ibid., pp. 26-32.

2. David O. Porter et al., "The Politics of Budgeting Federal Aid: Resource Mobilization by Local School Districts," a report prepared for the

SURC Policy Institute under Ford Foundation Grant #690-0506A, (January 1973), p. 28.

3. *Serrano v. Priest*, Cal. Rptr. 601, 487 P. 2d 1241, 1244 (1971).

4. Ellwood P. Cubberly, *School Finances and Their Apportionment* (New York: Teachers College, Columbia University, 1905).

5. For a review of "what we now know about what works and what doesn't" and a strategy for federal involvement in future R&D for developing effective programs, see Alice M. Rivlin, *Systematic Thinking for Social Action* (Washington: The Brookings Institution, 1970), pp. 64-120.

6. Porter, "Politics of Budgeting Federal Aid."

7. *Milliken v. Green*, 203 N.W. 2nd 457 (1972), rehearing granted Feb. 13, 1973.

8. Jesse Burkhead and Jerry Miner, *Public Expenditure* (Chicago: Aldine-Atherton, 1971), p. 286.

9. Ibid., p. 287.

10. Joel S. Berke and John J. Callahan, "*Serrano v. Priest*: Milestone or Millstone for School Finance," *Journal of Public Law*, Vol. 21, No. 1 (1972).

11. U.S. Department of Health, Education and Welfare, Office of Education, *Public School Finance Programs*, 1971-72 (Washington, 1972).

12. *Report of the New York State Commission on the Quality, Cost and Financing of Elementary and Secondary Education* (New York: The Fleischmann Commission, 1972), p. 205.

13. Twelve other states distribute additional state aid for special or exceptional educational programs through the general-aid formula, and five use both categorical aids and the general formula. New York is the only one of the fifty states that does not provide extra state aid for the education of the handicapped.

14. An additional twenty-one states provide aid for transportation services within the framework of the general-aid formula. Only Arizona, Iowa, Nevada, Rhode Island and Vermont do not provide transportation aid.

15. In this section data about the proportion of state/local revenues from state sources are from the National Education Association, *Rankings of the States, 1972* (Washington: The Association, 1972), p. 52. Data about categorical programs are from U.S. Department of Health, Education and Welfare, Office of Education, *Public School Finance Programs 1971-72* (Washington, 1973).

16. Charles Benson et al., *Final Report to the California Senate Select Committee on School District Finance* (Sacramento: California Senate Education Committee, 1972).

17. The Governor's Citizens' Committee on Education, "Improving Education in Florida," (Tallahassee: The Committee, March 1973).

18. Executive Office, Bureau of Programs and Budget, "School Finance Reform in Michigan—1971," (Lansing: Bureau of Programs and Budget, 1972).

19. Anthony Morley, "Minnesota," in *A Legislators Guide to School Finance Reform*, (Denver: The Education Commission of the States, August 1972), pp. 33-51.

20. New York State Commission on the Quality, Cost and Financing of Elementary and Secondary Education, *The Fleischmann Report*, Vol. I, (New York: Viking Press, 1973).

21. The proportion of students so selected would be based upon the proportion of third-grade pupils who scored at or below the third stanine—approximately the lowest quarter—on reading and mathematics tests currently administered in the Pupil Evaluation Program.

22. At present such units are not actually intermediate in character. They are Boards of Cooperative Educational Services (BOCES) that are dependent upon the willingness of local districts to use available services.

23. E. Perkins McGuire (chmn.), *Report of the Commission on Government Procurement* (Washington: 1972), Vol. 3, Part F.

24. See, for example, U.S. House of Representatives, Committee on Education and Labor, *A Compilation of Federal Education Laws*, Committee Print, 92nd Congress, 1st Sess., October 1971.

25. For a theoretical discussion of the necessity for federal funding of state and locally underfunded external benefits, see George F. Break, *Intergovernmental Fiscal Relations in The United States* (Washington: The Brookings Institution, 1966), pp. 105-106.

26. For a discussion of potential equalization roles for the federal government in the post *Rodriguez* period, see Joel S. Berke, "The Role of Federal Aid in the Post *Rodriguez* Period," *Journal of Education and Urban Society* Vol. 5, No. 2 (February 1973). For a discussion of current intergovernmental formulas and their relation to interstate capacity, effort, and need, see Anthony P. Carnevale, "Allocating Federal Aid to High Need Areas," *Journal of Education and Urban Society* Vol. 5, No. 1 (November 1972). For a theoretical treatment of the efficiency case for federal leadership in interstate revenue distribution, see Richard A. Musgrave, *The Theory of Public Finance: A Study in Public Economy* (New York: McGraw Hill, 1959), pp. 17-22.

27. Conclusions 1, 2 and 3 are found in Joel Berke and Michael W. Kirst, *Federal Aid to Education: Who Benefits? Who Governs?* (Lexington, Mass.: D.C. Heath, 1972); conclusion 4 is from Donald S. Van Fleet and Gerald Boardman, "The Relationship Between Revenue Allocations and Educational Need as Reflected by Achievement Test Scores," *Status and Impact of Educational Finance Programs* (Gainesville, Florida: National Educational Finance Project, 1971).

28. Michael W. Kirst, "The Politics of Federal Aid to Education in Texas," in Berke and Kirst, *Federal Aid to Education: Who Benefits? Who Governs?*, pp. 236-237.

29. Marilyn Gittell, *Six Urban School Districts* (New York: Praeger, 1968), p. 124.

30. David O. Porter et al., "The Politics of Budgeting Federal Aid." Resource Mobilization by Local School Districts," A Report Prepared for the SURC Policy Institute under Ford Foundation Grant No. 690-0506A, January 1973, pp. 132-133.

31. Moon Landrieu, as quoted in *The National Journal* IV, No. 51, p. 1922.

32. For discussion of federal general aid proposals in the 1950s and 1960s see James L. Sundquist, *Politics and Policy: The Eisenhower, Kennedy, and Johnson Years* (Washington, D.C.: The Brookings Institution, 1968).

33. *National Journal* IV, No. 51, p. 1907.

34. U.S. Congress, Senate, *The Elementary and Secondary Education Assistance Act*, 92nd Congress, Second Sess., S. 3779.

Chapter Nine

Political Implications
of Serrano

Arnold J. Meltsner
University of California, Berkeley
Robert T. Nakamura
Dartmouth College

When the California State Supreme Court found inequalities in educational opportunity—as a function of local wealth—to be unconstitutional, courts in a number of states quickly followed suit. Similarities in conditions stimulated similarities in judicial responses. But although courts have been moved by the pleas of plaintiffs from low-wealth schools, policymakers have been slower in their response.[1]

Policymakers have long been aware of inequalities that have provoked judicial action. Indeed, the thrust of most past state efforts has been toward reducing such inequities through the establishment and refinement of foundation support levels; but reforms have been slow and their effects only partial. Substantial inequalities have persisted because political conditions have sustained their maintenance. Inequalities that hurt some also help others.

With some local variations, political conditions that sustain stagnation are remarkably similar from state to state. The foundation plan itself produces inequalities that promote stakes in its maintenance. Differentiation among the providers of educational services—teachers, administrators, and other specialties—divides their interests and efforts.[2] Decentralization of school districts creates differing geographic interests—urban, rural, suburban—requiring special adjustments. Legislators, while agreeing on deficiencies in the current financing system, remain divided about alternatives.

To assess the prospects for future reforms, we have selected the California case for special attention.[3] As the first state to face court-ordered reform, California policymakers are in the midst of a controversy that their colleagues in other states are just beginning. Although specific debates will undoubtedly vary from state to state, we can expect some similarities: The beneficiaries of the current system will not relinquish their advantages without a fight; specific interests will seek special adjustments for themselves (urban factors, rural poverty factors); and compliance will be muddled by on-going controversies over taxation. The response of California decisionmakers to these factors provides clues to the response of other states.

Of course, not all states facing court-ordered equalization will respond in the same fashion. Political outcomes are likely to be tailored to idiosyncratic circumstances of different states. For example, states that already rely heavily on sales taxes may be faced with the problem of creating a major new revenue source, such as an income tax, to fund equalization. In such areas, a statewide property tax may be a more likely solution than the adoption of a new tax. In other areas, particularly sparsely settled rural states without substantial industrial facilities creating vast disparities in local wealth, the simpler expedient of creating larger school districts may be the least costly political solution.

Across the nation finance reform will be a function of a set of general political features of educational finance and the incentives and activities of political actors such as interest groups. One point of our analysis of California reform alternatives is to show the influence of specific political factors on the shaping of policy. Despite the possibility of substantial policy variations, these political factors constitute an irreducible force that can and will dampen the effects of a seemingly sweeping court decision.

A working assumption of many *Serrano* watchers is one of great expectations—the creaky and unfair system that pays for our public schools is in for a major overhaul. Our assumption is different—the system is going in for a tuneup. Policymakers who have struggled for years to achieve significant school finance reform will appreciate the difference.

We are not professional pessimists, but as observers of educational politics we are not sanguine about the future either. Over the decades, the politics of educational finance has been more a matter of nonevents, of interest in reform with little actual reform. Each year many bills are suggested, few pass, and change comes in bits. Thus in this chapter our task will be twofold. First we will place in perspective the prospects for major reform in California by examining limitations on policy and political features that sustain these limitations. Second, we will examine the current array of policy alternatives and suggest likely points of consensus; we then conclude with observations about the political future of educational finance.

A Landmark?

If one judges by the reams of papers that have been written, the meetings of coalitions of lawyers, and the symposia for confused professionals, *Serrano v. Priest* is a big case and is having a big welcome. But will it have the outcome that some of its architects intended? Will it "break the logjam of the status quo and thus free the state from a politically immovable system"?[4] If breaking the logjam means that political actors will use the *Serrano* decision as a resource for trying to change the current system, the answer is yes. Needing every resource they can get, these actors want to counteract the prevailing indifference toward school finance issues. *Serrano* will help to focus attention on school finance reform. It may even shift legislative energies from welfare, heroin, and mass transportation to at least a modicum of concern about our schools. It will expand the base of political support beyond the little band of experts who have worried for years about the inadequacies and inequities of the current system.

Even this increased attention and political support will be insufficient for coping with the political legacy of paralysis. Although the court shifted the legislative agenda, it did not provide the political muscle to alter the political forces behind the "immovable" system in any significant way. One problem is the inability of the judiciary to legislate and administer with finesse. Even if the California Supreme Court had mandated specific financing remedies, which it did not, the judicial system is not capable of controlling, for example, the many ways that local school officials and parents can imagine for countering the best of intentions. Another problem is the openness of the *Serrano* decision itself. Since a myriad of policy options could conceivably satisfy the court, no particular policy with its underlying political interests is favored. Thus, the legislature may worry about what the court will settle for in reducing the influence of community wealth. The outcome, however, will not hinge on such anticipations of judicial desirability but on the realities of political feasibility.

Although we are not back to square one and we can expect some changes in favor of low-wealth school districts, the great expectations *Serrano* generated will not be met. We will not see the demise of the property tax, for example, because legislators find it hard to agree on alternatives. Similarly, full state assumption of fiscal responsibility for local schools is out of the question. The arguments will be clothed in the ideology of local control, but it will be the state's tight fiscal purse that governs. Certainly some impoverished districts will get more over the next few years, but school budgets will not double, or increase over 50 percent. Moreover, it is doubtful that our urban and rural poor will suddenly make great advances in educational achievement because of marginal equalization changes. In short, *Serrano* is not a panacea for all of the fiscal problems of our schools. What it does is to set the agenda for policymakers considering new policies in the context of enduring political features.

ENDURING FEATURES

Why Nothing Happens

One important feature is legislative paralysis. Why does nothing or very little happen in educational finance? Usually, it is easier to explain why something happens rather than the other way around. But let us attempt several complementary explanations by examining equalization as one component of financial reform.

Suppose we assume that politics is entirely motivated by material concerns, by self-interest with respect to taxes and expenditures. In this model of politics, organized and articulated interests hover around political actors and determine policy. When nothing happens, we conclude that supporters of equalization are few, not well-organized, and not articulate. In other words, although the poor school districts may have an interest in equalization, they are doing little about it. At the same time, the rich districts, who fear a loss of their tax advantage, are active and successful in opposing reform. As a legislative staff member said, "These pockets of wealth will really scream if you introduce a statewide property tax."

Now if we can put aside the assumption of group interests and also assume that political actors respond to symbols and their own beliefs about schools, we have another explanation for the paralysis. Accountability, decentralization, and efficiency are important symbols to many. When school districts violate these symbolic commitments, some policymakers either oppose equalization and increased state support, or offer only lukewarm support for what they perceive as a failing system. Perceptions of what is really wrong with schools may differ. Some legislators feel the real problem is one of accountability:

> In the present system, you just can't have accountability. It doesn't matter who the management is. It's a question of who gets to operate the guillotine. . . . Nobody is happy with the schools. [A Republican senator.]

> Teachers should be made more responsible for good teaching results. They should be made accountable for their actions. [A Republican member of the Assembly Education Committee.]

> The whole school system should be made more accountable. [A Democratic Assemblyman.]

Others feel the answer lies in decentralization:

> Education must come closer to the people in the community. [A Democratic Assemblyman.]

Another popular symbol is efficiency:

> The main problem is that better business management is needed in the schools. [A Republican Assemblyman.]

> Before we blindly apportion more of the people's money, the time
> has come to see how much the school districts themselves can do to
> narrow the revenue gap through the revision of business practices.
> [Governor Reagan in his 1971 State of the State message.]

Whatever their individual diagnoses, these policymakers feel that the problems of schools are not all financial. If schools are failing, by whatever standard, why give them more money? This common refrain stultifies action.

Aside from the predispositions of political actors and the contest of organized interests, paralysis is also explained by a conflict over basic and widely held values. Equalization highlights the conflict between equality and freedom. We may subscribe to equality but we also cherish the individual's right to live where he wishes and to send his children to the school of his choice. If a parent wants to live in Beverly Hills and pay more for his house to get an excellent school district with a property tax advantage, why shouldn't he? Just like the parent who wants the best education for his child, the legislator expresses his concern for equalizing educational expenditures and at the same time does not want to diminish the best education of the schools in his district. The conflict is resolved by doing nothing.

Education Is a Second Priority

Another feature is that more money for schools and fiscal reforms are the second priorities of most participants. The governor places property tax relief before concern with schools. Voters turn down school tax increases. Although many legislators are aware of financial crisis and the inadequacy of current financial arrangements, they have other concerns: the impending election, health and welfare reforms, partisanship, the form of property tax relief. Similarly, teacher organizations—the California Teachers Association, California Federation of Teachers, United Teachers of Los Angeles—have other first priorities: the protection of tenure and salary and benefit gains. School districts, and their organizations, tend to have numerous and divergent interests. The wealthy districts want to stay wealthy. Some resist unification; others resist decentralization. State Superintendent of Public Instruction Wilson Riles strongly supports financial reform, but it is one priority among many: increased school support, early childhood development programs, and accountability.

The only actors left who make reform their first priority are the educational finance experts and a few legislators. Some experts are employed by legislative committees, by the Legislative Analyst, by the Offices of Senate and Assembly Research, and by the Departments of Education and Finance. They have knowledge without a vote and are limited by the competing priorities of their employers.

Although we have few laws of politics, it is reasonable to expect that the more comprehensive the reform, the more political support will be required.

To shake the foundation of the foundation plan, to eliminate aid to the rich, to shift the financing of schools entirely to the state, political priorities must also shift. Despite *Serrano*, these priorities have not shifted, and lacking requisite political support, policymakers continue tinkering at the margins.

Constituency and Complexity

California uses a foundation plan to finance elementary and secondary education at the present time. In principle, this scheme resembles the systems used in all other states that rely upon a combination of state and local tax sources. At a minimum such a plan sets a state guaranteed support level per pupil. If local districts are too poor to meet this amount with a reasonable tax effort, then they are eligible for state aid. Typically the state-set minimums fall far short of actual educational costs, and inequalities in local-district resources produce a pattern of unequal expenditures and tax rates. Although these generic similarities have produced common court actions of the *Serrano* type, each state's foundation scheme produces different constellations of beneficiaries.

California's scheme is complex in its apportionment formulas, and it creates a large number of specific categories of beneficiaries. The richest districts receive basic aid, an allotment that goes to all students regardless of local wealth, as well as the benefits of their substantial tax bases. There are also categoric aid programs, which are state grants of money for specific purposes, such as reading teachers. Furthermore, a system of permissive overrides (local tax increases allowed by the state legislature without voter approval) has developed for special purposes, including adult education, teacher retirement and fringe-benefit programs, education of the retarded, and meals for needy pupils. In short, each state must contend with a functioning system, producing numerous specific benefits with real constituencies for its continuance. When organized, these constituencies favor marginal changes, such as teacher groups wanting increased salaries and benefits, but few press demands for wholesale restructuring of the system.

When chronic demands for more money and adjustments in interdistrict spending inequalities are made, policymakers respond by reducing their political costs. It is easier for the legislature to pass overrides and for local districts to use them than it is to confront the taxpayer head on. For those who want change and those who do not, the response is the same: tune up the foundation plan.

In addition to the constituency basis of incremental reform, complexity breeds another source of resistance. No single court case can banish the fear of tampering with the many volumes of the state's education code. Knowledge about the effects of broad changes is bound to be scarce and imperfect, but information about small changes is relatively precise since it relies on past experience. Lacking a clear majority for major changes and fearing to make errors that will be difficult to correct, legislators rectify the most glaring, agreed-upon defects through small patches on the current system. Since these efforts are cumulative, the resulting education code becomes even more complex and lengthy over time. The process proliferates interests, increases stakes in current methods, and reduces the likelihood of comprehensive reform.

Weak Supporters and Strong Opponents

An important feature of California education finance politics is the weakness of proponents and the strength of opponents of reform. The opponents have been relatively successful because of their own effective efforts and through the inadequacies of disorganized, discredited, and divided supporters of reform. Support, such as it is, comes from three sources: the school lobby, education finance experts, and such beneficiaries as parents and local taxpayers in low-wealth school districts.

The school lobby is numerous and diverse. At last count there were twenty-three separate groups officially listed as seeking to influence education legislation. This figure includes four teacher organizations, five administrator groups, and three kinds of school board associations. From time to time, these groups are joined by representatives drawn from various elements of the state's thousand-plus school districts. Despite their numbers, the school lobby is far from a decisive force in educational finance.

The political conditions that bred the large school lobby militate against its unity. The inclusive education code, which regulates every facet of education, and prevailing differences between labor and management encourage organizations along mutually exclusive lines: teachers, administrators, and school boards. Often these groups are at odds with one another, at both local and state levels, over questions of tenure, collective bargaining, and accountability. Another source of division is the decentralization of school districts into geographic units of varying size, wealth, and educational needs. Differences in condition often breed conflict, and the school districts are no exception. According to our previous survey of California educational actors, superintendents in low-wealth districts are almost twice as likely as their counterparts in high-wealth districts to favor equalization of expenditures per pupil, 80 percent to 45 percent. Similarly, they are much more supportive of ending basic aid and using the money for equalization purposes (low wealth, 59 percent; high wealth, 26 percent).[5]

There have been attempts at unity; recently Wilson Riles sparked the creation of the Education Conference of California, which includes thirteen of the state's major education associations. The hope is that massive state aid can defuse potential internal conflicts. Although it is still too early to gauge the success of this effort, we should remember that a new organization cannot erase the fundamental differences in constituencies.

In addition to internal divisions, the school lobby suffers from other liabilities. In our interviews, many legislators expressed distrust of what they perceived to be the "education establishment" and its narrow conception of individual interests. Whether well-founded or not, these perceptions weaken the influence of organized schoolmen. Symptomatic of the school lobby's diminished influence is the weakening of the California Teachers Association (CTA), once the largest and wealthiest of the providers of educational services. In the past, the CTA succeeded in passing a number of popular initiative measures, relying on its large membership, large campaign expenditures, and voter acquiescence to win at the polls what they could not win in Sacramento. Its recent and positive effort, Proposition 8, which would have mandated a large increase in state support, failed resoundingly in a statewide election. Simultaneously, the influence of CTA's vast research organization was undermined by substantial staff increases in both the legislature and the governor's office; CTA lost its monopoly on providing policymakers with educational finance information.

Another source of finance reform support comes from the educational finance experts. They are the technical staff working for the legislature, the governor, and superintendent of public instruction. They keep various reform proposals alive hoping that eventually their employers will gather the requisite political support.

The largest group of potential supporters includes the politically inactive beneficiaries of reform—the parents and local residents in low-wealth districts. Effective political action depends heavily on a high level of interest and knowledge about finance legislation, which they lack. The complexity of finance issues itself reduces the likelihood of effective public mobilization. Moreover, schools perceived to be failing have few friends, and disgruntled parents rarely see their interests as related to what happens in Sacramento. Dissatisfied wealthy families exit to private schools; dissatisfied poor families agitate for greater control through vouchers and decentralization. The low-wealth school districts themselves are in a difficult position; they have few resources to devote to lobbying. At best their superintendents intermittently plead by phone with their representatives for more money. Moderate-wealth districts, especially large, unified, urban districts, do not have much to gain through political action on behalf of equalization measures. If they act at all, it is to secure special adjustments for themselves.

Unlike beneficiaries of potential reform, beneficiaries of the present system guard their privileges through energetic political action. They have strong incentives to act—usually monetary—as well as diverse political resources, strong allies, and a clarity of objectives.

The present system of inequalities favors wealthy school districts, farmers, some large landholding business, and, of course, local parents from wealthy districts. When threatened, these school districts quickly and effectively organize. For instance, they formed and funded Schools for Sound Finance a short time after the introduction of a statewide equalization measure in 1971.

They had a lot to lose. Many of the other interests affected by equalization through tax increases are already organized: The farmers have the Farm Bureau, the Grange, the Wine Institute; the large landholders have the California Taxpayers' Association; Pacific Gas and Electric, Standard Oil of California, and the Southern Pacific Railroad maintain individual lobbies.

Because any major school finance measure entails infusions of state money, opponents of reforms can usually depend on the help of Governor Reagan[6] and many Republican legislators who seek to hold down the costs of government. The opponents can also use their diversity to gain access to many different types of legislators—those representing basic aid districts, farm areas, and districts with large business installations. Although diversity is a liability for supporters of reform, dividing their energies and efforts, it is an asset for opponents because it expands the scope of their influence. Legislative success requires a series of concurrent majorities (at committees, floor votes, conferences, and the governor's office), but defeat requires only breaking the chain. The side with access and influence in a variety of sites can stop legislation.

Finally, the opponents of reform have clear objectives. They are merely interested in deterring legislation that hurts them. Although the question of what is desirable divides supporters, the question of what is not desirable is easily answered and acted upon.

Partisanship

The importance of partisanship in educational politics has been increasing over the past decade. We found substantial differences between the parties in both attitudes and actions in educational finance.[7] Democratic legislators are twice as likely as their Republican colleagues to perceive a majority of schools as spending inadequately (Democrats 80 percent, Republicans 33 percent). Democrats express more concern about interdistrict inequalities than Republicans (Democrats 85 percent, Republicans 50 percent). And they are more willing to equalize expenditures per pupil (Democrats 79 percent, Republicans 62 percent). Furthermore, Democrats are more likely to support school measures with their votes. In analyzing a set of education votes taken in the legislature during the 1969 and 1970 sessions, we found that Democratic membership correlated strongly (0.75) with proeducation voting.

Some policy concerns, of course, do receive bipartisan support. Consider the recent organization of LEARN (Legislators for Educational Assistance Right Now). It is a bipartisan effort lobbying their colleagues and the governor for increased school support.

When legislators find themselves in disagreement along partisan lines, it is usually on the question of funding level and source. The Democrats are more supportive of large infusions of new state money than are Republicans. Furthermore, there are partisan differences on the size of future tax increases and the form of taxation. The Democrats are more supportive of larger tax increases, with a heavier reliance on progressive taxes, such as the income tax. By contrast, the Republicans favor smaller tax increases—and consequently smaller increases in state support for schools—and prefer excise taxes.

Means of Conflict Resolution

The best strategy for educational finance entrepreneurs lies in designing a policy that uses specific features to attract and unify a majority coalition while avoiding measures that would mobilize all of the potential opponents. We have argued that potential supporters are at best a disunited band of disparate interests; this is scarcely a coalition in search of a policy. Instead, policy must be used to actually create the coalition of supporters through judicious use of specific appeals. Success will depend upon formulating proposals that fall short of a wholesale restructuring of the present system; after all, the status quo yields substantial benefits to many politically potent groups. Assuming that the incremental approach to finance reform continues, proposals should also be evaluated by their potential for growth. Not only is it desirable to have growing revenue sources but it is important to introduce structural changes that can improve the equity of educational opportunities over time.

Policy payoffs will differ with respect to their school lobby and elected policymakers. Since conflicting school groups contend over distribution of resources, their support could be gathered by using specific incentives, such as special adjustments for urban differences, "grandfather clauses," and lengthening the period of implementation for the wealthy. For state policymakers, the level of support and the forms of taxation have to be reconciled. Here conflicts over funding could be resolved by splitting the difference on the amount of money and settling for a mutually acceptable form of taxation.

The tactics of hammering out attractive proposals are fairly well known. Bargains are struck among potential supporters, tradeoffs are made between first- and second-priority items, contestants split the difference. Once a proposal is formulated that accommodates a core of supporters, policy entrepreneurs engage in an exercise of salesmanship and side-payments to gather additional support. The strategy of building coalitions through formulating attractive proposals comes from being aware of the enduring features—paralysis, the second-priority, complexity, weak support and strong opposition, and partisanship. Having discussed these features, we are now in a position to analyze the likely points of short-term policy consensus.

LIKELY POLITICAL CHOICES

Although individual bills die annually, policy components persist over a number of sessions. The problems do not go away, nor do the solutions. In 1972, 657 education measures were submitted to the California state legislature. From our interviews with legislators, staff members and lobbyists, we have selected eight measures as representative of the major school finance alternatives facing policymakers. They are representative because they contain some of the recurring policy components of school finance measures: the scope of state responsibility, equalization, property tax relief, time adjustments, changes in the tax structure, condition adjustments, and local control.

Although all of the following policy alternatives have been drawn from the California experience, many of their features are applicable to other states. There are only a limited number of *general* approaches to equalization. Costs will vary in direct proportion to the extent and generosity of new state minimums. And the interest groups activated will be motivated by uniform desires to maximize gains or minimize losses. Furthermore, there are natural tradeoffs associated with school finance measures; the desire for expenditure controls on local districts is usually reconciled with the need for some growth through linkage with an inflation factor. The range of possible side-payments is similarly limited; an urban factor will be widely used as a means of getting support from specific legislative delegations, and "grandfather clauses" might ease the transition for the hitherto rich districts. Finally, under most circumstances legislators are similarly influenced by the popularity of property tax relief, although they may be split on means of raising revenues.

By identifying the range of policy alternatives and relating their support to specific constituencies, we hope to map the political environment of the issue of educational finance as well as specify the areas of general agreement and possible means of conflict resolution. We have grouped these policy components and related them to specific legislative alternatives to illustrate points of consensus and contention (see Table 9-1) and to allow policymakers to select which components are worth pursuing. We will approach our discussion in order of descending agreement and importance.

Increased State Responsibility

In educational finance, policymakers are laboring to satisfy a variety of taskmasters—courts, citizens, and school people. The courts tell them that they must devise a system in which educational programs will not vary as a function of local wealth. Taxpayers' groups tell them that citizens are mobilized in a "property tax revolt." And the school lobby pleads for more state money. Under these circumstances, an increased state role seems to be an attractive solution. There are substantial variations, however, among the competing proposals to increase the state's responsibility.

All of the measures agree that the state should assume a larger responsibility for the funding of elementary and secondary education. Currently the state pays about 35 percent of these costs. Governor Reagan has conceded the need for 50 percent funding; the Assembly Education Committee envisions 65 percent; and Senator Collier, Chairman of the Senate Finance Committee, would have the state pay 100 percent of the costs. All of these plans increase the state's percentage share and total state dollars, but not all of them would increase the total amount of money available to local school districts.

Table 9-1. School Finance Measures and Policy Components in the California Legislature, 1972

	Increased State Responsibility	Equalization	Property Tax Relief	Time Adjustment	Change in Tax Structure	Condition Adjustment	Local Control
AB 212 Greene/Dent (previously 1406)	X	X	X	X	X		X
AB 1283 Assembly Educ. Comm. (Santa Cruz)	X	X	X	X	X	X	X
SB 1171 State Board (Teale)	X	X	X	X	X	X	X
SB 102 Collier (Gross Receipts)	X	X	X		X		
Watson Initiative	X	X	X	X	X		
AB 1000[a] Moretti (Assembly Democrats)	X	X	X				
SB 1351 Reagan Tax Plan	X	X	X	X			
SB 90[a] CTA (Dills)	X	X		X		X	

[a]Original bills as of the summer of 1972.

Senator Collier's plan would not appreciably increase school support, and an example of a larger state role with an actual *decrease* in educational spending is provided by the Watson Initiative. This initiative constitutional amendment qualified for the November 1972 ballot and was defeated. Although its specific history is of little general interest, the Watson Initiative is representative of a larger class of proposals capitalizing on perceived discontent with schools and the property tax. By cutting and freezing local property taxes and not completely offsetting these cuts with increased state contributions, the Watson Initiative would have reduced school support by $771 million in 1973-74. If the state could not make up the difference, many school budgets would have had to be slashed. The Oakland Unified School District, for example, would have experienced a 27 percent cut in a projected $71 million budget.[8]

Admittedly, neither the Collier bill nor the Watson Initiative had much legislative appeal. Senator Collier stated at his bill's introduction that its purpose was to stimulate the legislature to "think big" about major structural reform rather than to pose an immediate solution. The extralegislative route, through the initiative process, chosen by Assessor Watson, testifies to his limited official support. The existence of these alternatives, however, shows that an assumption of greater responsibility and compliance with *Serrano* can occur without vastly increasing the amount of money available for local education.

The remaining proposals would provide more money (from $210 million to over $1 billion) for schools as an adjunct to increased state responsibility. Two of these are tax bills—proposed by Governor Reagan and Assembly Speaker Moretti—and they contain $210 million and $500 million, respectively, for schools. The authors have stated that this money should go for compliance with the *Serrano* decision, which means that it would go to low-wealth school districts. Similarly, the other bills (State Board, Greene/Dent, CTA, and Assembly Education Committee) are essentially distribution schemes that would apportion the bulk of their benefits to low-wealth school districts, with some adjustments.

Our survey of California legislative attitudes shows support for an increased state role. Founded on three related beliefs—schools need more money, local resources are inadequate to meet this need, and the state should increase its contributions—65 percent of our legislative sample felt the schools were in the midst of a fiscal crisis. This feeling was stronger among Democrats (77 percent) than Republicans (50 percent). Local sources are perceived as exhausted; 94 percent of all legislators felt it was not feasible to increase local property taxes for schools.

Support for increased state aid to one-half or more of local costs came from 53 percent of our sample. Again, Democrats (64 percent) were more likely than Republicans (41 percent) to favor such increases. No one interviewed expressed support for less than a 50 percent state share, although 47 percent felt that the state should not be pegged to any specific share.

Among the interest groups, the school lobby is behind an increased state role. For instance, 91 percent of the school superintendents responding to our questionnaire favored a state role of 50 percent or more. The 50 percent target is also a major annual demand of the California Teachers Association.

Business and farmers' groups—California Taxpayers' Association, the Farm Bureau, the public utilities—have been relatively silent about the desirability of a larger state role. They have been vocal, however, about not wanting to pay the costs.

Full state funding seems to be the least likely alternative. It would entail a major new tax—such as the gross receipts tax—or a large increase in existing taxes. The Urban Institute estimates that a 125 percent income tax increase would be necessary *to replace* local property taxes for education in California.[9] Since the school lobby mobilizes on behalf of increased money, a measure that required drastic shifts in taxation without substantial increases would not have the necessary appeal. In short, full state funding could not mobilize an effective school constituency.

Given these dispositions, it is likely that the state will increase its percentage contribution to somewhat over 50 percent and increase state money by at least $200 to $400 million. The bulk of the benefits will be given to low-wealth school districts.

Equalization

All the measures contain at least an element of equalization. Our data indicate that 68 percent of the legislature said they were very concerned about interdistrict expenditure inequalities; 71 percent favored measures designed to reduce these disparities. On the other hand, although a large majority of legislators are concerned about these inequalities, we found no consensus on remedies.

There are three basic approaches available to policymakers: first, raise the state guaranteed minimums, closing the gap between the richest and poorest districts; second, some redistribution of district resources, taking money from the higher wealth districts and giving it to the lower wealth districts; and third, a total leveling of educational expenditures on a statewide basis.

Raising the floor. This alternative can be considered the minimum response to the problem of interdistrict inequalities of expenditures per pupil. Although participants realize that this is not a substantial reform, they argue that it moves in the direction of *Serrano* by reducing the greatest inequalities. Most of the plans raise the foundation plan minimums, for example, from the current $355 per ADA in elementary schools to: $687 (Reagan); $650 (State Board); $550 (Greene/Dent); $440 (CTA); and $650 (Assembly Education Committee). The amounts vary, but the common feature is raising the floor for minimum expenditures to a more realistic support figure. The costs associated with such a raise are reasonably low. A staff report of the President's Commission on School Finance estimated an increase to the average expenditure would have meant an expenditure of $141.7 million; raising all districts in California to the amounts spent by the highest 10 percent was $1.382 billion.[10]

An example of a simple raise in the floor is Governor Reagan's measure, which would merely increase the minimum without concomitant changes in district resources. He also proposes a constitutional amendment to end basic aid, which now aids the rich districts. This approach would close the greatest disparities—between the very richest and poorest districts—while leaving the remaining districts relatively unaffected. Some of these measures also have features that redistribute resources among districts and equalize district taxing power.

The low political costs of "raising the floor" have the minimum of political dislocations. This option avoids the expensive enterprise of raising expenditures in a large number of school districts. The floor approach can be funded out of modest increases from existing tax sources, thus avoiding the politically difficult problems associated with proposals requiring major tax increases and broad shifts in the basis of school support through equalizations of district wealth. The governor and a number of Republicans favor this approach because it does away with dramatic disparities at a minimum of state expense.

The very features that constitute the advantages of the floor approach—low costs and limited effects—also form the basis of the opposition. An equalization measure, without broad grants of additional money, cannot secure the cooperation of either the school lobby or many key Democratic legislators. They argue that a school finance measure should involve a major shift in resources, broad enough to help the bulk of schools. Although the need for increased state support is most acute in low-wealth schools, it is by no means absent in average wealth districts. School groups—the California Teachers Association, California School Boards' Association, Association of California School Administrators, and the State Board of Education—want more state money for the bulk of school districts. In the case of urban schools with relatively high wealth and expenditures, the demand for increased state support has the backing of a number of strategically placed legislators, particularly those from San Francisco whose school district would lose over $10 million in state money with the end of basic aid.

Partial redistribution of resources. These are the "Robin Hood" measures. They take resources from the high-wealth districts and redistribute them to the others. Specific techniques vary from proposal to proposal. Two of the measures—Greene/Dent and State Board of Education—use a statewide property tax, a uniform statewide levy that raises money from everyone and redistributes it on a per pupil basis. Another technique, used by the Assembly Education Committee bill, redistributes half of each district's assessed valuation over a five-year period. Instead of directly equalizing expenditures, this approach equalizes district taxing abilities by redistributing a substantial portion of local wealth.

Redistribution measures have several advantages. First, they mobilize a large number of beneficiaries to work for their passage. Second, they generate increases in funds available to schools by increased taxes on a hitherto privileged minority. When applied to a redistribution of local resources, equalization reduces some of the pressures on the state's general fund, since all additional costs are no longer borne by a tax increase alone. Third, such measures offer property tax relief to low- and average-wealth school districts. And fourth, these reforms retain some measure of local control over educational expenditures— actually augmenting the discretion of low-wealth schools to spend more money. Support for these redistribution schemes comes from several quarters: the community of educational finance experts; Superintendent Wilson Riles; the legislative education committees; and, if they can be effectively mobilized, the low-wealth school districts (91 percent of their superintendents in our sample were in favor of a statewide property tax).

Opposition to redistribution stems from those who may lose and those who do not want to pay more for schools. By enlarging the category or beneficiaries, these measures increase the expense. The Republican governor and his legislative allies, generally opposed to large-scale general tax increases, will be in opposition. So will many major taxpayers and their associations, and individual landholders, such as the railroads and corporate farmers. Equalization in this redistributive form also hurts a number of high-wealth school districts. They will be joined by the urban schools who will either lose or have little to gain but still consider themselves needy.

Total leveling of educational expenditures. Senator Collier's proposal is an example of this approach. Under his measure, a gross receipts tax would replace the current sales tax, and the funds generated by this change would be augmented by a statewide property tax on business property. As a package, this bill is a big moneymaker, estimated at about $4 billion. These funds would be used for a full state assumption of educational costs, totally replacing the local residential property tax as a source of school support. Presumably this money would be apportioned on a per pupil basis, with some adjustments for special conditions.

Obvious advantages are its simplicity, equality, and totality of its residential property tax relief. Hawaii is the only state at present with full state funding of local education. Disadvantages are those normally associated with drastic changes: the problem of passing such a massive tax increase and the elimination of local financial discretion.

Big proposals generate big opposition. Opposition can be expected from both Democratic and Republican legislators for such a major tax increase and shift. Naturally, the high-wealth schools will mobilize against this measure. It is doubtful that the governor would support such a major increase in the state budget. Again, the owners of business property would mobilize through their associations—California Taxpayers' Association, the Farm Bureau, and the Wine Institute—as would individual large and well-represented groups of businesses. Such opposition is not likely to be countered by an effective coalition of supporters. School groups would not support such a measure, which takes away many local privileges, without concomitant increases in state support. Full state enforced equalization is a measure without a real constituency.

Since there will be some equalization, let us summarize the prospects of the three approaches:

1. Some variant of the "raise the floor" approach seems most likely. The governor, school groups, and legislators would support raising the foundation plan levels.
2. A partial redistribution scheme is next; it would probably take the form of a statewide property tax because of past exposure.
3. The alternative of full state equalization is not likely in the near future.

Property Tax Relief

Property tax relief is wedded to educational finance reform. Although it is reasonably attractive to many of the major participants, educational finance reform does not seem to have much public appeal. Thus policymakers tie reform and its concomitant tax increase to the more politically attractive issue of property tax relief. Since schools are one major user of local property taxes, some of the energy expended on behalf of tax relief spills over into school finance reform; Governor Reagan spoke for many when he said, "A major part of any tax reform has to be the solution to school financing."

Property tax relief means allowing some citizens, such as the elderly, to pay less, while others pay more. Relief usually means shifts in existing tax burdens, which reduce the visibility of property taxes. Reforms are usually more inclusive, entailing such things as statewide equalization of burdens and rate. Property tax relief should not be confused with reform.

Whatever the origins and doubtful reality of the property taxpayers' revolt, it is a widely recognized political fact in Sacramento and other state capitals. Legislators believe it is infeasible to increase property taxes, despite the evidence of annual increases. The governor and prominent Democratic legislators have said that relief is one of their highest priorities, and each group has introduced its own version of property tax relief. School groups have recognized the legislative appeal of property tax relief and have touted their own measures as offering such relief.

The order of political priority is clear: property tax relief is first, and educational finance reform is second. The two competing major tax bills—proposed by Governor Reagan and Speaker Moretti—illustrate this relationship. Governor Reagan increases taxes by $1.2 billion, and gives $900 million to property tax relief and $210 million to schools. Assembly Speaker Moretti's plan has a $1.4 billion tax increase, with $900 million for relief and $500 million for schools. Similarly, the persistent demand for expenditure controls by political leaders is rooted in a desire to prevent schools from using state money without offering property tax relief, or preventing tax rates from increasing along with state increases.

Although the popularity of property tax relief is undisputed, there are variations in the relief plans. The three complementary approaches are state exemptions, tax rate control, and splitting assessment rolls.

State exemptions. State-created exemptions allow local taxpayers to deduct a portion of the value of their taxable property, and the state compensates local governments for losses in revenue. The obvious attraction of this method is that relief is granted directly by the state, and state political leaders can claim the credit. Additionally, political decisionmakers can give relief to reasonably precise subsets of property taxpayers, including or excluding small or large propertyowners, renters, and the elderly. Both Governor Reagan and Speaker Moretti's bills adopt this approach but differ on the method for computing the exemption.

Tax rate control. Another means of tax relief accomplishes its ends through adjustments in local tax rates. Under these approaches, the extent of relief would be geographically determined, with the most relief going to districts that are taxed at relatively high rates. There are three general ways to grant this type of relief: first, set a maximum rate in all districts (Watson Initiative); second, impose a uniform statewide property tax (State Board; Greene/Dent); and third, simply mandate tax reductions in some districts through legislative action. The last approach is contained in the Assembly Education Committee bill. Using state money to offset losses in local revenue, this measure would mandate local property tax decreases of 40 to 50 percent.

Split assessments. This idea has been around for some time. It would divide the assessed valuation of local districts into business and residential property. Once this is accomplished, the business part would be used as a source of increased property tax revenues. The advantages are numerous. First, a major source of interdistrict wealth inequities is the location of business and industrial facilities. Second, the major political difficulty with the property tax as a revenue source lies with the difficulties in raising homeowners' taxes. And third, taxing business puts the burden on property that may produce income. For these reasons and others, the Legislative Analyst proposed this measure several years ago. Recently, Senator Collier's school finance measure added a sweetener by eliminating residential property taxes for education.

On the other side of the political ledger, our data indicate little legislative support for split assessments; only one-third of legislators expressed approval of such a plan. Additionally, if apartments are considered businesses, then renters would bear a large portion of the relief granted to homeowners. Obviously farm groups and business interest groups would also be in opposition. Operating on our premise that major policy changes create major political opposition, this approach is an unlikely immediate possibility.

Time Adjustments

To control the future use of the property tax, there are two types of time adjustments: inflation factors and expenditure controls. In practice, these features are usually combined in the same proposals. Nearly everyone agrees on the priority of property tax relief, and they realize that increasing school expenditures (or those of other local governments) would eventually nullify exemptions or tax decreases. Furthermore, the agreement on an expanded state role makes the state sensitive to local expenditures since it will have to come up with more money over time. The collective fears of many were expressed by one liberal Democratic legislator who said, "K-12 is a bottomless pit for state money." A condition for increased state support, given the priority of lasting property tax relief and larger state responsibility, appears to be the imposition of expenditure controls.

The school groups and their friends argue that they must have some room for increases, given the permanence of some rate of inflation. A lobbyist for the California Teachers Association said, "It's generally recognized around here that you can't have tax relief without controls; an inflation factor would make them livable." Hence a compromise may be struck by considering expenditure controls and inflation factors as necessary political complements.

These time adjustments are subject to different applications. Two competing types are currently under consideration: first, adjustments that would apply equally across the board to rich and poor districts, maintaining existing inequalities; and second, adjustments that permit a faster rate of growth in poor districts, while freezing the rich districts in place. Without going into detail, the first type is contained in the governor's proposal, which would freeze district tax rates and apportion increases based on current levels of expenditures; and the second type is contained in the Assembly Education Committee bill.

Change in the Tax Structure

The two major tax measures would make no change in the existing tax structure. They rely on increases in existing taxes for their revenue. A large part of any new funds for schools in both the Moretti and Reagan tax measures will come from increases in the sales tax. Some further money is generated by increases in bank and corporation taxes. One major point of difference between these measures is Moretti's use of the income tax, while the governor's measure contains no such element. In any event, these competing partisan measures agree that an old tax is a good tax.

The sales tax is the line of least political resistance. First, the practical economic advantages are well known: it raises a lot of money (in California a 1 percent increase yields $485 million additional revenue without appreciable additional effort). Second, legislators perceive sales tax increases as the most acceptable method of raising more money. During the deliberations on the Moretti tax bill, a number of legislators asserted that this was the least painful form of tax increase to their constituents. Whether founded or not, this impression persists. And third, there is the practical political matter of legislative acceptability. The Democrats want a tax increase and prefer other sources, but they will yield to the Republicans on source if that is the only means of marshalling the necessary support for an increase.

Of the proposals that involve changes in the tax structure, the statewide property tax has been around the longest time. Between 1961 and 1972 it has been part of at least eleven major school finance bills. It has never gotten beyond the committee stage; it has never been before the floor of either legislative house; it has never been before the governor. Leaving aside the technical advantages, this measure owes its longevity to the backing of respected educational finance specialists employed by the state government.

The long history of the statewide property tax makes it probably the best known of the various reform proposals. The frequent debates over its elements have made both the advantages and disadvantages, particularly in its effects on individual districts, well known to legislators. Our survey indicated that there is substantial support for a statewide property tax; 65 percent of school superintendents, 61 percent of the Democratic and 40 percent of the Republican legislators, and a substantial number of interest-group representatives all favor it. Furthermore, several major newspapers, the principal school groups—parent-teacher associations, California Teachers Association, California School Administrators' Association—and Governor Reagan have endorsed it.

But this support is deceptive. It has been contingent on a variety of specific factors, many of which are contradictory. In 1970, a statewide property tax at a low tax rate was part of the governor's tax program; it had the support of Republican legislators and the California Taxpayers' Association. The school lobby opposed it because it hurt the high-wealth districts without substantially benefiting the rest. The converse occurred in 1971; a statewide property proposal with a high rate was supported by the school lobby because of its new money and opposed by some Republican legislators and the California Taxpayers' Association for the same reason. For other political actors the statewide property tax has been appealing in the abstract but unpopular as a concrete proposal that asked them to hurt some of their constituents and put them in the unpopular business of utilizing a property tax. In short, the statewide property tax has had enough appeal and utility to stay alive politically but not enough, so far, to pass.

Two of the other proposals would also involve major changes.

Watson would have frozen local property taxes at a low rate of $2 for schools (K-12) and prevented any additional increase by withdrawing the voters' and legislature's power to increase the rate. Collier's gross receipts tax bill would require a major new taxing machinery to enforce it, as well as an end to local financial discretion. Under both measures, the legislature and the governor would be responsible for increasing educational funds. By withdrawing the element of local funding discretion, they would make state government the location of all future fiscal fights in education. There does not seem to be any real support among legislators for this increased responsibility. Indeed, the existence of so many permissive overrides is one index of their wish to escape such responsibility.

Condition Adjustments

Condition adjustments—special monies for special conditions—are a recognition that equalization creates new problems and does not solve old ones. Often called "urban factors," these adjustments can also apply to noncity problems. Much of what has been said about school finance reform is that inequalities of taxing power lie at the heart of school problems. This is not always the case; for example, a consultant to an urban Democratic assemblyman complained, "The problem with equalization measures is that they don't spend money where the educational needs are, they spend in a way that disregards the children with special educational problems." Similarly, an aide to a suburban Republican assemblyman stated, "The court made the wrong assumption, that rich districts are filled with rich people. So the legislature has to figure a way out."

Equalization imposes special liabilities on relatively well-off urban schools with high expenditures and special problems. Either they are actually hurt, as in the case of the governor's proposal, or left without increases, as in the case of the Greene/Dent bill. Urban legislators will not stand for this situation, and thus there will be an attempt at adjustments for special conditions.

There are at least two techniques for making these special adjustments. The California Teachers Association bill contained a provision that would give money to large unified districts of 40,000 pupils or more. Another approach was in San Francisco Assemblyman Willie Brown's Educational Improvement Act (now amended into the Assembly Education Committee bill). Known affectionately as "Brown's ripoff factor," it established specific criteria for additional money: family poverty, pupil transiency, and bilingualism. Under this plan, a number of rural districts containing poor farmworkers would benefit along with the cities. The State Board proposal offers some adjustments for exceptional and mentally retarded children.

No doubt such condition adjustments will be an important point of contention. If they are included, the urban school districts will support the total package. This support is important since they have numerous strategically placed representatives in the legislature. Thus such adjustments would be an important bargaining counter.

A number of participants will oppose concessions. The governor would probably balk at the expense: the Assembly Education Committee bill contains a buildup to $250 million by 1974-75, and the more modest CTA proposal has a pricetag of $30 million for large unified districts. Furthermore, other moderate-wealth districts would work for adjustments in their favor, and the more demands there are, the more difficult accommodations become.

Local Control

The notion of local control is so amorphous as to exclude it as an analytic concept. At one time or another it has meant control by parents, teachers, school district officials, school boards, and voters. It is used as an argument both for and against increased state funding for local schools. Yet this doctrine, and what it represents, has substantial legislative and popular backing. Consider this appeal to local control as voter control by an Assembly Revenue and Taxation Committee consultant arguing against the Watson Initiative:

> By denying people the voting power to tax themselves for services they desire, this initiative prevents people from providing for their needs at the local level. In short, the initiative encourages the centralization of government and guarantees the consequent loss of home rule.[11]

Governor Reagan has often stated his commitment to the notion of local school board control; as one of his aides told us; "The governor has strong values for local control, and he will veto a bill if it looks like it's going to take things away from local school boards." Whatever the local group in control, the doctrine of local control has a definite symbolic importance to policymakers.

Local control, for our purposes, means *exceptional* preservation of a district's discretion to spend more if it wants to. Using this definition, three of the proposals have elements that can be categorized as local-control options. Two of them—State Board and Greene/Dent—use power-equalizing features. The Assembly Education Committee bill uses redistribution of assessed valuation to the same end. Both of these types of bills enhance the ability of low-wealth school districts to increase their educational expenditures.

At the other extreme, the Collier bill and the Watson Initiative have no elements of local control. Under full state funding, expenditures will be equal, and school districts will be left without independent tax sources to increase their programs. Under Watson, the power of local voters—and by extension their employees and representatives—to raise property taxes and expenditures will be eliminated. We do not know the reaction of voters to the elimination of all local control, but we do know that many legislators are committed to retaining and even expanding local options.

Power equalizing. These measures would make it possible for districts to raise identical amounts of money with equal tax effort. The state would set a foundation plan minimum, which could be augmented by local choice. Districts wishing to spend more would raise their taxes by fixed increments, each addition yielding a uniform sum regardless of local wealth. In effect, rich districts would be paying more money for their increased expenditures than poor districts. The excess from the rich would go to the poor districts.

Naturally, the objections to this approach come primarily from the wealthy districts. Their representatives argue that poor districts have real incentives to increase expenditures, since the bulk of their increases would be borne by others; conversely, the wealthier districts have little incentive since much of their money would go to someone else.

Redistribution of assessed valuation. This proposal is the novel portion of the Assembly Education Committee bill. It would equalize the ability of a district to raise more money by redistributing 50 percent of all the district's assessed valuation, which would narrow the gulf between the rich and poor districts in their tax bases. The rich get to keep half of what makes them rich, and the poor augment their base from the other half; the middle districts also undergo some changes.

The political advantage of this approach is that the rich are not as severely disadvantaged as in the power-equalizing measures. They still retain half of their wealth and raise more per given tax rate than poor districts. The poor are also helped in that they have their base augmented. This measure hurts the rich the least, while it gives substantial resources to low-wealth districts because the present form contains a substantial infusion of state money—$1.5 billion in three years. As a legislative education specialist observed, "The assembly bill costs more than any other proposal, because the major beneficiaries are the very poor and very wealthy at the expense of the middle. Remember, the rich are not going to be paying increases, and the poor will be getting more money." Without this money, or with substantially reduced amounts, the amicability of losing schools would be reduced.

Both power equalizing and redistribution of assessed valuation require considerable state funds to make them palatable to the wealthy districts. At this point they do not seem likely to be adopted.

The Short-Term Option

To summarize, an educational finance proposal for the short term that is likely to attract a winning coalition will contain these components:

1. State responsibility of 50-60 percent with an increase of state money from $200-400 million.
2. Equalization by raising the floor of the foundation plan.
3. Property tax relief by state exemption.

4. Expenditure controls with an inflation factor.
5. No major change in tax structure and increased reliance on sales taxes. A statewide property tax, while possible, is not as likely.
6. A special condition adjustment factor, mainly for urban school districts, probably about $50 to $70 million a year.
7. Local control mainly left intact.

SB 90: A Postscript on the
Short-Term Option

Making judgments about political feasibility is a hazardous business because events are likely to overtake one's predictions before they are in print. After we had completed our forecast of likely political outcomes, a compromise proposal was finally worked out between Speaker Moretti and Governor Reagan. This measure was passed in the last days of the 1972 legislative session, after a process that one lobbyist described as a "Perils of Pauline" series of near deaths. The compromise, which was first amended into AB 1000 and later emerged from a conference committee as SB 90, successfully utilized the minimum existing consensus among participants. Predictably, it incorporated many of the features we listed as components of a short-term option:

1. An increase in state responsibility for local education to 43 percent and $225 million in additional state money for general school support.
2. Increased state equalization aid for the lowest-wealth school districts (raising the floor provided by the foundation plan).
3. $229 million for reducing tax rates in high-tax, low-wealth school districts and an increase in property tax exemptions for homeowners.
4. Limitations on the local district's ability to increase taxes (which can be justified only through inflation costs and enrollment growths) and a means of adjusting state aid for increases in local assessment and for inflation.
5. No major changes in the existing tax structure; costs will be borne by increases in the sales tax and minor changes in other existing taxes.
6. $82 million in special assistance to urban districts.
7. The current system of local school district control over education is left largely intact.

In addition to these features, important side payments were made including an early-childhood development program ($25 million) eagerly sought by Superintendent Riles.

SB 90 was designed to take advantage of the existing distribution of participant goals. The specialists who drafted the compromise considered their task as "hurting no one, not being inconsistent with *Serrano*, and passing a bill." They reasoned that many participants would settle for less than they hoped for, as long as this settlement did not foreclose future efforts. The logic of such a strategy is described by Eugene Bardach:

Invigorating the existing ecology means improving existing programs and practices in the eyes of at least some who are affected by the improvement and doing so without offending any of them. The concept is analogous, therefore, to the economic concept of a Pareto superior move, a reallocation of economic goods in such a way that at least one party is better off than previously and no one is worse off.[12]

SB 90 gives the low-wealth schools some increased aid without taking away the local tax base of wealthy districts. It provides politically attractive property tax relief without the disruptive necessity of passing new forms of taxation. And it makes a series of special appeals to specific groups: urban aid for powerfully situated legislators, early childhood programs for the respected Superintendent of Public Instruction, controls on tax increases for taxpayer groups, and an automatic cost-of-living increase for educators.

In the judgment of political leaders and their aides, SB 90 was as ambitious a reform as the existing political consensus would support. The bill's shortcomings reflect the absence of a constituency for more far-reaching solutions. Those few legislators and experts concerned with the enduring problem of interdistrict resource inequalities lacked sufficient numbers to have their views incorporated into the settlement. Such inequalities can be expected to generate demands for action in the future; after all, the lowest-wealth school districts, though better off, are still in tight financial straits. The competition for legislative attention between property tax relief and increased funding for education has not been settled, proponents of each have already signaled a resumption of their hostilities. In short, the explicit open-endedness of SB 90 as a temporary adjustment of the educational finance system is an invitation for future tinkering and new political demands.

Long-Run Implications

No doubt the likely policy menu is too constrained by short-term political forces. It does not please us nor will it please reformers, particularly those who had their expectations raised by *Serrano*. Increasing the state role, raising foundation levels, and eliminating basic aid of course does move in the direction of greater equalization. But will the courts buy it? The simple answer is that we do not know. The language of the *Serrano* decision might lead one to believe that they will not. If the court wanted the state to leave local school boards with 30-40 percent of the property tax to play with (despite expenditure controls), it would have said so. Substantial compliance may not be compliance.

Yet policymakers will be inclined to go the minimum substantial compliance route for two reasons. First, because *Serrano* has not changed the underlying political forces, a minimum program is the consensus program. Second, they have nothing to lose. Even if the court does send the legislature back to the drawing board, it will certainly allow sufficient time for the legislature to find an appropriate remedy before going into the legislation business itself.

There is, of course, the possibility of a more active judicial role. The court might respond to legislative intransigence with a simple decision requiring equal per pupil expenditures. From our experience with reapportionment decisions it is possible, but it is not likely; after all, courts are not insensitive to the difficulties posed by an education system in which poor children may live in wealthy districts, and some communities may choose to tax themselves more heavily for the sake of better schools. A broader decision might open up other vast and unwelcome territories; for instance, there are now already suits on inequalities in such areas as police and fire protection and even mental health facilities. Furthermore, the prospect of strong judicial action is not always sufficient incentive for legislative decisions. In 1971, the legislature and the governor willingly went to court over their reapportionment differences. Some policymakers may even prefer to let courts undertake unpopular reforms and take them off the hook.

From a policy perspective, one real danger is that the court would agree to a minimum program because it is a step in the right direction. As can be seen from numerous studies, there are other steps that could be taken.[13] A minimum program leaves much of the present financing structure intact. Without getting into the specifics, we believe a *change in that structure* is needed automatically allowing for continued improvement without the necessity for tinkering with the foundation plan every few years. Such a reform would slowly increase the financial resources of all schools and at the same time would reduce the financial disparities among schools. It would work toward equality of resources while recognizing the difficulty of achieving equality of results. (See Chapter 2, 4, and 5, above.)

In the future, a number of conditions would have to be met before major structural change would be politically feasible. First, the state's economy would have to improve so that revenue would increase and officials would not have to be scraping the fiscal barrel every budget year. Major reform costs more, and increased yields and new taxes would be required. Second, a partisan realignment of the executive and legislature is required. Much of the current frustration over financial matters in California is caused by a conflict between a Republican governor and a Democratic legislature. Although Democrats are generally more pro-school than Republicans, we favor no particular party; we only want a pro-school realignment. These partisan differences remain important even in light of an improved fiscal situation and the windfall of revenue sharing. The governor has already served notice that he intends to devote these resources to tax relief, and the Democratic leadership has worked to earmark substantial amounts for education. This leads us to the third condition: a genuine constituency for schools. Whether they are failing or not, schools need political support. Unless policymakers take steps to mobilize such a constituency, educational finance will continue to be everybody's second priority. The ephemeral coalitions that are built to pass isolated issues are not sufficient to sustain major reform.

As a not necessarily desirable side-effect, major reform will encourage political uniformity. Consider, for example, the situation of full state assumption of school finance. Much of the conflict, formerly decentralized to local boards and communities, will shift to the state. There will be one central target for political action. Teachers' groups, for example, rather than fighting with local administrators and boards or among themselves, will coalesce to bargain with the state legislature. At the same time, equalization will reduce the range of disparate interests of school districts. Differences in wealth will no longer divide and weaken them at the state level, and a cohesive school district lobby will be able to act in concert. Everybody will be in a better position to ask for more.

The state's response to these concerted demands will be an increased concern for administrative uniformity.[14] The adoption of a statewide uniform salary scale (recently resurrected in the Collier measure) is a possible outcome. Unification of school districts, an ancient goal of state officials, will increase because rich districts will not be so reluctant to accept poor districts. The state education bureaucracy will reinforce the tendency to uniformity, for example, by issuing standard operating procedures for the distribution of supplies. This uniformity in resources going into school districts will multiply the effect of the original reform measures.

Political and administrative uniformity, however, does not imply educational uniformity. Although schools will be neither lighthouses nor caves, their outputs will vary. Differences in educational achievement will persist, and policymakers, by their fine-tuning for special problems, will prevent the homogenization of the total educational system. In spite of the many variables influencing achievement, we will continue to believe that schools with more resources can do something about individual and societal differences.

In this chapter we have analyzed the area of consensus, the nature of specific appeals, and the range of acceptability. The question of which specific reforms and coalitions are worth pursuing is still unresolved. We do believe, however, that policymakers should not confine themselves to assembling winning educational finance packages based entirely on the existence of short-term supporters. A minimum or band-aid approach may seem the line of least resistance, but it is not necessarily the most productive in the long run. A simple raise in the foundation minimum without a concomitant redistribution of district resources may simply sap some of the energy for substantial reforms and not necessarily improve the lot of many schools. At the other extreme, a major effort to equalize the educational attainment among all the state's school-children—shifting the debate from equalization of resources to results—would spark an unproductive and irreconcilable controversy.

NOTES

1. We wish to thank Art Azevedo, Fred Campbell, Paul Holmes, and Gordon Winton for their helpful guidance; as full-time observers of the Sacramento scene, they saved us from making many errors. Eugene Bardach and David Kirp of the Graduate School of Public Policy, University of California, Berkeley, gave us useful comments.

2. See Nicholas Masters, Robert H. Salisbury, and Thomas H. Eliot, *State Politics and Education* (New York: Knopf, 1964); and Frank A. Pinner, John N. Collins, and William A. Sederburg, *The State and Education: Decision Making on the Reform of Educational Finances in Michigan* (Washington: The Urban Institute, November 1971).

3. California has been a regional leader in policy innovations of various sorts. See Jack L. Walker, "The Diffusion of Policy Innovations Among the American States," *American Political Science Review* (September 1969), pp. 880-899.

4. John E. Coons, William H. Clune III, and Stephen D. Sugarman, *Private Wealth and Public Education* (Cambridge: Belnap Press, 1970), p. 294.

5. The survey data used in this essay were taken from our research conducted in 1970-71 for the Urban Institute. See Arnold J. Meltsner, Gregory W. Kast, John F. Kramer, and Robert T. Nakamura, *Political Feasibility of Reform in School Financing: The Case of California* (New York: Praeger, 1973).

6. Of course, Governor Reagan is not like New York's Governor Rockefeller or Michigan's Governor Millikan, but he is typical of those governors who seek to hold the line on budgetary expenditures.

7. This is not always the case. Bailey and his colleagues found partisanship to be relatively unimportant in decisionmaking. See Stephen K. Bailey, Richard T. Frost, Paul E. Marsh, and Robert C. Wood, *Schoolmen and Politics* (Syracuse: Syracuse University Press, 1962), p. 14.

8. California Legislature, Assembly Committee on Revenue and Taxation, *Facts About Proposition 14*, Prepared by Committee Staff, September 7, 1972, pp. 7 and 10.

9. Betsy Levin et al., *Paying for Public Schools* (Washington: The Urban Institute, 1972), p. 31.

10. "Documentation of Disparities in the Financing of Public Elementary and Secondary School Systems, by State: A Commission Staff Report Submitted to the President's Commission on School Finance," *Review of Existing State School Finance Programs*, Washington, 1972.

11. California Legislature, Assembly Committee on Revenue and Taxation, *Facts About the Watson Initiative*, a preliminary report, December 26, 1971.

12. Eugene Bardach, *The Skill Factor in Politics* (Berkeley and Los Angeles: University of California Press, 1972), p. 184.

13. Although we do not necessarily recommend the proposal of Charles S. Benson and his colleagues, we feel that their attention to the time-phasing of reform is, in part, what we have in mind as a structural change. Their three years from an interim plan to full-fledged reform may be too short

to build political support, but their proposal is still worth considering; see Benson et al., *Final Report to the Senate Select Committee on School District Finance*, June 12, 1972.

14. California has already moved in this direction with its state textbooks and fiscal reporting procedures. One recent study, however, found "no correlation between level of state aid and state imposed limits on local district decision-making," cited in Levin et al., *Paying for Public Schools*, p. 54.

Chapter Ten

School Finance and Social Policy: Serrano and Its Progeny

David K. Cohen
Harvard University

Life is sometimes stranger than art. The California Supreme Court's historic ruling in *Serrano v. Priest* rested on venerable assumptions about the relation between schooling and poverty. But the decision was scarcely beginning to bear fruit when those assumptions were called into question—oddly enough, often by advocates of *Serrano*. The California court, for example, had argued that the state's school finance system was unconstitutional because it "invidiously discriminates against the poor."[1] Yet scarcely two years later, writing in an *amicus* brief for the plaintiffs in a subsequent case, several of the principal theorists of *Serrano* argued that the case was not "a poor man's complaint."[2] Similarly, the California court grounded its justification for intervening partly on the effects of differences in school quality on educational outcomes. "Education," it argued, "is a major determinant of an individual's chances for economic and social success."[3] But not long ago John Coons wrote that "no one can say how significant" is the effect of expenditures on outcomes: "Social science has much to say about the cost/quality problem, but the net effect is agnosticism."[4]

   The picture painted in the *Serrano* decision, then, was one of poor children concentrated in poor districts, deprived of opportunities for success in school and later life by a fiscal system that deprived their communities of adequate school revenues. But if we judged by what some advocates of *Serrano* wrote soon after the decision, it would be less clear that this line of litigation would particularly benefit poor people, or that it would have any positive effect on the outcomes of education. And while the Supreme Court's reversal of *Rodriguez* slowed the momentum of these cases, it did not explain these paradoxes or particularly clarify the issues. Since the problems are sure to be with us for some time, they bear exploration.

EQUALITY: PEOPLE OR GOVERNMENTS?

In the popular mind, to say nothing of the courts and the plaintiffs, *Serrano* was supposed to reduce educational inequality between rich and poor families. The idea that the case was a quick march in the war on poverty was partly due to the political climate of the last decade, in which most initiatives in education were concerned with the poor. But mostly the perception arose from *Serrano* itself, and the writing and litigation that swirled in its wake. The decision makes this connection explicitly, by asserting that the state's finance system "discriminates against the poor," and arguing that the system afforded greater opportunities to "affluent children."[5] The court accepted the plaintiffs' notion that the coincidence of poor people and poor districts was so great as to make a lawsuit on behalf of one effectively a lawsuit on behalf of the other.[6]

But the evidence on this point in *Serrano* was ambiguous, and subsequent efforts to discern the association between poor people and poor districts have had perverse results. There is little evidence of a uniform and powerful association between the wealth of school districts (which in these cases was measured by their total assessed property valuation per student), and the wealth of the people living in those districts (which is measured by average family income). Research in California, apparently ignored by the Supreme Court there, seems to show no association between personal and district wealth;[7] an investigation in Kansas indicates a negative relationship—districts with higher assessed valuations seem to have lower average income;[8] a study in Massachusetts reveals only a weak positive association between property values and personal income;[9] and a study in Connecticut revealed only a slight tendency for districts with higher property valuations to have a smaller proportion of families in poverty.[10]

This evidence hardly supports assumptions about a strong coincidence between poor people and poor districts. It suggests, rather, that the popular conception of wealth and education—which has rich families huddled in property-rich suburban bastions holding back a flood of disadvantaged families from property-poor central cities—is overstated. This situation owes something to the fact that many districts with low-income families also have valuable commercial and industrial wealth, and it also may be related to errors in the way property is assessed and income is measured. It certainly suggests the incorrectness of popular ideas about extreme residential economic segregation, which took such a strong hold in American thought in the last decade. The evidence suggests that poor people live in all sorts of unlikely places: the incidence of suburban poverty, for example, is considerable, and it not infrequently approaches that of central cities.[11] And finally, central cities often have considerable property-based wealth. In many cases, their problem is not low tax base but high levels of public service.[12]

But whatever the reasons, all of this created problems for the thinking that underlay *Serrano*. For by revealing the lack of coincidence between poor people and poor districts, it seemed to require choices where before everything appeared harmonious. Should the cases be redefined to concern only poor people? Or poor districts? Or should some new conception of poverty be framed that comprised both income and property?

The answer was never entirely clear in subsequent litigation—the cases and comment generally continued to confound individual and district wealth. But by the time *Rodriguez* was ready for a hearing before the U.S. Supreme Court, the leading theorists of the litigation at least had announced in formal pleadings that the case was not "a poor man's complaint."[13] Coons, Clune, and Sugarman argued that although the plaintiffs happened to be poor, "the evil attacked here is district poverty."[14]

"District poverty," they argued, has to do with the relative ease with which school districts can raise money for education. They pointed out that school districts with valuable property can raise money for education more easily than school districts with a weak tax base. They argued that these wealth differences were something over which local school governments and citizens had no real control but that the differences place vastly unequal constraints on the ability of governments to raise money for education and vastly unequal burdens on taxpayers.[15] In this view, therefore, the central issue in the cases was unfairness in the burden of taxation arising from accidents of geography, commercial and residential location decisions, and political boundaries.

The view that the central issue is one of fairness in taxation seemed to be shared by the courts involved after the California decision. For one thing, they all made a point of highlighting disparities in tax burdens. In the original *Rodriguez* decisions, for example, the court held that the plaintiffs had been denied equal protection under the fourteenth amendment specifically because:

> the current system of financing public education in Texas discrim-
> inates on the basis of wealth by permitting citizens of affluent
> districts to provide a higher quality education for their children
> while paying lower taxes.[16]

Furthermore, in all cases the lower courts made it clear that one element of an acceptable remedy was elimination of unfair tax burdens in supporting education. The courts defined this as "fiscal neutrality"—which meant any system of school finance that eliminated the correlation between district wealth and school expenditures.[17] By far the best example of this sort of remedy—and the one that figured most prominently in the litigation—is the district power equalizing scheme popularized by John Coons and his associates.[18] Under this scheme the total revenues of any district would be determined by the ratio of its tax rate to its taxable wealth: districts that sacrificed the same *proportion* of their wealth would (theoretically) produce the same revenues per student, because yield variations owing to local wealth would be eliminated by state subsidies. The scheme is designed precisely to eliminate the unequal tax burdens that property wealth variations impose on local governments and citizens; as Coons has pointed out many times, its purpose is to give poor districts as much freedom (that is, as much economic capacity) to decide about spending as wealthy districts have.

Thus, "district poverty" turns out to be a problem of differences in the fiscal capacity of local governments and in the burden of taxation. This conception of the problem, of course, implies that equality would be attained when all districts in a state had an equal opportunity—in the purely fiscal sense—to produce a given per-pupil outlay. One would evaluate the extent to which equality had been achieved by determining the extent to which given tax efforts resulted in equal tax burdens. John Coons has summarized the idea with his usual clarity:

> If governmental entities are empowered to decide about and administer childrens' education, they must be provided an equality of economic capacity to carry out that function.[19]

Not surprisingly, this view of the issues helped define the problem in terms of property assessments and property tax rates. These are the most common indexes of governmental wealth and fiscal burden, statistics are readily available, they are relatively easy to understand, and they have been a staple in discussions of school finance for decades. In addition, wealth is assessed and tax rates are fixed by state agencies. As a result, by settling on a definition of governmental wealth keyed to property values and tax rates, the plaintiffs had isolated what seemed to be a clear case of state action in wealth discrimination. As the Minnesota Court wrote:

> This is not the simple instance in which a poor man is injured by his lack of funds. Here the poverty is that of a governmental unit that the state has itself defined and commissioned.[20]

Despite the many advantages this approach offered, it created one very considerable problem: the value of property simply is not the only wealth-related influence on school revenues. Noneducation spendings and income are important influences on expenditures that are by no means fully captured by property assessments. Defining the wealth of governments in terms of property values tended to distract attention from these other influences on school revenues.

Consider noneducation spending first. Local wealth influences school spending in two quite different ways: the total amount that exists, and the amount available for schools. Because local governments vary in the amount of money allocated to noneducation services, the total taxable wealth is not the same as the total available to schools. Two school districts may have equal assessed valuation per capita, but unequal noneducation municipal services. If one district supports large safety, welfare, and municipal health budgets while the other has only minimal costs in these areas, the first community will have less capacity to raise school revenues. Although it has identical wealth, it has more revenue to raise per capita for other things. This problem of municipal overburden especially afflicts older municipalities, and it is every bit as real a constraint on the fiscal capacity of local governments as the absence of lush property values. If the object of reform is to eliminate differences in the economic capacity to support education, this would seem a prime candidate.

The level of noneducation spending has no role in the litigation considered here. The cases were restricted to education, no doubt on the ground that the courts would be much more likely to consider the issues and return a favorable result. Education is a governmental function highly esteemed by the judiciary, and one with which it had become familiar through earlier intervention. Less unfamiliar and less esteemed services such as sanitation, safety, welfare, and health seemed much less likely candidates for judicial scrutiny. And the complicated conceptual arsenal such a broad approach would require—including the hard-to-measure notion of overburden[21]—could only reduce the likelihood of successful judicial involvement.

As a result of this almost surely correct reading of the situation, cases were confined to schools. But as some academic advocates of the decisions sadly pointed out, excluding other wealth-related influences on school spending meant that communities with less nonschool costs per capita would retain a relative fiscal advantage in raising money for education simply because they have less money to raise for everything else.[22] Limiting the notion of fiscal neutrality to education thus partly frustrates the purpose of the litigation. As a result, even if *Rodriguez* had been upheld on appeal, equality of economic capacity would not have been attained.

A similar situation arose as a result of defining governmental wealth in terms of property. This made some sense as a way of presenting the courts with what appeared to be a clear and judicially manageable wealth classification. It also makes some sense in terms of inequality in school finance. There is a positive correlation between property assessments and expenditures (wealthier districts spend more, on the average),[23] and a negative correlation between wealth and tax rates (wealthier districts have generally lower rates).[24] This means that, in general, districts with greater property wealth are able to produce more revenue at lower rates than districts with less property wealth. It therefore follows that any scheme that removed the influence of differences in the value of property on decisions about school spending would reduce revenue inequalities related to wealth.

But this approach would not provide school districts with "an equality of economic capacity to carry out schooling."[25] Eliminating the influence of property assessments on school revenues would not eliminate the influence of wealth on revenues, because wealth and property are not identical. The available evidence is not as complete as one would like, but it seems to show that among school districts, average family income exerts an independent influence on school revenues of roughly the same magnitude as that of property assessments.[26] And although the average family income and total property assessments are not unrelated among school districts, the association is remarkably weak. As noted earlier, the correlation is never greater than 0.4, is often around 0.2, and sometimes appears to be lower or even negative.

As a matter of economics this is not exactly startling news. Property and income are different ways of measuring wealth, and there are plenty of reasons to expect their correspondence, especially at the aggregate level, to be much less than perfect. Some have to do with the composition of wealth at the individual level (the little old lady who owns a fine large home but lives on a modest pension); others have to do with the composition of the aggregates in question (districts with large numbers of low-income families often have considerable high-wealth industrial and commercial property). Whatever the reasons, though, the important thing is the results. For if property assessments and income have a roughly equal independent effect on revenues, implementing a conception of fiscal neutrality keyed to total assessed property values alone could at best do no more than eliminate half the influence of local wealth on school revenues. Precisely because the coincidence of poor people and poor districts is imperfect, fiscal neutrality as it was defined in these cases is an imperfect instrument for eliminating the influence of wealth on local school revenues.

Focusing the cases on a conception of governmental wealth defined in terms of property therefore turned out to be no minor tactical matter. Several commentators noticed this problem and suggested that the courts (or legislatures) should revise their definition of wealth, either by including income as well as property, or by improving the definition of property wealth so as to bring it into line with income, or both.[27] These suggestions make a good deal of sense as a matter of economics, but they leave something to be desired in the way of understanding the cases. They assume that the lack of attention to other forms of wealth was due to a fit of absentmindedness or perhaps to dozing in Economics I. It is more likely that income was avoided in these cases because of the dangers it suggested. For if income is a criterion of wealth, and if (as the lower courts said), the essential unfairness of the existing system is that it permits some people to educate their children in public schools at less sacrifice than others,[28] then it might be difficult to limit consideration of fiscal inequality to differences among districts. In the case of high- and low-income families within the same school district, the same tax rate is assessed against all. In theory, the same monies are expended on all students, but the tax burden on high-income families would be less, because their fiscal capacity is greater. Is this inequality in the burden of taxes any more fair than the inequalities that allow people in some districts to provide better education at less of a sacrifice than people in others? If income is the basis for computing tax burden, a reasonable case could be made that differences in tax burdens within districts were as great and as unfair as differences among districts. It therefore might be difficult to escape the impression that the appropriate plaintiffs are not just all people in poor districts, but also poor people in all districts.[29]

The idea is not without appeal, because if income is an accurate measure of wealth, independent of property values, and if the fundamental complaint is unfairness in distributing the burden of taxation, then it would be sensible to recognize that the problem of inequality included differences in the burden of taxes among *people*, rather than simply among *districts*. But this impression would surely have had an unhappy effect in court. If the courts had thought they were being asked to decide whether the burden of taxes on individuals were fair, they might have thought they were being asked to decide how much progressivity in taxation was required by the Constitution, and shied away. The fairness of tax burdens is commonly thought of as a political matter, and there is no easy way to imagine a standard of fairness the courts would think judicially manageable. Certainly the majority opinion in *Rodriquez* suggests sensitivity on this point.

If the above example shows that the courts are unwilling to entertain cases presented as a question of fairness of a tax system, it also shows that the decisions in *Serrano* and its progeny do contain the idea that certain sorts of taxation are unfair. Fiscal neutrality might, in fact, be construed as a declaration that the burdens of local school taxes should never be less than proportionally distributed with respect to wealth. Fiscal neutrality asserts that the percentage of wealth sacrificed to support education should be the same for poor and rich districts at any level of outlay. This suggests that the problem with using income as a measure of wealth was purely decorative: using income openly suggests that the issue is fairness to individual citizens, whereas using property and calling it governmental wealth suggests the issue is fairness to creatures of the state. If income were used as the measure of wealth someone would inevitably have pointed out that if fiscal neutrality does mean equal proportions of wealth sacrificed, it might not be so neutral after all. People with low incomes have less money to sacrifice in taxes than the affluent.[30] It might be argued that progressivity would be more fair, thereby opening a distinctly unjudicial can of worms. Casting remedy as "fiscal neutrality," and trying to separate the wealth of governments from the wealth of persons provided a device for apparently avoiding these problems.

The discussion throws a little light on the logic of *Serrano* and ensuing cases. In fact, the litigation presented an issue of the fairness of taxation. As the Texas court wrote, the state's school finance system violated the

Fourteenth Amendment because it permitted "citizens of affluent districts to provide a higher quality education for their children while paying lower taxes."[31] But while the issue was in good measure the fairness of a system of *producing revenue*, the cases by and large were offered and decided as though the question were the fairness of a system for *distributing education.* In effect, the special genius of these cases was that they presented what was in reality the judicial establishment of a standard of fairness in tax burdens as a decision concerning the distribution of schooling.

But this special genius did not come without a price. Improving the chances that the cases would succeed meant focusing them on the distribution of education. Achieving fiscal neutrality, on the other hand, would require self-conscious attention to problems of revenue production. Both elements were involved in the cases, but satisfying the Fourteenth Amendment provisions concerning the distribution of school aid does not necessarily imply fairness in the production of revenue. As a result, *Serrano* and its successor cases were marked by a continuing inner tension between these two elements.

All of this helps to illuminate the intellectual underpinnings of the litigation, and it suggests why the cases often seemed at cross-purposes with themselves. It also helps to explain a peculiar paradox—a growing awareness that focusing on property wealth would not eliminate inequality, but little sense as to exactly what might have been expected if victory in *Rodriguez* had ensued. This uncertainty arises in part from the weak development of the factual issues in the cases, and in part from the confused conceptions of wealth, burden, and taxes on which the cases rested. The courts seem to have been mostly unaware of the limits of the ideas with which they have worked, and of the empirical ambiguities of public finance.[32] Their confusions were reflected in the Supreme Court's opinion in *Rodriguez.* There was a good deal of disagreement about whether deciding for the plaintiffs could have been a good idea, but justices on both sides of the issue seemed unable to produce evidence about the actual result of an affirmative decision.

EQUALITY: WHAT IS THE PRINCIPLE?

To argue that *Serrano* and its successors were not all they might be is not to say that the lower court decisions were unwise. One might still argue that the principle of fiscal neutrality developed in the cases was sufficiently important to outweigh any of the practical limitations noted here. But exactly how does one separate a principle from the way it has been realized in practice? In moral philosophy it may seem easy, but in social practice the distinction is less certain. For example, in an even more famous decision, *Brown v. Board of Education*, there might seem to be an inherent principle of racial equality. Yet the decision was implemented in such a way that for many years for many thousands of black people there was little more than pain or travesty—certainly not much racial equality. Can the principle of *Brown* be summarized as racial equality, then, or must we say more—that the principle's definition changed as a result of practice, from hostility and condescension to a more active conception of equality? What would the principle be had black Americans not struggled to assert a particular conception of it in practice? If a principle seems to be inherent in *Brown*, a reasonable argument can be made that it is inherent mostly in retrospect, after being forged in the struggle over how a policy was to be implemented.

Caution about principles is particularly germane in the school finance cases. The lower court decisions left legislatures much room for maneuver in defining what neutrality would mean in practice. For another, the decisions were unclear about limitations on the principle of fiscal neutrality. The cases were carefully framed to exclude all governmental concerns but education, even though in many minds this was only tactical, to be abandoned in the future. The basis for limiting the cases to education was an elaborate body of legal and social theory designed to show that schooling is unique among public services in the degree to which it requires Fourteenth-Amendment protection. This theory was propounded in every favorable opinion (including the Supreme Court dissents), and its basic ideas center on what the California court termed education's "indispensable role" in the modern industrial state:

> First, education is a major determinant of an individual's chances for economic and social success in our competitive society; second, education is a unique influence on a child's development as a citizen and his participation in political and community life.[33]

The Minnesota Court held that education was "basic to the functioning of a free society and thereby evokes special judicial solicitude."[34] The Texas Court wrote of the "grave significance of education both to the individual and to our society...."[35] The New Jersey Court opined that since education is a "fundamental interest," the requirements for equality are much more stringent than for other public services.[36]

These ideas provided precisely the weapons with which the courts beat back arguments from defendant state agencies that equalizing school expenditures would require equalizing outlays for all public services—including fire, sanitation, health, and the like. The court in *Serrano* took note of this argument, and gave clear expression to the view that education is socially and therefore constitutionally unique:

> We unhesitatingly reject this argument. Although we intimate no views on other governmental services, we are satisfied that, as we have explained, its uniqueness among public activities clearly demonstrates that education must respond to the equal protection clause.[37]

Prophesy is always an uncertain line of work, but it takes little clairvoyance to see that if this view of education is the basis on which the school finance issue is pursued after *Rodriguez*, hopes for extending the principle of fiscal neutrality to other public services must be somewhat diminished. If fiscal neutrality is required because education is special among services, the chance of equality elsewhere would be much reduced. The entire issue, of course, turns on the notion that education is both unique among services and specially protected by the U.S. Constitution. The doctrine holds that schooling is of special importance—that it is a fundamental interest—because it has a crucial effect on later political participation and social and economic achievement. From the idea that schooling has such an effect it is inferred that students who get better education will have greater civic participation and economic attainment. From this, proponents of *Serrano* argued that careful scrutiny of educational inequalities was constitutionally required. Since the argument seems to rest on factual assertions about the effects of education, research on this matter became a central point of interest in all the decisions and in much of the comment about them. Although this may have been unavoidable, in my view it was an unfortunate distraction; the uses of the research were unwise, and evidence of an unfortunate way of thinking about equality.

The story begins with research on education, which seems to suggest that the lower courts' ideas on the effects of schooling cannot be taken for granted. Take, for example, the effect of schooling on economic success. People with more schooling earn more, on the average, than those with less. But this difference is not as great as most people seem to believe, and for the most part it seems causally unrelated to school. That is, once differences in inherited social and economic advantages are taken into account, years of school completed does not seem to have much effect on earnings. On the average, an extra year of elementary or secondary school seems to be worth several hundred dollars a year in earnings for white males.[38] Although this cannot be ignored, it doesn't, for example, suggest an enormous difference between the income of people who drop out of the tenth grade and those who go on to graduate—a fact confirmed by a recent study of the effects of dropping out.[39] Thus, in contrast to the lower courts' view of schooling as a "major determinant" of economic success, the research suggests that the economic effects of getting more public education is modest.

This does not mean that schooling doesn't "make a difference" economically. People who stay in high school longer do earn a little more than those who drop out; people who graduate from high school obviously have a much better chance of going to college than people who drop out, and the economic returns of college education are somewhat greater than those to elementary and secondary schooling. But the research does suggest that the economic difference schools make is not exactly overwhelming, and it often seems to indicate that (as in the case of drop-outs) schooling makes no appreciable economic difference at all.

When we turn from economic to social success, schooling seems noticeably more important. The principal measure of social success related to schooling is occupational status, and people who have more of one tend to have more of the other. But while people in occupations with greater prestige tend to have more schooling, the strength of the relationship is open to varying interpretations. For one thing, roughly half of the existing variance in occupational status among white American men cannot be explained by differences in how long they stayed in school, their families, or with any other attribute social researchers can measure.[40] Second, of the status differences that can be explained, slightly more than half seem to be related to differences in how long people stay in school, and slightly less than half are associated with inherited social and economic status. So compared with inherited status, schools are an important influence on occupational achievement. But it also means that schooling accounts for only a moderate portion—roughly one-quarter—of the total occupational status differences among American men.[41]

As in the case of income, this evidence does not show that schools "don't matter." It does raise questions, though, about their relative importance —in effect, there is evidence here for everyone. People who think that schools are important can point to the fact that their influence on occupational status is roughly equal to that of social inheritance. People who think that the importance of schooling is overrated can point to the fact that schooling accounts for only roughly one-quarter of the differences in occupational status and for little of the variation in income. People who have doubts about social science can point to the fact that slightly more than half of the occupational differences are unexplained by anything sociologists can measure.[42]

Whatever else might be said about this research on the effects of schools, then, it hardly provides an unambiguous foundation for the notion that schooling is a "major determinant" of social and economic success. In fact, one wonders how to distinguish a major determinant from a minor determinant, or how important education would have to be to social and economic success before it would qualify as a fundamental interest. The courts' discussions of education offered no clues on these points, because it is entirely unclear where importance begins and unimportance ends in such matters.[43]

The evidence on school effects was not, of course, relevant simply to arguments about whether education is a fundamental interest, for in the lower courts' view, the notion of the schools' importance was part of a system of expectations about the effects of the decisions. They expected social changes as a result of redistributing school resources—specifically, that changes in the allocation of money to districts in which poor children attend school would produce improvements in those childrens' life chances. But evidence on the effects of expenditures offers no support for this supposition.

This gloomy result seems to hold for any index of educational success we might relate to school expenditures. Among students from similar family backgrounds, their aspirations, their test scores, and how far they go in school seem to be unrelated to the amount of money spent by their schools.[44] This result derives from quite a variety of studies, and it holds also for the resources that money purchases. Students who attend school in lush suburban surroundings do not go further in school, or get better scores, or have higher aspirations than similarly situated students who happen to attend schools with meager budgets.[45] For students with the same sort of family background, differences in school facilities, programs, expenditures, curriculum, and teaching staff are unrelated to differences in academic ability, length of schooling, or aspirations.

None of this means that schools have no effect on students' aspirations or the length of their educational careers. Schools and the people in them obviously have myriad important effects, through the incentives and discouragements they dispense, as well as through the various ways in which they legitimize some activities for certain students and discourage them for others. Schools also have a considerable effect on society, because they are an important instrument for assigning status and because they tend to legitimize this in the eyes of all concerned.

If the research does not show that schools "don't matter," it does show that resource and money differences among them seem causally unrelated to the ways in which they do matter. There is no evidence that schools' wealth has a differential effect on students' test scores, aspirations, and educational careers. Indeed, the research suggests that what counts about schools may not be how much money they apply to students, but how they differentiate among them. In terms more congenial to lawyers, the ways schools influence students' life chances may have more to do with how they classify students than with the resources spent on them. Nothing in this idea encourages the notion that equalizing expenditures among school districts will much affect the distribution of opportunities for social and economic achievement. All the evidence suggests that it will not.

This notion did not go entirely unnoticed in the litigation. It is not surprising that such findings would provoke questions about the usefulness of redistributing school resources, or doubts about the wisdom of using school reform as a strategy for general social reconstruction. Nor is it surprising that while the lower courts in these cases noticed the research, their reaction was a mixture of impatience and incredulity. In general, they responded by dismissing it, and it is not hard to see why. The judge in the Minnesota case, for example, remarked that if there were not a strong correlation between expenditures and "educational effectiveness," it would mean that school boards have been "merely wasting taxpayers' money,"[46] a thought so odious that the court apparently could not think it.

If the courts were perplexed by the research, their difficulties hardly could have been relieved by its use in the arguments they heard. It was no surprise that state governments should defend existing arrangements, but it was a bit remarkable that they should argue against redistributing school revenues on the grounds that school resources had no differential effect on student's achievement.[47] After all, this research usually has been interpreted to mean that state and local school agencies are not doing their jobs—or cannot do them. And before *Serrano* state and local school officials regularly attacked such evidence as an untrustworthy guide to policy. Yet in *Serrano* and succeeding cases it was state and local school officials who clasped to their breasts that very evidence on the inefficacy of school resources. To compound the irony, they did so in order to resist the attacks of reform-minded attorneys representing poor children. Surprisingly, those attorneys—who in ordinary circumstances would have pointed approvingly to the research as evidence of the schools' incompetence in educating poor children—instead attacked it, trying to marshal evidence on the schools' effectiveness.[48] This unlikely charade culminated with the submission of *amicus* briefs attacking the *Serrano* principle in *Rodriguez* by several of the wealthiest school districts in the United States. Among their arguments was the idea that money may be unrelated to educational outcomes.

The difficulty with this tack, from the plaintiffs' point of view, was that attacks on the research could do no more than moot arguments about the effects of schooling. And since conflicting evidence would be cold comfort, they turned elsewhere. In an *amicus* brief filed before the U.S. Supreme Court in *Rodriguez*, John Coons and his associates rested their argument for the specially protected character of education almost exclusively on its political rather than its social and economic consequences. They argue that education is crucial to the exercise of political freedom, and that discrimination in the provision of education is therefore a violation of the First Amendment. The basis for their view was that "every decision concerning the distribution of education represents a choice about the locus of political influence in succeeding generations."[49] Contrary to the main thread of *Serrano* reasoning—and, indeed, to all earlier writing on the subject—the economic and social arguments simply never appeared as the major basis for asserting the special nature of education.

Again, it is not unreasonable to ask whether schooling does have such an effect on political participation. Would equalizing school finance affect childrens' chances for political participation? Is there any causal relationship between the resources schools apply to children and the "distribution . . . of political influence"? For what was asserted was not a political principle but a matter of fact—namely that fiscal inequality among schools attended by children produces political inequality later among adults. The plaintiffs and their *amici* assumed that people who get more costly education will thereby receive more of the wherewithal required to participate in public life. They argued that people whose education has been financially deficient will participate less, or less usefully, than they otherwise might.[50]

The one unambiguous fact is that on the average, people with more schooling do participate more in politics; adults who have completed college vote more frequently and are more active in public life than adults who only completed high school; high school graduates are more politically active than people who left school after the eighth grade.[51] But what is one to make of this? The cases in question do not concern students' right to a free college education, and the states have long required—and zealously enforced—twelve years of school for all students. If there were any indication that schools could reduce drop-outs by spending more money, the evidence on length of schooling and participation might seem relevant, but all the research shows that drop-out rates are unrelated to school expenditures.[52] In fact, the things most likely to improve school attendance seem to have more to do with changing schools' programs and practices than with changing their budgets.[53] In the absence of any evidence that redistributing school resources would in fact redistribute educational attainment, then, it is hard to see how redistributing money would affect the "distribution . . . of political influence."

The evidence is no more encouraging when we turn to the effects of educational resources on the quality of political knowledge or activity. There has been no research on the relationship between school expenditures on children and their later political behavior as adults. But the plaintiffs' view on this point went as much to the quality of the political education recieved by students and the character of their later political participation as it did to the amount of either education or participation. Coons argued that wealth discrimination among schools leads to the "deliberate creation of intellectual classes,"[54] and thus "corrupts the very sources of free discussion and civic virtue."[55]

The results of research on political socialization, however, stand in striking contrast to these ideas. Quite a substantial literature on political socialization has accumulated during the past two decades, and it provides no support for the notion that schools have much of a differential effect on political knowledge or attitudes.[56] In fact, the research seems to show that to the extent that schools influence political development, they do so quite uniformly. These studies show, for example, that once students' political ideas take shape—usually around the end of elementary school—they seem to undergo little subsequent change. Studies of high school and college students show that they tend to have the same patterns of political thought in the last year of school as in the first.[57] Evaluations of specially designed curricula, innovative schools, and novel school programs seem to show that their effect on political thinking and information is usually modest or nonexistent.[58] Even a study that compared the religious values of Catholics who graduated from public school with the values of those who attended parochial schools proved disappointing: only modest differences appeared, and in fact parochial education seemed to affect only children from very religious homes.[59] In general, then, the evidence suggests that family cultural and economic background has a marked effect on political values and thought, but that schools have little differential influence in this area.

This conclusion is nicely exemplified by one study that compared the effects of school resources on students' political development in two California school districts.[60] The districts were both located in the Los Angeles area; one spent roughly $150 more per pupil per year, and was more vigorously engaged in devising and promoting various educational innovations. The political thought and knowledge of students from the two districts were compared in grades six, nine, and twelve. Despite wealth differences, at grade nine there were no differences between the two districts in students' political thought and knowledge, and at grade twelve there were only a few trivial differences. There were consistent small differences at grade six but they favored the district with less resources.[61] The author of the study also noted that

> variations in educational inputs have little effect on those demo-
> cratic values that demand the most rigorous thought. Freedom of
> speech, minority rights and the rules of the game are all insensitive
> to district differences. That the districts have virtually identical
> impacts on sophisticated dimensions provides just another indication
> of the restricted influence the school exerts.[62]

Having found only small and inconsistent differences between the two districts, the study nonetheless sought to determine if these were at all related to the quality of teaching. Although it was found that the district with more money had teachers who were more highly paid and more qualified in terms of various professional criteria,[63] there seemed to be no relationship between these differences and the ways in which teachers thought or taught. The study concluded that "there is as tenuous a link between educational effort and teacher characteristics as there is between educational inputs and democratic socialization."[64]

This study, like other research on political socialization, provides no support for the notion that equalizing the revenues of school districts would change the distribution of political competence. In fact, it suggests quite persuasively that equalization would have no such effect. The evidence shows that schools do not have a pronounced differential effect on political ideas—that the chief differential influences on students' political development lie outside the schools. Furthermore, researchers are roughly agreed on the reasons why schools affect political socialization as they do. They relate to the ambiguous political situation of a state-operated socialization agency in a large, diverse and decentralized democracy, and to the "neutral" stance schools have adopted in response to conflicting pressures to take political positions in educating children. There is no readily available evidence suggesting that any of these constraints is related to the fact that some schools are rich and others are poor, nor does anything indicate that eliminating rich schools and poor schools would change the distribution of political learning or competence.

Both research and common observation suggest, however, that schools do have an effect on childrens' political learning. The research indicates, though, that the effect is quite uniform, in spite of considerable differences in schools' educational resources. Common observation suggests that whether or not schools are differentially effective in teaching particular political information or competence, they do teach that the existing political order is legitimate. But while these effects of schooling are far from trivial, they seem to be unrelated to whether schools are rich or poor.

This analysis raises several unsettling questions about the fundamental interest doctrine and the educational ideas on which it seems to rest. For one thing, it appears that the conception of schooling held by advocates of the *Serrano* principle was questionable. It is of course true that schools make a difference, even though there is little evidence that they exert many of their effects differentially. Without schooling the American people would not be as literate or well informed as they are—knowledge of European geography, after all, does not spring spontaneously to the mind of American twelve-year-olds, any more than does algebra or French. Thus it would be correct to say that schooling has had many of the effects contemplated by those who originally framed constitutional or statutory requirements for free public education.

The fact is, however, that these important effects of schools seem not to occur differentially. This is probably attributable to changes in schooling and society that have occurred in the last century. America now has a fairly uniform system of universal education, and although there are inequalities in its distribution, they are not nearly as great as in the past. Most American children now receive twelve years of schooling, and most receive it under conditions that seem to meet the criterion of a decent minimum (at least the criterion thought sufficient a few years ago). In addition, literacy and information no longer depend as heavily on schooling as they once did. Not long ago, if a child's family was illiterate, and if he was not exposed to substantial and sustained schooling, the chances were very good that he would be illiterate as well. But most American families are not illiterate now. Basic skills are increasingly taught in the media and sometimes on the job—and as a result, the schools' overall importance in teaching basic skills has been lessened. Since nearly everyone attends school anyway, the chances that they could be differentially effective have been sharply reduced.

We have, then, a curious paradox: schooling is important, it does affect children and society, but what seems to matter (at least for some outcomes), is the presence or absence of this more and more equally provided public service, not differences in its provision. This, in fact, is what one might expect of a more or less fully socialized public service, and in a society moving toward greater equality in such services, the paradox may gradually become commonplace.

Another paradox seems to inhere in the lower courts' conception of fundamental interest. For, if education were as important as they said, and if schools work in the ways they imagined, one wonders how any inequalities could be constitutionally tolerated at all. If schooling is a fundamental interest, are inequalities created by voting in school districts (say, under a district power equalizing scheme) any better for children than inequalities now created by voting in state legislatures? Children, after all, would be equally damaged by either arrangement, and their interests equally infringed. As a matter of logic, it seems impossible to distinguish the two under the fundamental interest doctrine, although as a matter of politics the usefulness of such a distinction is clear. It is hard to avoid the conclusion that if one took the lower courts seriously on their conception of fundamental interest, all inequalities in education would be gravely suspect. This is not something these courts dealt with, because for reasons of politics and tradition they wanted to preserve local choice in education. But if flows quite naturally from their opinions.

EQUALITY: WHO BENEFITS?

All of this raises serious questions about how fiscal neutrality would be good, and for whom. The earliest view advanced by plaintiffs was that the beneficiaries would be children from poor families, and that the benefit would be improved education and greater opportunities. But it no longer seems clear that poor people would benefit especially from these decisions, and as a result it was then argued that the real beneficiaries would be people in poor districts. One problem with this is defining what a poor district might be: it is not clear that the criterion of wealth the lower court decisions employed was either correct or wise as a matter of policy. Nor do we have a clear idea as yet of what the legislative response would be. This makes it a little difficult to figure out who actually would benefit from these decisions, or how much, or whether they should. Studies exploring the possible outcomes have often pointed up the uncertainty, and some have even argued that there is a good chance that benefits might be redistributed from the poor to the affluent.[65]

If the beneficiaries are unclear, so are the benefits. This issue arises first from the lack of any convincing evidence that fiscal neutrality would affect childrens' performance in school or later life. If there is serious doubt that differences in school expenditures affect school or adult performance, how can one maintain that poor children would benefit from these decisions?

One tack has been to argue that they would not—that the principal beneficiary would be education professionals. Since teachers' salaries are between 70 and 80 percent of schools' operating budgets, and since salaries tend to be lower in low-expenditure districts, one might argue that any increase in a given district's operating budget would be absorbed in this category of expense. "Poor" districts might wind up with more teachers, or better-paid teachers, or more of the facilities and materials that teachers like. If teachers' salaries and other formal qualifications are unrelated to the outcomes of schooling, one could conclude that school professionals, not children, would be the principal beneficiaries of redistribution.

Another tack has been to argue that social research is never conclusive, and that such negative inferences are premature or ill-founded. But that hardly helps decide what the benefit from these decisions will be. Instead, it simply would put the whole issue in a limbo from which, by definition, it could never return.

Still another response has been to point out that schools do more than affect achievement and economic opportunities. They are places where children live for roughly one-third of their waking lives for twelve years. Everyone knows that schools can be more or less stimulating, responsive, comforting, and intelligent. Why should children in poor districts not have the same opportunity as those in wealthy districts to enjoy high-quality schooling, even if it has no effect on their IQ scores or income? More expensive schools, after all, usually have better facilities, more qualified teachers, and more specialized staff. They probably are more comfortable places, and they often have better library and laboratory resources. One might well argue that children in poor districts should not be deprived of such advantages simply because of the accidents of wealth or residence.

It is not intuitively evident that this argument is wholly correct— some relatively wealthy schools are boring and unintelligent, and some relatively poor ones are not. But even if we admit that riches do not always have educational rewards, the argument seems plausible. As some advocates of *Serrano* asked, do not children have an equal entitlement to have money wasted on them, regardless of the accidents of their parents' residence? The query may seem frivolous, but that could hardly be further from the truth. For it asks whether we are willing to justify equal access to public resources only by the effect of those resources on social "outcomes," such as economic and social status. Is it sensible to argue for equality simply in terms of the private benefits to individuals or groups within the society, or in terms of the spillover effects on society? Would racial segregation seem any less unconstitutional if it had no effect on test scores? Is not equality valuable chiefly because it eliminates invidious distinctions within mankind?

The questions are important, because they return us to an ancient tendency in democratic thought—the idea that the benefit of equality must ultimately lie more in the elimination of irrational distinctions than in the personal consequences of redistribution. On this view, we would imagine the benefit of *Serrano* to lie in the introduction of rationality in school finance, and we would imagine the chief beneficiary to be society, rather than some smaller class of private persons. This line of argument has considerable appeal. One reason is intrinsic to the idea—if we rest the justification for equality on some notion of social efficiency, we may be surprised. Research could show that greater productivity would be achieved by spending on the rich and talented rather than the poor and disadvantaged. It already seems to suggest that equal spending on schools would not affect individual efficiency or productivity very much. Another reason for the idea's appeal is historical: in a society that increasingly substitutes organization for personality, and bureaucratic rationality for traditional elites, it is more and more difficult to support the feeling that inequality is justifiable and legitimate. Schooling has become less and less the business of families, voluntary associations, and communities, and more and more the property of large organizations and anonymous professions. Schooling has become less and less the induction of the young into a particular community and its unique culture by its elders, and more and more their processing into national society and its uniform culture by paid functionaries. Under these circumstances, differences among communities—whether related to wealth, or taste, or location—increasingly lose their legitimacy. Their social face validity simply erodes. As a result of modernization, courts, like everyone else, think that differences that once seemed legitimate should no longer exist.

All of these factors, then, conspire to carry advocates of *Serrano* back to the notion that citizens should have equal access to public resources, and that this equality is premised not on some notion of private benefit or social efficiency, but on the idea that invidious distinctions within humanity are foreign to a fair society. The difficulty is that this approach gives away one foundation of the cases—that equality is required because of the special importance schooling has for the opportunities of private persons and the efficiency of society. Regard the language of the California Supreme Court, as it sought to justify equality in educational finance:

> We, therefore, begin by examining the indispensable role which education plays in the modern industrial state.[66]

> Unequal education, then, leads to unequal job opportunities, disparate income, and handicapped ability to participate in the social, cultural, and political activity of our society.[67]

> ... education is essential in maintaining what several commentators have termed "free enterprise democracy"—that is, preserving an individual's opportunity to compete successfully in the economic marketplace.[68]

> In view of the importance of education to society and to the individual child, the opportunity to receive schooling furnished by the state must be made available to all on an equal basis.[69]

It almost seems that the classical doctrine of equal opportunity has no place in this universe of thought—the conception of equality-as-unfairness seems to have been driven out by the conception of equality-as-efficiency. After all, if we assert that children should have an equal chance to have money misspent on their education, we really are saying that considerations of schools' efficiency and effectiveness (while always present) are not important enough to affect decisions about the distribution of schooling. That seems to suggest that the rationale for equality in education must be like the rationale for equality in highways, or sanitation, or safety: all of these are important services, but we would not debate the provision of equal sanitation outlays for Chicago and Highland Park in terms of whether better sanitation affected the economic opportunities or health of the residents. Rather (in a society that generally is quite sanitary already), we would debate the issue in terms of whether equality in such things was desirable as a matter of fairness. The relevant question would not be whether equal sanitation produces more equally clean and industrious people, but whether equality in the provision of public services is an important enough political value to make us forgo other values, such as diversity, local initiative, or efficiency.

Such arguments became awkward in the framework of *Serrano* and its successor cases, because there the rationale for equalizing the provision of public services seemed to rest on the alleged importance of the "outputs" of those services. The lower court decisions tell us that equality in education is important because education is one of the principal social instruments for distributing private economic benefits; they tell us that equality is essential in education because when those private benefits are maldistributed, both the private efficiency and productivity of some citizens and the total efficiency and productivity of the entire society is disrupted and reduced; the decisions tell us, in a word, that equality in education is important because of what it does, rather than what it is. In the intellectual world of *Serrano*, it would seem almost quaint to announce that equality was required by our fundamental ideas of political fairness, rather than our calculation of social and economic outcomes.

Thus, while the courts have tried to ignore and dismiss some recent social research on schools' effectiveness, they have nonetheless adopted a thoroughly modern—one might almost say economic or sociological—approach to the question of equality. For nothing could be more compatible with such an approach than the notion that equality is justified by the production of social outcomes. This is only one aspect of a more general movement of social thought in America away from essentially political conceptions of equality of provision to economically oriented conceptions of equal results. It is revealing that while *Serrano* and its progeny sought to achieve a purpose we would identify with an older notion of equal opportunity—that is, equal access to educational resources—they tended to present the matter as one of equality in results.

This increasing emphasis on results is not an absolute novelty. For more than a decade now the courts have couched their arguments for educational equality in terms familiar to the social welfare professions and the social sciences allied to them. The essential point in all the arguments has been that greater equality is important because of the greater individual and social productivity it would bring, a notion familiar in liberal thinking of the last half-century. This tendency in American social thought is due in part to the defensive attitude egalitarians often suppose they must adopt in a manifestly unequal free-enterprise system—they hope to win support for equality by showing it is good for the system in its own terms. Thus, equality is advanced as though it will increase the productivity of workers and the efficiency of the system as a whole.

The tendency to focus on social and economic outcomes has been reinforced by the rise of the social sciences, and the increasing interest in rationalizing social policy. For the conception of society implicit in much social science centers around "input-output" conceptions of social process, which originated in economics. These notions legitimate the idea that social institutions should be thought of on the pattern of industrial organizations, and they focus attention on institutional "outputs." It is not difficult to see why such a conception of social process would have enormous appeal in industrialized societies; by now, the conception of institutions given in the input-output model of social process is so firmly rooted in the social sciences that it goes entirely unquestioned. The notion is, one would say, entirely natural—so much so that its appropriateness as the basis for research on schooling, for example, has been accepted for decades. As a result of the increasing social importance and currency of social research, this conception has become firmly fixed in the thinking of public officials of all sorts—including the courts. The consequence has been a gradual alteration in our thinking about equality, until nearly everyone feels perfectly comfortable with the notion that equality in education is required because the schools are the chief regulator of social outputs.

The irony, of course, is that the research on the effects of schooling organized on the input-output model shows that differences in resources and productive processes are unrelated to differences in outputs. This may mean that the schools could be good factories but are improperly arranged to be so, or it could mean that an input-output model is inappropriate to describe the process of schooling. In either event, this research does suggest the dangers inherent in the economic mode of thought about equality. For, to the extent that the courts or other public agencies frame their approach to equality in terms of efficiency in the production of social outcomes, just to that extent will arguments for equality seem to rest on social facts rather than political values. It is, of course, just this situation that has caused the widespread pained reaction to research suggesting that the differential effects of school expenditures are slight or nonexistent. This hostility on the part of the lower courts and other advocates of the *Serrano* idea arose from their sense that this research implied that equality was unjustified. The research, of course, means no such thing: the evidence that schools have little differential effect is at least equally useful as an argument that differences in school resources are a waste of money and should be eliminated. For if resources do not have much differential effect, what good reason is there for the state to create resource differentials?

If the lower courts' reaction had no logical connection to the objective policy implications of the research, though, it did arise from their correct perception that the research was at odds with the rationale for equality they had erected. For that rationale rested squarely on the idea that equality in education was required because of its economic and social outcomes. As a matter of logic, though, it would have made at least as much sense to reconsider that way of thinking about schools and equality as to attack the research that suggested its barrenness. Ironically, the Supreme Court opinions simply rehearsed arguments; the majority sought to sustain the advantages of wealth by pointing to scholarly uncertainty about the effects of schooling, and the dissenters replayed arguments about the social importance of schooling.

If I am correct, though, the benefit of fiscal neutrality really is fairness in financing and distributing public goods, and the chief beneficiary is society as a whole. This idea has been obscured by a confusion between the essentially political ideas on which the notion of equality is founded and the essentially economic conceptions of social process and outcomes that are widely used to justify liberal social policy. This confusion has so permeated the fabric of these cases that the entire argument for equality often seems to depend on a series of factual assertions about the effects of schooling, rather than on a system of political judgments about fairness in social relations.

CONCLUSION

The Supreme Court's decision in *Rodriguez* reveals some of the dangers this confusion between economic and political conceptions holds for proponents of fiscal neutrality. The Court's majority defended existing wealth-based inequalities in part by arguing that research was unclear about the social importance of education and about the differential effectiveness of schools. The defense of established privilege rested partly on research that questioned traditional assumptions about the importance of education and the effectiveness of egalitarian policy. While arguments against equality can always be expected to portray it as inefficient if not unworkable, they will be more damaging when egalitarians confuse equality with efficiency or effectiveness.

On the other hand, this problem could not easily have been avoided in the development of these cases. As observed earlier, in a society that is both very unequal and deeply imbued with the idea of efficiency, the pressures to justify egalitarian doctrine in terms of existing values is very great. The fact that this results in sometimes impossible contradictions does not remove the pressures, nor does it vitiate the great political appeal of the approach typified by *Serrano*. As the lower court decisions reveal, it is easier to speak convincingly about the virtues of equality on the grounds of effectiveness than on the grounds of political virtue.

If one must respect the solution to this dilemma represented by *Serrano* and its successor cases, one must also notice the difficulties it led to in the litigation, and in the Supreme Court's decision in *Rodriguez*. If one believes, as I do, that the provision of public services should not be differentially constrained by wealth, the decision at the very least has set back chances for a partial step in the right direction. However, if the reason for removing these wealth constraints is that they represent distinctions among persons and governments so irrational and unfair as to be inconsistent with democracy, then this decision offers an opportunity to rethink the ideas about equality and society that underlay the litigation. In view of the power of established intellectual traditions and political realities, and the consequent allergy to dealing frontally with arguments for equality, this may seem a quixotic idea. But as the resolution of *Rodriguez* suggests, it may be no more foolish than the roundabout sallies discussed in this essay.

NOTES

1. This quotation and all other references to the school finance cases are drawn from a most helpful compilation of decisions prepared by the Senate Select Committee on Equal Educational Opportunity, Part 7, "Inequality of Economic Resources," Washington, September 30, October 1 and 6, 1970; *Serrano v. Priest*, p. 485.

2. J. Coons, W. Clune, and S. Sugarman, in an *amicus* brief ("Motion for Leave to File Brief and Brief for John Serrano"), filed with the U.S. Supreme Court in its hearings of the *Rodriguez* case, p. 8.

3. Ibid., pp. 498-499.

4. J. Coons, W. Clune, and S. Sugarman, "A First Appraisal of Serrano," *Yale Review of Law and Social Action* 2 (Winter 1971): 114.

5. Quoted in *Serrano v. Priest*, p. 486.

6. Ibid.

7. D.L. Davis, "Taxpaying Ability: A Study of the Relationship between Wealth and Income in California Counties," in *Proceedings of NEA 10th Conference on School Finance*, 1967, pp. 199-203.

8. P. Ridenour and P. Ridenour, "*Serrano v. Priest*: Wealth and Kansas School Finance," *Kansas Law Review* 20 (1972): 213-226.

9. The evidence derives from an unpublished study being conducted by Stephan Michelson and Norton Grubb.

10. M. Churgin, P. Ehenberg, and P. Grossi, "A Statistical Analysis of the School Finance Decisions: On Winning Battles and Losing Wars," *Yale Law Journal* 81 (1972): p. 1326-8.

11. A nice summary of evidence on this point is provided in J. Berke and J. Callahan, "*Serrano v. Priest*: Milestone or Millstone for School Finance?" *Journal of Public Law* [Emory University Law School] (1972), p. 40, which

presents a helpful table summarizing the proportion of families earning less than $3000 annually for the central cities and suburbs of twelve major metropolitan areas. The table shows that although cities generally have a greater proportion of such families, the suburbs generally have half, or more than half, as great a percentage of such families as cities: for New York city it is 14 percent, and for the aggregate suburbs it is 7 percent; for Indianapolis it is 13 percent, and for the suburbs it is 12 percent; for San Francisco-Oakland central cities it is 19 percent and for the suburbs it is 14 percent. These suburban figures are averages, which means that there are plenty of suburbs that have as large or larger proportions of such families as their central cities.

12. Berke and Callahan, "*Serrano v. Priest*: Milestone or Millstone?" pp. 39-47.

13. Coons et al., "Motion to File Brief for John Serrano," p. 8. There is, however, a good deal of confusion on this point in the ranks of *Serrano*'s advocates. At a conference discussing the cases, Mr. Sidney Wolinsky, who was one of the principal attorneys for the plaintiffs in *Serrano*, summarized the central point of the litigation as the following request to the courts: "We ask that you not discriminate against poor kids." Lawyers Committee for Civil Rights Under Law, "School Finance Litigation: A Strategy Session," *Yale Review of Law and Social Action* 2 (Winter 1971): 161.

14. Coons et al., "Motion to File Brief for John Serrano."

15. The classical statement of this diagnosis is in J. Coons, W. Clune, and S. Sugarman, *Private Wealth and Public Education* (Cambridge: Belknap, 1970).

16. Senate Select Committee, "Inequality of Economic Resources," p. 526.

17. Ibid.

18. Coons et al., *Private Wealth and Public Education*, Chapter 6.

19. J. Coons, W. Clune, and S. Sugarman, "A First Appraisal of Serrano," p. 114.

20. Senate Select Committee, "Inequalities of Economic Resources," p. 495.

21. As the example suggests, it would probably be impossible to entirely sort out variations in spending that arose from differences in need for services from variations that arose from differences in taste or social priorities. This is one reason why it would be difficult to formulate a measure of overburden that fairly compensates for differences in spending due to need, but not those due to taste. Despite this, it is clear that the reason cities have greater per capita welfare costs has to do with something besides the tastes of taxpayers.

22. Berke and Callahan, *Serrano v. Priest:* Milestone or Millstone?" p. 66.

23. S.J. Weiss, *Existing Disparities in Public School Finance and Proposals for Reform* (Federal Reserve Bank of Boston, 1970), reports correlations of between +.40 and +.56 between property values per capita and revenues for the five New England states, which seems about typical. Churgin et al. report that variations in taxable property account for about 36% of the variations in spending (Churgin, et al., "Statistical Analysis of School Finance Decisions," p. 1328.)

24. Weiss, *Existing Disparities*, which reports correlations between −.56 and −.69 for the five New England states (Table IV, p. 21).

25. Coons et al., "A First Appraisal of Serrano."

26. I am indebted to Michelson and Grubb for this information.

27. See, for example, Churgin, et al. "Statistical Analysis of School Finance Decisions," pp. 1327, 1340-41.

28. See, for example, the view of the Texas court, cited at page 000 above.

29. If the line of reasoning that was so prominent in *Serrano* had been pursued (to the effect that the plaintiffs were poor people, not people in poor districts), it would have been hard to avoid this notion, at least as a matter of logic. If the wealth classification involved in *Serrano* was individual poverty— as the court and the plaintiffs seemed to think—then the only logical reason not to deal with intradistrict wealth differences was the assumption that the poverty of people and the poverty of districts was identical. There are, of course, plenty of good nonlogical strategic reasons to avoid the notion that within-district wealth differences were involved, as will become clear shortly.

30. It is hard, therefore, to understand why fiscal neutrality has been so widely accepted as a sensible standard of fairness. It is easy to see why it seems more fair than what exists, but if a few moments reflection on fiscal neutrality reveals that it is a scheme to ensure that taxation is never more than proportional, a few more minutes might make one wonder why proportionality might be a constitutionally required standard of fairness in school taxation.

31. Senate Select Committee, "Inequality of Economic Resources," p. 526.

32. On the matter of the tax implications of the lower court cases, see Berke and Callahan, "*Serrano v. Priest*: Milestone or Millstone?"; Churgin et al., "Statistical Analysis of School Finance Decisions," and D.P. Moynihan, "Equalizing Education—In Whose Benefit?" *Public Interest* (Fall 1972), pp. 69-89; A. Solomon and G. Peterson, "Property Taxes and Populist Reform," working paper #16, Joint Center For Urban Studies of Harvard and MIT, 1972.

33. Senate Select Committee, "Inequalities of Economic Resources," p. 498-99.

34. Ibid., p. 516.

35. Ibid., p. 524.

36. Ibid., pp. 558-559.

37. Ibid., pp. 506-507.

38. C. Jencks et al., *Inequality: A Reassessment of the Effect of Family and Schooling in America* (New York: Basic Books, 1972), pp. 220-225.

39. J. Bachman et al., *Youth In Transition* (3 vols.; Ann Arbor, 1972), Vol. III, pp. 144-446.

40. Jencks, et al., *Inequality*, Chapter 6. See also P. Blau and O.D. Duncan, *The American Occupational Structure* (New York: Wiley, 1968).

41. Ibid.

42. Ibid. Much of the controversy on this point revolves around the meaning of the unexplained variance, and how much it involves things like "luck" and "character." Since things like this cannot easily be observed or measured, the disagreements could go on almost endlessly.

43. The fundamental interest doctrine, of course, provides no way of knowing what "crucial" is. If one were thinking of all the influences on adult success, my argument that schooling is not crucial might seem sensible. But if one had in mind only those things we could measure and control, schooling might seem more important.

44. Jencks, *Inequality*, Chapter 5; H. Averch et al., *How Effective is Schooling?* (Santa Monica, Calif.: RAND, 1971); J. Coleman et al., *Equality of Educational Opportunity* (Washington, 1966); D.P. Moynihan and F. Mosteller, *On Equality of Educational Opportunity* (New York: Vintage, 1971).

45. Jencks, *Inequality*.

46. *Van Dusartz v. Hatfield*, in Senate Select Committee, "Inequality of Economic Resources," p. 515.

47. This appears to have been the argument of defendent agencies in every case heard thus far. See, for example, the brief submitted by eighteen states' attorneys general and other officials in *Rodriguez*, G.W. Leiberman et al., *Brief of Amicus Curiae in Support of Appellants*, October Term, 1972, especially pp. 48-55.

48. Another case of these unfortunate contortions was reported in the *New York Times* on Sunday, June 11, 1972. The report concerned a conference sponsored by the Lawyers Committee for Civil Rights, which is described as the coordinating agency for the school finance litigation. The conference attacked research that showed no differential effect of resources on school performance. The *Times* reported:

> A group of lawyers and educators have charged that too much credence is being given to "inconclusive" or "flawed" studies that minimize the influence of schools on student achievement or the value of racial integration in the schools.
>
> Social scientists and officials of the Lawyers Committee for Civil Rights Under Law said that they feared an overreliance on educational research by the courts or other branches of government, as well as by the public.
>
> Dr. Kenneth B. Clark, a psychologist who is a member of the New York State Board of Regents, said that some of the studies, including work by two Harvard professors, Daniel Patrick Moynihan and David J. Armor, represented a "sophisticated type of backlash."
>
> To counter the impact of some of these studies, the lawyers committee released an analysis of research by the Advisory Commission on Intergovernmental Relations that found that schools "do make a difference to student achievement," but the potential difference is limited.

49. Coons et al., "Motion to File Brief for John Serrano," p. 42. This notion, of course, was not absent from the earlier opinions and pleadings, but the balance of attention changed radically in the few years after *Serrano* was decided. Coons et al., for example, barely mention the social and economic arguments for fundamentality in their *amicus* brief.

50. Ibid., pp. 32-42.

51. Milbrath, L.W., *Political Participation* (New York: Random House, 1965, Chapter 5.

52. Jencks, et al., *Inequality*, Chapter 5.

53. Ibid., pp. 150-151.

54. Coons et al., "Motion to File Brief for John Serrano," p. 41.

55. Ibid., p. 39.

56. *The Harvard Educational Review* published a special issue on political socialization (vol. 38, no. 3, Summer 1968), which provides a useful overview of the field in essays by several leading scholars. In most work in this area, interest in the differential effects of schools is subordinated to work on the intergenerational transmission of political attitudes. See, for example, the essay by K. Jennings, and R. Miemi, "Patterns of Political Learning," p. 444.

57. R. Lane, "Political Education in the Midst of Life's Struggles," pp. 475-476.

58. Ibid., p. 476.

59. A. Greeley, and P. Rossi, *The Education of Catholic Americans* (New York: Aldine, 1968), p. 89.

60. R. Merelman, *Political Socialization and Educational Climates* (New York, 1971).

61. This finding seems bizarre, suggesting as it does that more effective political socialization occurred in the district with less resources. The author hypothesized that the differences were due to background differences among students, that these differences operate mostly during elementary school, and that the schools closed this gap during high school when politics is more deliberately taught. But there is no evidence from any sources that social class has less of an effect on learning during high school. In any event, the differences at the sixth grade were so small as to be significant statistically, but not educationally.

62. Ibid., p. 104.

63. Ibid., p. 169.

64. Ibid., p. 177.

65. See, for example, Churgin et al., "Statistical Analysis of School Finance Decisions"; Berke and Campbell, "*Serrano v. Priest*: Milestone or Millstone?"; Moynihan, "Equalizing Education"; and Solomon and Peterson, "Property Taxes and Populist Reform."

66. Senate Select Committee, "Inequalities of Economic Resources," p. 498.

67. Ibid., p. 409.

68. Ibid., p. 502.

69. Ibid., p. 500. This notion has been explored by Frank Michelman, "The Supreme Court 1968 Term, Forward: On Protecting the Poor Through the Fourteenth Amendment," *Harvard Law Review* 83, no. 7 (1969): 7-59.

Index

handicapped, 35; in Benson, 170; in Berke
and Goettel, 228; exclusion cases, 93
Hargrave v. Kirk, 94
Hartman, R.W. and Reischauer, R.D., 11
Hawaii: categorical funds, 231; local in-
volvement, 216; state revenues, 108
head tax, 139
Horowitz, Harold, 3

Iannaccone, J., 207
implementation: and statutory interest, 203
incentives: and disparity, 279
income: and education, 297
inequities: and Mr. Justice Stewart, 96;
social hierarchy, 7, 198
innovation: and expenditure, 210; in Pincus,
8; political ideas, 300

jurisdiction: concept, 204

Kansas: income and assessment, 288; post-
Serrano, 87

Landrieu, Moon, 248
lawsuits, equal protection, 34
Law v. Nichols, 93
Lawyers Committee for Civil Rights, 312
LEARN (Legislators for Educational Assist-
ance Right Now), 261-265
Legislative Analyst, 261
Levin, H.M., 15, 164, 193; predictive model,
188
local control, 278

McInnis v. Ogilvie, 76, 84
Marshall, Mr. Justice, 4, 90, 104
Martin, Roscoe, 214
Maryland: categorical aid, 231; school income tax, 66; state control, 200
Massachusetts: aid distribution, 206; property values and personal income, 288;
variable matching, 42
Meltsner, A.J. and Nakamura, R.T., 20
methodology: and Barro, 28; measurement
problems, 75
Michigan: and Berke and Goettel, 239;
defeated reform, 75; equalization plan,
78; fragmented politics, 207; post *Serrano*, 87; state control, 200; state data,
215

Millikin v. Green, 5, 98, 226
Minar, David, 205
minimum provision alternative, 67
Minnesota, 240; court role of education,
295; equalized school finance systems,
75; expenditures and educational effec-

tiveness, 298; post-*Serrano* decision, 87;
school services, 164; wealth discrimination, 290
Montana: level expenditures, 131
Moretti, O., 269
municipal overburden, 11; and tax, 168
Muskie, E., 250

National Advisory Council on the Education
of Disadvantaged Children, 189
National School Lunch Act, 208
NDEA (National Defense Education Act),
208, 243
NEFP (National Educational Finance Project), 35
Nevada: categorical aid, 231; level expenditures, 131; taxes, 109
New Hampshire: state revenues, 108
New Jersey: Court and equity, 295; defeated reform, 75; post *Serrano*, 87;
reform forces, 25
New York: aid distribution, 206; in Berke
and Goettel, 240; central city resources,
212; Fleischmann Comm., 32; fragmented politics, 207; percentage equalization, 44; political realism, 78; school
reform, 123; revenues, 108; state control, 200; variable matching, 42
NIE (National Institute of Education), 8
Nixon, R.M., 75
Northwest Survey Ordinance, 243

Office of Senate and Assembly Research,
261
Oakland Unified School District, 269
opportunity: locus, 136
Oregon: state revenues, 109

Pacific Gas and Electric, 265
partisanship, 265
performance: and categorical aid, 225; resources, 299
Pennsylvania: categorical aid, 231; variable
matching, 42
Perkins, Congressman, 75
PL 874, 244
Plessy v. Ferguson, 83, 193
policy: in Hartman and Reischauer, 97;
social, 169; and statewide property tax,
58; -making and states, 57; structural
change, 282; supplementation, 50
politics: and alternatives, 255-268; bargaining, 67; in Campbell and Gilbert, 203;
distribution of power, 218; realism, 78;
socialization, 301
Porter, David: allocation and resources, 225,
248

Rand Educational Policy Studies

John Pincus, *Editor*

Published

Averch, Harvey A., Stephen J. Carroll, Theodore S. Donaldson, Herbert J. Kiesling, and John Pincus. *How Effective is Schooling? A Critical Review and Synthesis of Research Findings.* Englewood Cliffs, New Jersey: Educational Technology Publications, 1974.

P. Carpenter-Huffman, G.R. Hall, G.C. Sumner. *Change in Education: Insights from Performance Contracting.* Cambridge, Mass.: Ballinger Publishing Company, 1974.

Pincus, John (ed.). *School Finance in Transition: The Courts and Educational Reform.* Cambridge, Mass.: Ballinger Publishing Company, 1974.

Other Rand Books in Education

Bruno, James E. (ed.). *Emerging Issues in Education: Policy Implications for the Schools.* Lexington, Mass.: D.C. Heath and Company, 1972.

Coleman, James S. and Nancy L. Karweit. *Information Systems and Performance Measures in Schools.* Englewood Cliffs, New Jersey: Educational Technology Publications, 1972.

Haggart, Sue A. (ed.). *Program Budgeting for School District Planning.* Englewood Cliffs, New Jersey: Educational Technology Publications, 1972.

Levien, Roger E. *The Emerging Technology: Instructional Uses of the Computer in Higher Education.* New York: McGraw-Hill Book Company, 1972.

About the Contributors

Stephen M. Barro, an Economist at The Rand Corporation, deals with the management of government programs in elementary and secondary education. He has a B.A. from the California Institute of Technology, M.A. from the University of California, and is presently a Ph.D. candidate in Economics at Stanford University.

Charles S. Benson, Professor at the School of Education, University of California, is doing research for the Ford Foundation and Carnegie Corporation. Dr. Benson received his B.A. from Princeton and his M.A. and Ph.D. from Columbia.

Joel S. Berke is Director of the Educational Finance and Governance Program of the Syracuse University Research Corporation. Dr. Berke obtained his B.A. from the University of Vermont, and his M.A. and Ph.D. at the Maxwell Graduate School of Syracuse University.

R. Stephen Browning is a staff attorney with the Lawyers' Committee for Civil Rights Under Law, Washington, D.C. Dr. Browning has a bachelor's degree from Indiana University, Masters in City Planning from Harvard University, and Juris Doctorate from the Indiana University School of Law.

Alan K. Campbell, Dean of the Maxwell Graduate School, Syracuse University, is the author of numerous books and articles on urban education. Dean Campbell obtained a B.A. at Whitman College, M.P.A. from Wayne University, and Ph.D. at Harvard.

David K. Cohen, Professor of Education and Social Policy at the Harvard Graduate School of Education, received his B.A. from Alfred University and his Ph.D. from the University of Rochester.

Dennis A. Gilbert has been employed at the U.S. Department of Labor and the Office of Senator Walter F. Mondale. He is a graduate of the University of Michigan and is currently a Ph.D. candidate in Social Science at the Maxwell School of Syracuse University.

Robert J. Goettel, Associate Director of the Educational Finance and Governance Program at the Syracuse University Research Corporation, obtained his B.A. and M.A. from the State University of New York, and his Ph.D. from Columbia University.

Robert W. Hartman is Senior Fellow at the Brookings Institution in Washington, D.C. Dr. Hartman has a B.A. from Queens College, and an M.A. and Ph.D. from Harvard University.

Henry M. Levin, an Associate Professor of Education at Stanford University, received his B.S. from New York University, and his M.A. and Ph.D. from Rutgers.

David C. Long is a Staff Attorney with the Lawyers' Committee for Civil Rights, Washington, D.C. Dr. Long has a B.A. and M.A. from the University of Hawaii and a J.D. from the University of Chicago Law School.

Arnold J. Meltsner is a political scientist and teaches at the Graduate School of Public Policy, University of California, Berkeley. He received his B.A., M.A., and Ph.D. from the University of California.

Robert T. Nakamura is a political scientist and teaches at Dartmouth College. He is currently completing his Ph.D. at the University of California.

John Pincus, an economist, is the Manager of Rand's Education and Human Resources Program. Dr. Pincus is a graduate of Colby College. He received an M.A. from Columbia, and an M.A. and Ph.D. from Harvard.

Robert D. Reischauer is a Research Associate at the Brookings Institution in Washington, D.C. Dr. Reischauer obtained his B.A. from Harvard and his M.I.A. and Ph.D. from Columbia.